Security Management

An Introduction

Second Edition

P. J. ORTMEIER, Ph.D.

Grossmont College
and
California State University

PEARSON

Prentice
Hall.

Upper Saddle River, New Jersey 07458

Library of Congress Cataloging-in-Publication Data

Ortmeier, P. J.
   Security management : an introduction / P. J. Ortmeier.— 2nd ed.
      p. cm.
   Includes bibliographical references and index.
   ISBN 0-13-113792-1
   1. Private security services—Management. 2. Buildings—Security measures.
   3. Industries—Security measures. 4. Corporations—Security measures.
   5. Security systems. 6. Computer security. I. Title.

   HV8290.O78 2005
   363.28'9'068--dc22

                            2004001282

Publisher: Stephen Helba
Executive Editor: Frank Mortimer, Jr.
Assistant Editor: Sarah Holle
Production Editor: Patty Donovan, Pine Tree Composition, Inc.
Production Liaison: Barbara Marttine Cappuccio
Director of Manufacturing and Production: Bruce Johnson
Managing Editor: Mary Carnis
Manufacturing Buyer: Cathleen Peterson
Creative Director: Cheryl Asherman
Cover Design Coordinator: Miguel Ortiz
Cover Designer: Amy Rosen
Cover Image: Varie/Alt/Corbis
Editorial Assistant: Barbara Rosenberg
Marketing Manager: Tim Peyton
Formatting and Interior Design: Pine Tree Composition, Inc.
Printing and Binding: R.R. Donnelley & Sons

Pearson Education LTD
Pearson Education Singapore, Pte. Ltd.
Pearson Education, Canada, Ltd
Pearson Education—Japan
Pearson Education Australia PTY, Limited
Pearson Educaçion de Mexico, S.A. de C.V.
Pearson Education Malaysia, Pte. Ltd.

PEARSON
Prentice
Hall

10 9 8 7 6 5 4 3 2

ISBN 0-13-113792-1

To Jake, Luke, Kelly, and Marcus

CONTENTS

CHAPTER 3   Legal Aspects of Security Management   57

CHAPTER 4   Risk Assessment, Planning, and Program Administration   87

CHAPTER 5   Physical Security

CHAPTER 6   Personnel Security

CHAPTER 7   Information Security

P R E F A C E

ORGANIZATION OF THE BOOK

The protection of people, physical assets, and information is a concern at every level of society. Whether an individual, a giant organization, or a nation, one's need for safety and security is fundamental. However, due to limited resources or lack of authority to confront numerous noncriminal risks, public law enforcement agencies are unable to provide adequate protection against the multitude of threats. In addition to crime, numerous hazards threaten personal safety and property. Natural disasters and environmental mishaps can be costly. Technological advances create opportunities for invasions of privacy and nonphysical intrusion into organizational databases. Terrorism has also emerged as a major threat to public safety and security. Consequently, security services have experienced tremendous growth, both in terms of the number of personnel employed and the financial investment in loss prevention and asset protection.

Security Management: An Introduction, 2nd edition, provides up-to-date information and expands on material presented in the first edition while it addresses security operations and management in the post-9/11 era. It utilizes a unique approach as it presents management strategies for loss prevention as well as an overview of the security field. The book is comprehensive and it highlights the multitude of security-related subjects while avoiding unnecessary discussion. It balances the business and legal orientations of security management and addresses security from public as well as private perspectives. The book also identifies over 20 security environments, applications, and services and examines issues encountered within these areas. The book incorporates the findings of the ASIS International/Webster University Education Symposium as well as the proceedings of the ASIS Academic/Practitioner Symposia. Although the ASIS symposia products continue to be works in progress, this book addresses and makes reference to the topics outlined in the ASIS recommendations for introduction to security courses for business students.

This book may be used as a text in security management, criminal justice, or business courses, or as a reference for security managers. Practitioners working within specific security venues can use the book to familiarize themselves with other applications in the security industry.

Those pursuing an ASIS International Certified Protection Professional (CPP) designation will discover that this book is a must read when preparing for the CPP examination. A recent CPP recipient stated that the book presents a systematic approach to the broad array of data contained within the scope of security management. The CPP declared that the book "contains a significant amount of information tested on the CPP examination" and it serves as a "guide" and "confidence builder" for the exam.

Reviewers refer to the book as excellent, balanced, well rounded, and efficient in identifying and explaining the significant topics in the security arena. Reviewers also indicate that the book presents valuable information for the front-line manager as well as the student of security management. One reviewer commented that the fundamentals of security management are rarely so well articulated.

Chapter 1 presents an introduction to the world of security management. It addresses the nature, scope, and history of security services, the essential elements of security, types of security organizations, regulation and professionalism, the impact of economic and social globalization, homeland security, and the future of security management. Chapter 2 identifies criminal as well as noncriminal threats to individuals and organizations. Chapter 3 confronts the legal issues associated with security management. Chapter 4 defines and outlines the process of risk management, security planning, and program administration. Chapters 5, 6, and 7 address the security management triad: physical, personnel, and information security. Investigations, criminal and business intelligence operations, and reporting are the subjects in Chapter 8. Over 20 identifiable security environments, applications, and services in specific settings are addressed in Chapters 9 and 10. Each chapter begins with a set of learning objectives and ends with a summary, a list of key terms, and discussion questions and exercises to enhance critical thinking and knowledge acquisition. A glossary of terms is provided and the appendices include a correlation of the ASIS Symposia topics with the book's contents and a sample safety and security survey instrument. Numerous additional sources of information on the topics discussed are presented throughout the text.

ABOUT THE AUTHOR

Dr. Ortmeier holds bachelors and masters degrees in Criminal Justice and a Ph.D. in Educational Leadership with an emphasis in Public Safety Training and Development. He is a U.S. Army veteran, a former police officer, a former vice president of United Security Systems, Incorporated, and he served as the coordinator of a criminal justice and security program at a midwestern college for 10 years. Dr. Ortmeier developed and implemented numerous courses and degree programs in law enforcement, corrections, security management, and public safety.

Currently, Dr. Ortmeier is the coordinator of the Administration of Justice Program at Grossmont College in the San Diego suburb of El Cajon, California. He also holds teaching positions at California State University-San Marcos, The Union Institute and University, and Webster University in San Diego.

Dr. Ortmeier is the author of *Public Safety and Security Administration* and *Policing the Community: A Guide for Patrol Operations* as well as several articles appearing in journals such as *Police Chief, The Law Enforcement Executive Forum, California Security, Police and Security News,* and *Security Management.* With Edwin Meese III, former attorney general of the United States, Dr. Ortmeier co-authored *Leadership, Ethics, and Policing: Challenges for the 21st century.* Dr. Ortmeier's publications focus on police field services, security operations, professional career education, management, leadership, and competency development for public safety personnel.

Dr. Ortmeier is a member of the Academy of Criminal Justice Sciences, the California Association of Administration of Justice Educators, the American Society for Industrial Security, and the American Society for Law Enforcement Training. His current interests include homeland defense and the development of leadership skills and career education pathways for public safety and security professionals.

ACKNOWLEDGMENTS

I wish to express my deepest appreciation to the many people who provided support and assistance during the development of the second edition of this book. Gratitude is extended to my friends at Prentice Hall, including Frank Mortimer, Sarah Holle, Barbara Cappuccio, and Tim Peyton, and to Patty Donovan and my other production and copy editors for their keen eyes, professionalism, and dedication. A thank you is also extended to Cindy McQuien for her assistance with the preparation of the manuscript.

I am extremely grateful to the manuscript reviewers for this edition: Holly Dersham-Bruce, Dawson Community College, Glendive, MT; Stephen Jones, University of Maryland, College Park, MD; Sean Gabbidon, Penn State University, Middletown, PA; Neal Strehlow, Fox Valley Technical College, Appleton, WI; and Donald Jenkins, Central Community College, Grand Island, NE.

I also appreciate the valuable contributions made by the reviewers of the first edition manuscript: Dr. Michael Moberly, Southern Illinois University, Carbondale, IL; Charles Biggs, Oakland City University, Oakland City, IN; Terrance Hoffman, Nassau Community College, Garden City, NY; and Kevin Peterson, Innovative Protection Solutions LLC, Herndon, VA.

Finally, I wish to express my heartfelt gratitude to my family, friends, and colleagues for their encouragement and patience.

CHAPTER 1

Introduction

LEARNING OBJECTIVES

After completing this chapter, the reader should be able to

- articulate the theoretical foundation for security.
- compare and contrast public law enforcement with private policing.
- describe the goals of security management.
- outline and describe the history of security services.
- demonstrate knowledge of the essential elements of security.
- describe the different types of security organizations.
- evaluate the roles of the security manager.
- discuss the importance of regulation of the security industry.
- evaluate professional certification and education programs for security personnel.
- describe the impact of globalization on security services.

THE CONTEXT FOR SECURITY

Theoretical Foundation

Societies were slow to develop protection for their individuals and groups. However, as the concepts of territoriality and personal property developed, human beings became more concerned with the protection of persons and property. As societies became more complex, unwritten behavioral rules and, ultimately, written laws were developed and formalized to proscribe (forbid) and prescribe (encourage) specific types of human behavior. Eventually, private and public security systems were created to deter offenses, enforce societal rules and laws, and provide protection for persons and property (Purpura, 2003; Simonsen, 1998).

The theoretical foundation for **security** is based on several behavioral assumptions, or beliefs about human behavior. First, individuals choose pleasure over pain and often make inappropriate decisions in search of gratification. Second, individuals commit crime when conditions exist that promote suitable targets of opportunity and the influence of social control is lacking. Third, although crime will exist to some degree in any society regardless of social controls (Hancock & Sharp, 2004), the opportunity for crime can be reduced through manipulation of the environment (American Society for Industrial Security, 1998; Crowe, 2000). Fourth, in addition to the threat of criminal behavior, numerous human activities and natural phenomena create situations through which great harm may occur if appropriate prevention and intervention strategies are not implemented (Hess & Wrobleski, 1996). Security is intended to provide these prevention and intervention strategies.

The theoretical foundation for security may also be viewed from the standpoint of the crime (or problem) analysis triangle. The triangle offers a simple mechanism to visualize and analyze crime, disorder, and potentially harmful events. Because all three elements (sides) of the triangle must be present for a crime or harmful event to occur, the elimination of any one of the three elements may prevent the crime, solve the problem, or mitigate harm caused by an event. If a potential victim implements measures to eliminate or reduce the opportunity for a crime to occur, the crime may be prevented. Improved locks and lighting, for example, can harden a target (victim) and reduce a potential burglar's opportunity to commit a burglary without detection (Meese & Ortmeier, 2004; Peak & Glensor, 2002).

Defining Security's Role

Since the terrorist attacks of September 11, 2001, security has moved from the periphery to the center, with government, private organizations, and individual citizens placing more emphasis on the need for security. However, even before

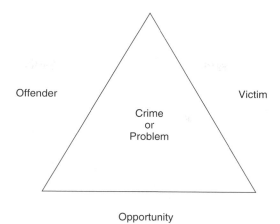

Offender

Victim

Crime
or
Problem

Opportunity

Figure 1–1   Crime (or Problem) Triangle

the horrific events of 9/11, the level of support for security from senior management in many organizations was increasing. Corporate executives realized that effective security protects the ultimate bottom line: that is, survival of the organization (Harowitz, 2003).

Security services today are sophisticated and complex and virtually defy a simple definition. In a sense, security is a concept in search of a definition (Simonsen, 1998). As an occupation, **security management** is multifaceted and interdisciplinary. Security involves the use of criminal and civil law, investigations, business management, policy formulation, psychology, sociology, and technology to protect persons and property. Contemporary security operations often focus on such diverse areas as fraud, disaster recovery and business continuity, energy management, fire prevention and protection, Internet and information protection, preemployment screening, executive protection, counterterrorism, business intelligence, environmental safety and crime, substance abuse, and workplace violence prevention.

Security is involved and interacts with every aspect of personal, organizational, and group life. Individuals strive to be safe and secure. Private businesses and corporations seek to prevent loss and protect property and human assets. Societies and political entities seek protection. Security operations include or collaborate with elements of the criminal justice system. Security cooperates with law enforcement in the crime prevention effort, interacts with the judicial system to assist in prosecution, and may, through a trend toward privatization of certain correctional services, be involved in the staffing and management of jails and prisons. In some areas, security's mission includes protection from hazardous materials, fire safety, and firefighting through industrial fire brigades. Security operations may also be used to generate revenue through the sale of products and services.

Security's Impact

The singularly most important and conspicuous purpose of security is that of protector or guardian. As the guardian against harm to people, property, and information, security is a service function with a tremendous impact. However, security's value may be difficult to measure or quantify. Therefore, security's impact may be determined more appropriately by what does not happen, rather than by what does (Sennewald, 2003).

Security may add value to an organization by aggressively seeking cost reduction initiatives. Security managers may cut costs through entrepreneurial ventures and articulation arrangements with other security service providers. Collaborative business arrangements and consortiums are formed to increase efficiency and reduce expenses. In Washington, DC, five independent high-rise building management groups entered into an agreement to share services provided by a third-party vendor (Dalton, 1995). Hospitals share services, including security services, with other hospitals (Colling, 1999). Multiple facilities with proprietary (in-house) alarm and video surveillance systems can collaborate to create a single central station to share in the cost or can charge member organizations for the service. Large facilities can utilize security personnel, instead of mailroom staff, to provide internal mail and delivery services, thus adding value to the organization by cutting delivery costs while increasing patrol activity.

Security involves government, nonprofit, and for-profit institutions. In an organizational sense, security is a function and responsibility that is woven increasingly throughout the operation of all public agencies and private institutions. As a function within an organization, security may be defined as a public or private service-related activity that provides personnel and equipment and creates policies and procedures designed to prevent or reduce losses caused by criminal action as well as by noncriminal events resulting from human error, emergencies, man-made and natural disasters, and business intelligence collection by competitors.

In the past, security's image usually reflected a poorly trained individual who earned near minimum wage and guarded a gate or patrolled a business at night (Hess & Wrobleski, 1996; Kakalik & Wildhorn, 1971; Simonsen, 1998). Most contemporary security personnel, however, are much more sophisticated. Security personnel are used for emergency response, access control, deterrence, investigations, and to protect persons and property. They monitor and operate security equipment utilized for access control, surveillance, fire protection, and patrol activities. Security managers are called upon to establish policies and procedures for disaster recovery, emergency management, fire prevention, security education, loss prevention, and asset protection. Ultimately, the goals of security promote a safe and secure environment and prevent loss. The result is maximum return on the investment of public or private dollars. An organization's management is legally and morally responsible for the safety and security of people and property. If an organization has a security problem, it has a management problem. Security management involves all those activities and objectives designed to meet asset protection goals to ensure that security problems do not materialize.

As the crime rate in the United States increased during the mid-twentieth century and law enforcement resources became increasingly strained, the public police were unable to effectively police private property. Additionally, many organizations realized that human and property assets required more protection. As a result, the security profession grew at an extremely rapid rate. In 1970, the number of security personnel in the United States, approximately 500,000, was about the same as the number of **public law enforcement** officers (Cunningham, Strauchs, & Van Meter, 1990). By 1991, the number of police officers increased to 580,000, while security personnel increased to 1.5 million. By the year 2000, the number of police officers increased to over 600,000 and security personnel numbered approximately 2 million. Currently, expenditures for security services are almost twice that of public law enforcement. Clearly, security services are the primary protective service in the United States (Fagin, 2003; Senna & Siegel, 2001).

The Contemporary Security Environment

The security environment depends on several factors. Every enterprise differs in its mission, culture, and in the way it conducts internal as well as external affairs. This difference is a result of a culture emanating from organization's history, personnel, and interrelationships. Organizational ethics also play an important role in the development of the security environment (Dalton, 2003). Some organizations have very strict policies regarding personnel behavior, while others do not. In addition, private enterprises generate rules, regulations, and standards of conduct that form the foundation for a private justice system (Schmalleger, 2004). These **private justice systems** codify and implement certain levels of punishment for misbehavior, much like criminal codes define and punish individuals for violation of societal rules. The security environment also depends on the relationship between security and public safety personnel. In the past, the relationship between public law enforcement and corporate security was often strained due to the low quality of some security personnel and the fact that many **private police** forces engaged in a protective function that many in public law enforcement believed fell under the purview of public policing.

Another compounding factor involves the relationship between security personnel and the organization being protected. Many security employees are contract workers provided by third parties. Following a trend in American business, numerous organizations are replacing some of their proprietary employees with contract workers. Loyalty to the organization, therefore, often remains with the contractor rather than with the site being protected. Finally, a major challenge for security management in the electronic age is the protection of proprietary information for the organization it services. Competitive pressures, foreign and domestic, combined with the ability to invade an institution or country electronically, pose enormous threats to national security and business enterprises.

In spite of any shortcomings within the security environment, the future seems relatively unlimited for the security profession and for individuals who choose security management as an occupation. Among other factors, constraints on public law enforcement budgets are likely to continue and necessitate increased use of private police (security) services. Security's positive impact in the modern world is without question. As security concepts are integrated into organizations, leaders are becoming more aware of the importance of security's value and contribution to the enterprise (American Society for Industrial Security, 1998).

Exciting career opportunities also exist in the security field (Harr & Hess, 2003). Salaries for security managers are generally competitive with those received in other professions. The results of a salary survey conducted in 1999 by the publisher of a security trade journal indicated that the average salary for security management personnel ranged from $30,000 to over $150,000 annually *(Access Control & Security Systems Integration,* 1999). A salary survey conducted in 2002 indicated that the highest average business-sector security manager salaries are earned in information technology ($109,105), followed by security professionals employed in the utilities and energy industry ($103,636) (Anderson, 2002). The salaries for chief security officer (CSO) positions in large multinational organizations is expected to reach $400,000 annually (Lohr, 2002).

SECURITY: A BRIEF HISTORY

Ancient Traditions

In early times, protection of persons and property was the responsibility of individuals, clans, or tribes. Social control was maintained through custom, and redress of grievances was handled informally by the individual or group. In 2100 B.C., customs were codified for the first time through the efforts of Hammurabi, the King of Babylon (site of present-day Iraq). The **Code of Hammurabi** represented the first written laws designed to prescribe the responsibilities of the individual to the group. The Code also specified a predictable punishment for each offense, thus reducing the possibility of barbarous and capricious punishment at the hands of revenge-seeking victims. In 1500 B.C., Egypt created a judiciary system, and in 1400 B.C., Amenhotep, pharaoh of Egypt, developed customs houses and marine patrols (American Society for Industrial Security, 1998; Schmalleger, 2004).

English Common Law

After the Norman Conquest in 1066 A.D., England developed a system of county (shire) government through which the King appointed a law officer (reeve) to act as the magistrate for each county. Thus, the shire reeve, forerunner of the

sheriff, was created and authorized by the King to make arrests. The shire reeve could deputize a posse to seek out criminals and enforce the common law of England.

The eleventh-century Norman Period also marked the beginning of an English court system. These courts formed a rudimentary criminal justice system. Decisions by judges became binding as precedent for future cases of a similar nature, thus establishing the foundation for the English common law. In 1215, the Magna Carta created by King John guaranteed basic civil rights to freeborn people. In 1285, the Statute of Winchester established a day and night watch for walled cities. Individuals took turns as nonpaid night watchmen in the community.

In the late 1600s and early 1700s, the industrial revolution dramatically transformed economic and social conditions. Villages became cities and crime increased. In response, the central government in England passed additional laws. The Highwayman Act of 1692 made provisions for **thief takers**, forerunners of the bounty hunters, who were compensated for capturing thieves and recovering stolen property. The law backfired because thief takers themselves stole property and sought the reward for its recovery. In response to the corrupt thief taker system, Henry Fielding, chief magistrate of the court on Bow Street in London, established a small group of salaried thief takers, known as the Bow Street Runners, to capture criminals. The unit's strategy was to arrive at the

Photo courtesy of Star Source International.

crime scene as quickly as possible, usually by running, to capture the criminal (Barlow, 2000; Fagin, 2003).

The American Experience

The criminal justice system in the United States developed primarily from the English common law structure. Most of the original American colonies were settled by the English. Thus, the colonists simply transplanted the laws of England onto American soil. As in England, the sheriff was the primary legal official. When the American colonies became a nation after the Revolutionary War, many states continued to observe English common law.

In the United States, as well as the world, the development of a formalized police service was slow. Historians trace the beginnings of police departments to Detroit in 1801 and Cincinnati in 1803, and the first national investigative agency to the U.S. Post Office in 1828. However, it is London, England, which is credited with the creation of the first full-time paid public police department in the world. Largely as the result of the efforts of **Sir Robert (Bobbie) Peel**, the British Parliament passed the **Metropolitan Police Act** on September 9, 1829. The Act authorized the establishment of the London police force.

Boston created the first formal police department in the United States in 1838 (Gaines, Kaune, & Miller, 2001; Senna & Siegel, 2001). New York City followed suit in 1844, San Francisco in 1847, and Dallas in 1856. At the federal level, an investigative arm was formed in the U.S. Treasury Department in 1864, and the Border Patrol was created in the U.S. Justice Department in 1882. However, public policing in the United States remained fragmented, decentralized, and often corrupt. Therefore, the security business in the United States grew rapidly to fill the void created by the limitations of public law enforcement.

In 1850, Henry Wells and William Fargo established two cargo companies. American Express operated east of the Missouri River, and Wells Fargo operated west of the Missouri River. In 1851, **Allan Pinkerton** established the first national private security and investigations company in the United States. The Pinkertons provided private police service to the railroads, offered detective services, and functioned as the intelligence arm of the Union Army during the Civil War. In 1853, August Pope patented one of the first burglar alarms. In 1858, Edwin Holmes introduced the first central station burglar alarms. In the same year, Washington Perry Brinks introduced the first armored carriages for the transportation of money and valuables.

Although public and private police agencies proliferated throughout the 1800s and early 1900s, policing remained primarily a local function controlled at the municipal level. Most police agencies were adjuncts of local political machines. Private police remained prominent until the early twentieth century. Former law enforcement officers began to enter the security services arena. In 1909, a former director of the U.S. Department of Justice's Bureau of Investigation formed the William J. Burns International Detective Agency (Schmalleger, 2003, 2004).

Between 1929 and 1939, private security employment declined as a result of the Great Depression. Between 1940 and 1945, due to the need to protect the United States' infrastructure and military and industrial facilities during World War II, the use of private security increased. After World War II, professionalism in law enforcement and private security grew because many returning veterans, who had acquired military police experience during and immediately after the war, selected police work and private security as occupations. In 1954, George Wackenhut, a retired FBI agent, formed the Wackenhut Corporation, an enterprise that became another one of the largest private security companies in the United States.

In 1955, a group of security professionals formed the **American Society for Industrial Security (ASIS)**. Today, ASIS International's membership exceeds 30,000, making it the world's largest organization of security professionals. Dedicated to protecting the people, property, and information assets of a diverse group of private and public organizations, its members include management professionals who formulate security policy and direct security programs in a wide range of businesses, industries, and government operations.

In 1965, a national commission was established to investigate the nature and extent of crime in the United States and develop recommendations for the improvement of the criminal justice system. The President's Commission on Law Enforcement and Administration of Justice, commonly referred to as the President's Crime Commission, issued its report in 1967 and recommended improvements in law enforcement, courts, and corrections services. In response to the President's Crime Commission report, Congress enacted the Omnibus Crime Control and Safe Streets Act in 1968 and budgeted billions of dollars to fight crime and make improvements in the administration of justice. Among its provisions, the Act established the **Law Enforcement Assistance Administration (LEAA)** in the U.S. Department of Justice. The LEAA was responsible for administering federal grant programs to local, county, and state governments to establish and improve police training programs and upgrade equipment and facilities. A major portion of the money was set aside for the **Law Enforcement Education Program (LEEP)**. LEEP provided grants and interest-free loans to pre-service as well as in-service law enforcement personnel to attend college. Colleges and universities throughout the country were also eligible for federal funding that enabled them to establish education programs in law enforcement and criminal justice (Fischer & Green, 1998; Ortmeier, 2002). Although no longer in existence, the LEAA and the LEEP helped to launch an era of professionalism in the public police service. However, virtually all of the federal dollars were directed toward improvement of the criminal justice system with a significant portion of the funds allotted to public law enforcement. Professionalism of private sector security services lagged because government funding was not available for training and education of private protection service personnel.

The Omnibus Crime Control and Safe Streets Act of 1968 also led to the creation of the National Institute of Law Enforcement and Criminal Justice. The institute later became the National Institute of Justice (NIJ). As an organization that still exists, the NIJ continues to provide financial support for criminal justice-related research efforts. Many of these research efforts address crime prevention, yet most of the financial support is directed toward local government crime-fighting efforts. Although the vast majority of crime prevention efforts and expenditures occur in the private sector, few government dollars are available for private prevention research efforts (Schmalleger, 2003, 2004).

Despite the federal effort and marked improvements in the quality and quantity of police services, the crime rate continued to increase between 1968 and the early 1970s. In response, the National Commission on Criminal Justice Standards and Goals was formed. One of the Commission's last reports, the **Task Force Report on Private Security**, was published in 1976. For the first time, a national commission recognized private security as an essential ingredient to public safety. The Task Force, through its report, recommended that the private sector be encouraged to improve the nature and quality of security services and complement the law enforcement community in its efforts to fight crime. Thus, the Task Force Report and other developments during the 1970s created an environment where security services began to assume a more direct role in the crime-fighting and prevention effort. During the last quarter of the twentieth century, the security industry continued to grow rapidly due to increasing concern over crime and the limited availability of law enforcement resources. By 2000, security personnel outnumbered law enforcement personnel by at least three to one (Collins, Ricks, & Van Meter, 2000; Fennelly, 2004; Senna & Siegel, 2001).

PRIVATE POLICE AND PUBLIC LAW ENFORCEMENT

As the private police (private security) arena continues to grow, its relationship with public law enforcement continues to evolve. The growth of private security during the 1970s and 1980s was identified as a major source of friction between private security services and public law enforcement. The public police, having enjoyed a dominant position in the provision of protective services, foresaw an erosion of their "turf" to private security. Additionally, the public police's view of security as inferior was often reinforced because security personnel lacked adequate training (Cunningham, Strauchs, & Van Meter, 1990). However, many experts today recognize that the private and public sectors can assist each other (Craighead, 2003; Schmalleger, 2003, 2004; Sennewald, 2003). Indeed, as early as 1976, the Task Force Report on Private Security promoted private/public collaboration and recommended that private security and public law enforcement work together in a complementary, rather than competitive, relationship to prevent crime and disorder. Still, major distinctions exist between the private and public policing sectors.

Private policing, or private security as it is known today, evolved gradually over a period of years. Currently, private police (security) personnel and operations provide most of the nonpublic police protective services in the United

States. As time progresses, more public police services are likely to be privatized (Schmalleger, 2004). Unlike the majority of public police services, security includes a multitude of specialties located in government as well as business and industry. Since security is both multidisciplinary and interdisciplinary, the contemporary security manager must draw upon several disciplines in an effort to prevent loss and protect tangible, intangible, and human assets. Security's authority is also quite distinct from that of public law enforcement. Except for some government operatives and a few privately financed security persons with statutorily mandated public police powers, the security person is concerned primarily with the welfare of a private client or group (Fischer & Green, 1998). Public law enforcement, on the other hand, is a function of the executive branch of government. Thus, public police officers are compensated entirely through public funds generated from tax revenues, grants, and other public sources. The publicly paid police officer is concerned primarily with the welfare of the general public. The **roles of public law enforcement** are to keep the public peace, maintain order, police public property, and respond to and investigate reported crimes on public and private property. The public police have no authority to enforce a private organization's policies and procedures.

Estimates of the number of separate and distinct law enforcement jurisdictions in the United States range from 17,500 (Gaines, Kaune, & Miller, 2001) to 20,000–25,000 (Inciardi, 2000). This includes agencies of national (federal), state, county, and local government. **National law enforcement agencies**, for the most part, have broad territorial jurisdiction and narrow subject matter jurisdiction. This means that federal agents generally have the authority to operate anywhere in the United States or its territories but are statutorily limited in the types of laws they may enforce. They do not have general police powers because the U.S. Constitution limits the authority of the national government.

In the aftermath of 9/11, the U.S. Department of Homeland Security (DHS) was created by the **Homeland Security Act of 2002** (United States Congress, 2002). The DHS represents the largest transformation of the national government since President Harry S. Truman merged the branches of the armed forces in 1947 to create the U.S. Department of Defense. On March 1, 2003, 180,000 employees in 22 separate federal agencies throughout several departments of government became part of the DHS. The primary mission of the DHS is to consolidate and better coordinate national (federal) efforts to combat terrorism and protect the United States against other threats to the homeland. Besides providing a better coordinated defense for the United States, the DHS maintains liaison with state and local governments as well as the private sector (United States Department of Homeland Security, 2003). Additional information regarding the DHS, its organizational functions, and the federal agencies it consumed is located in Chapter 9 under Government Security.

Contact the Department of Homeland Security at www.dhs.gov

Most public policing in the United States is not a national function. Rather, it is the responsibility of state, county, and local governments, where the jurisdiction of law enforcement agencies is the opposite of federal agencies. Whereas federal agencies have very broad territorial jurisdiction, **state, county, and local law enforcement agencies** have very narrow territorial jurisdiction. Their authority is generally limited to the boundaries of the municipality, county, or state. However, police agencies confined within state boundaries have very broad subject matter jurisdiction. They have general police powers and enforce a wide variety of state and local laws. They are usually the first responders to emergency and disaster scenes, including those caused by acts of terrorism.

State agencies include the **state police** and **highway patrol**. Some states have one or the other, while a few states have both. Where both types of agencies exist within the state, the state police are generally responsible for policing state government property and providing executive protection for the governor. The primary responsibility for state highway patrol agencies is traffic law enforcement. Highway patrols function as the state police in states that do not have a separate state police agency. The Texas Rangers are credited with being the first form of state police organization. Many states also operate a form of state bureau of investigation. Often an arm of a state's department of justice, a state bureau investigates major, multijurisdictional, and organized crimes.

Historically, the chief law enforcement officer in a county is the sheriff. The sheriff and the sheriff's deputies provide public law enforcement services throughout the county and may, in some jurisdictions, staff county jails. The sheriff usually patrols rural and unincorporated areas of the county as well as municipalities that do not have a police department (Schmalleger, 2004).

Local, or municipal, police departments provide police service to villages, towns, and cities. These agencies generally confine themselves to the city limits and are led by a chief who is politically appointed by the mayor, city council, city manager, or a police commission. In some cities, the police chief is provided with civil service protection.

In addition to national, state, county, and local police, other law enforcement (public police) agencies have been created for special or limited purposes. Airport, school, university, transit, port authority, and public housing police agencies are examples of special purpose agencies. Limited purpose agencies are often restricted in the types of public laws they can enforce. Alcohol beverage control, parks and recreation, conservation, fish and game, and Native American tribal police are examples of agencies with limited police powers (Barlow, 2000).

Despite the differences between the private and public policing sectors in the primary duties and responsibilities (generally, private versus public interests), the relationship between the sectors has evolved positively since the 1980s. ASIS International and the International Association of Chiefs of Police (IACP) have joined forces through Operation Cooperation, a call to action that encourages public law enforcement and private security professionals to work together. The impetus behind partnership creation is the growth in security services coupled with the success of community policing in forging alliances with citizen groups. Activities associated with Operation Cooperation include networking, information and resource sharing, crime prevention, training, joint operations, and the development and promotion of state and federal legislation of mutual interest ("Operation Cooperation," 2001).

Cooperative relationships between and among private security organizations, government operations, and public law enforcement demonstrate a growing trend toward **private/public interdependence.** Joint public and private ventures, investigations, emergency planning efforts, and crime prevention programs, and the privatization of some public police services are mutually advantageous. They are illustrative of a trend toward maximization of private and public security resources (Fischer & Janoski, 2000; Hess & Wrobleski, 1996; Schmalleger, 2003, 2004).

Some public police agencies have multiplied their capabilities by establishing collaborative relationships with private security. Many security companies possess technology and resources that surpass those of their local police agency counterparts. Private security personnel can also assist the police by collecting and forwarding information and extending surveillance activities beyond that which can be conducted by police agencies (Meese & Ortmeier, 2004). Information collection and surveillance can provide critical intelligence to assist with community policing and counterterrorism efforts.

The vital role of private security in crime prevention efforts should not be overlooked by the public police. The security professional may be the one person in society who has the knowledge and technology to effectively prevent crime (National Advisory Commission on Criminal Justice Standards and Goals, 1976). Since the resources of the public police are limited, it is in the best interests of public safety for police agencies to initiate cooperative efforts with the private sector to increase the quantity and improve the quality of crime prevention services (Lyman, 2002; Meese & Ortmeier, 2004; National Advisory Commission on Criminal Justice Standards and Goals, 1976).

SECURITY MANAGEMENT: ESSENTIAL ELEMENTS

The management of security operations may be categorized according to the security functions performed. These functions include the essential elements of **physical security**, **personnel security**, and **information security**. *Physical security* refers to tangible objects, such as walls, fences, locks, and building design, that promote the protection of persons and property. It also includes lighting, surveillance and alarm systems, and security personnel devoted to access control activities. The physical safety and security requirements for persons and property are balanced with operational needs and the aesthetic qualities required in the environment. Good physical security protects a facility and its people. It can affect a potential criminal offender's perception of a possible crime target.

The protection of electronic systems from loss due to accidents, natural disasters, or unauthorized access is another function of physical security. Computer systems, data, software, transmission lines, airwave frequencies, voice communications, electronic mail, and Internet servers must be protected. Revolutionary changes in technology have radically changed the nature of business and the environment in which business and government operate. As a result, special attention must focus on the protection of these systems. Security measures must also be designed and implemented to protect the operation itself. In other words, an organization's processes must be protected. Without redundant systems, such as backup power supplies, temporary inactivity may occur in a critical stage of the operation, resulting in expensive downtime.

Personnel security involves the protection of persons associated with the organization as well as protection from individuals who might harm the organization. Protection of employees, customers, and guests is inherent in the security function. Unique strategies may be required to protect dignitaries, corporate officers, and celebrities. Personnel security also involves hiring the right people and maintaining their integrity. It includes the utilization of an effective pre-employment screening process as well as policies and procedures to reduce the opportunity and motive for employee theft and poor productivity.

Information security (INFOSEC) is the third leg of the security management triad. Other than death or injury to a person, the greatest single threat to any individual, agency, institution, or nation is the loss of intellectual property or proprietary and confidential information. All stages of the information cycle must be protected. The methods used in the creation, processing, storage, retrieval, transmission, dissemination, and disposition of information in any form must be secured. The level of protection required at each stage depends on the information's value to the organization, the ability of an outsider to duplicate the information, and the potential harm that could result if the information is acquired by the wrong individuals, organizations, or nations.

Other elements of security management, often considered subsets of physical, personnel, and information security, include **technical security** and **operations security (OPSEC)**. Usually associated with protection against technical threats such as electronic eavesdropping and computer hacking, *technical security* is used to describe the development and implementation of countermeasures identified in risk assessments and security surveys. The principles of technical security involve understanding the threat, predicting the likelihood the threat will become an actual loss event, projecting the impact the loss will have on the enterprise, and preventing the loss if possible (American Society for Industrial Security, 1998).

Operations security (OPSEC) is the process utilized to deny potential adversaries information about capabilities and/or intentions by identifying, controlling, and protecting evidence of the planning and execution of sensitive activities (OPSEC Professionals Society, 2000). It is used to analyze operations and identify vulnerabilities from an adversary's perspective (Hess & Wrobleski, 1996). OPSEC strategies also evolve from a risk assessment or security survey.

OPSEC is the process used to protect critical information by changing or concealing indicators that might disclose the information protected (Pitorri, 1998). OPSEC may also be used to refer to all measures designed to protect the operation through which information proceeds. Sometimes OPSEC is used to refer to administrative countermeasures, such as procedural controls and policies, designed to complement physical security measures (Simonsen, 1998).

SECURITY ORGANIZATIONS

An important consideration for any security manager is the decision relating to how the security operations should be structured and who will perform security-related tasks. Proprietary (in-house) personnel may be used, or a contract service (outside vendor) may provide security services or personnel for a fee. Some security operations use a combination of proprietary and contract services (Canton, 2003; Hess & Wrobleski, 1996). Still others may prefer to blend or merge the security operation with another department within the parent organization.

Contract Security Services

In contrast to a proprietary security program, which is controlled directly by the protected organization, a firm that provides security services to other organizations for a fee is referred to as a **contract security service**. Virtually any security function can be performed by a contract service. Security services provided under contract include personnel, patrol, alarm systems, armored delivery, consultants, executive protection, pre-employment screening, drug testing, and investigative services. With respect to investigations alone, contractors may provide services and specialties in such areas as criminal defense, personal injury, surveillance, expert testimony, workers' compensation and insurance fraud, hazardous waste disposal, undercover operations, trademark infringement, stalking prevention, and personal protection.

The component of the contract service industry that experienced the most growth in the past 25 years is the uniformed security personnel business. Downsizing by many U.S. corporations during the 1980s and early 1990s resulted in layoffs for many proprietary security personnel. Many of these security officers were replaced with less expensive contract officers. Additionally, as governmental budgets stabilized (or in some cases, decreased) and the fear of crime and terrorism increased, many organizations began to employ contract security firms to protect personnel and reduce liability by creating a safer workplace.

The trend toward personnel outsourcing and the use of temporary employment services in the United States has created tremendous demand for contract security services. From a consumer standpoint, there are advantages as well as disadvantages to the use of a contract service, particularly the employment of security personnel. Some of the advantages include the following.

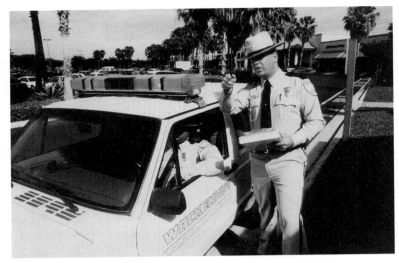

Photo courtesy of Wackenhut Corporation.

- Lower cost. Expenses can be as much as 20 percent lower than proprietary services, not counting the costs associated with benefit packages (health insurance, retirement, vacation, etc.).
- Administrative unburdening. The contractor is responsible for hiring, training, equipping, scheduling, supervising, evaluating, and terminating employees.
- Flexibility. As personnel needs change, the number of contracted personnel required can be increased or decreased easily.
- Fewer direct personnel problems. Problem contract employees may be replaced through a phone call to the contractor. Problems associated with unionized employees, wrongful termination lawsuits, and unemployment benefits are reduced or eliminated.
- Objectivity. Contract employees are likely to be more objective and less susceptible to collusion with nonsecurity employees of the host company or agency (Fischer & Green, 1998; Maurer, 2000b).

The disadvantages associated with the use of contract security personnel include higher attrition, inadequate training, and the contractor's failure to conduct thorough background investigations on employees (Maurer, 2000b). Ultimately, outsourcing security personnel and services is a management decision that should not be taken lightly. Careful consideration should be given to the needs of the organization. Cheaper is not necessarily better. If a contract service is used, the host organization should specify the qualifications, training, wage, supervision, and evaluation requirements in the contract.

Proprietary Security

Security organizations that function within and for a parent agency, business, or institution are referred to as **proprietary security** or *in-house security.* These security units provide services similar to those offered by contract providers. However, in proprietary security, personnel are employees of the organization where they actually work and are not under contract through a third-party agency or business. There are several advantages to the use of proprietary personnel.

- Higher quality. Personnel are generally paid more. This may result in a higher quality of personnel.
- Loyalty to the organization and site where employed.
- Low attrition. Higher pay and benefits promote retention. In some contract organizations, the turnover rate may approach 300 percent.
- Stability. Where a stable workforce, with knowledge of the facility and its personnel, is an important consideration, a contract guard service is not recommended.
- More direct control and supervision over the security force.
- High morale and motivation (Fischer & Green, 1998; Maurer, 2000b).

Hybrid Security Organizations

Some organizations employ contract as well as proprietary personnel and benefit from the advantages of both. A **hybrid security organization** employs a permanent proprietary security staff as well as contract security personnel to supplement in-house operations. All major airlines, for example, employ a behind-the-scenes in-house security staff. They also employ contract personnel to monitor the X-ray equipment used to screen passengers, visitors, and carry-on packages prior to admittance to aircraft boarding areas.

The Virtual Security Organization

Some agencies and businesses do not have distinct security departments. They may have a **virtual security organization** through which security function is integrated with the entire operation or merged with another department, such as human resources, health and safety, environmental services, or risk management. Economic conditions and budgetary constraints associated with consolidation and efficiency may force integration of a security component with another operational unit within an organization. Actually, as a function, security crosses departmental lines anyway. Security should be an integral part of every facet of the enterprise (Kovacich & Halibozek, 2003; Ortmeier, 1999).

ROLES OF THE SECURITY MANAGER

Since security management is a multifaceted occupation, the **roles of the security manager** are varied. The security manager simultaneously assumes managerial, administrative, preventive, and investigative responsibilities. As a manager, the security professional is responsible for selecting, training, scheduling, supervising, and evaluating security personnel. The manager is responsible for issues related to productivity, morale, compensation, well-being, and professional growth of security personnel as well as safety and security indoctrination and training of all employees. Employee attitudes and expectations toward authority are changing. Workforce diversity is commonplace and workplace violence has become a major issue. Organizations are also requiring higher productivity and improvements in the quality of output.

In the role of an administrator, the security professional is responsible for the establishment of security's organizational vision, mission, goals, and objectives. The security administrator must create a vision for the security operation as well as administer the day-to-day operations of the department. This involves planning, financial control, public relations, and community liaison activities. Security managers have become risk managers. They must anticipate, analyze, and protect an organization from virtually every conceivable threat, from liability to terrorism.

As a primary prevention officer of an organization, the security manager is ultimately responsible and accountable for prevention of loss from any source. It is the manager's responsibility to recognize and appraise hazards, and initiate action to reduce or remove the risk of loss. A high number of arrests for crimes committed on the premises is not a good measure for security program effectiveness. The measure of the best security program is how many crimes are prevented! When a loss does occur, the security manager must investigate and determine the cause. Conducting background investigations on prospective employees and auditing the site to ensure security measures are working is also part of the investigative function (Fischer & Green, 1998; Maurer, 2000a).

The security manager is not a police officer. Security management and public policing are not synonymous. The language of the security manager is the language of business, loss prevention, and asset protection, not law enforcement. Similarities between public policing and security in the actual functions performed often end with appearance and structure. Although security personnel are involved in the detection and investigation of crime and the arrest of suspected criminal offenders, most of a security person's time is spent on preventive efforts to reduce losses from noncriminal sources (Burstein, 1996). In fact, former law enforcement officers do not always make the best security managers. Individuals and organizations that employ security personnel prefer individuals with specialized training, education, and experience in security services rather than in law enforcement. Security management and business skills, such as planning, accounting, budgeting, public relations, and value-added contribution techniques are not taught in police academies. In a study conducted by the author, consumers of security services as well as security professionals preferred management candidates who possessed knowledge of security and skills in general business practices, personnel management, labor relations, planning, threat assessment, and policy formulation. Much less emphasis was placed on criminal law enforcement skills (Ortmeier, 1996b). In the post-9/11 environment, security knowledge and business skills remain important, with increased emphasis placed on intelligence (information gathering) capabilities and investigative skills (Harowitz, 2003).

REGULATION OF THE SECURITY INDUSTRY

Although security operations and personnel are employed in public as well as private environments, most regulatory recommendations and initiatives have focused primarily on the private security industry. This has been due, in large measure, to the general lack of minimum selection, training, compensation, and employee retention standards for private sector security personnel. The need for minimum standards and regulatory oversight has also been cited in several research studies. The first major research study of the private security industry in the United States was conducted by the Rand Corporation in the early 1970s. Funded through a grant from the U.S. Department of Justice, Rand researchers discovered poor training of, and abuses of authority by, private security officers. The Rand report noted that the typical private security officer of the 1970s was an undereducated, untrained, very poorly paid, undersupervised, aging white male. The Rand report solutions to private security's personnel problems focused on licensing security businesses and registration of security officers (Kakalik & Wildhorn, 1971, 1972; Purpura, 2003).

From 1972 to 1977, the Private Security Advisory Council (PSAC) produced advisory reports to the Law Enforcement Assistance Administration (LEAA). Through the LEAA, the PSAC published model state statutes for licensing burglar alarm companies and security officers, a code of ethics for security operations and management personnel, standards for armored car and armed courier services, guidelines outlining the scope of authority for security personnel, and areas of the public police–private security conflict (U.S. Department of Justice, Private Security Advisory Council to the Law Enforcement Assistance Administration, 1977).

In 1976, the Task Force on Private Security of the National Advisory Commission on Criminal Justice Standards and Goals determined that the security industry was significantly underregulated and its protective services function was underestimated. The Task Force Report recommended minimum training and regulation standards. The Task Force on Private Security represented the first national effort to set standards and goals for the regulation of the security industry. The Task Force Report stated that virtually every aspect of society was in some way affected by private security. Specifically, the Task Force placed emphasis on licensing security businesses; uniform minimum security personnel selection, training, and registration standards; codes of ethics and conduct; increased cooperation with the public police; improvement of security alarms and other crime prevention systems; state regulation; and continuing professional education and training (National Advisory Commission on Criminal Justice Standards and Goals, 1976).

Subsequent to the publication of the Task Force Report, the U.S. Department of Justice, through the LEAA, funded two studies of the private security industry. The results of these studies, the Hallcrest Report (1985) and the **Hallcrest Report II** (1990), reaffirmed the need for training and regulation of the security industry. The Hallcrest Report II contained numerous findings, recommendations, and forecasts relative to private security. The report addressed general and economic crime; selected crime concerns, including unethical business practices and terrorism; the dimensions of protection; security personnel issues; security services and products; comparisons of public police and private security; and future research needs (Cunningham & Taylor, 1985; Cunningham, Strauchs, & Van Meter, 1990).

The need for minimum regulatory standards may be apparent to some. After all, the security industry fulfills a vital function, and security personnel are responsible for the protection of persons and property. In many cases, security officers carry lethal weapons and exercise authority over others, and the potential consequences of negligent behavior are great. Nevertheless, regulation of the industry has been slow in its development. Viewed primarily as a state function, comprehensive regulation of the industry is not common, and mandatory minimum training standards are not required in several states. In some states, a person could be employed as an armed security officer although no background check, training, or licensing is required.

Although uniform minimum standards are lacking and only about half of all states require training (Hall, 2003), approximately three-fourths of the states have some form of legislation that regulates and licenses security personnel and organizations (Fischer & Green, 1998). However, most existing laws focus on contract rather than proprietary security services. Training requirements also vary. Some state training programs are consistent with the minimum standard recommended by the 1976 Task Force Report on Private Security. The Task Force recommended a minimum of 8 hours of formal preassignment training coupled with an additional 32 hours of in-service training, 16 hours of which could be supervised on-the-job training (National Advisory Commission on Criminal Justice Standards and Goals, 1976).

In California, contract personnel are required to complete a 3-hour preassignment course on security officer powers to arrest. Armed contract personnel must complete an additional 24 hours of firearms training through which the trainee must achieve an 85 percent minimum score on a written test and a qualifying score on a firearms range skills test. Additional instruction and licensing are required for contract security personnel who wish to possess a baton or a chemical weapon.

Since January 1, 2003, security personnel subject to licensing in California can no longer operate with a temporary 120-day license while a criminal history verification is being conducted. A licensee can be employed as a contract security officer only after the criminal history check is completed and the registration credential is issued by the state's Bureau of Security and Investigative Services. Additionally, effective July 1, 2004, preassignment training for licensed security personnel increased from 3 to 8 hours, with an additional 32 hours of training required within the first 6 months of employment (California State Bureau of Security and Investigative Services, 2003). For licensing requirements in other states, readers are advised to consult laws in their respective jurisdictions.

To date, there are no federal laws regulating private security. The first federal government effort to regulate the security industry commenced with the introduction of a bill by former vice-president Al Gore when he was a senator from Tennessee. If passed, the bill would have required minimum standards for proprietary and contract security personnel working in U.S. government operations. Subsequent initiatives by Congressmen Matthew Martinez (D, OK) in 1992 and Dan Sundquist (R, TN) in 1993, and Senator John Edwards (D, NC) in 2003 did not result in the passage of any federal law regulating the industry.

A Private Security Officer Quality Assurance Act was considered by the U.S. Congress. Commonly referred to as the Barr-Martinez/DeWine bill, the proposal required authorization to function as a private security officer. Under the Act, applicants for licensure would have been required to submit fingerprints routed to the FBI by a state clearinghouse for a criminal history check. Results of the check would be forwarded by the FBI to the state regulatory agency that has licensing authority over the applicant.

The National Association of Security Companies (NASCO) endorsed the Private Security Officers Quality Assurance Act. In addition, the National Association of Security and Investigative Regulators (NASIR), founded in 1993, was formed in response to the need for regulators to share information and address common concerns. NASIR's membership includes representatives from more than 30 of the 40 states that regulate private security in some form.

On April 2, 2003, U. S. Senator Carl Levin (D, MI) introduced a bill, the Private Security Officer Employment Act of 2003, to permit review of FBI criminal history records of applicants for private security officer employment. Cosponsored by Senators Lamar Alexander (R, TN), Joseph Lieberman (D, CT), Mitch McConnell (R, KY), and Charles Schumer (D, NY), the bill was read twice and referred to the Senate's Committee on the Judiciary. If passed, the legislation would allow employers of contract as well as proprietary private security personnel to request a FBI criminal database search for prospective and existing security employees. Requests by employers would be made through their state's identification bureau or similar state agency. Employers would not be granted direct access to FBI records. Rather, state agencies would serve as intermediaries between employers and the FBI. The program would be financed through reasonable fees charged to employers seeking the criminal history searches.

Although some form of regulation may be necessary in the security industry, there is disagreement with respect to the form it should take. The recent emphasis on states' rights, deregulation, and less governmental interference with private industry may delay the development of uniform regulatory and training standards for private security well into the twenty-first century. At least one security consultant intimates that various states use licensing requirements more as a source of revenue than as a means to screen and qualify applicants. Further, the consultant recommends that the industry regulate itself because employers, not the state, are ultimately responsible for the quality of personnel (Sennewald, 2003). However, uniform minimum selection, training, and licensing standards for security personnel are unlikely without some form of state or federal legislation mandating such standards.

PROFESSIONAL CERTIFICATION AND EDUCATION PROGRAMS

In spite of the lack of uniform governmental standards for the regulation of the security industry, organizations within the industry, as well as private and public instructional providers, have voluntarily developed certification, training, and education programs. Diligent efforts on the part of ASIS International led to the development of a professional code of ethics and the **Certified Protection Professional (CPP)** program. To acquire the CPP designation, the candidate must meet minimum experience and education criteria and pass a professional certification examination. The program focuses on security management and is administered by a professional certification board under the auspices of ASIS International. Additional certification programs offered by ASIS International include the Physical Security Professional (PSP) and the Professional Certified Investigator (PCI) designations. Similar efforts to improve the quality of security personnel have been articulated through programs developed by the International Foundation of Protective Officers (focusing primarily on security officers), International Association of Hospital Security, United Security Professionals Association (financial security), Academy of Security Educators and Trainers, International Association of Professional Security Consultants, and International Association of Computer Systems Security (Simonsen, 1998).

Very few security education programs existed until the late 1970s. Since that time, associate, baccalaureate, and master's degree programs have been developed at several colleges and universities. Some of these programs prospered, while others were eliminated due to low enrollments. Those that prospered maintain a close working relationship with security companies and executives in responsible charge of the security function in private corporations and public agencies. The key to successful security education programs lies in the strong linkages between instructional providers and the employer-consumer. Academic program advisory committees, made up of representatives from employer groups, function as recommending bodies and monitor instructional programs to ensure quality competency development that meets the contemporary needs of those who employ security personnel.

One of the criticisms leveled against many security education programs is that faculty tend to be former law enforcement officers who have little experience in, or formal education related to, prevention and business management techniques. Most law enforcement efforts are directed toward apprehending an offender after a crime has been committed. Security education program faculty should have training, education, and experience with the provision of security services or the management of security operations. Another criticism relates to the placement of academic security programs within higher education institutions. Most are housed in criminology departments or are adjuncts to law enforcement and criminal justice programs. Since security is a business-related function, academic programs might be more appropriately placed in colleges of business (American Society for Industrial Security, 1998; Chuvala & Fischer, 1991; Longmore-Etheridge, 2000). Alternatively, security education programs and students located in criminal-justice-related academic departments would benefit from articulation of security subjects with business subjects. Students majoring in security management might also be allowed to include appropriate business courses in their degree programs.

Education as well as certification programs are important ingredients to professionalism. Education programs assist individuals with acquisition of the philosophy and knowledge specific to a discipline. A legitimate certification program ensures that members of a profession are competent to practice in the field. The contemporary security manager can no longer survive simply with a high school diploma and 20 years' experience in the military or public law enforcement (Simonsen, 1998). Many professional career development and life-long learning opportunities exist today, and they are available through a variety of mediums. A complete list of security education and certification programs is beyond the scope of this book. However, additional information regarding such programs may be obtained by contacting ASIS International or the National Academic Consortium for Homeland Security.

Information regarding specific security training, education, and certification programs may be obtained by contacting ASIS International at www.asisonline.org or the National Academic Consortium for Homeland Security at www.osu.edu/homelandsecurity/NACHS.

IMPACT OF GLOBALIZATION

Technological advances and economic globalization have given rise to new challenges for security management (Kovacich & Halibozek, 2003). In many areas, economic competition has replaced political and military power. Industry is globalizing, with many American companies conducting business in numerous foreign countries. Approximately 70 percent of every new dollar earned by American corporations has global trade as its source (Badolato, 2000). Competitive pressures have forced many businesses to decentralize, enter global markets, create virtual corporations, and collaborate in joint ventures. This trend creates new business vulnerabilities.

The safety and security of almost all aspects of an organization's property and personnel are impacted by globalization. Businesses are threatened with economic espionage, foreign control, executive kidnapings, terrorism, and narcotics trafficking. Conducting business in foreign countries is challenging and can be hazardous. Special attention must be given to the political climate, currency exchange rates, availability of labor, compliance with local laws and international treaties, cultural and language differences, organized crime, personal and executive protection, physical security, and disaster preparedness (Ortmeier, 1999).

Today's security manager must be able to function in a global, high-technology environment. The world is experiencing fast-paced human evolution as well as some revolutions. Societies are evolving as they confront and experiment with the concepts of terrorism, diversity, human rights, democracy, and commerce in a high-tech information age. With the demise of the Cold War, espionage activities have shifted from the theft of nation-state political secrets to theft of economically significant proprietary information and intellectual property. The political, economic, human, and technological revolutions of the twenty-first century have a tremendous impact on, and can pose tremendous threats to, business and governmental operations (Kovacich & Halibozek, 2003). To appropriately confront the ever-changing world order, the security professional must be knowledgeable and understand, appreciate, and manage new world implications and requirements.

American companies must mitigate risks as they conduct business in foreign countries. Security professionals in these companies must ensure that personnel do not violate the U.S. **Foreign Corrupt Practices Act (FCPA)**. This federal law prohibits payment of bribes by U.S. companies to foreign government officials. In some countries, bribes are encouraged, even solicited, by officials as a fee for doing business in that country. However, fines of up to $250,000 and/or imprisonment of up to 5 years may be levied against individuals prosecuted and convicted under the Act. According to the law, a bribe or corrupt payment is defined as the fee paid directly to a foreign official to obtain work permits for individuals not otherwise eligible, have a police officer ignore an infraction, win approval of a government contract, have illegal items distributed in the mail, or encourage an official to give special privileges to the American company. The FCPA does not prohibit administrative fees (grease payments) designed to expedite an approval or paperwork process.

Problems with the FCPA may be avoided through a strong compliance program. Accurate records must be maintained to document the company's transactions. Background checks on foreign officials and a program of internal controls help prevent violations of the FCPA.

In addition to the business-related challenges posed by globalization, the phenomenon creates numerous challenges for government security and law enforcement operations as well. Not only do commercial, travel, and communications activities span the entire globe, the spread of crime and disease are no longer controlled by international boundaries. Nations and their citizens are less independent. Indeed, they have become more interdependent. And, although globalization is advantageous in many respects, effectively confronting transnational criminality and numerous negative international political and social issues demands creativity and responses beyond those developed through conventional law enforcement and security means (Adler, Mueller, & Laufer, 2003).

THE FUTURE OF SECURITY MANAGEMENT

The security profession has grown tremendously over the past 35 years. Security personnel currently outnumber law enforcement officers by at least three to one. Expenditures for private security are more than double that of public law enforcement (Senna & Siegel, 2001). This is in stark contrast to the early 1970s, when the number of personnel and the dollars spent on security services were roughly equivalent to public law enforcement. The growth trend is likely to continue well into the twenty-first century. Many organizations rely heavily on security services. In addition, the responsibilities assumed by asset protection personnel are expanding rapidly (Davidson, 2003). Security departments provide vital and unique services to the progressive organization that go beyond traditional uniformed officer presence and enforcement of policies, rules, and regulations. They gather and disseminate important information for an organization that is not available through any other source. In many organizations, the security professional's responsibilities are expanding to include facilities management. In these organizations, the security professional is responsible for maintenance, landscaping, food service, and numerous other functions that were not a part of the security manager's job description in the past. Thus, security's value-added presence is expanding and becoming more important to an organization's survival (American Society for Industrial Security, 1998; Dalton, 2003; Fischer & Janoski, 2000).

The future holds great promise for security management and for those who wish to pursue a career in asset protection. However, the twenty-first century security professional will also face great challenges. The changing nature of the workplace, ethical considerations, advances in technology, increased diversity, privatization of public services, terrorist activities, and the globalization of business activities will perpetuate the evolution of the security field. Security personnel at all levels must acquire new, more sophisticated skills to compete and demonstrate the competencies necessary to prevent losses in the future. Specialized training, education, and experience in loss prevention will be a necessity rather than a luxury. Traditional security and safety methodology must be supplemented, and in many cases replaced, with radically redesigned loss prevention processes. Security managers can no longer afford to be satisfied with the status quo, but must think strategically to meet new organizational demands. As part of the executive management team, security professionals are required to operate within an increasingly diverse workforce. Security managers must possess the multidimensional competencies of loss prevention expert, intelligence gatherer, investigator, administrator, visionary planner, financier, resourceful inventor, and effective communicator (Fischer & Janoski, 2000; Harowitz, 2003).

Rapid information exchange and cost effectiveness lie at the heart of all successful contemporary businesses. With many corporations entering the global marketplace, security managers must constantly reevaluate their function's ability to reduce costs, secure the exchange of critical data, and measure performance. Corporate cost-reduction pressures and management's desire to centralize or decentralize control exacerbate the security manager's challenges. In response to these challenges, the security operation must function as other successful groups function in the global economy's information age (Pearson, 2000).

In spite of the challenges, the prospects for growth of security services and products appears very optimistic. The privatization of certain public services, such as jail and prison management, will continue to expand. Security systems integration, security management, and a global security marketplace represent other segments of the security business that may experience tremendous growth (Bailin, 2000). Increased use of technology will also be part of security's future, as will increased collaboration and cooperation between and among business and governmental units (Harowitz, 2003). As the security profession becomes even more complex and sophisticated, security managers will be chosen from the ranks of those with specialized training, education, and experience in security services rather than retired law enforcement officers (Maurer, 2000c). Security managers are also likely to assume a broader range of responsibilities, as evidenced by position titles that reflect facilities, continuity of operations, and risk management functions. In light of a promising future, the security professional of the twenty-first century is extremely well positioned to make tremendous positive contributions to the world, community, organization, and the profession (Kovacich & Halibozek, 2003).

SUMMARY

The theoretical foundation for security is based on several assumptions, not the least of which is the belief that many losses can be prevented and that criminal behavior may be deterred through appropriate security-related activities. Numerous intentional and unintentional hazards threaten people, property, and information. Security's mission is to prevent these hazards from materializing.

Although their histories are intertwined, private security and public law enforcement differ greatly in approaches and focus. Security services focus on prevention of loss from any source, while the public police react primarily to reported crimes and public disorder. Security is provided through contract services, proprietary and hybrid security organizations, and virtually through other elements of an enterprise.

The security manager simultaneously assumes the roles of a manager, administrator, prevention person, and investigator. Although a national quality control standard for security personnel does not exist at this time, numerous states and many professional security organizations have developed statutes and standards for regulating security services. The professional groups as well as colleges and universities also provide security-related training and education programs. Technological advances, terrorism, and economic globalization create new challenges for the security manager. As old threats are mitigated, new threats develop. Thus, expansion of security services appears inevitable.

KEY TERMS

American Society for Industrial Security (ASIS)

Certified Protection Professional (CPP)

Code of Hammurabi

contract security service

Foreign Corrupt Practices Act (FCPA)

Hallcrest Report II

highway patrol

Homeland Security Act of 2001

hybrid security organization

information security

Law Enforcement Assistance Administration (LEAA)

Law Enforcement Education Program (LEEP)

Metropolitan Police Act

national law enforcement agencies

operations security (OPSEC)

personnel security

physical security

Pinkerton, Allan

private justice system

private police

private/public interdependence

proprietary security

public law enforcement

roles of public law enforcement

roles of the security manager

security

security management

security services

sheriff

Sir Robert Peel

state, county, and local law enforcement agencies

state police

Task Force Report on Private Security

technical security

thief takers

DISCUSSION QUESTIONS AND EXERCISES

1. Discuss the theoretical foundation for security and the reasons for the tremendous growth in security services.
2. Compare the authority of the public police with that of private security.
3. List and describe the goals of security management.

4. Describe the development of security services.

5. What are the essential elements of security?

6. List and describe types of security organizations.

7. The security manager functions in several roles. Identify and describe each of these roles.

8. Why are certification and education programs important for the security profession?

9. What impact does business and information globalization have on the provision of security services?

2

Threats to Safety and Security

LEARNING OBJECTIVES

After completing this chapter, the reader should be able to

- identify and describe threats to safety and security.
- discuss the nature and importance of unintentional threats against an organization.
- discuss the importance of accident prevention.
- describe the fire triangle and classifications of fire.
- distinguish between natural and environmental disasters and civil disorder.
- analyze factors that create civil liability.
- demonstrate knowledge of substance abuse prevention, intervention, and treatment strategies.
- discuss the nature and extent of crime.
- list and describe types of crime.
- evaluate crime prevention strategies.

INTRODUCTION

Numerous threats and hazards jeopardize the safety and security of people, property, and information. Some threats involve the ability or an expression of intent to harm or destroy. Other threats are inadvertent (unintentional), yet they pose a source of danger. A materialized threat can emanate either intentionally or unintentionally from a human agent or from a natural cause. A fire, for example, can result from arson activity (intentional) or through an accident or natural phenomenon (unintentional). Loss prevention and asset protection strategies in the security arena must often focus on potential harm that could emanate from a variety of sources, such as accidents, human error, fire, natural and environmental disasters, civil liability, substance abuse, civil disorder, and crime. Thus, the security manager is generally concerned with a wide variety of potential threats and hazards.

ACCIDENTS

An **accident** is an unfortunate event caused unintentionally by a human agent. A majority of accidents result from carelessness or failure to have or enhance safety rules. In addition to the possibility of personal injury or death, direct costs associated with these events include increases in insurance premiums and worker's compensation claims. Indirect costs include lost productivity. Accidents resulting in medical emergencies can occur at any time, and employees should be trained to respond properly.

To assist in the creation of a safe work environment, Congress passed the **Occupational Safety and Health Act** in 1970. The act established the Occupational Safety and Health Administration (OSHA) and outlined specific requirements for employers. The act imposes upon an employer a general duty to provide a work environment that is free from recognized hazards that are causing, or are likely to cause, serious bodily injury or death to employees. In addition to the general duty, an employer must comply with specific OSHA promulgated safety rules. The act also prohibits any employer from discriminating against or discharging an employee who exercises rights under the act. More specifically, employers must know and comply with OSHA regulations and standards; eliminate hazards and provide a safe and healthy work environment; establish a record-keeping and reporting system covering all work-related injuries, deaths, and illnesses; conduct periodic safety and health inspections and correct any hazards found; allow OSHA to inspect their facilities; provide protective equipment; keep workers informed of their rights, the company's safety record, and safety standards; develop and enforce safety and health standards; and provide safety training for employees.

Enforcement of the act may involve OSHA inspections and citations of employers for breach of the general duty; breach of specific safety and health standards; or failure to document incidents, maintain appropriate records, or conspicuously post notices required under the act. The penalties for violations of the act can be both civil and criminal (Mann & Roberts, 1997). Initially, the cost of OSHA compliance can be considerable. Strategically, however, the cost of organizational operations can be reduced significantly because accidents, long-term illnesses, and deaths resulting in liability are decreased. Thus, sick time, medical claim costs, and wrongful death suits are reduced or eliminated. The security element of an organization is often responsible for OSHA regulation enforcement and compliance, as well as for employee training.

HUMAN ERROR

Losses may occur mistakenly and unintentionally through **human error**. Inaccurate record keeping and the inadvertent discard of valuables are commonplace. Shrinkage (loss of assets) within a retail organization, for example, is not always the result of internal or external criminal action. Merchandise may be inadvertently under-rung at a cash register. Damaged merchandise may be discarded without proper documentation, and defective merchandise may be destroyed when it could be returned to the manufacturer for credit. Thus, human error can increase the cost of operations (Fay, 2000).

THE THREAT FROM FIRE

Few events can cause as much personal injury or property damage as a fire. Approaches to fire safety include strategies for **fire prevention** as well as **fire protection** and suppression. Fire prevention refers to policies and practices that focus on preventing a fire from occurring. Fire protection involves minimizing personal injury and damage to property once the fire has started.

The three components of the **fire triangle** are heat, fuel, and oxygen. The components must be present in appropriate amounts and under specific conditions for a fire to occur. Prevention strategies involve control of the fire triangle. Fuel and oxygen are usually present. In addition, numerous heat sources are available to complete the fire triangle and ignite the fuel. Prevention strategies are designed to limit fuel and heat exposure. Flammable materials (fuel) should not be stored or placed near heat sources. Ignition resistant firewalls can prevent the spread of fire between adjacent occupancies. Heat sources, such as cigarettes, can be reduced or eliminated (Fischer & Green, 1998). Fire prevention also involves training and education of individuals as well as organizations as to the nature, extent, and realities of fire and its prevention. **Products of combustion** include flame, heat, smoke, and invisible toxic gases. Fire suppression involves control and elimination of the products of combustion. Limiting exposure to all products of combustion is extremely critical to human life. Exposure to flame and heat may cause serious injury and death within a very short period of time.

Smoke obscures vision and exit routes. Toxic gases displace life-sustaining oxygen, and most fire deaths result from the inhalation of these gases.

The **classification of fire** is determined in accordance with the type of combustibles involved.

Class A: ordinary combustibles such as paper and wood

Class B: flammable liquids such as gasoline

Class C: electrical

Class D: combustible metals

Once a fire starts, suppression strategies are used to minimize the damage and spread of fire. These strategies include the use of personnel and fire protection and suppression equipment such as alarms, extinguishers, sprinkler systems, and fire-fighting equipment. Strategies also include the use of fire escapes, exit routes, evacuation procedures, and fire doors to help contain the fire (Fischer & Green, 1998).

Fire can be devastating. During a 3-year period beginning in 1990, four major wildfires destroyed nearly 4,300 structures in California. These well-known fires include the following:

• June 1990, Santa Barbara—641 structures destroyed
• October 1991, Oakland-Berkeley Hills—2,900 structures destroyed
• October 1993, Laguna—330 structures destroyed
• November 1993, Malibu, Topanga Canyon—323 structures destroyed

Fire also poses a tremendous threat to life safety. In some cases, loss of human life and personal injury can be unimaginable. On February 20, 2003, a fire broke out during the rock band Great White's concert in The Station nightclub in West Warwick, Rhode Island. Pyrotechnics (fireworks) used during the band's performance inside the club ignited combustible interior building materials. Within minutes, flames engulfed the club. Most concert-goers were unaware that the flames were not part of the show. Subsequently, 99 people died and nearly 200 more were injured in a frantic struggle to escape the aging wood frame building. The West Warwick fire was the deadliest nightclub fire in the United States since the Beverly Hills Supper Club fire in Southgate, Kentucky, killed 165 in 1977 (Zuckerman, 2003).

In late October, 2003, three major fires in the California county of San Diego killed 16 people, including a firefighter, and destroyed nearly 2,500 homes and businesses. One of the fires, designated the Cedar Fire, was the largest in California history. It consumed almost 300,000 acres in less than three days. The Cedar Fire's origin was traced to a lost hunter who lit fires to alert rescuers of his location (*End in Sight,* San Diego Union Tribune, 2003).

NATURAL DISASTERS

A **natural disaster** involves any sudden, extraordinary misfortune in nature. Types of natural disasters include tornadoes, earthquakes, hurricanes, forest fires, landslides, tsunamis, coastal erosion, floods, storms, and extreme temperatures. Any natural disaster can result in injuries, death, and property loss. Contingency plans should be developed in advance of any natural disaster. These plans should involve an assessment of the potential risk, prioritization of tasks necessary to prevent or reduce losses, preparation for various disaster scenarios, and a plan to recover from the disaster (Haddow & Bullock, 2003).

Security managers are responsible for loss prevention and asset protection. Since human assets are the most valuable, systems must be in place to protect people from the negative impact of natural disasters. History is replete with numerous examples of the heavy toll natural disasters levy on human existence. Extreme heat, earthquakes in California, hurricanes in the Southwest, and tornadoes in the Midwest pose threats annually. In 1995, nearly 700 Chicagoans died as the result of exposure to extreme heat. In a 2-week period between July 19 and August 1, 2000, a heat wave was blamed for 149 deaths in the central plains and northeastern United States. A tornado touched down in Fort Worth, Texas, on March 28, 2000, killing 4 people and injuring 36. Although weather conditions indicated a tornado was possible, no one could predict if or where the storm would hit. Ultimately, downtown Forth Worth bore the brunt of the storm that shattered windows in high-rise buildings, overturned vehicles, and uprooted trees (Hawkins, 2000). On December 16, 2000, unseasonable tornados killed 11 people and left numerous others injured in Alabama. May 2003 was one of the worst months for tornados in recorded U.S. history. From Colorado to Virginia over 300 twisters caused millions of dollars in damage, killed nearly 50 people, and injured hundreds more.

During December 2000, severe cold and heavy snowfall covered much of the continental United States. Storms paralyzed ground transportation and caused considerable delays with air travelers during the pre-holiday season. Businesses were impacted negatively, since holiday shoppers were unable to reach retail establishments and shipping was delayed (Conlon, 2000). Ice and snow across the southern plains of the United States damaged power lines and left almost 600,000 homes and businesses without electricity. A thick coat of ice stretching from New Mexico to Arkansas created massive traffic jams and stranded thousands of people. At least 37 deaths were attributed to the severe winter weather conditions (Barnes, 2000). On December 30, 2000, a blizzard struck the northeastern United States. The storm created whiteout conditions and left 9 to 18 inches of snow between Delaware and Maine. The gigantic blizzard disrupted holiday travel and commerce, with major urban areas such as New York City hard hit by the storm (McFadden, 2000; Revkin, 2001). On February 17, 2003, a blizzard in the Midwest and Northeast regions of the United States was blamed for at least 28 deaths (Petterson, 2003).

ENVIRONMENTAL DISASTERS

An **environmental disaster** includes exposure to hazardous materials, conventional and nuclear power failures, and gas line or water main breaks. Sometimes referred to as technological or man-made disasters, environmental disasters also include nuclear accidents, terrorist incidents, and the use of nuclear, biological, chemical, or radiological weapons (Haddow & Bullock, 2003). Hazardous materials emergencies require extreme care due to the volatile nature of most toxic gases, chemicals, liquids, and corrosive materials. Failure of utilities may also be life-threatening, and backup systems and procedures should be preplanned.

Environmental disasters are caused by the impact of human action on the natural environment. These events become more commonplace as the human population increases. Currently, the world's population exceeds 6 billion, and approximately 100 million people are added to the population each year.

Environmental legislation has been enacted in many jurisdictions in an effort to prevent damage to biological and ecological systems. The first recorded environmental legislation in America occurred in 1626, when the Plymouth Colony enacted ordinances that regulated harvesting and conservation of timber on colonial land (Rettie, 1995).

Numerous local, county, state, and federal statutes exist that are designed to protect the environment. In some cases, statutes provide for criminal prosecution as well as compensation under civil law. Under these laws, civil and criminal liability may be incurred for conduct resulting in air and water pollution, improper pesticide distribution and use, excessive noise, and possession or emission of regulated chemicals. Corporations as well as individuals may be held civilly and criminally liable for violations. The laws hold corporate officers and other employees liable if they know or should know environmental laws are being violated. Specific intent to commit a crime is not required (Epstein, 1998). Simply stated, an **environmental crime** is any human activity that violates an environmental criminal statute (Clifford & Edwards, 1998).

Although many countries may be environmentally conscious, activities in some countries create international environmental problems. A **transborder** flow occurs when an event in one country impacts the environment in another country. Transborder flows of toxic substances occur when pollutants originate in one country and move to other countries through water and air currents, living organisms, and deliberate transportation. Transborder flows of some economic decisions have produced devastating human and environmental consequences for almost 500 years. Through direct political and military control, such as colonialization, less developed areas of the world have been victimized when economic decisions originating in developed countries deplete resources in underdeveloped nations. Transnational corporations as well as powerful nations can penetrate international borders to exploit human and biological environments in host countries (Michalowski, 1998).

Occasionally, environmental disasters arise from unlikely sources. In May 2000, National Park Service personnel started a controlled burn to clear brush near the Bandelier National Monument near Santa Fe, New Mexico. As warm winds reached speeds of up to 55 miles per hour, the fire burned out of control. The wildfire caused the evacuation of nearly 25,000 area residents, including the entire population of 11,000 of Los Alamos, New Mexico. Over 200 homes and an unknown number of other buildings were destroyed by the fire.

CIVIL LIABILITY

Civil liability has become a major concern for public as well as private organizations and institutions. Simply stated, civil liability may occur when a person is harmed or injured through the action or inaction of another. Huge jury awards and out-of-court settlements have been granted to plaintiffs who file and prove claims of sexual harassment, unsafe environments, negligence, wrongful death, defects in design, manufacture and packaging, failure to warn, invasion of privacy, use of excessive force, personal injury, violations of civil rights, and conspiracy to defraud. Incidents that precipitate these claims involve intentional or unintentional wrongs, failure to protect, and failure to exercise a reasonable standard of care.

Plaintiffs often sue for **punitive damages** as well as **compensatory damages**. Juries assign punitive damages to punish the respondent in a lawsuit, thus sending a strong message of disapproval. Compensatory damages are designed to compensate the petitioner for actual losses incurred. The large non–class-action lawsuit jury awards in 2000 exemplify the trend toward multimillion dollar compensatory and punitive damage assessments.

- Although subsequently overturned, $474.7 million was awarded to Anna Nicole Smith, a former *Playboy* model, who accused the family of her late husband, oil tycoon J. Howard Marshall II, of conspiring to cut her out of Marshall's will.
- A $341.7 million judgment against the Iranian government was awarded to former Associated Press reporter Terry Anderson, who was held hostage by Iranian-supported terrorists in Lebanon for 7 years.
- $328 million was awarded to the parents of 10-year-old Jeffrey Curley of Cambridge, Massachusetts, against the two men who were convicted of raping and murdering Jeffrey.
- $327 million was awarded to the families of a young couple killed in Israel in 1996 by Iranian-backed terrorists. The judgment was the second largest award against the Iranian government in 2000.
- $268.7 million was awarded to the family of a teenager who died from an overdose of medication after an operation.
- $268.6 million was awarded to a South Dakota woman who was seriously injured and widowed by a driver under the influence of drugs.

- A $240 million judgment against the Disney Corporation was awarded to two men who claimed Disney stole their idea for a sports complex.
- $113.5 million was awarded to the family of a murdered woman after the woman's husband tried to obtain money from the deceased woman's trust fund.
- A $111.5 million judgment against Bear Stearns Company was awarded to a multimillionaire who lost $300 million in high-risk currency futures trading.
- $105 million was awarded to the father of a man who was sexually molested by a South Carolina school teacher decades earlier.
- $105 million was awarded to a man who was seriously injured when a tire-rim assembly system broke during a tire change. The judgment was against Bridgestone-Firestone (Sukiennik, 2001).

Liability may arise from situations and events associated with errors and omissions, as well as claims of wrongful termination, workplace violence, and sexual harassment. In many cases, liability attaches to an incident even though an individual is not at fault or did not intend any harm. This type of liability is referred to as **strict liability**. In other cases, organizations or third parties may be held liable for the actions of others with whom they have a relationship. This is called **vicarious liability**. Avoiding, reducing, or mitigating liability involves the development of a comprehensive plan to prevent incidents that create liability and to take action to limit liability once an incident occurs. Appropriate strategies involve adequate physical and information security as well as a human resource management plan that includes proper selection, training, supervision, and discipline; policy review and revision; and legal support. Liability can also be transferred, to some degree, through the purchase of appropriate amounts of liability insurance (Canton, 2003; Cheeseman, 2004; Sennewald, 2003). Examples of the negative impact of liability as well as policies and procedures designed to mitigate liability are presented throughout this book.

SUBSTANCE ABUSE

Substance abuse refers to the inappropriate ingestion of toxic and controlled substances into the human body. Substance abuse has become increasingly costly in both economic and human terms. According to the U.S. Department of Health and Human Services, drug use among 12- to 17-year-olds increased dramatically and drug abuse in the workplace became more common during the 1990s. A majority of drug addicts in the United States may be employed full-time ("Most drug abusers . . .," 1999; "Picture of drug use . . .," 2000). This situation creates serious problems for society, the employer, and the individual.

Chemical abuse is pervasive and far-reaching. It accounts for a large proportion of present-day criminal law violations, and it places a tremendous strain on the criminal justice system. It is often a contributing factor in many types of crimes, including burglary, robbery, smuggling, theft, and murder. Drug law violations clog courtrooms, and drug-related convictions crowd corrections programs and facilities. Substance abuse may lead to even greater destructive consequences than other so-called victimless crimes. Lost productivity, wasted human potential, disease, violence, fragmented families, and economic loss are but a few of the negative consequences of chemical abuse (Schmalleger, 2003).

Commonly abused substances include alcohol, hallucinogens, amphetamines (stimulants), depressants, and tranquilizers that are swallowed; PCP, cocaine base, and cannabis (marijuana) products that are smoked; heroin, which is injected; and methamphetamine and cocaine hydrochloride that may be snorted or injected. The **symptoms of substance abuse** include significant changes in personal appearance, sudden and irrational flare-ups, unusual degrees of activity or inactivity, as well as sudden and dramatic changes in discipline and job performance. Physically, the abuser may have dilated pupils or may wear sunglasses at inappropriate times. The abuser may have needle marks or razor cuts, or may wear long sleeves to hide such marks. Borrowing money, stealing, and frequent association with known substance abusers or dealers are also strong indicators.

A person exhibiting the symptoms of hallucinogen use, such as LSD, peyote, and psilocybin, may have dilated pupils, sweat excessively, hallucinate, and have increased respiratory and heart rates. The symptoms associated with PCP use often include high pain tolerance, great physical strength, hallucinations, unpredictability, aggressive and extremely violent behavior, excessive sweating, drowsiness, nystagmus, paranoia, confusion, blank stares, muscle rigidity, unusual gait or convulsions, and a possible chemical odor on the breath or body. Symptoms of stimulant use, such as cocaine, amphetamines, or methamphetamine, include restlessness, talkativeness, trembling, dilated pupils, sleeplessness, hyperactivity, and increased respiratory and heart rates. Finally, symptoms of depressant use, such as barbiturates, sedatives, or tranquilizers, include slurred speech, poor coordination, unsteadiness, intoxicated behavior with no odor of alcoholic beverages, nystagmus, and decreased respiratory and heart rates.

Public substance abuse prevention and treatment strategies include programs such as Drug Abuse Resistance Education (DARE) for juveniles and law enforcement's emphasis on drug law enforcement and interdiction ("Truth, DARE and consequences . . .," 1998). The DARE program and law enforcement, by themselves, have had little appreciable impact on reducing illicit drug use. One study indicated that the impact of each dollar spent in drug treatment produces approximately the same results as seven dollars spent for law enforcement. Government efforts to reduce illicit drug use apparently have the greatest impact when treatment and law enforcement strategies are used conjunctively (Mishra, 1998; Rand Corporation, 1999).

On November 7, 2000, California voters overwhelmingly approved Proposition 36, a measure designed to divert many drug offenders from the criminal justice system into treatment programs. Under the law, those convicted of illegal drug possession for the first or second time, as well as some drug-related parole violators, are referred to treatment rather than receive a criminal justice sanction. This law does not apply to drug dealers. The law represents an experimental shift away from drug law enforcement toward treatment and rehabilitation (Ainsworth, 2000).

Private strategies include prevention and treatment programs sponsored by health care organizations, private rehabilitation facilities, and employer-sponsored employee assistance programs. Appropriate employer responses to substance abuse involve a written and communicated company policy, documentation of incidents of abuse in the workplace, and employer interventions through counseling, treatment, probation, and termination. Currently, private employers have no legal right to intervene unless the substance abuse affects job performance and safety. Drug testing in the workplace is increasing, although the legality of such testing has yet to be firmly established. Local statutes and case law should be reviewed, and a legal opinion obtained prior to implementing or modifying any drug-testing program.

CIVIL DISORDER

Civil disorder occurs when an individual or group disrupts the normal peace and tranquility of a community or the operations of a business or organization. The perpetrator's activities may be legal or illegal. Strikes and labor disputes, demonstrations, special events such as sports activities, concerts, parades, and riots are all examples of civil disturbances.

Although most civil disorder events are peaceful, a nonviolent group could become violent if conditions conducive to violence exist. The potential for property loss, injuries, and death is tremendous. The Los Angeles riot that occurred subsequent to the acquittal of police officers involved in the Rodney King incident in 1992 began as a demonstration. It became a riot and resulted in over $1 billion in losses, with 10,000 businesses destroyed, at least 1,300 injuries, and 44 deaths. The damage and casualties were greater than that which occurred during the Watts Riot in Los Angeles in 1965 and the Detroit riots in 1967 ("Path of destruction," 1992).

Even joyous events sometimes transform into disastrous riots. On June 19, 2000, hundreds of celebrators threw rocks, set fires, and looted subsequent to the Los Angeles Laker's National Championship basketball victory. Two police vehicles were destroyed by fire and several businesses were vandalized and looted. As with natural disasters, contingency plans should be developed to deal with civil disorder and minimize property loss and casualties.

Although much has changed since the early days of labor unrest, a potential problem for many organizations involves labor disputes. When planning is inadequate and responses inappropriate, the stage for disaster is set. The organization is often faced with millions of dollars in losses, negative publicity, and consumer disconnect. As evidenced by the history of labor unrest, merely assigning security personnel to the entrances of the organization's facility is not enough. A comprehensive labor dispute contingency plan is essential and must contain several possible courses of action. The strategy should include liaison with public law enforcement, appropriate security personnel, vulnerability assessments, evidence collection, intelligence operations, and good media relations.

Preestablished liaison with and commitment from law enforcement and other public safety agencies ensures response if demonstrators engage in illegal activities. Adequate, well-trained security personnel can deescalate conflict through self-restraint and not be intimated by demonstrators. Regular vulnerability assessments of the facility, homes of employees, distribution points, and off-site meeting facilities are a necessity. During a strike, labor unions often claim unfair labor practices on the part of management. Organizations should document the illegal activities of strikers through the use of audio and video tape, still photographs, and personal affidavits. The documentation can be used as a defense in subsequent litigation stemming from the unfair labor practices claims. Intelligence operations at local gathering places outside the facility assist management and security personnel to anticipate problem situations. Media relations are also important. Liaison should be established with news organizations, and managers should be trained on how to respond to media inquiries. Finally, management and security personnel should avoid confrontations with the disputants that might create long-lasting resentments. In most cases, union workers will resume employment when the labor dispute is settled. Tensions between management and union workers can taint labor relations in the future (Taylor, 2000).

CRIME

Although a majority of most security managers' time is likely spent dealing with noncriminal matters, crime prevention and the detection of criminal activity are major security concerns. All types of **crime** are potential threats. However, security personnel most often deal with the prevention and detection of crimes involving theft (larceny), burglary, trespassing, vandalism, embezzlement, computer crime, substance abuse, assault, robbery, and various forms of fraud and economic crime. (Hess & Wrobleski, 1996; Simonsen, 1998). One study indicated about 79 percent of employees steal from employers, resulting in losses of more than $120 billion each year (Slater, 2000).

Crime is a complex concept, and an inclusive definition of crime is often difficult due to the competing theories about what causes it. In addition, behavior that is codified as criminal today may not be criminal tomorrow. The public's perception and attitudes toward criminal behavior also change over time. Property crime offenders were severely punished at one time and, in some cases, as severely as violent offenders. Today, most property crime offenders are treated much less severely than their violent criminal counterparts (Siegel, 2001).

Scope of Crime

In 1929, the Attorney General of the United States and the FBI were authorized by Congress to develop and implement a uniform system for the collection and dissemination of crime statistics. The system was built upon the recommendations of earlier efforts by the International Association of Chiefs of Police (IACP). The system was designed to identify major crime trends by comparing seven crimes included in Part I of the **Uniform Crime Report (UCR)** contained in *Crime in the United States.* Part I, or **Index crimes**, included the violent crimes of murder, forcible rape, robbery, and aggravated assault as well as the so-called nonviolent crimes of burglary, larceny (theft), and auto theft. These offenses represented the types of crime most likely to be reported to the police. In 1979, arson was added to the Index crimes list. Crimes not listed in Part I were included in Part II of the UCR. The UCR includes information regarding the crime rate based on the number of reported crimes per 100,000 population.

Crime statistics included in the UCR are supplied to the FBI voluntarily by law enforcement agencies. Initially, approximately 400 agencies reported their crime statistics to the FBI. By 1971, approximately 8,000 of the estimated 20,000 law enforcement agencies in the U.S. reported crimes. In 1994, 16,313 agencies submitted crime reports. Because police officers rarely observe a crime when it occurs, law enforcement agencies rely on citizens and victims to report criminal activity (Schmalleger, 2004).

According to reported statistics, the crime rate began to increase significantly in the 1960s. Campus unrest, anti–Vietnam War protests, urban riots, and the increase in the number of young men in the population contributed to the increase in the crime rates. Crime rates in the United States reached a peak in 1980 and began a slow decline in 1981 (U.S. Department of Justice, Bureau of Justice Statistics, 1992). Factors contributing to the decline have been attributed to tougher sentences, community policing, and a decline in the number of men in the Index-crime–prone age group of 14 to 24 (Dorning, 2000; "Is LA's crime honeymoon over? . . .," 2000). However, with the potential increase in the number of males in their late teens and early 20s on the horizon, many experts predict that the crime rate will rise again (Arner, 2000a). Additionally, if certain negative political, social, and economic conditions develop, some experts predict a dramatic increase in both violent and property crimes by 2010 (Schmalleger, 2004).

A major criticism of the UCR is that it includes information on crime reports submitted to the FBI voluntarily by law enforcement agencies, and all agencies do not currently report such data. In addition, police agencies are not able to report crimes that are not reported to them (Senna & Siegel, 2001). In an effort to obtain more detailed information on the nature and extent of crime in the United States, the U.S. Department of Justice conducted victimization surveys beginning in 1972. The major purpose of the surveys was to uncover unreported crimes and the reasons for not reporting. The results of the victimization surveys reported twice as much overall crime than was reported in the UCR's statistics, with theft-related offenses four times higher than official records. Burglary was the most commonplace reported crime. Reasons given for not reporting included a victim's perception that nothing would be accomplished, the incident was not serious enough for police attention, and fear of reprisal. Surveys conducted in the late 1990s indicated that only about 40 percent of all crime and 20 percent of all theft-related crimes were reported to the police (U.S. Department of Justice, Office of Justice Programs, Bureau of Justice Statistics, 1997).

Today, **National Crime Victimization Survey (NCVS)** information is collected by the U.S. Department of Justice's Bureau of Justice Statistics in cooperation with the U.S. Bureau of the Census. The NCVS collects data annually from a sample of approximately 50,000 households containing more than 100,000 individuals age 12 or older. The NCVS does not measure murder, kidnaping, crimes against commercial establishments, public drunkenness, drug abuse, prostitution, illegal gambling, con games, or blackmail. The NCVS is not without its critics either. There is, for example, the potential for false or exaggerated reports made by the victims to the interviewers, and no attempt is made to validate victims' claims. The UCR is still the most accurate database in terms of crimes reported to the police.

In response to criticisms of the UCR and the NCVS, the FBI introduced and began accepting crime data for the **National Incident-Based Reporting System (NIBRS)** in January 1989. The traditional UCR system required a summary of the number of occurrences of Part I offenses as well as arrest data for Part I and Part II offenses. As an alternative to summary reporting, the new enhanced UCR, or NIBRS, was developed to deal with the volume, diversity, and complexity of crime. The NIBRS requires more detailed reports. Agencies collect data regarding individual crime incidents and arrests, and submit reports detailing each incident. The incident-based reporting provides much more information (Schmalleger, 2004).

Among the major changes introduced in NIBRS is the substitution of Part I and Part II offenses with Group A and B offenses. While existing Part I offenses focus on eight street crimes, the new Group A expands to 22 offenses and widens criminological interest to include economic crime. Detailed information is provided for each occurrence of these crimes. Included among the 52 data elements collected is information detailing the circumstances of the crime, offender characteristics, arrestee data, victim information, and offense and property data. Less detailed information is required for the 11 offenses in Group B. This group focuses generally on nonviolent and less serious offenses, such as bad checks and criminal trespass.

Other new features of the NIBRS include new offense definitions. Rape, for example, in addition to cases involving force, has been expanded to include cases in which consent was not given due to temporary or permanent mental or physical incapacity. In addition, there are new UCR codes, and all crimes occurring during the same incident are recorded. The NIBRS has also introduced a new category called crimes against society. It provides an additional category to complement the existing crimes against property and crimes against person categories and includes crimes such as gambling, prostitution, and drug sales and use. Finally, the NIBRS provides the means for distinguishing between attempted and completed crimes, and expands data on the victim-offender relationship. Although the system was intended to be fully operational by the end of 1999, states have been slow to convert to the new system.

In 1995, the NCVS redesigned its questionnaires to include more detailed information on interaction between victim and offender, victim crime deterrence efforts, perceived effectiveness of crime deterrence efforts, bystander behavior, perceived alcohol and drug use by offenders, and suspected offender gang involvement (Ortmeier, 2002; Schmalleger, 2003, 2004).

> Additional information regarding crime statistics and trends may be obtained by contacting the FBI at www.fbi.gov.

Although the overall crime rate has been declining since the early 1980s, public opinion polls indicate that citizen fear of crime remains high. Many people, for example, may keep guns in their homes as protection against the nighttime intruder, although burglars rarely enter a home if it is likely to be occupied. Myths abound for many types of crime, and unrealistic fear creates a false sense of insecurity and may negatively impact the quality of life for many people.

Contrary to common belief, the overall rate of household burglaries has been declining since the early 1970s. Yet, burglary remains an attractive crime for the offender. The arrest rate for burglary is relatively low. A burglar evaluates potential targets based on their contents and any security measures on the premises. Two-thirds of all residential burglaries occur when no one is home. People become creatures of habit, and it is not difficult for a burglar to identify the routine of a residential target. The proportion of daytime burglaries has increased, primarily because more women have entered the workforce and the residence is unoccupied during regular daytime business hours (Hakim & Blackstone, 1997).

Economic Crime

Generally, an **economic crime** is defined as a violation of criminal law designed to reward an offender financially (Siegel, 2001). Organizations, businesses, governments, and other enterprises are easy targets for economic crime. Intellectual property in the form of trade secrets, copyrights, patents, client lists, financial information, and technical and strategic plans may be of interest to competitors and foreign governments. Products can be tampered with, hijacked, grey- or black-marketed, and counterfeited. Information can be acquired electronically through computers and the Internet. Technology can be acquired by reverse-engineering a product, surveillance, undercover work, hiring an employee away from a company, disingenuous contract negotiations, and bribery.

The most prevalent economic crimes involve some form of fraud. Investment fraud occurs when bogus stocks are sold. Warranty fraud takes place when merchants fraudulently claim a product is under warranty and they obtain replacement parts under a warranty exchange program. Telemarketing fraud, which involves telephone sales of high-priced, low-value items, targets the elderly and many businesses. Workers' compensation fraud resulting from faked injuries and illnesses costs businesses millions of dollars each year. As much as 10 percent of every health care dollar spent may be attributable to fraud. Fraudulent schemes utilizing the Internet, as well as computer hacking of all types, are growing rapidly. Fraudulent checks, credit card scams, and fraudulent loans threaten financial institutions. Embezzlement, padding expense accounts, and lost production time also result in financial losses to businesses and cause a drain on the U.S. economy. Occupational fraud committed by an occupational subculture that encourages, and in some cases requires, illegal behavior of its members may account for over $400 billion dollars in losses to American companies annually (Coleman, 1994).

A form of economic crime that is becoming more prevalent is **identity theft**. The crime is committed when an imposter fraudulently uses another's personal identification information to obtain credit, merchandise, or services in the name of the victim. The personal identification information often stolen and used by criminals includes driver's license and social security numbers, addresses, phone numbers, and dates of birth. In some cases, the perpetrator obtains the personal information through the Internet or by accessing an organization's client account information. Other methods include theft of personal mail, eavesdropping, searching a person's trash for personal information, or simply observing the victim enter personal data on a form or at an automatic teller machine (ATM). In most cases, victims of identify theft are unaware that they are being victimized until they receive bills and invoices for goods and services they have not purchased (Schmalleger, 2003).

Additional information regarding identify theft, its prevention, and how to report it can be accessed on the Federal Trade Commission's website at www.consumer.gov/idtheft or on the Social Security Administration's identify theft website at www.ssa.gov/pubs/idtheft.htm.

The noted criminologist Edwin Sutherland introduced the phrase **white collar crime** and defined it as an offense committed by a person of respectability and high social status in the course of an occupation (Sutherland, 1949). Later, James Coleman (1994) expanded the definition and defined it as a violation of the law committed by a person or group of persons in the course of an otherwise respected and legitimate occupation or financial activity. White collar crime includes political corruption, bribery, illegal business practices, price-fixing, tax evasion (as compared to tax avoidance), fraud, identity theft, misrepresentation of facts that leads to financial gain, embezzlement, and other economic crime such as industrial espionage, computer-related crime, and theft of proprietary information. White collar crime accounts for a greater total financial loss to the American people than does street crime. If deaths resulting from known, yet uncorrected, workplace safety hazards were included in the statistics, white collar crime would account for a death rate which is higher than the nation's murder rate.

White collar crime is also a national security issue. The greatest single threat to the security of the United States today may be white collar crime, including economic crime and industrial espionage. By the mid-1990s, losses from economic crime in the United States increased to over $60 billion. Industrial espionage agents target intellectual property such as trade secrets, financial information, corporate tactical and strategic plans, and technology. Many foreign businesses and some foreign governments are actively involved in industrial espionage against United States businesses (Coleman, 1994).

Case histories of economic crime depict the seriousness and magnitude of the problem. For example, in 1997, Volkswagen (VW) agreed to pay General Motors (GM) $100 million to settle a lawsuit stemming from a 4-year old allegation that VW stole trade secrets from GM. VW also agreed to purchase over $1 billion worth of parts from GM over a 7-year period. The settlement was one of the largest in corporate espionage history. VW did not admit any wrongdoing but acknowledged that it was possible that GM proprietary information may have been transferred when several GM executives defected to VW (Meredith, 1997).

Counterfeiting and piracy of American products cost billions of dollars in lost sales each year and threaten the brands and reputations of businesses. Generally of inferior quality, counterfeit products are purchased by unsuspecting customers who file consumer complaints against the legitimate companies when defective products are discovered. The problem impacts traditional product-based industries such as clothing, cosmetics, pharmaceuticals, beverages, and motorbikes, as well as the high-tech software, electronics, sporting goods, and entertainment companies. In some countries, counterfeiting and piracy of goods takes place in state-owned factories that have the capacity to replicate legitimately produced foreign brand products ("China's piracy plague," 2000). In violation of copyright laws, millions of Internet users routinely duplicate copyrighted material every day. Computer software, photographs, movies, books, even cross-stitch needlework patterns produced by a South Carolina company are copied illegally. The South Carolina company, Pegasus Originals, estimated a $200,000 loss in 5 years, due largely to Internet piracy. Utilizing traditional methods, photocopies and tape recordings degrade (become less and less clear) with each copy of a copy. However, with the Internet and digital technology, every copy is of the same quality as the original. The Internet also allows for much wider distribution than a manual person-to-person format. Once an item is placed online, literally hundreds of thousands of people can download and copy the copyrighted item in an instant.

Many cyberspace copyright infringement legal battles pit large corporations against each other. In its copyright infringement lawsuits, the music recording industry sued two large targets: MP3.com and Napster.com. MP3.com allowed Internet users to download music while Napster allowed users to exchange their digital music files with each other. On September 6, 2000, a federal judge ordered MP3.com to pay almost $250 million to the Universal Music Group for intentionally violating copyrights. The Recording Industry Association of America claimed it lost over $300 million in sales due to Napster activities (Balint, 2000).

All forms of economic and white collar crime appear to be on the rise, and fraudulent activities have been discovered in the highest echelons of some large corporations. In addition to the various methodologies previously discussed, the United States has witnessed a marked increase in corporate accounting infractions and similar financial frauds. In 2002 alone, malfeasance by many corporations and high-level executives led to criminal investigations and charges, guilty pleas, and convictions for stock manipulation and insider trading. Details about fraudulent schemes emerged from major corporations such as Enron, WorldCom, Tyco International, ImClone, Adelphia, and the accounting firm of Arthur Andersen. Many corporate executives became wealthy at the expense of employees and investors. As a result, corporate boards and executives, as well as auditing firms, face greater scrutiny, new laws, and more stringent industry standards (Foss, 2003).

Public law enforcement may be ill-equipped to combat most economic and white collar crime. Unlike most street crime, economic crimes harm a great number of people over an extended period of time. Thus, the damage is less apparent (hidden) and often indirect. Societal reactions to economic and white collar crime are also diluted. Prison sentences are rare. More common punitive sanctions include restitution, fines, censure, and disapproval. Most of these sanctions are imposed by regulatory agencies rather than the criminal courts. Unless the offenses are made public, most economic and white collar crimes are handled internally, with corporations and organizations utilizing private disciplinary mechanisms (Siegel, 2001).

Organized Crime

Organized crime is defined as any relatively permanent group of individuals that systematically engage in illegal activities and provide illegal services. Organized crime is a continuous conspiratorial activity with economic gain as its primary goal. It involves the coordination of numerous persons in the planning and execution of illegal acts or the pursuit of legitimate goals through unlawful means (Siegel, 2001). Organized crime's existence is maintained through the use of threats, intimidation, force, monopoly control, and corruption. Revenues from illegal activities are used to develop legitimate businesses to use as covers for more illegal activity. The image of organized crime, often referred to as the Mafia or La Cosa Nostra, portrays people of southern European ancestry, under the direction of a godfather, engaging in organized illegal activity. This may have been true in the early days, because authorities trace the beginnings of organized crime in the United States to the Prohibition Era (1919–1933) when Southern European immigrants became involved in bootlegging activities. During this period, the manufacture, distribution, and sale of alcoholic beverages in the United States were illegal. Due to consumer demand, the alcoholic beverage bootleggers went underground, and criminals organized to meet the public's demand. Contemporary organized crime crosses all ethnic and cultural lines. The groups are involved with illegal drugs, gambling, loan-sharking, prostitution, labor racketeering, intellectual property theft, stock fraud, and various other illegal activities (Albanese, 1996; Siegel, 2001).

Sometimes colloquially referred to as "the mob," organized crime group activity has expanded into the world of economic and white collar crime. An example of the mob's influence came to light in November 1997, with the arrest of 18 people who were allegedly involved with a stock price-fixing scheme. Members of the Genovese and Bonanno crime families collaborated with HealthTech International, Inc., a Mesa, Arizona, health and fitness center company, to artificially inflate the company's assets and stock prices. Through the scheme, stockbrokers convinced unwitting buyers that the company's assets were eight times their actual value. As a result, the company stock's trading value increased over 250 percent and participants in the scheme stood to gain enormous profits through the sale of the inflated stocks.

In June 2000, federal authorities raided numerous locations across the nation and arrested over 100 people in what the authorities referred to as one of the largest securities fraud cases in United States history. Members of New York's five organized crime families allegedly banded together in an unprecedented joint venture to scam $50 million through the stock market. In the federal indictments and criminal complaints that followed, authorities charged that gangsters recruited stockbrokers to inflate the value of companies in which the mob families had secret ownership. Through promoters, the brokers inflated the value of the stocks. Unsuspecting investors bought stock in the underfunded companies. One shell company had only $2,000 in actual assets, but was able to generate $90 million from stock sales before collapsing (Smith, G.B., 2000).

Organized crime is constantly expanding its range of illegal activities. Foreign criminal organizations, through their increasing use of computer technology, have become a direct threat to the security of the United States. Sophisticated criminal organizations can penetrate innocent computer databases, influence financial markets, and destabilize countries and entire regions of the world. In addition, international criminal organizations counterfeit money, CDs, and software; smuggle aliens, weapons, and precious gems; and kidnap and transport women and children for various forms of sexual servitude. In response, the United States created an international task force to eliminate barriers among agencies and countries that fight different types of organized crime. The interagency task force is also charged with fighting international trafficking of women and children and the smuggling of aliens ("Global crime cartels are tech-savvy, U.S. says," 2000).

Street Crime

What is commonly referred to as **street crime** includes offenses such as murder, forcible rape, robbery, aggravated assault, burglary, auto theft, larceny, and arson. These crimes are listed in Part I of the UCR, a document published annually by the FBI, as discussed earlier in this chapter. Often referred to as Index crimes, or the leading criminal indicators, the list includes serious crimes against persons and property most often reported to the police. Statistics on these crimes typically appear in the news broadcasts. The public's perception is that street crime of a felonious nature accounts for the largest percentage of crime in the United States. However, most crime in the United States is not of the street crime variety (Albanese, 2000).

Most street crimes are committed by youthful offenders. Young men, teenagers to young adults, tend to commit most of the crime in the streets. Throughout the latter half of the twentieth century, juvenile gangs (groups of associates) became a major problem in urban, as well as some suburban and rural, areas (Siegel, 2001). Although some gangs include adult members, most are teenagers. Specific problems associated with gangs include the use, distribution, and sale of controlled substances. Illegal drug trafficking provides an economic foundation for organized gangs. Other problematic areas include turf conflict, where rival gangs, using public areas as private space, compete for the same area (Barlow, 2000). Gangs have also infiltrated businesses, the military, and public law enforcement agencies (Newman & Kurtis, 1997).

Bombs, Bomb Threats, and Weapons of Mass Destruction

In 2003, the United States entered into a war in Iraq to remove President Saddam Hussein and his regime from power. Hussein's government was credited with the development and use of weapons of mass destruction (WMDs). The development and illegal use of bombs and WMDs is not new. They have been used by individuals, drug traffickers, organized crime, dictators, and terrorist groups for some time. Relatively inexpensive to produce, these devices and agents are commonly used by perpetrators who wish to be far from the scene when the detonation takes place. The Unabomber sent pipe bombs through the mail to specific targets. The deaths resulting from the bombing of the World Trade Center in New York City in 1993, the Alfred P. Murrah federal office building in Oklahoma City in 1995, and a nightclub in Bali, Indonesia, in 2002 demonstrated the catastrophic nature of explosives assembled for mass murder in a single event. The Tokyo subway sarin nerve-gas attack in 1995 also enlightened the world about the damage that can be created through the use of nuclear, biological, and chemical (NBC) weapons.

Although the majority of bomb threats are a hoax, they should be treated seriously. In most jurisdictions, the threat itself is a crime. In the event a person has reported a suspicious package, it should be treated as an actual explosive device. Upon arriving at the scene where a suspicious package is reported, the initial responder should contact the person who reported the package so the person can direct emergency personnel to the location of the item in question. A safe distance around the package should be established. Personnel should not handle, touch, smell, or attempt to dismantle any suspected or known explosive device. Bomb disposal experts or explosive technicians should be summoned. Personnel should use land-line telephones rather than cellular phones or radios for communication because of the possibility of a radio-activated device (California Commission on Peace Officer Standards and Training, 1999). Electric and gas utilities should be disconnected, a no-smoking policy must be enforced, and any flammable combustibles in the vicinity of the device should be removed.

If a bomb threat call was received and no suspicious package has been located, a search for the device must be conducted. Contrary to early practices, the best people to conduct the initial search for a suspicious package are people who live or work in the area. These people are familiar with the area and are more likely to observe something that is out of place or does not belong to an occupant. If a suspicious package is located, an evacuation is necessary.

It is also important to interview the person who received the bomb threat. If the threat was received via telephone, the interview should focus on what the caller said, the sound of the caller's voice, and any background noises apparent to the listener. If an explosive incident has occurred, personnel should treat the affected area as a crime scene unless determined otherwise.

Bomb searches must be carried out with extreme caution. Ideally, two persons familiar with an area should search for a suspicious package. After entering an area or room, the searchers should stand quietly with eyes closed and listen for clockwork devises or any unusual sounds. The area should be divided into two equal parts. Searchers will start at the perimeter, searching from the bottom and working up, from the ground (floor) level to hip height, waist height to ceiling, ceiling area (light fixtures, air ducts), and any area behind a false or suspended ceiling. Searchers should work back-to-back, working toward each other, from the perimeter to the center of the area of room being searched. After the search is completed, the area (room) should be posted with a sign or marker indicating a search has been completed in the area. If a suspicious package is located, the area should be evacuated to a safe distance and bomb disposal experts summoned to remove the package. (U.S. Department of the Treasury, Bureau of Alcohol, Tobacco and Firearms, 2000).

Terrorism

Although the number of terrorist attacks declined significantly in 2002 (Dunphy, 2003), the United States, along with many other countries, finds itself immersed and preoccupied with the terrorist activities of other nations as well as of small groups and a few radical individuals (Maniscalco & Christen, 2002; U.S. General Accounting Office, 2001). Yet, terrorism is not a new phenomenon. It has been one of the darkest features of human behavior since the beginning of recorded history. Individuals and groups have committed incredible atrocities in the name of promoting or defending a greater good. Terrorists have severely disrupted the well-being and peace of mind of everyday people, and they have destabilized entire societies (Martin, 2003).

There is considerable disagreement on the definition of terrorism, largely because a definition depends on an interpretation of the motivation of the participants. What is terrorism to one person may be a selfless act to another (Barlow, 2000). Thus, defining terrorism is not a simple process (Martin, 2003). Broadly speaking, terrorism involves the use of violence or threats to intimidate or coerce. Terrorism may be the product of an individual or a group. Within this context, terrorists could include idealistic and political groups; economic opportunists; urban groups, such as predatory, ethnic, and economic gangs; career criminals; domestic violence perpetrators; and some firearms rights, anti-abortion, pro-choice, animal rights, and environmental activists. In addition, drug cartels are involved in what has come to be known as narco-terrorism. Drug cartels terrorize politicians, kidnap and execute government officials and corporate executives, and extort services and economic resources from international business concerns. Within a narrow context, terrorism is defined as an act of violence committed against an innocent person, or noncombatant, for the purpose of achieving a political end through fear and intimidation (Deutch, 1997; Siegel, 2001). The definition of terrorism continues to evolve as terrorists and their motives, targets, and methods change. Terrorists, both domestic and foreign, include individuals, street gangs, political and religious zealots, and highly organized national and international organizations (Maniscalco & Christen, 2002; Simonsen & Spindlove, 2000).

Terrorist acts may be classified as domestic or international. In 1995, Timothy McVeigh bombed the Alfred P. Murrah federal office building in Oklahoma City. One hundred sixty-eight men, women, and children died as a result of the bombing. McVeigh was subsequently convicted in U.S. District Court in Denver and executed for the killing of several federal law enforcement agents who were present in the building at the time of the bombing. A terrorist group, the Aum Shinrikyo cult, was responsible for a sarin nerve-gas attack in a Tokyo subway in March 1995. The attack killed 10 commuters and left nearly 5,000 ill (Deutch, 1997; Gaines, Kaune, & Miller, 2001).

International terrorists do not confine themselves to a nation-state. There were 273 terrorist attacks classified as international terrorism in 1998 (U.S. Department of State, 1999). Numerous examples of international terrorism activity surfaced over the past several years. Osama bin Laden, an exiled Saudi Arabian financier, is alleged to be responsible for a worldwide terrorism conspiracy. Bin Laden and his Al Qaeda organization were implicated in the 1993 bombing of the World Trade Center in New York City, the 1998 bombings of the U.S. embassies in Tanzania and Kenya, as well as the attack on the U.S.S. *Cole* on October 12, 2000. The *Cole,* a U.S. Navy ship, was refueling in Aden, Yemen. The bombing of the *Cole* left 17 sailors dead (Sniffen, 2000).

Of course, the most devastating terrorist attacks to occur on United States soil took place on September 11, 2001. Terrorists connected with Osama bin Laden hijacked four commercial aircraft, two of which were flown into the twin 110-story towers of the World Trade Center in New York City, one into the Pentagon, and one into the ground in rural Pennsylvania. Subsequently, the World Trade Center towers collapsed on themselves. Approximately 3,000 deaths resulted from the 9/11 terrorist attacks ("America under attack," 2001).

A year after the 1995 Oklahoma City bombing, Congress passed and the president signed the Anti-Terrorism and Effective Death Penalty Act of 1996. The law:

- allows victims to sue countries that sponsor terrorism.
- establishes a special "removal court" to oversee the deportation of aliens suspected of terrorists activities.
- provides immigration officials with more authority to deport aliens convicted of any crime.
- forbids fund-raising activities in the United States by any foreign group identified by the U.S. Government as engaged in terrorist activities.

Although not included in the new law, the Clinton administration wanted to expand the power of federal authorities to increase their ability to surreptitiously monitor suspected terrorists through the use of electronic surveillance equipment (Gaines, Kaune, & Miller, 2001).

According to the U.S. Commission on National Security, 21st Century, a new national security structure is necessary to replace the institutions that combated the threat of terrorism during the 40 years of the Cold War. Emerging technology and expanding economic growth promote new and different threats. Computer technology allows hackers to penetrate American businesses and vital public safety infrastructure databases. A foreign or domestic hacker, utilizing a computer, could manipulate and destroy vital and top secret information, create havoc with air traffic control systems, deactivate public utilities, and slow emergency communications systems. The Commission predicted that people are more likely to die in large numbers on American soil if precautionary measures are not implemented. New-age terrorism requires government and military capabilities characterized by stealth, speed, accuracy, mobility, and intelligence that are different from counterterrorism mechanisms used in the past.

Private, nonmilitary counterterrorism strategies will also be required (Kreisher, 1999).

Few experts argue that the threat of terrorism is not escalating. However, a lack of preparedness to prevent terrorism or mitigate the damage from acts of terrorism exists in many areas. Some fail to recognize that weapons are plentiful and prevention strategies are often inadequate.

The weapons of terrorism range from traditional low-technology firearms and improvised explosive devices (IEDs) to information warfare and weapons of mass destruction (WMDs), sometimes referred to as weapons of mass effect (WMEs). The threat of the use of WMDs is particularly frightening. Many nation-states as well as non-state organizations either possess or have access to nuclear, biological, or chemical (NBC) devices that have the potential to cause loss of life and property destruction on a scale never before experienced. As the threat of terrorism increases, organizations will find it necessary to implement terrorism prevention procedures and install NBC detection devices at or near facility perimeters (Hutchinson & Warren, 2001; Maniscalco & Christen, 2002; Nason, 2000).

Due to limited resources and poor intelligence capabilities, law enforcement agencies and security organizations have not been able to prevent many terrorist attacks. However, the events of 9/11 provided the catalyst to create more proactive terrorism-prevention strategies. In response to the 9/11 attacks, Congress enacted the **USA PATRIOT Act of 2001**. Officially known as the Uniting and Strengthening America by Providing Appropriate Tools Required to Intercept and Obstruct Terrorism Act of 2001, the law dramatically increased the criminal investigative authority of local, county, state, and federal law enforcement agencies. The law strengthens law enforcement's ability to jail suspects, broadens search and seizure authority, enhances the power of prosecutors, promotes the sharing of intelligence, and provides for more restrictive border security (U.S. Congress, 2001). In 2003, the U.S. Senate voted to retain the Patriot Act's 2005 sunset provision and passed a limited version of the act. Many lawmakers expressed concern that the 2001 law jeopardized civil liberties.

The terrorist attacks of 9/11 represent the most destructive criminal event perpetrated on U.S. soil to date (Schmalleger, 2004). Experts suggest that the United States and its foreign interests will continue to be a preferred target for international terrorists (Martin, 2003). Reaction from the United States is likely to be swift and certain. The emerging issue of individual rights and freedom versus collective security and crime prevention will challenge everyone (Schmalleger, 2004). Critics argue that public pressure to combat terrorism can result in measures designed to curtail civil liberties, such as the right to privacy, due process, and freedom from unreasonable searches and seizures. However, if current terrorism patterns continue, U.S. citizens may wish to sacrifice some liberties in exchange for safety and security (Gaines, Kaune, & Miller, 2001; Meese & Ortmeier, 2004).

Additional initiatives to combat terrorism include various laws passed to reinforce security in the United States and elsewhere. Major among these initiatives are the Aviation and Transportation Security Act of 2001 and the Homeland Security Act of 2002. These laws and other U.S. responses to terrorism are discussed elsewhere in this book.

Victimless Crime

Often referred to as public order offenses, **victimless crime** generally includes offenses in which the participants enter into the activity voluntarily (Siegel, 2001). Offenses such as illegal gambling, pornography, drug use, illicit sexual behavior, public drunkenness, disorderly conduct, and vagrancy are often included in the victimless crime category. Some people suggest that many of these crimes should be decriminalized because enforcement of laws against such activity diverts public safety resources away from suppression of more serious crime, invades the privacy of individuals, and sets the stage for corruption in the legal system. Another consequence is the secondary criminogenic effect. Under this theory, enforcement of victimless crime laws indirectly leads to other crime, such as burglary, when a drug addict steals to support a habit. Others argue that society should retain and strictly enforce these laws. They contend that victimless crime destroys the morale fiber of society and leads to more serious offenses.

Whether one favors decriminalization or enforcement of victimless crime laws, behavior associated with such activity poses unique challenges to the security professional and business organizations. Since people engage in the behavior voluntarily, the participants often do not concede that their actions are criminal in nature, nor do they believe harm occurs as a result of their actions. Such attitudes exist in the American workforce, resulting in behaviors that threaten productivity, health, and safety (Cole & Smith, 2001).

Workplace Violence

Due to the dramatic increase in reported violence in the workplace in the late twentieth century, a new category of crime was created. **Workplace violence** is now a commonly used term defined generally as violence upon a person that occurs in the workplace. It may stem from an employment relationship, unsafe working conditions, or a relationship that exists outside the workplace. Workplace violence can occur during a robbery or other commercial crime, in employer-directed activity, in a domestic or misdirected affection situation, during a terrorist act or hate crime, or during a strike or civil disturbance (Hess & Wrobleski, 1996; Johnson, Klehbauch, & Kinney, 1994).

Although workplace violence has generated tremendous publicity in recent years, homicides on or off the job are more closely associated with personal human relationship problems. Actually, one is more likely to be assaulted, beaten, or killed in one's home by a family member or acquaintance than anywhere else or by anyone else in society. According to some state statutory provisions, domestic violence is a crime committed against an adult or fully emancipated minor. These laws apply to a present or past relationship of an intimate nature. Victims may include a present or former spouse, a cohabitant who is not an ordinary roommate, persons in dating or same-sex relationships, or a person with whom the perpetrator has had a child.

Domestic violence presents problems for organizations, since violence originating in the home and other areas outside the workplace can extend to the work site (Lynch, 2000; May, 2000). The perpetrator of workplace violence need not be an employee. In many cases, the offender is not an employee. Either the offender enters the workplace to commit a business-related crime, such as robbery or burglary, or the offender is in some way connected to an employee. In a personal relationship, the persons involved are usually aware of the name and location of each other's employers. If the relationship deteriorates, the aggressor knows where and when to locate the victim (Craighead, 2003).

There are no absolutes and no exact answers to the issues and the problems of workplace violence. However, precautionary measures can be taken. One approach is to use noninvolved third parties to mediate disputes. The mediation approach may resolve conflict well in the workplace, where the disputants know each other and tensions usually build over long periods of time. Another approach focuses on company-sponsored retraining and fair hearings to thwart potential violence due to layoffs and terminations. In addition, pre-employment screening tests can help identify violence-prone individuals and anger management training can help prevent workplace violence by those already employed (Siegel, 2001). Additional policies and procedures for preventing or minimizing the damage from workplace violence are addressed in Chapter 10.

Causes of Crime and Prevention Strategies

This section presents a brief summary of some of the causes of crime and strategies for preventing criminal activity. The exact causes of crime are not actually known, although there are many different views and theories on what causes crime. The causes of crime are not explainable in specific terms or through single theories. Many theories do not account for the negative case. This phenomenon is illustrated by the individual who is exposed to the theoretical cause, but does not commit a crime. In spite of the difficulties, crime causation is generally explained in terms of psychological, sociological, physiological, economic, drug use, demographic, urbanization, cultural, and expectations theories (Siegel, 2001).

Psychological theories of crime causation fall into two basic categories. They are the ego-state and personality-disorder theories. Sigmund Freud, the father of ego-state theories, believed that an individual's personality was divided into three parts: the id, the source of all basic drives such as hunger and sex; the ego, developed during infancy and early childhood, that provides the id with a conscious avenue to acquire satisfaction of the drives; and the superego, the conscience that inhibits immediate satisfaction of the id. According to the theory, criminal behavior results from a conflict between the id and the superego. Crime occurs because the satisfaction of the basic drives are inhibited by limited avenues for success. When the desires of the id are in conflict with societal demands, impulses of the id are repressed. If the individual is unable to repress these impulses, criminal behavior may result.

The second set of psychological theories focus on personality disorders. A mental deficiency may promote subnormal rather than abnormal behavior. A sociopathic personality disorder may create a repressed conscience. The sociopath is hostile and aggressive on occasion and usually wants immediate satisfaction of desires. A psychotic person loses touch with reality. The criminally insane are people with psychotic personalities.

Sociological theories evaluate the impact of external forces on the individual. Thus, ecological, cultural, and social influences may contribute to delinquent behavior. Ecological influences involve the environment in which one lives or works. Cultural influences include subcultural norms of a group that contribute to crime and delinquency. Notable among cultural theories was Edwin Sutherland's theory of differential association, a theory postulating that excessive exposure to a set of values, whether the values are acceptable to society or not, reinforces behaviors consistent with those values. Other social influences that contribute to delinquent behavior include an abnormal family life as well as problems in school, work, or a recreational setting.

Physiological theories include those that focus on heredity, biochemicals in the human body, and anthropology. Heredity theories propose that behavior is inherited. These theories disregard the role of external forces in contributing to delinquent behavior. Biochemical theories focus on hormonal imbalances in the human body and the influences of secretions of the endocrine glands. Anthropological theories, first developed by the Italian pioneer criminologist Cesare Lombroso in the nineteenth century, correlate specific physical features with criminal behavior. According to Lombroso, unattractiveness may produce unpleasant social experiences. The socially unattractive person reacts with antisocial behavior.

Other theoretical causes of crime include economic theories that emphasize the role of unemployment and poverty, drug culture theories that focus on the enforcement of drug laws as high drug prices cause users to commit secondary crime to support a drug habit, and demographic theories that suggest the amount of crime depends upon the changing composition of the population (young people tend to commit most street crime). Urbanization theories postulate that more people are concentrated in smaller areas, thus causing tension. Cultural theories focus on culture conflict within a society. Expectation level theories are explained by the disparity between the rich and the poor. As the gap widens between the poor and the affluent, and the ability to become affluent diminishes, frustration among the poor grows and the poor commit crime (Brown, Esbensen, & Geis, 1996; Siegel, 2001).

In the final analysis, most crime is probably multicausal. It is difficult to isolate single causes in an individual case and treat the cause. This is very problematic for the criminal justice system because effectively dealing with the causes of crime may be beyond the control of public safety agencies. They deal with crime primarily after the fact. Thus, most crime prevention becomes an individual, familial, organizational, and community responsibility.

Crime prevention strategies include education, treatment, diversion, rehabilitation, and deterrence through law enforcement and security. Prevention of crime in organizations involves comprehensive loss prevention and asset protection tools, policies, and procedures. In addition, prevention of serious street crime, which always impacts individuals and organizations in a negative way, requires early intervention in the delinquency cycle. When one realizes that crime is caused by a complex array of risk factors, it is not difficult to understand why single-focus intervention strategies are unlikely to succeed. Crime prevention must involve comprehensive intervention approaches that address multiple risk factors. To be effective, these strategies require collaboration between and among individuals, groups, and institutions. As mentioned previously, it is extremely unlikely that a single cause contributes to delinquent or criminal behavior. Therefore, it is important that individuals, families, social services agencies, schools, public safety organizations, security professionals, and businesses work together to prevent or reduce the likelihood of criminal behavior. To date, the criminal justice system has experienced little notable success with preventing the reoccurrence of criminal behavior by those who have been exposed to the system. Intervention as well as deterrence through security before a crime is committed may be the best strategy for solutions to crime prevention (Wasserman, Miller, & Cothern, 2000).

SUMMARY

The possibility of accidents, human error, fire, natural and environmental disasters, liability, substance abuse, civil disorder, and crime pose threats to individuals, organizations, and nations. The majority of loss events caused by these threats can be prevented if adequate precautionary measures are taken. Carelessness causes most accidents, errors, and fires. The damage from natural and environmental disasters can be minimized. Liability can be mitigated. Substance abuse can be prevented and substance abusers treated. The damage from civil disorder can be decreased if adequate contingency plans are in place and activated when the need arises. Many crimes against persons and property can be prevented, and offenders quickly apprehended, if comprehensive strategies are developed to deter, deny, detect, and detain those who persist in the violation of society's criminal laws.

KEY TERMS

accident	classification of fire
causes of crime	compensatory damages
civil disorder	crime
civil liability	crime prevention strategies

economic crime

environmental crime

environmental disaster

fire prevention

fire protection

fire triangle

human error

identity theft

Index crimes

National Crime Victimization Survey (NCVS)

National Incident-Based Reporting System (NIBRS)

natural disaster

Occupational Safety and Health Act

organized crime

products of combustion

punitive damages

street crime

strict liability

substance abuse

symptoms of substance abuse

terrorism

transborder

Uniform Crime Report (UCR)

USA PATRIOT Act of 2001

vicarious liability

victimless crime

white collar crime

workplace violence

DISCUSSION QUESTIONS AND EXERCISES

1. Individuals, businesses, public agencies, and nations are threatened by numerous criminal and noncriminal hazards. List these hazards and describe the ramifications of each.

2. What factors tend to create liability for an organization? How might these factors be minimized?

3. Describe the types of crime security personnel encounter most often.

4. Do prevention strategies prevent crime or merely shift criminal activities to other potential victims?

Legal Aspects
of Security Management

LEARNING OBJECTIVES

After completing this chapter, the reader should be able to

- describe the judicial system of the United States.
- outline the judicial process for civil as well as criminal cases.
- distinguish a tort from a crime.
- discuss types of situations conducive to tort liability.
- list and describe the essential elements of a contract.
- describe types of administrative law.
- contrast real and personal property.
- articulate the importance of employment law.
- demonstrate knowledge of labor law as it applies to security services.
- list and describe types of crime.
- evaluate incidents to determine if a crime has occurred.
- compare arrest authority of public police with private security.
- demonstrate knowledge of laws of arrest, search, and seizure.
- evaluate trends in security legislation.

INTRODUCTION

The legal aspects of security management involve a mixture of criminal, civil, and administrative law. Therefore, security managers encounter relatively unique legal obligations and are faced with a multitude of legal issues and decisions. People, physical property, and information must be protected without incurring civil liability or violating anyone's rights. Personnel matters must be dealt with in a manner consistent with existing labor laws. Security managers must enter into and audit contractual agreements. They must also prevent and investigate crime and collect and preserve evidence that may be used in a criminal prosecution.

Organizational activities must be monitored to ensure compliance with a wide array of local, state, and federal laws. Consequently, the contemporary security manager must be well versed in the law and anticipate situations in which expert legal representation is necessary. This chapter is devoted entirely to the judicial process and the legal concepts that engulf the security management profession.

JUDICIAL SYSTEMS

To fully appreciate the legal considerations involved in security management, one must possess knowledge of the nature of judicial systems and processes. Courts vary in their authority. In addition, procedural rules and **degrees of proof** required vary significantly between civil law and the administration of criminal justice. The judicial process in the United States is also adversarial. In a criminal case, the government, through state and federal prosecutors, must establish proof of guilt beyond a reasonable doubt. Defendants and their defense attorneys work to refute the government's case. In a civil case, a plaintiff sues a respondent to enforce an obligation or receive compensation, and the degree of proof required is much less. The adversarial process requires an impartial person (or persons) to function as a referee to ensure that the parties follow the rules. Judges and juries function as the referees (Rutledge, 2000). The courts impact the legal system and society in a significant way. The courts determine guilt or innocence, reach findings in civil cases, and issue decisions that impact the process through which criminal as well as civil cases pass.

In America, the Massachusetts Bay Colony formed a combined legislature/court in 1629 to make laws, conduct trials, and impose sentences. By 1776, all American colonies had established court systems. After the American Revolution, the colonial courts formed the foundation for state court systems. A growing population, the settlement of the West, and the movement toward urbanization led to an increase in civil lawsuits and criminal arrests by the late nineteenth century. To service the need, state legislatures and constitutions created numerous courts and a variety of court structures. The federal court system was established by the U.S. Constitution, the Federal Judiciary Acts of 1789 and 1925, and the U.S. Magistrate's Act of 1968 (Law Enforcement Assistance Administration, 1976). Throughout the twentieth century, court systems in the United States became more uniform and streamlined. Today, the federal court system has three levels, and state systems have three or four levels of courts.

There are two basic types of courts: **trial courts** and **appellate courts**. Criminal and civil trials take place in trial courts. They have original jurisdiction in these cases. Appellate courts, on the other hand, with rare exception, do not originate or try cases. They only review cases and decisions appealed to them from trial courts or lower appellate courts. Appellate courts review the **transcript** (written record) of the trial court proceeding as well as written briefs submitted by the parties in the action. The appellate court may also entertain short oral arguments from the petitioner and the respondent or their representatives. Appeals from trial courts proceed through either a state or federal appellate review process and may culminate at the **U.S. Supreme Court**.

The federal court system consists of 95 **U.S. district courts** (trial courts) situated in 13 **U.S. court of appeals** circuits. The U.S. Supreme Court functions as an appellate court. It reviews constitutional challenges to federal and state statutes, as well as appeals from criminal and civil trial court cases brought before it through state appellate courts or one of the 13 U.S. courts of appeal. In the case of state court judgments, an appeal from a state's **court of last resort** is a matter of right when the validity of a federal statute is questioned in a state court or when a state **statute** is challenged because it is alleged to violate the U.S. Constitution (Cole & Smith, 2001; Fagin, 2003).

The U.S. Supreme Court has no authority to make a final determination in a state case. The Court may affirm (let stand) the decision of the lower court or reverse the decision and remand (return) the case to the lower court for a decision not inconsistent with the U.S. Supreme Court's opinion. If the constitutionality of the entire state court case is at issue, the charge against a defendant in a criminal case must be dismissed. If only a portion of the **evidence** is declared inadmissible, the state court may order a new trial based on admissible evidence only. A new trial does not violate the Fifth Amendment double jeopardy clause, since there has not been a final judgment in the case and the new trial is considered *de novo* (new), as if the original trial had not taken place.

The **intermediate appellate courts** in the federal system are the U.S. courts of appeal. They have appellate jurisdiction over all U.S. district court decisions except when a three-judge district court has enjoined (stopped) enforcement of a federal or state statute on grounds of unconstitutionality, and the case proceeds directly to the U.S. Supreme Court; when a U.S. district court declares a federal statute unconstitutional and the United States is a party to the action; or when a case requires immediate settlement because of imperative public importance (Rutledge, 2000).

The U.S. district courts are the trial courts of general jurisdiction in the federal system. They have trial jurisdiction over civil actions involving copyrights, patents, postal matters, civil rights, and almost all other civil and criminal cases arising under the laws and treaties of the United States and the U.S. Constitution. They have concurrent jurisdiction with the states in criminal cases when a criminal act violates federal as well as state law. U.S. district courts have jurisdiction in civil cases in which the dollar amount in dispute is over $10,000 and the parties to the action are residents of different states.

The U.S. Magistrate Courts have authority to issue federal warrants, set bail, hold **preliminary hearings** in federal cases, and conduct summary trials for minor federal crimes in which the defendant waives the right to a trial in U.S. district court. Other specialized federal courts include the U.S. Court of Claims, which hears financial lawsuits against the United States, the U.S. Court of Customs and Patent Appeals, the U.S. Tax Court, and military and territorial courts.

State and local courts try criminal and civil cases arising out of incidents occurring within the state and cases involving violations of state and local laws. Each state has a court of last resort, usually called the state supreme court. Appeals from these courts are taken directly to the U.S. Supreme Court, the highest court in the United States. All states also have some form of intermediate appellate court. They review decisions on appeal from state trial courts. Appeals from state intermediate appellate courts are taken to the state court of last resort.

State trial courts generally fall into two categories: general jurisdiction and limited jurisdiction. **Courts of general jurisdiction** may try any state criminal or civil case brought before it. **Courts of limited jurisdiction** are restricted in their authority. These courts adjudicate small civil claims, typically try **misdemeanor** cases, and conduct preliminary hearings in **felony** cases. If, as the result of a preliminary hearing, the court of limited jurisdiction determines that probable cause exists to hold the defendant on the felony charge, the defendant's case is transferred to the state court of general jurisdiction for arraignment and trial.

Figure 3–1   Court Systems

Examples of courts of limited jurisdiction include municipal, juvenile, and small claims courts. Some states have merged the courts of limited jurisdiction with the courts of general jurisdiction. The merger can result in a tremendous expenditure reduction. Subsequent to a merger, the state has one trial court level, referred to as a district, county, circuit, or superior court, which assigns cases to criminal, civil, juvenile, or probate dockets, departments, or divisions (Adler, Mueller, & Laufer, 2003; Cole & Smith, 2001).

BURDEN AND DEGREES OF PROOF

In an adversarial legal system, opposing parties in a dispute operate under varying burdens and degrees of proof. In criminal cases, a defendant is presumed innocent until proven guilty. The prosecution has the burden to proceed first with a criminal complaint and the burden of establishing guilt beyond a reasonable doubt. This is the strictest degree of proof. It does not imply a mere possible doubt, nor does it mean that guilt must be established beyond any doubt. Rather, guilt must be established in the mind of the finder of fact in such a way that the fact finder is morally certain that the defendant committed a criminal act.

Unlike criminal prosecutions, where convictions may result in imprisonment or execution, lesser degrees of proof are required in proceedings where one is not subject to culpability for a criminal act. Lesser degrees of proof include clear and convincing evidence, proof by a preponderance of the evidence, and *prima facie* proof. The clear and convincing standard of proof is used to establish a probability that the evidence presented is based on fact. This standard is used, for example, to determine if a juvenile under a designated age appreciated the wrongfulness of an act.

The third highest degree of proof is based on a preponderance of the evidence standard. This degree of proof is met if the evidence demonstrates a probability—at least a 51 percent likelihood—that the facts in issue are true. This standard is used in civil lawsuits.

Finally, prima facie (on its face) proof is the standard used to establish, through a slight showing, that the circumstances in a particular situation are as they appear. Thus, a slight showing may allow the fact finder to draw a certain conclusion, if no contradictory evidence is present. This standard, or degree, of proof is used in a preliminary hearing in the pretrial phase of a criminal prosecution (Rutledge, 2000).

THE JUDICIAL PROCESS

Criminal Cases

In a criminal case, initiation of the pretrial process is made through a physical arrest or issuance of an arrest warrant. A criminal citation is issued in lieu of an arrest for minor offenses. If arrested, the arrestee is "booked." A booking is the official recording of the arrest in the records of the arresting law enforcement agency. If the arrestee cannot be released on recognizance (ROR) without a bail hearing, and a judge is not immediately available, the arrestee may be detained in a jail for a reasonable time (about two court working days) until a first appearance before a judge. At the **first (initial) appearance**, the arrestee is informed of the charge(s), advised of rights under the Constitution, and, if possible, bail is set. In some jurisdictions, the first appearance is referred to as the **arraignment on the complaint**, which should not be confused with a postindictment or postinformation proceeding, called an arraignment. The first appearance is a nonadversarial proceeding.

In federal felony cases, a formal charge against the accused must be issued by a federal grand jury in the form of an **indictment**. In state cases, the prosecuting attorney may present the case to a county grand jury for possible indictment, or may file an information, which is a formal charge for a felony issued from the prosecuting attorney's office subsequent to a preliminary hearing. The formal charge for a misdemeanor case is usually called a criminal complaint.

Many states do not utilize a grand jury. In lieu of a grand jury proceeding, a preliminary hearing is conducted to determine if probable cause exists to hold the accused to answer to the charge. The preliminary hearing is an adversarial proceeding. During this hearing, the prosecution must establish a prima facie case, which means that on the face of the evidence presented, probable cause exists that a crime occurred and the defendant committed the offense (Acker & Brody, 1999).

If probable cause is established at the preliminary hearing, the case proceeds to the arraignment. At the arraignment, the accused is asked to enter a plea. The pleas available include guilty, not guilty, not guilty by reason of insanity, or no contest (nolo contendere). If the defendant pleads not guilty or no contest and proceeds to trial, the defense attorney usually files pretrial motions to have the charges dismissed, suppress prosecution evidence as inadmissible, discover evidence the prosecution has, or delay the trial. Motions may also be filed to change the venue (location) of the trial, consolidate multiple charges arising from a single criminal transaction, sever multiple counts or defendants, and disclose the identity and location of an informant. In many states, the arraignment occurs prior to the preliminary hearing.

If the case qualifies for, and the accused selects, a jury trial, the next step is jury selection. An initial list of potential jurors is selected from property tax records or from a list of registered voters or vehicle owners, or from the department of motor vehicle's list of those who hold driver licenses. From the initial list, a jury pool (venire) is randomly selected. Members of the jury pool receive jury duty notices and are asked to report to a court facility. From the jury pool, a jury panel of approximately 30 people is randomly selected and referred to a courtroom for trial jury selection. Members of the jury panel are interviewed by the judge, prosecution, and defense during a **voir dire examination** (*voir dire* means to speak the truth) to determine their suitability for service on the trial jury. Potential jurors may be excused from the jury panel for cause or due to a

peremptory challenge. **Challenges for cause** are not limited. However, peremptory (no cause or reason need be given) challenges are limited in number, usually to 6 to 10 challenges, depending on the seriousness of the criminal charges.

Once the trial jury is selected, the jury is sworn in (impaneled) and the government presents its case. During the opening statement, the prosecutor explains to the court what evidence will be presented as proof of the allegations in the complaint, indictment, or **information**. Subsequently, the defendant or the defendant's attorney outlines how the allegations made by the prosecutor will not be proven. Following the opening statements, the prosecution and the defense present their cases. A witness is examined directly by the side calling the witness, followed by cross-examination from the opposing party. **Impeachment** (reducing a witness' credibility) is the intended outcome of cross-examination.

When the defense rests its case, the prosecutor may offer rebuttal evidence to respond to the defendant's proof. If the prosecutor offers rebuttal evidence, the defendant may present a surrebuttal to refute the prosecutor's rebuttal evidence. States vary regarding the number and order of closing arguments. Nearly all states allow the defense to make a final argument (summation) first, followed by the prosecution. A few states permit three arguments (summaries) at the end of the trial (Schmalleger, 2003, 2004). Where three arguments are permitted, an opening argument is made by the prosecution. The prosecutor summarizes the evidence presented, states how the evidence has satisfied the elements of the charge, and asks for a finding of guilty. This is followed by an argument from the defense. This is similar to opening argument by the prosecution, except the defense asks the court for a finding of not guilty. Finally, during the closing argument by the prosecution, the prosecutor may reply to statements in the argument made by the defense (Rutledge, 2000).

After all closing arguments are presented, the judge instructs the jury (if any) regarding the points of law that apply in the case. These instructions are critical to the final determination in a jury trial. As exemplified by the Charles Keating, Jr. fraud case, an appellate court may reverse a conviction if the judge's instructions are improper. Keating was convicted in 1992 in Los Angeles Superior Court of fraud involving the sale of $200 million in worthless bonds that ultimately led to the collapse of the Lincoln Savings and Loan Company. Public funds in the amount of $3.4 billion were used to keep the entire savings and loan industry from collapsing. According to the appellate court, the judge in the Keating state trial, Lance Ito (the judge in the O. J. Simpson trial), presented faulty instructions to the trial jury. Ito did not instruct the jury to consider whether Keating intended to swindle the investors (Krasnowski, 2000).

Subsequent to the judge's instructions to the jury, the jury retires to deliberate. These deliberations are not public, and the jury may be sequestered. A unanimous verdict by the jury is required in criminal cases.

If the jury's verdict is not guilty, the defendant is released. Not guilty verdicts are final. If the defendant is found guilty, the judge may order the probation department to conduct a presentence investigation. The results of the investigation assist the judge in determining the most appropriate sentence. At sentencing, the judge may impose a fine, jail or prison sentence, probation, suspended sentence, or may order an execution. Postconviction remedies for the defendant include appeal and habeas corpus actions when all other appeal remedies are exhausted (Rutledge, 2000).

Civil Cases

In civil cases, a complaint (lawsuit) is initiated by a plaintiff, claiming a civil wrong committed by the respondent in the case. The respondent files an answer to the plaintiff's claim and states a defense against the complaint. A civil lawsuit is not a criminal prosecution. Therefore, neither a state's prosecuting attorney nor the U.S. Attorney represent either party in a civil case.

Procedurally, a civil suit parallels, but does not replicate, a criminal proceeding. Pretrial motions requesting discovery of the opponent's information are filed by both parties. Jury selection follows a procedure similar to that which occurs in criminal cases. At trial, opening statements are made by the plaintiff (or plaintiff's counsel) and the respondent (or respondent's counsel). The plaintiff's case is presented first, followed by the respondent's case. Direct and cross-examination of witnesses is similar to criminal proceedings, although evidentiary rules, testimonial privileges, and prohibitions against admission of hearsay evidence are more relaxed. Both sides make closing statements, the judge provides instructions to the jury, and the jury deliberates to reach a verdict. Unlike criminal cases, where unanimous verdicts are required, substantial majority verdicts are permissible in many civil cases. The function of the jury in civil lawsuits is to find, by a preponderance of evidence, for or against the plaintiff. Civil liability, rather than criminal culpability, is the issue in civil cases (Rutledge, 2000).

Additional information about the judicial process as well as legal concepts and laws may be obtained through resource linkages provided by the American Bar Association at www.abanet.org.

TORT LAW

A **tort** is a civil, rather than criminal, wrong for which the law provides a remedy. Unlike a crime, which is a public wrong against society, a tort is a private wrong committed against a person or property, excluding breach of contract. The wrong, committed without just cause, must have caused physical injury, resulted in damage to an individual's property, or deprived someone of personal liberty and freedom. In some cases, an act may violate the criminal law and also provide the foundation for a tort action. In addition, a tort may be intentional (willful) or unintentional (accidental). **Intentional torts** include activities such as assault (the open threat of bodily harm against someone), battery (any harmful or offensive bodily contact), wrongful death (causing another's death through reckless conduct), false imprisonment (the unlawful violation of the personal liberty of another), and fraud.

Intentional torts also include defamation of character, invasions of privacy, and misappropriation of the right to publicity. Defamation involves damaging a person's reputation by making public statements that are both false and malicious. Defamation can take the form of libel or slander. Libel includes statements in print, writing, pictures, signs, or publications that injure the reputation of another. The words can also be read aloud by a speaker or broadcast for the public to hear. Slander is speaking defamatory words intended to prejudice others against an individual, jeopardizing reputation or means of livelihood. Intrusion into one's privacy or private affairs, public disclosure of private facts about a person, false publicity about a person, or using a person's name or likeness without permission are considered invasions into privacy. As a general rule, certain public officials and celebrities are unable to claim defamation of character or invasion of privacy. Because of their status, public officials and celebrities are not protected from derogatory statements because the person making the statement is exercising the first amendment right to freedom of speech.

Employers may be sued for defamation when they provide derogatory information to a perspective employer regarding a current or former employee. Usually, the truth of the information provided is a complete defense to the lawsuit. However, even when the disclosure is truthful, statements made in a malicious or reckless manner may establish the foundation for a punitive damage award to the plaintiff (current or former employee defamed). Generally, the respondent in a defamation lawsuit will be unable to establish a defense if any of the following conditions exist:

- Actual malice on the part of the information provider is established.
- False defamatory information was published intentionally.
- False defamatory information was provided to someone who has no legitimate reason to receive it.
- False defamatory information was published recklessly, without regard to its truthfulness.
- False defamatory information was published for other than legitimate reasons.

There are situations other than employment reference inquiries that may give rise to liability for defamation. These situations include statements made in the course of an employee misconduct investigation and accusations of misconduct directed toward a customer or client of a business. Truth of the statement may be a complete defense to a defamation lawsuit (Inbau, Farber, & Arnold, 1996). However, employers and security personnel are cautioned to refrain from making specific accusations, either verbally or in writing. Even when an adequate defense is available, the costs associated with litigating a defense can be considerable.

The tort of misappropriation of the right to publicity applies to those situations in which a person uses another living person's name or identity for commercial purposes. In the United States, people have the exclusive right to profit from the commercial use of their names and personalities during their lifetime. This is particularly true of well-known individuals and celebrities. In such cases, a plaintiff can sue for recovery of unauthorized profits acquired by the offending party, and the plaintiff can obtain an injunction against the offender to prevent unauthorized use of the plaintiff's name or identity in the future (Cheeseman, 2004).

Unintentional torts evolve from those situations in which a person fails to exercise ordinary and prudent care and thus injures someone. The accused may have failed to perform an act that a reasonable person, in similar circumstances, would do, or may have done something that a reasonable person would not do. In these situations, the actor is said to be negligent. Most professional liability suits are based on an alleged act of **negligence**. Commonly referred to as malpractice, all professional liability claims are based on improper performance of the act. Malfeasance is the performance of an act in a wrongful and unlawful manner. Misfeasance is the performance of a lawful act in a negligent manner.

Professionals can be civilly liable if their actions or omissions meet the four requirements necessary for the legal definition of negligence. The person charged with negligence owed a duty of care to the accuser (duty), the provider breached the duty of care to a person (derelict), the breach of the duty of care to the person was a direct cause of the person's injury (direct cause), and there is a legally recognizable injury to the person (damages) (Simonsen, 1998).

Managers and organizations may also be civilly liable for numerous personnel-related and management-related practices. Liability may be incurred when an employee is found to be negligent when acting within the scope of employment (vicarious liability). Management may be liable for negligent hiring, training, supervision, and retention, as well as for wrongful termination of personnel. Organizations and individuals may be held liable for invasion of privacy, malicious prosecution, defamation of character claims, foreseeable acts of violence, false arrest and false imprisonment, use of excessive force, and failure to protect confidential information (American Society for Industrial Security, 1998; Cheeseman, 2004).

The increasing number of liability-related lawsuits should be a concern for professionals. To protect themselves against criminal or civil charges, people should practice good human relations, become familiar with relevant federal and state laws, make every reasonable effort to comply with those laws, and adhere to a professional code of ethics and standards of conduct (Simonsen, 1998).

CONTRACT LAW

A **contract** is a legally binding voluntary agreement between two or more parties through which specific promises are made for a valuable consideration. A legally binding contract contains four basic elements: an agreement, a consideration, legal subject matter, and contractual capacity of the parties. The agreement is an offer by one party and the acceptance of that offer by another party. The offer, which relates to some present or future action, must be communicated, made in good faith and not under strain or as a joke, and clear enough to be understood by both parties, and it must define what both parties will do if the offer is accepted. An offer may be withdrawn before a valid acceptance. In addition, the acceptance must be absolute and in accordance with the terms of the offer. If the acceptance adds to or modifies conditions made in the original offer, the addition or modification constitutes a counteroffer for another contract. Mutual assent is part of the agreement and is evidenced by an offer and acceptance. For a contract to exist, both parties must agree to and fully understand the terms and conditions of the agreement.

The consideration is something of value that is bargained for as part of the agreement. When a contract is made, each party agrees to do or provide something for the other. The exchange of promises is called a consideration. The agreement must also involve legal subject matter; that is, it must be for legal services or purposes. Contracts are not valid and enforceable in court unless they are for legal purposes. For example, a contract that provides that a manufacturer can intentionally provide a defective product for a retailer is illegal. In this case, the contract would be void. It would be set aside and treated as though it had never existed. A legally unenforceable contract should not be confused with breach of contract. Breach of contract may be charged if either party fails to comply with the terms of a legally valid contract.

The parties who enter into the agreement must also be competent and possess the capacity to enter into a contract. If any of the parties are incompetent at the time a contract is made, the agreement is voidable. The contract may be set aside or invalidated. Incompetent parties include persons under 18 years of age, or the age of majority, who are not emancipated, as well as some mentally incapacitated persons. Emancipated minors are individuals between the ages of 15 and 18 who are married, in the armed forces, or self-supporting and no longer living under the care and control of their parents or guardians. Similarly, the persons entering into the contractual agreement must be capable of fully understanding all of its terms and conditions. A person declared insane or mentally incompetent by a court may not enter into a legally binding contract. In some cases, mental incompetency extends to those under the influence of drugs or alcohol at the time the agreement is made.

Contracts may be expressed or implied. An **expressed contract** can be written or oral, but all terms of the contract are explicitly stated. An **implied contract** is unspoken and results from the actions of the parties. Conduct of the parties, rather than expressed words, create the contract. The contract is valid if both parties understand the offer, both are competent, and the services provided are legal. State laws prescribe which contracts must be in writing to be enforced.

A promise by a third party to pay for the services of another must be in writing to be enforceable by a court. Likewise, financial arrangements must be in writing according to Regulation Z of the U.S. Consumer Protection Act of 1968. This law is also known as the Truth-in-Lending Act. Under the law, the agreement must be in writing and must contain information regarding the fees for services, amount of any down payment, date each payment is due, date of the final payment, amount of each payment, and total interest charges to be assessed. The purpose of this type of legislation is to protect consumers from fraudulent, deceptive, or hidden finance charges levied by creditors. The written agreement can also be used by creditors to collect outstanding debts.

Finally, contracts may include special clauses that stipulate liquidated damage arrangements and limitations on damages. Special clauses may also include hold-harmless and indemnification language. Hold-harmless clauses are included when one party assumes liability for another party to the contract. Indemnification clauses are included when one party agrees to reimburse the other party for expenses associated for any loss, damage, or liability claim (American Society for Industrial Security, 1998; Cheeseman, 2004; Mann & Roberts, 1997).

Although security managers are likely to engage in numerous contractual relationships, the most probable situation involves a contract for some type of security service. Outsourcing (utilizing contracted vendors) for security services and personnel has become common. Potential outsourcing situations include facility reviews, program planning, security system design and installation management, system monitoring, training, investigations, and security personnel (Maurer, 2000b).

In business and government environments, electronic mail (e-mail) is sometimes used to negotiate and agree on contract terms. Assuming all the elements to create a contract are present, an e-mail contract is valid and enforceable. To ensure that the contract meets a state Statute of Frauds documentation requirement, the parties to the email contract should print and retain a paper version of the electronic contract. Likewise, to overcome evidentiary problems in the event of a lawsuit, the parties should print and retain paper versions of any prior e-mail contract negotiations. The Electronic Signature in Global and National Commerce Act, enacted by Congress and signed by the president in 2000, provides that an electronic signature has the same force and effect as a manually pen-inscribed signature on paper (Cheeseman, 2004).

Since security executives of large organizations often manage several contracts, periodic review of contractual arrangements is appropriate. In some cases, restructuring contracts can result in considerable cost savings. As an organization's operation grows through mergers and acquisitions, the decentralized approach to security service-provider agreements may not be efficient or cost effective. One major financial institution, headquartered in Pittsburgh, Pennsylvania, with 10 geographic regions spanning several states, decreased the number of contractors, obtained volume discounts, and reduced the organization's annual contracted security expenses by 9 percent. A review of existing contracts, operations, billing rates and structures, and bid solicitation procedures analysis was implemented. Surprisingly, the financial institution's management discovered that a single vendor was not the most cost-efficient solution. However, the organization was able to reduce the 14 original contractors to 4 (Mann, 1999).

Another type of contract a security manager may encounter, particularly in private industry, is a noncompete agreement. If a former employee takes critical proprietary information from the former employer to a competitor, or uses the information to start a competing enterprise, the former employer can lose trade secrets and market share. To prevent this type of knowledge transfer, employers often require employees to sign a noncompete agreement. Such agreements prohibit direct competition or knowledge transfer by the former employee.

Although the courts generally do not uphold contracts that restrict a person's ability to obtain employment, they do accept contracts designed to protect a company's legitimate business interests. Protectable business interests include trade secrets, intellectual property, and business goodwill arising from the name, location, or reputation of the company. Some courts also hold that an employee's unique skills acquired on the job are a protectable business interest.

When noncompete agreements are enforceable, the enforcement is not unlimited. The noncompete restriction is limited to a reasonable period of time, generally not more than two years. Most courts also restrict enforcement to the geographic area where the former employee worked and had client contact.

Noncompete agreements are upheld in most states if the contract is confined to legitimate business interests, states the irreparable harm to be suffered by disclosure, narrowly defines the scope of the restrictions to a reasonable time and place, and describes the prohibited conduct. The agreement should include a statement that lack of immediate enforcement of the agreement does not constitute a waiver, an acknowledgment by the employee that the restrictions are reasonable and necessary, and a statement that the agreement applies if the employee either resigns or is terminated.

Some companies prefer to use a nonsolicitation agreement rather than a noncompete agreement. Instead of completely prohibiting competition, a nonsolicitation agreement only restricts a former employee from soliciting the former employer's clients or employees.

Enforcement of noncompete or nonsolicitation agreements necessarily involve litigation through the courts. A former employer commences proceedings by obtaining a temporary restraining order (TRO), good for about 10 days, or a preliminary injunction, which remains in place until a trial determines the outcome (Bland & Harkavy, 2000).

Occasionally, a former employee has extensive knowledge of and experience with a former employer's operations and trade secrets and, given the nature of a new position with a competitor, it is inevitable that disclosure will take place. The former employee may have knowledge of operational and strategic plans, intellectual property, pricing structures, and other forms of proprietary information. In these situations, a former employer may ask a court to prevent a former employee from working for a direct competitor. Although not a noncompete agreement, the legal principle involved here is referred to as the *inevitable disclosure doctrine.* As with noncompete agreements, the doctrine's enforcement is not limitless, and some courts are reluctant to enforce it unless there is evidence of actual misconduct on the part of the former employee (Halligan, 2000). Whether a former employer creates and seeks relief through a noncompete or nonsolicitation agreement, or through the doctrine of inevitable disclosure, state statutes and case law should be researched to determine applicability in local jurisdictions (Bland & Harkavy, 2000).

ADMINISTRATIVE LAW

The branch of public law created by administrative agencies and presented in the form of rules and regulations that dictate the duties and responsibilities of individuals and organizations is referred to as **administrative law**. Administrative agencies derive their authority from state and federal statutes that authorize the agency, often referred to as a department, commission, bureau, or office, to regulate conduct involving safety, education, welfare, national security, taxation, environmental and consumer protection, transportation, communications, labor relations, commerce, and trade. Because societies are complex, countless administrative agencies have been created to regulate and control human and organizational behavior. Since the legislative process takes a great deal of time, legislatures pass enabling statutes that create these agencies and empower them with broad discretionary authority to formulate and implement public policy, which has the impact of law, within very short periods of time.

Administrative agencies are usually granted executive powers, such as the power to investigate and prosecute violations of statutes and administrative regulations and orders. The agency may issue an administrative subpoena for specified information. Administrative agencies may also conduct physical inspections (searches) of business and governmental premises and facilities. However, the executive powers granted to administrative agencies are subject to certain constitutional constraints. Administrative inspections or searches, for example, are subject to the same restrictions placed on other government agents by the Fourth Amendment to the U.S. Constitution (Cheeseman, 2004).

Although subject to judicial review, the actions of administrative agencies can disrupt daily activity and business operations if, in the minds of agency representatives, conduct does not conform to the requirements of the regulations. Security professionals must acknowledge the power and control administrative agencies retain and ensure that human and organizational behavior conforms to regulatory requirements.

PROPERTY LAW

Although property rights hold a unique position in the American society, the term *property* is not easily defined. Property includes almost every right that the law protects, except that afforded to one's personal liberty. Property rights protect lawful possession, use, and ownership. In the United States, property is a legally protected interest or group of interests, including the exclusive right of a private person to control private property, as well as the right of a political unit (city, county, state, nation) to control public property for an economic good (Mann & Roberts, 1997).

Property can be tangible, such as an automobile or building to which an interest holds a possessory right or title. In contrast, intangible property does not take a physical form. Stock certificates, proprietary information, intellectual property, copyrights, and patents represent property interests that, although not physical, are legally protected by law. As technological knowledge expands more rapidly and data processing and communication systems become more sophisticated, the classifications of personal property broaden. The rise in patent applications, for example, can be explained partly by new classes of discoveries and innovations that have been granted protection.

Although the U.S. patent system has existed for over 200 years, biotech companies could not patent genetic discoveries until 1980. Patents on software were not allowed until 1981. In 1998, patent rights were expanded to include business methods (Jones, 2000). The protection and enforcement of property rights on patents of this nature are also more difficult. Since most new patents apply to intangibles such as ideas and information stored in electronic mediums, security is more difficult to achieve and competitors often battle over exclusive rights. Millions of Internet users routinely reproduce or misuse copyrighted material (Balint, 2000). In some high-profile lawsuits in 2000, Amazon.com claimed its one-click ordering system patent must force Barnesandnoble.com to use two clicks. Priceline.com sued Microsoft and its Expedia subsidiary for infringement on Priceline.com's name-your-price auction model, a business methods patent (Jones, 2000).

The most significant distinction in property law emanates from the difference between **personal property** and **real property**. Personal property includes virtually anything, tangible or intangible, other than land and anything in it or permanently attached to it (real property, real estate). When real property, such as minerals or buildings, are extracted or removed from land, they are theoretically transformed into personal property. Important legal considerations emanate from the distinction between personal and real property. Transfer of title to personal property is relatively simple and is typically controlled by a uniform commercial code. Transfer of real property (real estate) is much more formal and includes the delivery of an instrument referred to as a deed. In some cases, an individual, political entity, or corporation (considered a "paper" person in the eyes of the law) may have a legal right to possess, rather than own, property.

Renting a vehicle (personal property) or leasing a building (real property) represent contracted possessory rights rather than ownership. Under the terms of the contract, the lessee is subject to agreed-upon conditions of use, and the lessor retains ownership rights.

Whether personal or real, tangible or intangible, property can be insured, either by the owner or by the person who holds a possessory right to the property. Insurance refers to a contract of the insured within a group of contracts held by the insurer to distribute (spread) the risk, damage, or loss among a large group of contract holders. Virtually any commercial activity can be protected by insurance coverage. A business can obtain insurance to protect itself from damage or loss to tangible assets, to protect it from strict liability, intentional or unintentional torts, and negligence, or to shield itself against financial losses due to fire, death of an executive, or dishonest employees (Cheeseman, 2004; Mann & Roberts, 1997).

The concept of property is extremely important in a democratic and free society such as the United States. In a sense, property rights are almost sacred to many people. Security managers, therefore, should familiarize themselves with the nature, scope, rights, and legal consequences associated with personal and real property law.

EMPLOYMENT LAW

Employment law covers a vast array of common law and statutory provisions that regulate the employment relationship. Employment laws include labor laws, employment discrimination laws, and laws that are created to protect employees. Originally, labor laws were created to restrict worker efforts to unionize, strike, or picket to obtain better working conditions or higher wages. Injunctions were used in peaceful labor disputes. However, in 1932, the U.S. Congress enacted the Norris-LaGuardia Act, which withdrew federal court power to issue such injunctions in nonviolent labor disputes. More importantly, the act declared that labor was free to organize and form unions without employer interference.

In 1935, Congress enacted the National Labor Relations Act. The act outlined the federal government's support for collective bargaining and unionization. The act also established the National Labor Relations Board, which was tasked with the responsibility to monitor and administer regulations relative to employee rights.

The Fair Labor Standards Act (FLSA) was passed by Congress in 1938. The act forbids the use of oppressive child labor, and it established minimum wage and overtime pay for workers. Under the FLSA, an employer cannot require a nonexempt employee (nonmanagerial worker) to work more than 40 hours per week unless the employee is paid one-and-a-half times the regular pay for each hour worked over 40 (Cheeseman, 2004). In 2002, a federal trial jury in Portland, Oregon, found Wal-Mart Stores, the world's largest retailer and private employer, guilty of pressuring employees to work unpaid overtime. More than 400 current and former employees from almost two dozen Oregon Wal-Mart Stores sued the retailer for violating state and federal wage laws. More than 35 similar lawsuits were filed against Wal-Mart in 30 other states. Those suits, from New York to California, involved thousands of workers seeking millions in back pay. Other suits and complaints against Wal-Mart alleged that the company discriminated against female workers and that Wal-Mart thwarted employee efforts to unionize (Armour, 2003; "Wal-Mart loses overtime pay lawsuit," 2002).

In 1947, Congress passed the Labor-Management Relations Act, otherwise known as the Taft-Hartley Act. This law prohibits unfair union practices and amends the National Labor Relations Act to prohibit certain types of union activities.

In the area of employment discrimination law, a number of federal and state statutes prohibit discrimination in employment on the basis of gender, race, religious preference, national origin, age, or disability. Paramount among these laws is the Civil Rights Act of 1964, the Americans with Disabilities Act of 1990, and the Civil Rights Act of 1991. Additional laws afford an employee a number of job-related protections. Employees have a right to a safe and secure workplace, compensation for work-related injuries, financial security upon retirement or loss of employment, and protection against unfair dismissal from employment. The latter group of laws include the **Occupational Safety and Health Act** of 1970, the federal **Employee Polygraph Protection Act** of 1988, the Family and Medical Leave Act of 1993, and numerous other laws related to employee privacy, drug and alcohol testing, and workers' compensation (Cheeseman, 2004; Mann & Roberts, 1997). Additional information regarding these laws as well, as examples of the legal issues associated with the employer-employee relationship, are presented in Chapter 6, "Personnel Security."

CRIMINAL LAW

Sources, Definitions, and Classifications of Crime

Sources of criminal law include the U.S. Constitution, federal statutes, state constitutions and statutes, county and municipal ordinances, judicial decisions (case law), and **common law** (law based on custom or tradition). Statutes and ordinances are the product of a legislative activity. Common law originated in England and formed the foundation for early U.S. law.

There is no universally accepted legal definition of crime (Senna & Siegel, 2001). Generally, a crime is as an offense against society. When a crime is committed, the offender commits an offense against the society that has designated the offender's behavior criminal. Therefore, if a person violates a state criminal law, the offender has harmed all the citizens of that state, regardless of who the specific victim is. When one commits a violation of the federal criminal law, the offense is committed against all the citizens of the United States.

In a more expanded form, a crime may be defined as an intentional act (actus reus), or omission to act, in violation of the criminal law, committed without defense or justification and punished by society as a **felony**, **misdemeanor**, violation, or **infraction**. The essential elements of the crime include a culpable mental state, guilty mind (mens rea), or criminal intent (a design, resolve, or purpose of the mind), an act or omission to act, and a causal legal connection between the intent and the act itself. The corpus delicti (body) of a crime includes injury, loss or harm, and the existence of a criminal agent as its cause. In a criminal case, the prosecution is required to prove the elements as well as the corpus delicti of a crime.

Mens rea (guilty mind) is the element of a crime that focuses on the offender's intent to commit a criminal act. Generally, a person cannot be convicted of a crime unless the act or omission involved negligence, recklessness, or knowledge, or was committed intentionally or willingly (Senna & Siegel, 2001). Types of intent fall into four basic categories: general, specific, transferred, and **criminal negligence**. General criminal intent may be inferred from merely doing the act. Specific criminal intent requires a specifically intended and desired result. With transferred (constructive) intent, a person may be liable for unintended consequences, such as when A shoots at B, misses, and kills C, an unintended victim. Criminal negligence is the failure to exercise the degree of care that a reasonable and prudent person would exercise in similar circumstances. A person who operates a motor vehicle while under the influence of alcohol or drugs does so in a criminally negligent manner.

For criminal liability to attach, one must be the actual cause (cause-in-fact), as well as the proximate (legal) cause, of the events leading to the result. To be the **proximate cause** of an event, the actor can foresee (anticipate) the result. One is liable if a reasonable and prudent person would have foreseen the possible consequences of the act or omission (Brody, Acker, & Logan, 2001; Senna & Siegel, 2001). In some employer-employee relationships, the employer may also be vicariously liable for the actions of the employee when the employee commits an unlawful act within the scope of employment, even though the employer had no knowledge that the act was being committed. Some crimes, referred to as *strict,* or *absolute, liability* offenses, require no culpable mental state and present a significant exception to the principle that all crimes require a proximate causal connection between the act and intent. Strict liability offenses make it a crime simply to do something, regardless of the actor's intent. Such offenses are based upon the presumption that causing harm is in itself blameworthy (Schmalleger, 2003, 2004). Corporations, as fictitious legal persons, can also be held criminally liable for the acts or omissions of their managers, agents, and employees (Cheeseman, 2004).

Offenses are classified as felonies, misdemeanors, violations, or infractions. Felonies usually carry a potential penalty of a fine, over one year in prison, or death. Misdemeanors carry a potential penalty of a fine or up to one year in county jail. Violations or infractions carry a potential penalty of a fine and are not usually punishable by imprisonment (Ortmeier, 2002; Nemeth, 2004; Rutledge, 2000).

Specific Crimes

The type of behavior identified as criminal, as well as the name and classification given to each offense, is determined by individual jurisdictions. The federal government and each of the states have their own criminal codes. Thus, the names given to crimes and the elements of the crimes may vary (Senna & Siegel, 2001). The following is an overview of several of the major crimes and their elements. Readers should consult their respective state criminal codes for jurisdiction-specific crimes and elements.

Crimes Against Property   Offenses contained in the **crimes against property** category include those in which the victim is not present or is unaware that the crime is being committed. The typical target of these crimes is tangible or intangible property.

- Theft (larceny). This crime involves the intentional taking of personal property of another with the intent to permanently deprive the owner of the property. The distinction between misdemeanor (petty) and felony (grand) theft depends on the dollar value specified in the statute.
- Vehicle theft. This involves theft of a vehicle and is usually specified as grand theft, regardless of the vehicle's value.
- Fictitious check. This crime involves writing a no-account check or willfully, with intent to defraud, writing or delivering a check, knowing there are insufficient funds for payment in full.
- False pretenses. Anyone who knowingly, by false pretense or fraud, procures property of another commits the offense of false pretenses.
- Embezzlement. This crime involves fraudulent appropriation or unauthorized disposition of property by a person to whom the property has been entrusted.
- Breaking and entering. This crime involves forcible entry into a structure intended for human occupancy without the permission of the owner or lessee and destroying property of value in or around the structure.
- Burglary. This crime involves entry into a structure with the intent to commit a felony or steal property of any value.
- Arson. This crime includes those situations in which the offender willfully and maliciously sets fire to any structure, forestland, or property.
- Forgery. This crime involves the false making or major alteration of any document which, if genuine, would carry with it a legal obligation or responsibility.

- Extortion (blackmail, or theft by intimidation). This crime involves withholding or obtaining property of another through the threat of some future harm.
- Trespassing. This crime involves a willful encroachment upon any land or building after receiving notice to the contrary by the person in lawful possession of the property.
- Vandalism (malicious mischief). This crime involves the malicious defacing, damaging, or destroying of another's personal or real property.

Crimes against Persons   **Crimes against persons** include those offenses committed by physical contact with the victim, in the presence of the victim with the victim's knowledge, or by placing the victim in fear of an immediate harm.

- Assault. This crime involves an attempted battery or placing someone in fear of an immediate battery.
- Battery. This crime involves the willful and unlawful use of force or violence on another person. Battery requires some physical contact with the victim (Brody, Acker, & Logan, 2001). Several states do not differentiate between assault (conveying a threat) and battery (requiring physical contact) (Simonsen, 1998). The designated crime of battery does not exist in these states. Rather, battery is merged within, and represents a form of, assault. Thus, the crime of battery is replaced with a more serious form (degree) of assault (Brody, Acker, & Logan, 2001).
- Domestic violence. This crime occurs when one willfully inflicts injury upon one's spouse, the father or mother of one's child, or a cohabitant in a relationship of an intimate sexual nature.
- Terroristic threat. This crime involves a threat to commit an act of violence or other harm. Examples include bomb threats or threatening an individual with some future physical harm.
- Robbery. This crime involves the felonious taking of property in the victim's presence by the wrongful use of force or fear.
- False imprisonment. This crime involves detaining or restricting personal liberty against the will of another.
- Kidnaping. This crime involves the forcible abduction of a person to another location. Taking a hostage or using a victim as a shield also constitutes kidnaping in many states.
- Rape. Generally, this crime involves any unconsented-to sexual penetration upon the person of another.
- Unlawful sexual intercourse (statutory rape). This crime involves the act of sexual intercourse with a person under the statutory age of consent who is not the spouse of the perpetrator.
- Homicide (unlawful). Homicide is simply defined as the killing of a human being (or fetus in some states) by another human being. However, all homi-

cides are not unlawful: Excusable homicides include accidental killings, and justifiable homicides include court-ordered executions. If a homicide is not excusable or justifiable, it is unlawful.

- Murder (first degree). This crime involves the intentional, willful, deliberate, or premeditated killing of a human being (or, in some states, a fetus) with malice aforethought or causing a death which results during the commission of an inherently dangerous felony listed in the first degree murder statute (the Felony Murder Rule). Malice aforethought is expressed or implied when the killer manifests a deliberate intent to kill or when the circumstances attending the killing demonstrate an abandoned or malignant heart (Raymond & Hall, 1999).
- Murder (second degree). This crime involves an intentional, unlawful killing of a human being (or fetus) with malice aforethought but without premeditation.
- Manslaughter (voluntary). This crime involves the intentional, unlawful killing of a human being without malice aforethought but in a fight or in the heat of passion.
- Manslaughter (involuntary). This crime involves the unlawful killing of a human being without malice aforethought in the commission of an unlawful act not amounting to a felony or in the commission of a lawful act in an unlawful or negligent manner. Vehicular manslaughter (motor vehicle homicide) is an example of involuntary manslaughter.

Obstruction of Justice   Obstruction of justice offenses include those crimes that obstruct or hinder the administration of justice process.

- Perjury. This crime includes willful lying under oath or affirmation, or under the penalty of perjury.
- Subordination of perjury. This crime involves soliciting someone else to commit perjury.
- Bribery. This crime involves giving or offering anything of value to an official with a corrupt intent to influence any act, decision, vote, opinion, or other official function or duty of such person. Requesting or acceptance of a bribe is also a criminal offense on the part of the official.

Crimes against Children   Many states have statutes that focus on crimes against children. Examples include child endangerment, physical abuse, lewd acts upon a child, molestation, child pornography, unlawful sexual intercourse, and failure to make a report of suspected child abuse.

Sex Crimes   In addition to the crime of rape (listed in the category of crimes against persons) and unlawful sexual intercourse (listed in crimes against children), many states, such as California, place sex-related crimes in a special category. These sex crimes include indecent exposure, sodomy, incest, failure to register as a sex offender, assault with intent to commit rape, spousal rape, and sexual battery (California Commission on Peace Officer Standards and Training, 1999).

Controlled Substance Crimes   Controlled substance crimes involve acts such as the possession, sale, transportation, manufacture, furnishing, or administering of controlled substances listed in applicable state and federal statutes. These crimes include possession of drug paraphernalia and being under the influence of, or cultivating, a controlled substance. These crimes focus on narcotics, cocaine, heroin, controlled substances, amphetamines, barbiturates, and marijuana.

Liquor Law Violations   Liquor law violations include selling to, or possession by, minors under a designated age; sale and consumption during statutorily restricted hours; sale to an intoxicated person; and sale of liquor without a license.

Driving under the Influence   Normally found in motor vehicle codes, driving under the influence (DUI) or driving while intoxicated (DWI) statutes focus on the operation of a motor vehicle while under the influence of alcohol or drugs.

Weapons Violations   The possession of certain types of weapons by ordinary citizens is prohibited by law. Crimes in this category include possession of specified handguns and long guns, certain types of knives, nunchakus, metal knuckles, and explosives. Many laws also prohibit carrying weapons concealed.

Other Crimes

- Criminal attempt. This crime involves an attempt to commit some other crime coupled with an act completed toward the commission of the intended crime.
- Solicitation. This crime involves soliciting (requesting) another to commit an intended crime. Statutes often limit solicitation to specific types of serious crime and sex or drug offenses.
- Conspiracy. This crime involves two or more persons who agree to commit any crime coupled with an overt act in furtherance of the **conspiracy.**
- Disturbing the peace. This crime includes unlawful fighting in a public place, challenging another person in a public place to a fight, maliciously and willfully disturbing another person by loud and unreasonable noise, or using offensive words in a public place that are inherently likely to produce an immediate violent reaction.
- Unlawful assembly. This crime involves two or more persons assembled with the intent to do an unlawful act or a lawful act in a violent manner.

- Riot. This crime involves two or more persons acting together without authority of law to use any force in a manner calculated to inspire terror.
- Interference with judicial proceedings. This crime involves offering false evidence or bribery of a judicial officer, juror, or witness.
- Interference with law enforcement. It is a crime in many jurisdictions to resist, delay, or obstruct a public officer, peace officer, or emergency medical technician in the course of employment (Acker & Brody, 1999; Nemeth, 2004; Raymond & Hall, 1999).

LAWS OF ARREST

An arrest involves the taking of a person into custody for the purpose of answering to a criminal charge. Effecting an arrest is a risky proposition. The arresting person risks injury, possibly death, to self, the person being arrested, and others. Further, in probably no other situation is the risk of a lawsuit greater, especially when the arresting person is not a public law enforcement (peace) officer. Potential civil causes of action, not to mention criminal charges, against a non–peace officer can be extremely damaging. To avoid liability, some organizations do not allow non–peace officer personnel, such as security officers, to effect an arrest under any circumstances (Canton, 2003).

Laws of arrest differ between public peace officers and private citizens. In the vast majority of situations, security personnel operate as private citizens unless statutory authority as peace officers is granted to them. The brief discussion that follows describes the essential distinctions between peace officer and **private citizen powers to arrest**. Also included is a discussion on use of force and detention authority. State and local laws should be consulted for jurisdiction-specific powers to arrest and use of force guidelines.

A peace officer may arrest if the officer observes a felony being committed. The officer may arrest for a felony not committed in the officer's presence if there is probable cause to believe that a felony was committed and that the person arrested committed it. Probable cause is established when the amount of evidence present would cause a reasonable person to believe a crime has been committed. Probable cause requires more than mere suspicion but less than absolute proof (Purpura, 2003).

A peace officer may also arrest for a misdemeanor the officer observes. In most states, if the misdemeanor is not committed in the officer's presence, an arrest cannot be made unless a misdemeanor arrest warrant is on file for the person arrested or an exception is noted in an applicable statute. A peace officer is protected from criminal and civil liability for false imprisonment or false arrest if the officer arrests according to legal guidelines and a subsequent investigation reveals no crime was committed.

Generally, a private citizen (person not a peace officer) may arrest if the private person observes a felony being committed. For a felony not committed in the private person's presence, an arrest can be made if the felony was, in fact, committed and the arresting person has probable cause to believe that the person arrested committed the offense. In some states, the person arrested must have, in fact, committed the felony. A private citizen may also arrest for a misdemeanor the private citizen observes. However, private persons have no authority to arrest for a misdemeanor not committed in their presence. Also, unlike peace officers, private citizens are not protected from criminal or civil liability due to false imprisonment or false arrest.

Although advisable, verbalizing "You are under arrest for . . ." is not necessary to produce an arrest situation. Actions may communicate an arrest. Restricting a person's (subject's) liberty or freedom of movement can be viewed by the courts as an arrest. If the subject reasonably believes that an arrest has taken place, whether or not arrest language is communicated, an arrest has been made. Finally, except for those private persons who may be granted limited or special public peace officer status, private citizens are not required to advise an arrestee of any rights as outlined in the Miranda admonition (Purpura, 2003).

Subsequent to an arrest by a private person, the public police must be contacted and custody of the arrestee must be transferred to the police as soon as possible. In some jurisdictions, the public police cannot refuse to take custody of a subject arrested by a private person.

A person may use reasonable nondeadly force when lawfully arresting another person. If the person being arrested resists, the person making the arrest can use whatever force is reasonably necessary, including deadly force, to protect themselves or an innocent third party from serious bodily harm or death. A person may also use nondeadly force in the protection of property. The use of reasonable, non-deadly force is justifiable to protect property when the actor believes such force is immediately necessary to prevent or terminate an unlawful entry or trespass or the unlawful taking (theft) of tangible, movable property (Nemeth, 2004).

As part of an investigation into missing or possibly stolen company property, an employer may discuss such matters with an employee during the employee's paid work hours. Case law is divided on the issue of whether an employee may be detained during the investigative process. Obviously, nonforcible detention is permissible during work hours. An employer has the right to conduct investigations regarding conditions of employment and personnel fidelity during the course of employment. However, if force or the threat of force is used to detain the employee, the employer may be subject to a liability risk resulting from a claim of false imprisonment.

When the person being detained is not an employee, an authorized temporary detention is usually limited by statute to retail merchants and their agents. Such statutes generally allow detention for a reasonable period of time to ascertain ownership of merchandise. The phrase *retail merchants and their agents* is noteworthy. In some jurisdictions, case law suggests that contract security personnel supplied to a merchant by a vendor are not agents of a merchant within the meaning of the statute and, therefore, do not have any detention authority (Inbau, Farber, & Arnold, 1996; Simonton, 1998).

EVIDENCE LAW

Evidence is used to make decisions in a judicial proceeding. Evidence includes testimony, writings, material objects, and other items presented to the human senses as proof of the existence or nonexistence of a disputed fact. The rules of evidence govern admissibility of testimony, writings, and material objects in judicial proceedings. Evidence is offered in court as an item of proof to establish a fact, to impeach a witness, to rehabilitate (support) a witness, and to assist in determining an appropriate sentence. Evidence must be relevant, competently presented, and legally obtained. Evidentiary rules are often described as the rules of exclusion because their language describes what evidence cannot be used because its use would violate a statutory or constitutional safeguard.

Sources of evidence law include the state and federal evidence code provisions regarding witness competency, the introduction of writings, privileged communications, and hearsay evidence, as well as penal (criminal) code provisions regarding accomplice testimony, invasion of privacy, and wiretapping. The U.S. Constitution, state constitutions, and case law regarding search and seizure, interrogation issues, and interpretation of evidence-related statutes are also important sources of evidence law (Nemeth, 2001).

Classifications of evidence include the following:

- Testimonial evidence (testimony). Testimony is given by a person who has knowledge of the issues being tried in a case.
- Documentary evidence (writings). This includes any documented or tangible form of communication offered as evidence in court.
- Physical evidence. Examples of physical evidence include proceeds from a crime, tools (instrumentalities) of a crime, items that are illegal to possess (contraband), and physical evidence that establishes the identity of the perpetrator.
- Demonstrative evidence. Examples include objects and materials such as maps, models, charts, diagrams, displays, and computer simulations that are meant to portray or enhance the meaning of evidence presented.
- Relevant evidence. Evidence that has any tendency to prove or disprove a disputed fact in a case is relevant evidence.
- Material evidence. Important (weighty) evidence is material evidence.
- Admissions and confessions. An admission is a statement by a suspect acknowledging some fact in a case. A confession is a statement by a suspect admitting liability for a crime.

- Hearsay evidence. This type of evidence includes any out-of-court statement, presented in court by someone other than the original declarant, that is offered to prove the matter stated in court. Subject to certain exceptions, hearsay evidence is inadmissible.
- Direct evidence. This is evidence that directly proves a fact without drawing inferences from other facts.
- Circumstantial evidence. This type of evidence tends to prove a fact through inference or logical association with another fact.

SEARCH AND SEIZURE

The prohibition against unreasonable search and seizure is derived from the Fourth Amendment to the U.S. Constitution. However, this prohibition applies only to governmental intrusion by public law enforcement. Searches conducted by private individuals, including private security personnel, although considered unreasonable if conducted by a public peace officer, are not subject to any judicially interpreted exclusionary rule. Thus, unreasonable searches conducted by private persons are not unconstitutional. However, private persons may be subject to a civil lawsuit for invasion of privacy.

As a general rule, public peace officers may conduct legal searches

- subject to a valid search warrant.
- incidental to a lawful arrest. This search is limited to a search of the arrestee and the area within the arrested person's immediate reach, for weapons, contraband, and means of escape.
- with consent from a person authorized to consent to the search.
- in fresh (hot) pursuit or if an exigency or public safety emergency exists.
- when items are in open (plain) view.
- of a motor vehicle when probable cause exists or the vehicle is in police custody and an inventory is necessary for safekeeping of the vehicle owner's possessions.
- for weapons on a suspicious person to protect peace officers or other prospective victims ("stop and frisk") (Acker & Brody, 1999).

The application of the Fourth Amendment depends upon whether the person claiming protection under the amendment can claim a justifiable, reasonable, or legitimate expectation to privacy that has been invaded by government action. Absent any established exception to the contrary, courts have held that the process of determining which warrantless searches are unconstitutional requires a balancing of the public's interests against the Fourth Amendment interests of the individual. In one landmark court case, a public hospital employee, who was aware of the hospital's policy providing for random spot inspections of packages, refused to permit inspection of a closed knapsack. The hospital's policy provided for an alternative procedure, through which an employee could check packages before entry and thereby avoid any possibility of an inspection. The appellate court ruled in favor of the hospital when it held that, in light of the public's interest in controlling pilferage from public institutions, the noncoercive search tactics used, and the availability of an alternative procedure, the individual employee's expectations of privacy were considered to be unreasonable (*Chenkin v. Bellevue Hospital Controller, N.Y.C.,* ETC., 1979).

A **private person's search authority** is limited. Private persons may search

- incidental to a lawful arrest. The search of the arrestee is generally limited to a search for weapons only.
- another person if an expressed or implied limited search privilege is granted through a waiver by the person subject to search.
- with the consent of the person being searched.
- to protect human life in an emergency such as a fire.
- an employee's workspace, when there is no reasonable expectation of privacy.
- employee lockers and desks if the employer, with the employee's knowledge, retains a duplicate key. Furthermore, if an employee, after signing a waiver to search as a condition of employment, refuses to consent to a search, the refusal may provide grounds for termination when the possibility of termination is included in the waiver's language.

Conversely, if any of the circumstances outlined above are absent, a private person shall not search

- another person or their possessions without permission.
- an employee or the employee's personal possessions or workspace without uncoerced consent.
- an area where another person has exclusive dominion and control.
- a suspicious and potentially violent person unless statutory authority for a "stop and frisk" exists.
- an area retained under a lease agreement, such as a hotel room or apartment (Inbau, Farber, & Arnold, 1996).

U.S. law recognizes each person's right to exist without unwarranted intrusion or undesired publicity. Subject to the limited exceptions previously discussed, the government does not have the right to search a business without a search warrant unless the business is regulated, such as firearms dealers, mines, and liquor stores, and case law and statutory provisions support the warrantless searches. Similarly, absent any established legal authority or well-communicated policy, private organizations cannot search a person or the person's personal workspace without subjecting itself to a tort claim for invasion of the right to privacy (Cheeseman, 2004).

LEGISLATIVE TRENDS IN SECURITY MANAGEMENT

Numerous recent federal and state legislative initiatives address safety and security concerns. As exemplified by lawmaker activity in a number of states, critical issues are being addressed in the areas of security personnel, school security, the use of defibrillators, pre-employment screening, identity theft, digital signatures, drug testing, computer security, workplace violence, private prisons, closed-circuit television (CCTV), and privacy.

In 1999, legislatures in five states passed laws affecting the requirements, duties, and responsibilities of security personnel. Fifteen states enacted legislation relating to school security. Four of those states passed legislation allowing release of juvenile crime records to school officials. Many states established school security programs. Included are school safety centers that collect information on school-related crime and use the information as the basis for prevention efforts and safety plans. To encourage life-saving efforts, 28 states passed laws granting immunity from liability to individuals and organizations who administer or use defibrillators to revive persons suffering from cardiac arrest. Twelve states passed legislation requiring or expanding pre-employment screening efforts to those employed in public or private schools, day-care centers, and nursing homes. A Colorado law grants immunity to employers who provide derogatory, yet truthful, information to a prospective employer on a former employee's work-related abilities, habits, or grounds for termination.

Also in 1999, several states enacted legislation making it illegal to use or attempt to use another person's identification or financial information. Seven states, as well as the U.S. Congress, passed laws authorizing the legal use of electronic (digital) signatures in lieu of physically handwritten signatures. New drug-testing laws provide for denial of workman's compensation claims and support disciplinary efforts against employees who test positive. The employee must be given fair written warning of the policy and the drug test must be administered and evaluated according to statutory guidelines. Other laws enacted relate to computer crime, workplace violence, the administration of private prisons, and restrictions on the use of CCTV in areas where the subject has a reasonable expectation to privacy. Numerous other privacy-related laws restrict access to patient medical records and driver license information. Future legislative efforts will continue to focus on school security and workplace violence, as well as on electronic commerce and the future of copyrights, contract law, and intellectual property in the electronic domain (Anderson, 2000).

The twenty-first century presents new legal challenges for the security management professional. The elimination of, and alterations to, nation-states and societies, the changing nature of the workplace, increased use of high technology, terrorism, and the expansion of global competition help to create an environment in which the legal aspects of security management constantly evolve (Kovacich & Halibozek, 2003). In response, numerous legislative initiatives, as evidenced by laws associated with subjects such as cybersecurity, counterterrorism, and homeland defense have been proposed and passed. The progressive, informed, and visionary security manager takes advantage of any opportunity to learn about new laws and their implications.

SUMMARY

The judicial process in the United States is adversarial. Complex criminal and civil judicial proceedings take place in a wide variety of federal, state, and local trial and appellate courts. Prosecutors in criminal cases and plaintiffs in civil cases have a burden to proceed first. In criminal cases, a defendant can be formally charged through an indictment from a grand jury or through an information or similar complaint filed by a prosecutor. Civil actions are initiated through a complaint filed by a plaintiff. Trial juries are randomly selected initially, then proceed through a final selection during a voir dire (to speak the truth) examination.

A tort is an intentional or unintentional civil wrong for which the law provides a remedy. A contract is a legally binding voluntary agreement between parties. Administrative law agencies promulgate rules and regulations that prescribe duties and responsibilities of individuals and organizations. Property law focuses on possessory and ownership rights associated with real and personal property. Employment law regulates the relationship between an employer and an employee. The criminal law embodies a broad spectrum of behaviors deemed impermissible in society. Punished as felonies, misdemeanors, violations, or infractions, crimes are categorized in several ways. Paramount among the categories are crimes against property and crimes against persons. In most jurisdictions, private citizens have the authority to effect an arrest. However, the arrest authority of a private citizen differs from that of a public law enforcement officer. The rules of evidence and search and seizure place constitutional limits on the collection and admissibility of evidence. Legislatively, numerous federal and state initiatives will continue to address safety and security issues.

KEY TERMS

administrative law	contract
appellate courts	court of last resort
arraignment	courts of general jurisdiction
challenges for cause	courts of limited jurisdiction
common law	crimes against persons
conspiracy	crimes against property

criminal negligence	peremptory challenge
degrees of proof	personal property
employment law	preliminary hearing
expressed contract	private citizen powers to arrest
evidence	private person's search authority
felony	proximate cause
first (initial) appearance	real property
impeachment	solicitation
implied contract	statute
indictment	tort
information	transcript
infraction	trial courts
intentional torts	unintentional tort
intermediate appellate courts	U.S. court of appeals
misdemeanor	U.S. district court
negligence	U.S. Supreme Court
obstruction of justice offense	voir dire examination

DISCUSSION QUESTIONS AND EXERCISES

1. Describe the judicial system in the United States. Include types, levels, and jurisdiction of courts in the description.
2. Compare and contrast civil with criminal pretrial and trial processes.
3. Distinguish a tort from a crime and describe types of situations that give rise to tort liability.
4. Why should a security manager, or any person nominally in charge of a loss prevention function, be familiar with contract, property, administrative, and employment law?
5. What constitutes criminal activity? In other words, what are the essential elements of a crime?
6. Compare the arrest powers of the public police with that of private security.
7. Under what circumstances may a private security person search another person? (employee workspace? another's briefcase or handbag?)
8. Under what circumstances may conversations be monitored, physically or electronically?

CHAPTER 4

Risk Assessment, Planning, and Program Administration

LEARNING OBJECTIVES

After completing this chapter, the reader should be able to

- define risk and risk assessment.
- list and describe five distinct types of risk that threaten individuals and organizations.
- discuss management techniques associated with risk elimination, reduction, and mitigation.
- evaluate risks to determine vulnerability, probability, and criticality of loss.
- conduct a risk assessment utilizing subjective as well as objective measurements.
- conduct a security survey.
- analyze needs identified through a risk assessment.
- develop appropriate courses of action to eliminate, reduce, or mitigate risks identified in a risk assessment.
- discuss the importance of the budget process.
- demonstrate knowledge of Crime Prevention through Environmental Design (CPTED).
- discuss the procedure for protection plan implementation.
- evaluate protection systems.
- demonstrate knowledge of emergency planning.

INTRODUCTION

A major focus for security management is the concept of risk. Subjective information as well as objective measurement instruments (such as a security survey) are used in an essential first step of a planning process designed to identify and assess the threat posed by each risk source. As the planning process proceeds, the security manager must make recommendations and determine the financial impact of any potential risk mitigation strategy. Planning activities also involve preparation for emergency situations and consideration of anticrime measures available through environmental manipulation. Once a plan of action is approved, the security manager is responsible for program implementation, administration, and evaluation of results.

THE CONCEPT OF RISK

Risk Defined

Risk may be defined as the possibility of suffering harm or loss, exposure to the probability of loss or damage, an element of uncertainty, or the possibility that results of an action may not be consistent with the planned or expected outcomes. A decision maker evaluates risk conditions to predict or estimate the likelihood of certain outcomes (Robbins & Coulter, 2003). From a security perspective, risk management is defined as the process involved in the anticipation, recognition, and appraisal of a risk and the initiation of action to eliminate the risk entirely or reduce the threat of harm to an acceptable level. A risk involves a known or foreseeable threat to an organization's assets: people, property, information, or reputation (Fay, 2000; Hess & Wrobleski, 1996; Simonsen, 1998). Risk cannot be totally eliminated. However, effective loss prevention programs can reduce risk and its impact to the lowest possible level (Fischer & Janoski, 2000). An effective risk management program can maximize asset protection while minimizing protection costs (Kovacich & Halibozek, 2003).

Types of Risk

Generally, risk is associated with natural phenomena or threats created by human agents. Natural risks arise from earthquakes, volcanic eruptions, floods, and storms. Risk created by human beings include acts or failures to act that lead to crime, accidents, or environmental disaster. As many as five distinct types of risk threaten individuals and organizations. **Pure risk** exists when there is a potential for injury, damage, or loss with no possible benefit. Potential medical claims resulting from accidents may be classified as pure risks. The threat of criminal attack or natural disaster are also examples of pure risk. These events increase operating costs, a form of loss. **Dynamic risk** exists when threat conditions fluctuate. Examples include areas of the world that are subject to weather extremes, communities that depend on seasonal tourism, or changing political conditions. A **speculative risk** exists when there is a potential for benefit or loss, depending on the consequences of an activity or inactivity. New product research and development as well as business ventures into new markets are examples of speculative risk. A **static risk** is constant and unchanging. If a critical component needed to manufacture a product is provided by a single patented source, the risk associated with the loss of the supplier is static. The risk is always present. Loss of the sole source means the product manufacturing process is stopped. Finally, some threats involve **inherent risk**. These risks are unavoidable because of the nature of the business, such as transportation and mining, or because the business is involved in an extremely competitive marketplace.

Failure to recognize and take action against a risk is potentially costly for any organization. Materialized risk increases the cost of doing business, may increase insurance premiums, and exposes the organization to criminal as well as civil liability. In addition to direct costs associated with a reduction in organizational assets, indirect costs are incurred when the organization experiences loss of market, reputation, or competitive edge. Losses in shareholder equity and reductions in productivity also result. A risk event may adversely impact profitability for private business and affect a public organization's ability to render services (American Society of Industrial Security, 1998; Fay, 2000; Fischer & Green, 1998).

Risk Management Techniques

Risk management is a process that has been used by insurance companies for decades. It involves deliberate actions aimed at loss prevention and mitigation. Through risk management, security professionals anticipate, recognize, and analyze potential risks and loss-creating threats, and implement strategies to mitigate loss and damage. A comprehensive risk management program involves

- the identification of risks and vulnerabilities through continuous threat assessment.
- analysis of the risks and vulnerabilities identified.
- optimization of cost-effective risk management alternatives designed to avoid, reduce, spread, or transfer identified risk (Fischer & Janoski, 2000).

Externally, a risk management program utilizes the society and its legal system to protect assets against threats. Internally, a risk management program incorporates administrative controls as well as physical, personnel, and information security policies and procedures to protect assets against threats and hazards (Kovacich & Halibozek, 2003).

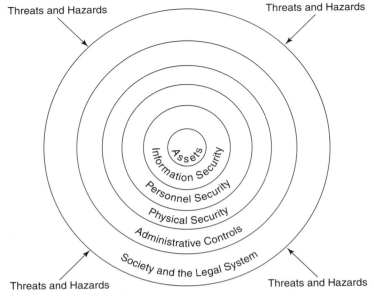

Threats and Hazards

Threats and Hazards

Threats and Hazards

Threats and Hazards

Assets

Information Security

Personnel Security

Physical Security

Administrative Controls

Society and the Legal System

Figure 4–1   Risk Management/Asset Protection System

Elimination, Reduction, Mitigation   Risk management techniques involve elimination of the risk if possible, reducing the probability that a loss will occur, and mitigating the damage if a threat materializes. Total elimination of risk is difficult, although mitigation of risk is possible in some cases, given the right circumstances. Removing all flammable materials from a facility will eliminate the threat of fire fueled by the flammable materials. It will not, however, eliminate the threat of fire fueled by a different source. Implementing an effective access control system may reduce the possibility of criminal attack. Appropriate disaster planning may mitigate damage, minimize injuries, and save lives in the event of a hurricane, tornado, or earthquake.

Vulnerability, Probability, Criticality   The security professional must consider three factors that influence risk management decisions: vulnerability (exposure), probability (likelihood), and criticality (impact). Each of these factors must be considered and the cost of asset protection balanced against the potential for loss. First, the security manager must consider vulnerability to loss. If an individual or organization is vulnerable, it is exposed to the possibility that the risk or threat will materialize. Little or no physical security certainly exposes physical assets, personnel, and information to attack. Second, the probability of loss must be considered. The security manager must consider the likelihood a threat will materialize and pursue measures to prevent an incident or mitigate the negative impact of an event (Fay, 2000). A facility, because of a general lack of physical security, could be extremely vulnerable to criminal action. However, if the facility is located in an area that has experienced an extremely low crime rate, the probability of criminal attack may be negligible. In this case, the cost of additional physical security measures may outweigh the benefits.

Finally, the security professional must consider criticality of a loss if the loss did occur. In other words, the manager must foresee the likely impact and consequences associated with the loss. If a product research and development organization stores all of its data in a database at a single location and the database is completely destroyed during a flood, the loss to the organization would be devastating. If a subsidiary or vender to a manufacturing firm is the sole supplier of a component critical to the manufacturing process, what impact would a personnel strike at the subsidiary's or vendor's facility have on the ability of the manufacturing firm to assemble product and service customers?

In summary, vulnerability to loss as well as the probability and criticality of loss must be considered when making risk management decisions. All three factors are equally important. The sophisticated security manager analyzes the risk and allocates resources for maximum benefit (Fischer & Green, 1998). Realistic asset protection and loss prevention can be achieved when limited security resources are allocated according to need and the potential consequences of a materialized threat (Jopeck, 2000). In some cases, a thorough risk assessment reveals a low probability that a breach of security or disastrous event will occur. However, the security manager should not disregard low-probability risks, because failure to protect against such risks can be a fatal error. The impact of the bombings at the World Trade Center in New York City in 1993 and at the federal building in Oklahoma City in 1995 provide ample evidence of the consequences associated with disregarding low-probability risk (Garcia, 2000).

RISK ASSESSMENT AND THE SECURITY SURVEY

As a method for identifying and evaluating risks, a **risk assessment** involves a critical, objective analysis of an organization's entire protective system (Jacobson, 1997). Continuous risk assessment enables the security professional to provide sound data upon which to solicit funding and make informed decisions regarding the allocation of scarce resources (Jopeck, 2000).

The Guidelines Commission of ASIS International developed a recommended practice advisory for conducting general security risk assessments. The following is a brief outline of the Commission's recommended approach. Additional information regarding the guidelines can be obtained by contacting ASIS International at 703-519-6200 or www.asisonline.org. The approach is aligned with planning processes discussed later in this chapter.

- Develop an understanding of the organization and identify the human, physical, and information assets at risk.
- Specify loss risk events and vulnerabilities.
- Establish the probability of loss risk and determine the frequency of loss events.

- Determine the impact of loss events, including the financial, psychological, and other costs associated with a loss event.
- Develop options to prevent or mitigate losses.
- Study the feasibility of implementing each option.
- Perform a cost-benefit analysis (ASIS International Guidelines Commission, 2003).

The processes and instruments utilized during the risk assessment depend on the situation. It is necessary to collect and analyze relevant data. This data may be collected utilizing subjective as well as objective techniques (Fay, 2000). **Subjective (qualitative) measures** include the use of forecasting, employee surveys, expert opinion, and the **Delphi technique**. The Delphi technique involves a process through which several individuals or experts provide input on a given issue and ultimately arrive at consensus on a prediction or list of needs and priorities (Bunning, 1979). **Objective (quantitative) measures** include the use of audits, marketing, operations research, incident and statistical reports, threat assessment, investigations, risk analysis, inspections, and security (loss prevention) surveys.

A **security survey** is used to evaluate an entire organization to identify risks and security deficiencies. The survey must be comprehensive, and it should identify

- assets (people, property, information) to be protected.
- anything (or anyone) that could adversely threaten the well-being of the assets.
- the vulnerabilities (weaknesses) that could conceivably be exploited by the threats (Fischer & Janoski, 2000).

The results of the survey are used for risk assessment as well as safety and security planning (Jopeck, 2000).

A survey instrument (checklist) is often used to conduct a security survey. The security survey should assess several areas of concern. Every facility faces a multitude of security threats. Each potential threat must be analyzed in terms of its source (internal or external) as well as the goals, tactics, capabilities, and motivation of any criminal perpetrators (Garcia, 2000). The nature of the organization and its activities as well as the country within which the organization is located must be considered. The availability of public services, utilities, and health care, along with political and economic conditions, must be evaluated. The general area or neighborhood surrounding the facility must be analyzed. Consideration must also be given to area crime rates, aesthetic qualities, and susceptibility to catastrophic events such as floods. The perimeter near the facility should be evaluated in terms of its parking, fencing, landscaping, and signage. The survey of the building itself should include points of entry, exits, access control, locks and keys, alarm systems and lighting, and vulnerability to intrusion.

Restricted areas within the facility must be identified. These include computer and data storage areas, key storage areas, mechanical and utility rooms, telecommunication rooms, mail rooms, and executive office suites. Alarm and surveillance systems, fire protection, personnel security, and information protection must be reviewed. The procedures for investigations and the collection of business and criminal intelligence, as well as reporting systems, operations, and liaison activities, must be evaluated.

A review of organizational policies includes an analysis of procedures used in the management of human resources and in the protection of property and information. A review of safety procedures should include mechanisms for prevention of accidents as well as fire safety and emergency plans. An assessment should be made of the number of security personnel required and of personnel responsibilities and training requirements. The survey should also assess the indoctrination and education of all employees regarding security and safety policies and procedures (Ortmeier, 1999).

Some surveys uncover surprises that are really not unique. In one organization, a man posing as a repair person was caught attempting to steal proprietary information. He was able to escape without being identified. The incident was not reported when it occurred but was disclosed when employees were interviewed during the course of a security survey. The incident proved that the organization was the target of competitive intelligence operatives. The discovery led to the development of business counterintelligence procedures and counterintelligence training for employees (Jopeck, 2000).

As organizational stakeholders, all employees should be consulted during the security survey. Employees typically know where vulnerabilities lie and people are an excellent source of information. Input from employees also assists with the creation of employee ownership of the security program. Ownership, or buy-in, with employees is critical to program success.

At a minimum, the survey should address the general area or neighborhood surrounding the facility, as well as the perimeter, buildings, restricted areas, organizational policies, safety, personnel, and security education. The approach to a security survey may vary. Objective as well as subjective measures may be used to collect information. Emphasis should be placed on the physical environment, effectiveness of security personnel, policies and procedures, and management's attitude toward the loss prevention function. A comprehensive survey instrument should be used in the actual on-site survey. A sample safety and security survey instrument is included in this book (Appendix B). Since each type of organization has special needs, it may be necessary to customize the survey instrument to accommodate organizational requirements (Collins, Ricks, & Van Meter, 2000; Craighead, 2003; Schaub & Biery, 1994).

The risk assessment process is widely recognized and has been adopted by private industry, public law enforcement, and all levels of government. Therefore, the sources of information for determining the probability of loss and the actual frequency of risk events are extensive. Local police crime statistics, the Uniform Crime Report (UCR), the National Crime Victimization Survey (NCVS), and criminal intelligence reports are excellent sources. An organization's internal documents (e.g., incident reports, complaints received) and civil claims can provide critical risk assessment data. Information about general economic conditions, the threat of natural disasters, and industry trends are also vital to the risk assessment process (ASIS International Guidelines Commission, 2003).

PLANNING

A plan involves the detailed formulation of a program for action (Fay, 1999). There are several categories of plans. A **single-use plan** is used once and no longer needed when the objectives of the plan are accomplished. Budgets and special projects are examples of single-use plans. A **repeat-use (standing) plan**, on the other hand, may be used several times. Repeat-use plans are implemented each time a given situation or incident occurs. Unless modified, repeat-use plans change little over time. Examples of repeat-use plans include policies, procedures, and methods for achieving objectives. A **tactical plan** is short range and scheduled to be implemented within a short time frame. A **strategic plan** is long range and involves implementation over a period of years. A **contingency plan** is one that will be implemented only if a certain event, such as a natural disaster, occurs (Meese & Ortmeier, 2004; Perry, 1996).

Plans define an organization's goals, establish strategies for achieving those goals, and they integrate and coordinate organizational efforts (Robbins & Coulter, 2003). Plans are developed and implemented to project revenue and expenses, control access, create security awareness among constituents, protect people and property, prepare for emergencies, and recover from unfortunate events (Fay, 1999).

All **planning** processes include at least three common elements. The **elements of planning** include a needs (or risk) assessment, the development of alternative courses of action, and selection of an action plan. The first step is to establish the existence of a need for a plan. In security management practice, the risk assessment and analysis determines the need. A thorough examination of existing conditions as well as the prediction of potential threats will help determine if an actual need exists or if a perceived need is simply based on unnecessary desires or special interests. Assets requiring protection, potential threats, and vulnerabilities are identified and assessed (Jopeck, 2000). Thus, the practitioner must realistically identify the threats against the organization, its people, and its property.

After needs are identified, objectives for meeting the needs are outlined. For the security manager, this involves qualifying and quantifying the risk and the development of action plan countermeasures that correspond to the threats identified in the needs assessment (Jopeck, 2000). Action plans must include measurable objectives. Decisions on courses of action and the selection of the most appropriate action plan will be based on an analysis of current and forecasted conditions. Each alternative must be analyzed and evaluated to determine

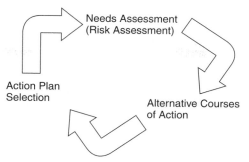

Figure 4–2   The Planning Process (common elements)

probable undesirable as well as desirable consequences. This will involve conscious consideration and selection of a course of action among available alternatives to produce the best possible outcomes.

CompStat (Computer-driven Statistics) shows tremendous promise as a planning and management tool. CompStat was made famous through its application in the New York City Police Department during William Bratton's tenure as NYPD's commissioner in the mid-1990s. CompStat technology and management helped New York City reduce its crime rate significantly. Prior to CompStat's integration into NYPD's tactical and strategic planning processes, the department collected crime data, but the statistics were 3 to 6 months old before they were compiled and analyzed. CompStat technology, and the interactive managerial communications that accompanied it, provided current, almost real-time statistical information. The information provided a framework for more effective deployment of police resources and accountability for results.

CompStat is applicable in the private as well as the public sectors. Security managers may wish to develop and implement a CompStat-style incident tracking system. Coupled with a comprehensive data collection system (i.e., detailed reports that include when, where, who, what, how, and why an incident occurred), security-related incidents can be coded, automated, and analyzed quickly utilizing CompStat computer technology. Appropriately applied, CompStat planning and management processes increase efficiency and cost-effectiveness, and they can have a dramatic positive impact on profitability (Henry, 2002).

The decision-making process and the decisions made are not always popular. The impact a decision has on the organization, its people, its clients, and the community will require careful consideration. Change causes stress and anxiety. However, if well thought out, each decision may be viewed as an opportunity for development, progress, and advancement of individual as well as organizational goals and objectives. The plan must project an implementation schedule, identify who is responsible for its implementation, monitor and evaluate its progress, and establish the criteria for evaluating the plan.

The financial impact of each action plan must also be determined. This requires a **budget** for each alternative action plan. Budget preparation is an integral part of the planning process. It is an essential planning tool tied to the established goals and objectives developed as alternative courses of action. The budget is a plan expressed in financial terms. An analysis must be made of the cost versus the benefit of each threat countermeasure. Industry standards indicate that the protection cost should be less than 2 percent of the value of the asset to be protected. Higher protection cost percentages are justifiable only if special circumstances exist. Countermeasure expenditures exceeding 5 percent of the value of the protected item are rarely justifiable (American Society for Industrial Security, 1998).

A **cost-benefit analysis** provides a useful decision-making tool when one considers the commitment of funds or other resources. The analysis is a systematic process through which one attempts to determine the value of the benefits derived from an expenditure and compare the value with the cost. The cost-benefit analysis usually involves three steps.

- The identification of all possible consequences of an expenditure.
- The assignment of a monetary value to each consequence (cost and benefit) associated with the expenditure.
- The discounting of anticipated future costs and revenues accruing from the expenditure to express those costs and revenues in current monetary terms (ASIS International Guidelines Commission, 2003).

The cost-benefit analysis can assist with the calculation of the **return on investment (ROI)** of security-related expenditures and the **value-added contribution (VAC)** of the security program. ROI refers to the net savings that result when security measures are in place. The VAC refers to those anticipated threats that do not materialize because of the security program (Dalton, 1995).

The ROI and VAC can be difficult to quantify unless one has a baseline for comparison. A reduction in the number of thefts after protective measures are placed in service is quantifiable. Savings can also be estimated in such diverse areas as illicit drug use and employee attrition (Jones & Arnold, 2003). However, without a basis for comparison (i.e., how much overall crime is prevented), security's productivity can be questioned because its VAC is unquantifiable in specific terms (Harowitz, 2003; Johnson, 2003). Thus, selling the security program and its budget can be challenging. To overcome the challenge, the security manager must be creative. The manager must also be assertive and pursue collaborative asset protection linkages and advocates with personnel in other organizational units, such as operations, sales, marketing, human resources, information technology, and community relations (Sommer, 2003).

Areas to consider in budget preparation include past operations, present conditions, and future expectations. Vulnerability to loss as well as the probability and criticality of loss must be considered. Revenue forecasts and projected expenditures are also useful ingredients to budget preparation. The budget process should be continuous, flexible, and responsive to the changing needs of the organization.

There are several types of budgets. A **traditional budget** is a simple percentage increase over the last budget. A **line item budget** includes a description of items and the cost of each item. Line item budgets provide detail and clarity, and are easy to audit. Their disadvantages include inflexibility and isolation from the objectives. A **performance-based budget** includes measurable units tied to objectives that allow for a cost-benefit analysis by program type. The disadvantage to this type of budget is that some items, such as how many crimes or accidents are prevented as a result of money spent on a security system, are not easily measured. With a **zero-based budget (ZBB)**, each program within a budget period must justify its existence and expenditures (Perry, 1996). Budgets are used to forecast expenditures and revenues, and as quantitative standards against which one can measure and compare resource consumption (Robbins & Coulter, 2003). The type of budget selected will depend on the circumstances, information needs, and organizational policy.

Regardless of the type of budget used, the elements of a budget should include an accounting for personnel services, operating expenses, supplies and materials, capital outlay, and miscellaneous expenditures. The personnel services portion of the budget includes identification of the types and number of persons required as well as **personnel expenses** associated with salaries and wages, including statutorily mandated payroll taxes, discretionary personnel-related expenses such as health insurance and retirement, and overtime pay for hourly employees.

Operating expenses include such items as rent, utilities, contract services, training, insurance, professional fees, pre-employment screening, and memberships in professional organizations. **Supplies and materials expenses** include objects with an expected life of one year or less. This category includes office supplies, computer software, and fuel.

Capital expenditures are depreciable assets. They are objects with an expected life of one year or more. Large capital expenditures may require a separate capital budget and are usually amortized over a period of years. Examples include vehicles, computers, pagers, and buildings. The **miscellaneous expense** category of the budget includes any item not appropriately placed in one of the other categories. Travel and depreciation of capital assets are placed in the miscellaneous category (Price, Haddock, & Brock, 1996).

To select the most appropriate action plan, all stakeholders should be involved in the decision-making process. In other words, a determination of available resources must be made and consumers should be interviewed to solicit input before countermeasures are implemented. Support must be generated for the recommended plan. Effective implementation will depend on organizational support. Positive employee and constituent relations requires that they be involved in the decision-making process or, at the minimum, be informed of future plans. People often experience difficulty with change, whether the change is viewed negatively or positively.

When an entire community may be impacted by a plan, information should be disseminated, on a need-to-know basis, to generate public support. This can be accomplished through the media, public speaking engagements in community forums, and at meetings of professional organizations. Support from the persons responsible for approval of the budget is also necessary. A strategy must be developed to justify the budget to all the major stakeholders. They will want to know what value the proposed plan will contribute to the goals and objectives of the organization or agency.

Security professionals are always challenged to do more with less. Stakeholders and shareholders alike pressure senior management to survive, compete, and seek new ways to reduce expenses, increase revenue and profit, and improve the quality of products, personnel, and the workplace. Change in a competitive environment increases stress, the likelihood of uncivil behavior, and excuses for wrongdoing. The potential for workplace violence also increases. Simultaneously, organizations are faced with a complex web of environmental, health, safety, and security regulations, compliance issues, legal constraints and confrontations, increased risk exposure, and decreased employee morale and loyalty. Consequently, increased pressure is placed on the security manager to widen the span of control and accept more responsibility for the bottom line. The security manager's dilemma, however, can be transformed into a window of opportunity for growth and can lay the foundation for justification of security expenditures. If security managers expand their range of skills, embrace technology, and confront business issues in an intelligent manner, they can convincingly describe and demonstrate security's tremendous return on investment (Caldwell, 2000).

If the plan involves other organizations and agencies, liaison should be established with them. For example, corporate security departments tend to be more effective when liaison is established with relevant public safety agencies. Similarly, if resources are to be shared through a consortium, the planning process must involve the other organizations impacted by the plan. Liaison with other agencies is a necessity. Given the reality of terrorism and that the crime rate, although declining in recent years, remains relatively high, cooperation between and among law enforcement and security operatives is essential. Strong alliances have already developed between the public and private sectors in many areas of the United States (Operation Cooperation, 2001). Public-private partnerships such as the Virginia Police and Private Security Alliance (Bentley, 1997) and the East Bay Public Safety Corridor Partnership in San Francisco (U.S. Department of Justice, Bureau of Justice Assistance, 1997), and the use of private security on public transit systems are but a few examples of how cooperation and complementary relationships can benefit all citizens (Moses-Schulz, 1997).

At a minimum, liaison activities, such as NYPD's Area Police–Private Security Liaison (APPL) project, allow security executives to share information and network to facilitate the distribution of intelligence alerts (Henry, 2002). Truly, liaison activities help to create a foundation upon which the public police and security organizations can multiply their capabilities (Meese & Ortmeier, 2004).

CONTINGENCY PLANNING

There may be several versions of each type of **contingency plan.** Some plans are simple, while others are complex. The response to an accident requiring basic first aid may be relatively simple, while a response to an environmental disaster may be very detailed and complex. Disasters can impact an entire community or region. Therefore, a contingency plan should address all conceivable variables and requirements. A chain of command designating authority relationships must be created. This includes command staff as well as a designated emergency coordinator. The plan must state its purpose, the types of emergencies covered, and the transition process from normal to emergency operations. Plan execution instructions and supporting information must be included. Maps and information on procedures, local resources, mutual-aid agreements, and liaison personnel are essential. The locations of the emergency control and operations center must be identified and communications channels should be described in the plan. Provision must be made to secure vital agency and organizational records and databases. This includes data files, incorporation certificates, bylaws, client lists, stock records, board meeting minutes, and financial records. Emergency shutdown procedures, personnel protection systems, the roles of supervisors, emergency evacuation routes, and shelter locations must be specified. All contingency plans should be contained in a manual, and employees must be trained regarding their response in the event of a disaster. Finally, the plan should be tested periodically to ensure organizational readiness and to assess the need for changes to the plan (Haddow & Bullock, 2003; Meese & Ortmeier, 2004; Papi, 1994).

CRIME PREVENTION THROUGH ENVIRONMENTAL DESIGN

Crime Prevention through Environmental Design (CPTED) is based on the theory that the environment can be protected, and crime prevented, through the proper design of facilities and communities. Emphasis is placed on effective use of architecture, building codes, and defensible space. Security and safety concepts are incorporated into the planning of the facility or community. In conjunction with community policing programs, CPTED may be applied to residential and business areas to increase public safety and reduce citizen fear of crime.

Risk assessment and security planning through CPTED have been very effective in preventing and deterring crime. Alternatively, poor security planning not only fails to prevent and deter crime, but also encourages it, because the facility design attracts criminal activity. Failure to design residential and business environments with effective safety and security measures also creates a liability connection between victims of crime and property owners, managers, organizations, and landlords.

CPTED is not new. In prehistoric times, cave dwellers cleared areas in front of their caves and stacked rocks around the perimeter to mask their space and warn intruders. During the early Greek empire, temple designers used environmental concepts to affect and control behavior. The temples were built of a type of stone that contained phosphorous and reflected a golden light shortly after dawn and just before dusk. During medieval times, height was used as a defensive tool. Sleeping quarters were high above ground level and whole communities were surrounded by high walls (Crowe, 2000).

Beginning in the 1970s, the National Institute of Justice sponsored research and promoted crime prevention strategies that use CPTED and community policing to make neighborhoods safer. Results indicate that proper design of the physical environment can control and prevent crime. Private individuals and businesses working in conjunction with the police have reduced fear of crime and deterred criminals. They have also used government building codes and agency inspection power to discourage illicit drug use and other criminal activity (Fleissner & Heinzelmann, 1996).

CPTED supports the movement toward community- and problem-oriented policing. Alternately, community policing and problem solving reinforce the concepts of CPTED (Scott, 2000). Although long in coming to policing, when used in conjunction with community policing programs CPTED can increase public safety (Kroeker, 2001). Utilizing CPTED concepts, the police may actually be able to predict where crime is most likely to occur. After high-risk areas are identified, the police can work closely with individuals and businesses to prevent and control crime (Meese & Ortmeier, 2004).

The conceptual thrust of CPTED is that an environment can be manipulated to produce behavioral effects that prevent crime and improve the quality of life. The environment includes people and physical and social surroundings. The design includes all those activities, structures, and policies that seek to positively impact human behavior as people interact with the environment. CPTED focuses on the physical aspects of the environment as well as on what social scientists, public safety and security personnel, and community organizations can do to safely meet the needs of legitimate users of a space. Traditional target-hardening techniques, such as natural and artificial barrier systems, access control, and surveillance, are used to reduce the threat from criminal offenders. However, the CPTED concept is applied beyond the use of target hardening. It also involves strategies developed, implemented, and evaluated by security and law enforcement personnel, as well as by the community, to allow for the least restrictive human interface with the barrier systems (Harrell & Taylor, 1996).

CPTED is based on certain assumptions relating to how space is to be designed and used. First, all human space has a designated purpose that lays the foundation for the social, legal, cultural, or physical definitions that prescribe desired and acceptable behaviors. Second, facilities and communities are designed to support and control the desired behaviors. The basic concepts of territorial reinforcement, access control, and surveillance are inherent in the approach. These basic concepts are accomplished through any combination of the following:

- A clear border definition of the controlled space. Public and private spaces must be clearly delineated.
- Clearly marked transitional zones. The user must be forced to acknowledge movement into the controlled space.
- Relocation of gathering areas. The design must formally designate gathering areas in locations with good access control and natural surveillance capabilities.
- Safe activities in unsafe locations. Safe activities serve as magnets for normal users and communicate to abnormal users that they are at greater risk of detection.
- Unsafe activities in safe locations. Vulnerable activities should be placed within tightly controlled areas to help overcome risk and make normal users feel safer.
- Use of space to provide natural barriers. Conflicting activities may be separated by distance and natural terrain to avoid fear-producing conflict.
- Improved scheduling of space. The effective use of space reduces actual risk as well as the perception of risk for normal users.
- Appropriate space allocation and design increases the perception of surveillance.
- Reduction in isolation and distance. Design efficiencies and improved communication systems increase the perception of surveillance and control (Crowe, 2000).

One of the most significant shifts in modern thinking about crime prevention is that individual action in a vacuum often increases risks to safety and security. However, the mobilization of all stakeholders in a collaborative effort to prevent crime and disorder creates an environment in which success is more likely (Fennelly, 2004). From a CPTED perspective, this means effective communication and collaboration between and among business organizations, public agencies, security managers, architects, and others to engineer safe and secure environments (American Institute of Architects, 2003).

Good planning will dictate the tactical implementation of CPTED concept design strategies. Risk and crime analyses, demographic and land use information, and resident or user interviews should be utilized to plan security controls. CPTED is not a substitute for a comprehensive loss prevention program. However, it can reduce the opportunity to commit crime when implemented in the context of a program designed to prevent crime while providing freedom from interference for legitimate users. CPTED concepts and strategies may be accomplished in a variety of ways. Since each situation is unique, CPTED design concepts should be applied as appropriate planning warrants (Crowe, 2000; Jeffery, 1972).

PROGRAM IMPLEMENTATION AND ADMINISTRATION

The Administrative Process

The administrative process involves two or more people working collaboratively to accomplish a predetermined vision. The process emerges from the need to cooperate with others on complex, difficult, or multiple tasks to achieve common objectives of an organization, community, or society. To understand and appreciate the nature of security management, it may be helpful to review the general characteristics of public and private **administration** as well as the specific principles of organization and management.

The characteristics of **public administration** include being the following:

- Public affairs-oriented: Public administration focuses on the management of public agencies and organizations.
- Impartial and fair: All citizens are entitled to a particular government service and must be treated in a uniform manner.
- Apolitical: The policies of government may be political, but the detailed execution of these policies is administrative.
- Public-service oriented: Public administration exists to serve the public, and profit is not a motive for its operations.
- Publicly funded: Funds for public administration are appropriated by law and derived primarily from tax revenues.
- Publicly documented: Administrative records and financial documents are public information that must be made available for review by all citizens.
- Accountable to the public: Public administration is subject to legislative and judicial review at all times.
- Selectively staffed (civil service): Qualified personnel are selected on the basis of demonstrated merit through civil service examinations.
- Hierarchical: Public agencies are official and formal and consist of levels of positions.

The characteristics of **private administration** include the following:

- Private enterprise: Private administration exists to fulfill a private rather than public obligation or interest.
- Private or corporate ownership: Private individuals, groups, or stockholders own private organizations.

- Competitiveness: The organization may be in competition with other enterprises engaged in producing the same product or service.
- Profit incentive: Except for certain nonprofit private organizations, the incentive is to generate net profit.
- Financing regulated by market price: Revenue is based on the ability to sell the product or service.
- Privacy of information and records (within limits): Information is proprietary and the property of the owner(s).
- Accountability to owners and stockholders: The organization and its employees are held accountable to the organization's owners rather than the public.
- Some freedom in selection and termination of employees: The organization is not bound by civil service rules related to hiring or termination of employees.
- Freedom to regulate work methods and organization: The organization is not bound by civil service regulations (Perry, 1996).

In some areas, the distinction between public and private organizations is blurred. Privatization of public services is one example. However, similarities as well as differences continue to exist. They differ because public agencies are usually financed through tax revenues, while private organizations are financed through profits from business operations. Private organizations may enforce regulations not under the authority of public governmental entities. The statutory authority granted to private individuals and organizations to arrest, search, and to enforce the law also varies between and among government jurisdictions.

From a structural standpoint, the traditional principles of organization in the administrative process include the following:

- Similar tasks are grouped together.
- Specialized units or departments are created when necessary.
- Lines of demarcation between responsibilities are clearly established.
- Communication channels are established.
- Structure and common terminology are used.
- Unity of command is developed (one person, one boss).
- Span of control is exercised for effective supervision.
- Each task is assigned to someone (responsibility).
- Supervision for each person is required of someone.
- Authority is commensurate with responsibility.
- Individuals and organizational units are held accountable for tasks.

The level of complexity within an organization depends on the amount of horizontal and vertical differentiation that exists. Horizontal differentiation is usually based on activity. This activity may be associated with the type of clientele, style of service, geography, time, or process. Vertical differentiation is based on levels of authority.

Small departments, agencies, or businesses may be simple or very complex in organizational design. Some organizations have narrow spans of management control, with tall structures and many levels. Other organizations increase the span of control and decrease the organization's vertical structure, thus reducing levels of management. There is no one-size-fits-all structure, and there are advantages and disadvantages associated with each. Tall organizations with narrow spans of control, for example, place fewer demands on supervisors while increasing problems with vertical communication (Lewis, Goodman, & Fandt, 2001; Swanson, Territo, & Taylor, 1998). The most appropriate organizational structure is the one that best facilitates organizational performance (Hodge, Anthony, & Gales, 2003).

Organizations may also be differentiated by line, staff, function, or project orientations. Line activity refers to those elements that perform tasks for which the organization was created. Staff activity refers to those elements that support the line, such as communications networks. Functional structures, although complex, improve communication between elements because delegation of management authority extends beyond normal spans of control. Business intelligence activities, for example, may cross all lines of authority. The essence of the project structure is that elements from various segments of the organization may be assigned to task forces that address a specific problem. The task force is dissolved when the problem is solved.

The structural component of an organization is often represented in the form of an organizational chart. However, the introduction of computer technology changed the way many institutions operate. Many organizations moved away from the hierarchial or military structure model to a flatter, more collegial organization built around shared information (Hellriegel, Slocum, & Woodman, 2001). As a result, middle management, which used to function as the conduit between higher management and line personnel, has been eliminated in many organizations. Each member of the organization becomes a member of a team that is more innovative, participatory, flexible, and adaptable.

Subsequent to the terrorist events of September 11, 2001, many organizations reassessed the structure of their human operations. As a result, some organizations have distributed their workforces over wider areas, when appropriate, creating decentralized networks of workplaces in which human activities are grouped according to common tasks. The approach favors preparation for possible disasters, shortens worker commutes, and makes more efficient use of space. This organic organizational design also provides for greater flexibility in an era of environmental uncertainty (Robbins & Coulter, 2003).

While an administrative structure depends on adopted principles of organization, the fluid and dynamic process of administration is addressed through the principles of management. The traditional (classical) principles of management

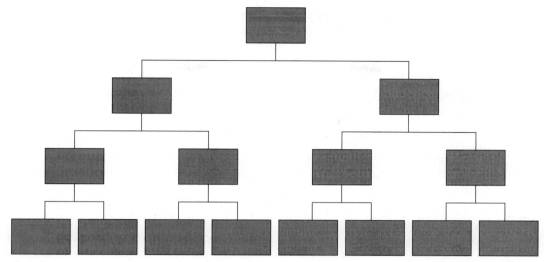

Figure 4–3 Tall organizational structure with narrow span of control and high vertical complexity.

include planning, organizing, staffing, directing (leading), coordinating or controlling (evaluation), reporting, and budgeting (POSDCORB). Planning involves forward thinking and selection of courses of action based on an identified need. Organizing involves the collection and development of physical, financial, and human resources necessary to achieve the goals articulated in the planning process. Staffing is the process of hiring, training, and rewarding people for doing the organization's work. Directing (leading) involves guiding people to achieve the goals of the organization. Controlling (evaluation) involves comparing actual performance with planned performance (Mosley, Megginson, & Pietri, 1993; Robbins & Coulter, 2003; Sennewald, 2003).

The traditional principles of management, as formulated in the POSDCORB model, provide a useful framework for describing the administrative process. However, the realities of modern administrative practice are not quite as simplis-

Figure 4–4 Flat organizational structure with wide span of control and low vertical complexity.

tic as the descriptions of the POSDCORB management functions might lead one to believe. Simple, clear-cut steps to management do not exist. Realistically, managers often perform a little of each function simultaneously as they plan, organize, staff, direct, coordinate or control, report findings, and budget resources. Management functions may actually defy any sequentially ordered application. In a twenty-first century environment, management is usually a process, rather than a series of activities. Therefore, to effectively address issues of trust, ethics, accountability, work–personal life balance, and global changes, modern managers must be aware of and creatively utilize numerous management models (Robbins & Coulter, 2003).

Whether a business or agency conforms to traditional or more modern principles of organization and management, four common elements exist in all administrative processes. These include planning, implementation, ethical leadership, and evaluation. Using the common elements as a focal point, planning involves need assessment, alternative action plan development, and selection of an action plan. Implementation (operationalizing the plan) includes all activities designed to organize, staff, acquire equipment and facilities, develop policy statements, and allocate and deploy resources. Leadership involves supervision and maintenance of ethical standards. Evaluation focuses on monitoring progress, control, and follow-up (Meese & Ortmeier, 2004; Ortmeier, 1999).

Organization, Staffing, Equipment, and Facilities

The first major step in the implementation of the action plan selected is to organize the operation according to the plan. The organizational structure, or framework, of a business or governmental agency will vary depending upon its size, location, budget, and methods of operation. The second major step in the implementation of the action plan is to staff the department, agency, or business. Regardless of the type of organization, basic elements exist in the management of human resources. These include the process of determining how many people the operation needs, what they will do, and how they will be hired, trained, led, and evaluated. Human resource management is discussed in detail in Chapter 6.

The third step in the implementation process is to acquire necessary equipment and facilities. Equipment and facilities represent high-dollar cost items in the budget. Careful planning may avoid the pitfalls of overextension. A lease arrangement may be a viable alternative to purchase. With respect to physical facilities, the location selection process should receive special attention. Area crime rates and availability of public services should be researched. Equipment typically utilized in a security environment includes communications hardware, alarm systems, firearms, and vehicles. The quality and expected life span of each item as compared to price should be a consideration. Competitive bidding, references, as well as the requirement for performance and service contracts are essential ingredients to successful equipment and facilities acquisitions.

Policies and Procedures

The fourth step to implementation of the action plan is the development of policies and procedures. Written policies and procedures provide uniform guidelines for handling various types of situations. A **policy** is a general statement describing how anticipated situations should be handled. A **procedure** outlines a series of steps to be followed consistently in a definite order (Fay, 1999; Robbins & Coulter, 2003). Sometimes they are written in response to an incident that has occurred but for which there is no existing policy or procedure.

Policy statements focus on a wide range of personnel issues, such as selection, discipline, promotion, and termination. They often address behavioral problems associated with substance abuse, sexual harassment, discrimination, as well as use of force. Thus, policies can be used to help create accountability for behavior (Dalton, 2003). Policies can also be used to describe general goals. As exemplified by the following list, policy statements address a wide range of topics and issues.

- affirmative action
- conflicts of interest
- drug and alcohol abuse
- equal employment opportunity
- equal employment opportunity for the disabled, Vietnam-era veterans, and special disabled veterans
- ethics
- firearms
- general practices
- harassment
- health, safety, and the environment
- information security
- Internet use
- investigations
- political contributions
- protection of assets
- security
- sexual harassment
- smoking
- special project security
- travel and entertainment
- use of force
- U.S. sentencing guidelines
- workplace violence (Fay, 1999)

Most existing organizations have numerous policy statements in place. Existing policies may require periodic revision to accommodate new variables, and additional policies may be created as new situations arise.

Although policies and their presentation format may vary between organizations, each statement should include the title of the policy statement, the name of the issuing department, an effective date, the name of the persons responsible for approving the policy and the statement, and the purpose of the policy stated in clear, concise terms. The statement should also include the scope of the policy. In other words, to whom does it apply? This is followed by the policy statement itself, the procedure for implementing the policy, and a list of definitions if uncommon terminology is used.

Procedures outline specific operational protocol and describe detailed responses to incidents or events. As exemplified by the following list, procedures often cover a wider range of activities than do policies.

- AIDS contact
- antieavesdropping
- antistalking
- attack avoidance
- auto theft prevention
- background checking
- bank security officer
- bomb threats
- burglary prevention
- canine security
- civil process acceptance
- classification of sensitive information
- cleaning crew access control
- clear desk
- computer virus protection
- conference security
- driving safeguards
- duress alarm
- electronic information security
- electronic mail protection
- emergency calls
- employee access control
- executive protection
- fire responses by security officers
- flag etiquette
- guest security

- handling classified information
- hazards identification
- information protection at the office
- Internet protection
- intranet protection
- lost and found
- medical emergencies
- office building evacuation
- office inspections
- office security management
- password protection
- property removal
- rape avoidance
- repair crew access control
- security program auditing
- sexual harassment reporting
- substance abuse program audit
- telephone answering
- two-way radio (Fay, 1999)

Contract Services (Outsourcing)

A contract vendor may be appropriate for certain types of security services. When a vendor is used, the contract should specify salaries and wages, insurance coverage, liability limits, employee screening procedures, audit rights for the contractee, performance standards, and procedures for compensation adjustments. A contract should also contain letters of authorization. If a premium wage rate (a rate above the prevailing wage) is specified, the contractor should be audited to ensure payment of the premium rate. The contractee should consult with an insurance expert to determine the type and amount of insurance required of the contractor. Some contractors are underinsured and underfinanced, and they do not have the resources to withstand a lawsuit. Indemnification permits the contractee to be reimbursed for expenditures incurred as a result of the contractual relationship (Cheeseman, 2004). Through an **indemnity/hold harmless clause,** the contractee is held harmless in the event of a wrongful act by a contract employee. A preemployment screening procedure should also be specified in the contract.

The contractee should reserve the right to audit the contractor to prevent unscrupulous activities on the part of the contractor. Performance standards and training must be included in the contract. An adjustment of compensation clause allows the contractee to reduce compensation to the contractor for failure to meet obligations expressed in the contract. Letters of authorization should be included to specify what the contractor can do on the contractee agency's or corporation's behalf. The letters should detail contractor limits of authority (Dalton, 1995; Johnson, 2003).

EVALUATION

Achieving excellent performance in any organization involves special attention to the **evaluation** process. Even carefully developed plans can fail without an evaluation of progress and outcomes. After a plan is implemented, the evaluation and control process begins. The process is exercised continuously throughout the life of the operation. Evaluation involves measuring performance, comparing performance with stated objectives, reporting results, and taking corrective action, if necessary. In essence, it involves a return to needs or risk assessment and planning and the completion of the administrative process (management cycle).

Evaluation has both predictive and after-the-fact aspects. Through predictions, the evaluator attempts to anticipate the possibility of undesirable outcomes and prevent deviation from established standards. Crime prevention is an example of predictive evaluation. After-the-fact evaluation analyzes an event or deviation from established standards to determine what corrective action is required (Lewis, Goodman, & Fandt, 2001). A determination of the cause of a theft is an example of after-the-fact evaluation.

The first step in the evaluation process is to measure performance based on the standards (objectives) established during the risk assessment and planning process. The standards are units of measurement that serve as reference points for evaluating results. **Tangible standards** are quite clear, specific, identifiable, and generally measurable. They measure quantity and quality. They may be used to assess incident reduction efforts, appraise individual employee performance, or as an ingredient in the budget process. Tangible standards are expressed in terms of numbers, dollars, physical properties, and time.

Numerical standards are quantifiable, such as the amount of crime reduction or number of personnel who successfully complete a training program. Examples of monetary standards include the impact of a budget or payroll and maintenance costs. Physical standards refer to quality, durability, and other factors related to physical composition. Vehicle durability can be determined with physical standards. Time standards refer to the speed with which a task might be completed.

Intangible standards relate to human characteristics that are difficult to measure. They take no physical form, yet they are just as important as tangible standards. Examples of intangible standards are a desirable attitude, high morale, ethics, cooperation, and the organization's reputation. In some cases, crime prevention cannot be measured utilizing a tangible standard. It is difficult, if not impossible, to measure the amount of crime that has been prevented unless a number of criminal incidents occurred before a prevention program was initiated. Thus, measuring a monetary **return on investment (ROI)** for security-related expenditures is often a challenge. Security's value-added contribution (VAC) to the organization is often incalculable (Dalton, 1995). In many situations, security's VAC may be more qualitative than quantitative. Employees and clients may feel safer and experience less fear of crime. Thus, morale, productivity, and the quality of organizational life improve.

Methods for measuring performance include personal observation, written and oral reports of subordinates, automatic recording systems, inspections, tests, and surveys. Whatever method is used, performance standards should be based on realistic targets. Failure to meet a performance standard can result from a variety of causes. Identification of causes rather than the symptoms is extremely important if appropriate corrective action is to be taken. Those closest to the situation should be consulted to determine why the performance standards are not being met. Participation of all affected by the measurements is an essential ingredient in this process. The sooner a deviation from a standard is identified, the sooner the situation can be corrected. Evaluation and assessment, therefore, is a continuous process (Lewis, Goodman, & Fandt, 2001).

After a careful analysis of any deviation from a performance standard, corrective action may be necessary. Modifications to the original plan should not be viewed negatively. Objectives and standards stated in the original plan are often based on forecasts. If the deviation is extreme, it may be necessary to evaluate the planning process itself. There may be several reasons why a deviation from an established standard has occurred. It is possible that the standards could not be achieved because they were based on faulty forecasts or assumptions or because an unforeseen problem arose that distorted the anticipated outcome. Failure might have occurred in some other activity that supported the activity being evaluated. It is also possible that the employee who performed the task was unqualified, not given adequate directions, negligent, or did not follow required directions or procedures (Goetsch & Davis, 1995).

Quality performance standards are probably the most difficult to measure. Quality can be an elusive concept and it means different things to different people. Basically, quality means the product or service meets or exceed predetermined expectations. **Quality assurance,** continuous quality improvement, and total quality management (TQM) initiatives involve approaches to administration that attempt to maximize effectiveness of an organization through the continual improvement of the quality of its people, processes, products, and environment. To ensure quality performance, initiatives must be based on decisions founded on facts rather than on intuition. Participants must also take personal responsibility for quality, improve teamwork and commitment, and focus on the end user and service (Haberer & Webb, 1994; Lewis, Goodman, & Fandt, 2001). Quality assurance is a way of life, not a program (Peters, 1987).

Quality assurance initiatives involve goal setting, trust, cohesiveness, increasing information flow, and resolving conflict. To succeed, quality assurance initiatives must incorporate an internal and external customer focus, an obsession with quality, long-term commitment, teamwork, employee involvement, and empowerment. They must incorporate education and training, freedom from control, and unity of purpose. The initiatives must also use the scientific approach to decision making and problem solving.

Some managers make errors when implementing quality assurance initiatives. They attempt a quality initiative by delegating responsibility to an outside expert rather than applying the leadership necessary to get everyone within the organization involved (Clemmer, 1992). Employees must learn how to be team players. An organization must often undergo a cultural change before teamwork can succeed. Creating teams before learning about teamwork and quality assurance methods will be counterproductive and will create more problems than the teams will solve.

Organizations must develop quality initiatives concurrent with plans for integrating them into all elements of the organization. None of the approaches to quality management is truly a one-size-fits-all proposition. Quality programs must be tailored to fit organizational needs. According to Goetsch and Davis (1995), quality initiatives should include commitment, team building, training, vision and guiding principles, broad objectives, communication, a plan for implementation, project identification, feedback, and modification of the organizational infrastructure as necessary.

It is a long-established fact that human beings are resistant to change. Security personnel are no exception. The injection of quality assurance initiatives into the security function results in a major change in the way many agencies and firms conduct business. Attitudes do not change rapidly. Nor do they change without reasonable justification. Concrete evidence of the benefits of quality assurance initiatives can enlighten and convince security personnel that quality service is what helps gain public and consumer trust and support for the organization and the people in it. If not appropriately implemented, quality assurance initiatives become just another management fad that can damage, rather than assist, an organization (Dalton, 1995; Lewis, Goodman, & Fandt, 2001).

Traditional organizational performance measures have focused on financial and statistical results. However, a consequence of a narrow focus on financial return and statistics is that it may encourage organizational leaders to lie, distort, or misrepresent data to demonstrate favorable results. This phenomenon is evidenced by the corporate scandals of the early twenty-first century. Investors and other stakeholders have learned, however, that numerical measures are only as accurate as the people who compile them. Ethical managers will ensure that adequate controls are in place to discourage attempts to distort or manipulate data (Robbins & Coulter, 2003).

SUMMARY

Risk is defined as the possibility of suffering harm or loss, exposure to the probability of loss or damage, an element of uncertainty, or the possibility that the results of an action may not be consistent with expected outcomes. Risk management techniques involve elimination, reduction, and mitigation of risk, as well as a determination of asset vulnerability and the probability and criticality of loss.

Risk assessments are accomplished using a variety of subjective and objective measures. Typically, a security survey is conducted utilizing a security survey instrument. The risk assessment and security survey represent the initial step in the planning process. The initial step is followed by the development of alternative courses of action and selection of the action plan. The potential financial impact of each plan must be determined through the creation of a budget.

CPTED methodology is used to design facilities and communities with safety and security in mind. Program implementation involves the development and acquisition of an organizational structure, staff, equipment and facilities, and policy and procedure statements, as well as the use of contract security services when appropriate. Security program administration emerges as a mechanism to cooperate with others to achieve organizational goals. Quality service is assured through a comprehensive evaluation process, coupled with a determination of the VAC the security element presents.

KEY TERMS

administration

budget

capital expenditures

CompStat

contingency plan

cost-benefit analysis

Crime Prevention through Environmental Design (CPTED)

Delphi technique

dynamic risk

elements of planning

evaluation

indemnity/hold harmless clause

inherent risk

intangible standards

line item budget

miscellaneous expenses

numerical standards

objective (quantitative) measures

operating expenses

performance-based budget

personnel expenses

planning

policy

private administration

procedure

public administration

pure risk

quality assurance

quality assurance initiative

repeat-use (standing) plan

return on investment (ROI)

risk

risk assessment

risk management techniques

security survey

single-use plan

speculative risk

static risk

strategic plan

subjective (qualitative) measure

supplies and materials expenses

tactical plan

tangible standards

traditional budget

value-added contribution (VAC)

zero-based budget (ZBB)

DISCUSSION QUESTIONS AND EXERCISES

1. Describe five types of risk and discuss management techniques for eliminating, reducing, or mitigating each risk type.

2. How is an asset evaluated to determine its vulnerability, probability, and criticality of loss?

3. Contrast subjective with objective risk assessment measurements. Which is more appropriate in a security setting? Why?

4. Describe the process for analyzing needs identified through a risk assessment.

5. How many courses of action should be developed to eliminate, reduce, or mitigate risk? Explain your response.

6. What role does the budget assume in action plan development, selection, and implementation?

7. What is CPTED, and how is it applied?

8. Why is program evaluation important? Who should be involved in the evaluation process?

CHAPTER 5

Physical Security

LEARNING OBJECTIVES

After completing this chapter, the reader should be able to

- describe the basics of defense.
- demonstrate knowledge of outer and inner perimeter controls.
- analyze the protective value of building exteriors and interiors.
- discuss the importance of lighting as a deterrent as well as a detection mechanism.
- demonstrate knowledge of different types of locking devices.
- list and describe types of visual assessment, surveillance, and alarm systems.
- describe the access control function of security personnel.
- evaluate the need for security personnel.
- demonstrate knowledge of security force management principles and techniques.
- design a training program for security personnel.

INTRODUCTION

Physical security is the first line of defense against a potential threat. Facility perimeters, tangible property, personnel, and information are protected using an appropriate combination of the elements of lighting, hardware, equipment, human agents, policies, and procedures. These elements form protective barriers and systems that harden the target against the potential threat.

BASICS OF DEFENSE AND LEVELS OF PROTECTION

The **basics of defense** involve the use of systems and countermeasures such as policies, procedures, people, equipment, architectural design, and strategies to prevent loss and deter, detect, deny, delay, or detain the person or agent that may cause harm to the enterprise. The basics of defense involve the use of any combination of alarms, barriers, devices, and personnel designed to control access. The mere presence of appropriate controls may deter intruders and thus divert them from the protected area. If intruders are not deterred, controls such as alarms and surveillance systems may detect the intruder's presence. Physical security measures may also deny access. At the very least, the control system may delay access until protective personnel arrive. If all systems fail to prevent intrusion, it may be necessary (in rare circumstances) to detain a human agent that poses a potential threat.

The level of asset protection depends on the types of systems and countermeasures utilized. Further, the amount of protection provided depends on how the systems and countermeasures are monitored and maintained. No protection system is 100 percent defeat-proof (Gigliotti & Jason, 1999). However, appropriate risk assessment strategies can help one visualize the level of protection that is practical and necessary.

Level 1—Minimum Protection. Designed to *impede some unauthorized external threat activity.* Includes the use of simple locks and physical barriers.

Level 2—Low-Level Protection. Designed to *impede and detect some unauthorized external threat activity.* Includes the use of basic local alarms, physical barriers, security lighting, and high-security locks.

Level 3—Medium Protection. Designed to *impede, detect, and assess most unauthorized external threat activity.* Includes the use of high-security physical barriers, remote alarm systems, security personnel, and a basic communications system.

Level 4—High-Level Protection. Designed to *impede, detect, and assess most unauthorized external and internal threat activity.* Includes the use of perimeter alarms, surveillance systems, security personnel, advanced communications systems, access controls, high-security lighting, coordination with local public law enforcement, and formal contingency plans.

Level 5—Maximum Protection. Designed to *impede, detect, assess, and neutralize all unauthorized external and internal threat activity.* Includes the use of on-site armed security response personnel and sophisticated alarm systems (Gigliotti & Jason, 1999).

The strategy for defense of any asset focuses on the outer perimeter and progresses through the inner perimeter, building exterior, areas within a building, and specific rooms. In this sense, countermeasures form concentric circles of protection around an asset (see Chapter 4). This layered effect provides a greater degree of protection than a single layer and does so at reasonable expense. Since several different types of countermeasures may be necessary to combat each threat, the countermeasures should complement rather than compete with each other. By utilizing design concepts embodied in the principles of Crime Prevention through Environmental Design (CPTED), countermeasures can be integrated with other facility design requirements. Thus, the initial cost of physical security measures is lowered and the need for security retrofits is reduced (Crowe, 2000).

PERIMETER CONTROLS

Perimeter controls fall into two basic categories: outer and inner controls. Outer perimeter controls focus on the neighborhood or community within which an enterprise is located. If a new facility is planned, management is well advised to conduct a site survey to determine the availability of public services, analyze crime rates, and evaluate threats from noncriminal agents and from events such as natural disasters. Natural barriers should not be discounted. In some instances, natural barriers such as streams, lakes, and rugged terrain are excellent perimeter controls. Outer perimeter controls need not be obtrusive. The perimeter control could be a clear zone. In fact, an outer perimeter that is open and clear of unnecessary obstructions may deter a would-be intruder because the intruder has nowhere to hide.

The inner perimeter includes territory or property owned or operated by the enterprise. Landscapes and parking lots fall into this category. Proper landscaping can promote safety and security while remaining aesthetically pleasing. Careful planning and design of the landscape is essential. Bushes and trees often provide hiding places for would-be intruders or predators. Parking lots should be well lit and not located in remote areas unless surveillance is possible (Fischer & Green, 1998). Perhaps the most cost effective of all security countermeasures, adequate signs serve as deterrents, help to create psychological barriers to human threats, and assist with pedestrian and vehicular traffic control.

BUILDING EXTERIORS AND INTERIORS

The building exterior, often referred to by architects as the *envelope,* includes the walls, doors, windows, and locking devices designed to provide exterior protection. Exterior walls should be constructed of intrusion-resistant and impact-resistant materials. This also applies to walls in common with adjoining occupancies. Access to a business can be gained easily if the common wall with an adjacent business is constructed merely of wood or metal studs and drywall, plaster, or paneling.

Exterior doors should be solidly constructed. Hinges with nonremovable pins should be located on the inside. Door frames, locks, and panels are also extremely vulnerable to attack. The frame of the door should resist prying or spreading with a crowbar. Exterior door locks should be high-quality and intrusion-resistant. Although high-quality modern door locks are pick-resistant, many can be slipped or pulled if the tools required are available. Door panels should be solid and 2 inches thick. Steel plates may be used to reinforce door interiors. Windows in door panels can be reinforced with bars or steel mesh or constructed of impact-resistant materials.

Other exterior openings larger than 96 square inches should receive special attention. Air ducts, elevator shafts, skylights, and windows should be covered with security glass or protective screening and, if possible, be alarmed. Unauthorized human intrusion into a building is often accomplished by entering through a window. The roof and main floors should be hardened and alarmed, if possible. The roof of a building is often overlooked when protection features are incorporated into building design. Usually constructed with lightweight and easily penetrated materials, a roof is rarely alarmed, and visibility of the roof is restricted. Therefore, intruders may gain access to a building through the roof without detection. Likewise, floors, especially those in multistory buildings, provide access if adequate security does not prevent access from an occupancy located below the protected enterprise.

If the interior of a building has been designed properly, activities may be assigned to functional areas based on their level of risk and vulnerability to loss. Sensitive and high risk areas should be located deep within the building and away from the building's exterior. These areas can be target hardened with intruder, fire, and disaster resistant materials as well as alarm and access control devices and personnel (Hess & Wrobleski, 1996).

LIGHTING

One of the best and least expensive security mechanisms is effective lighting. Lighting should be considered an inner as well as an outer defense. Many crimes are committed because the opportunity for detection is limited. Light increases the likelihood of detection. Continuous lighting is necessary for secured areas. Portable lights should be available for special needs. Standby or emergency lighting is used when extra light is required or electric power failures necessitate use of an alternative power and illumination source.

Perimeter lighting involves the use of streetlights, floodlights, searchlights, and fresnol lights (which provide a long, narrow, horizontal beam without glare). Floodlights are typically used at facility boundaries to deter intruders. Parking lot and building exterior lights should be 50 feet apart and 50 feet high. Building exterior openings, doors, and windows should be illuminated also. Wiring for lights must not be exposed to damage or a possible intruder. Light fixtures should be tamper-resistant. A backup power supply or generator should be available to support emergency lights in the event of a commercial power failure.

The amount of illumination required depends on the purpose of the lighting. In operations areas such as workspaces, the amount of lighting and brightness required is usually much higher than for security purposes. Protective lighting must be of sufficient brightness to permit adequate human or technological surveillance, illuminate exit routes, identify hazards to prevent personal injury, and create a psychological barrier to unauthorized intrusion. Protective lighting must also be positioned to avoid glare that might reduce visibility for security personnel and others with authorized access to a facility.

The cost effectiveness of lighting as well as the amount of illumination and glare produced by lighting depend on the type of lamp selected. Commonly referred to as bulbs or tubes, lamps generally fall into six categories. The oldest and most common type is the incandescent lamp, which produces light by heating a filament. Although inexpensive to purchase initially, the incandescent lamp is the least efficient and most expensive in the long term because most of the energy consumed by the lamp creates heat rather than light. Mercury vapor lamps produce a strong light with a bluish cast, have a long lamp life, and can tolerate low temperatures. However, they have a long start-up time. Florescent lamps are typically of a mercury vapor type and are highly efficient. Florescent lamps are temperature sensitive and have limited value in cold climates. Metal halide lamps are expensive, but they depict true colors and can tolerate low temperatures. However, like mercury vapor lamps, metal halide lamps require considerable start-up and restart time. Therefore, they are not practical where continuous lighting is necessary. Frequently used in transportation environments or areas where fog is common, sodium vapor lamps emit a soft yellowish light that penetrates moisture. Produced as low-pressure or high-pressure pressure lamps, sodium vapor lamps are more efficient than mercury vapor. Quartz lamps are excellent sources of illumination for perimeter control systems. They emit a very bright white light, and start-up time is short.

FENCES

Although fences typically provide minimum security, they define the perimeter, delay an intruder, channel employees and visitors to appropriate areas, and act as a platform for alarm sensors. Depending on the aesthetic qualities desired, fences may be constructed of wood, masonry, or wire. Wood, stone, brick, and masonry fences possess aesthetic qualities not typical of wire fences. However, unlike wire fences, solid barriers obstruct visibility of the area outside the fence. If concealment of inside activities to passersby is a consideration, solid walls are very effective.

Chain link fence is the most commonly used type of fence. It requires little maintenance, is simple to erect, and provides for greater visibility than wood or masonry. To be fully effective, chain link fences should be constructed of #11 gauge or heavier wire, at least 8 feet high, with mesh of 2 square inches or less. For maximum security effectiveness where appearance is not a concern, barbed, razor ribbon, or concertina wire may be added to the top of the 8-foot chain link fence. The bottom of the fence can be secured to prevent lifting or crawling under by tying the lower edge of the fence to rigid metal straps. If the earth below the fence is loose or subject to erosion, the fence should be buried and secured below ground level. Culverts may be installed to prevent washouts during rainstorms.

Every opening in a perimeter barrier fence presents a potential security risk. These openings should be kept to a minimum, and access through gates should be controlled. Obviously, there should be sufficient openings to accommodate the safe and efficient movement of pedestrian and vehicular traffic. A careful analysis of needs and traffic patterns will determine how many openings are necessary. Gates may be used to secure openings when not in use. Security personnel or technical surveillance may be used to monitor open as well as secured gates.

To maintain the protective integrity of a fence, alarm sensors may be added. Electromagnetic and fiber optic cables, taut wire, and various other types

Chain link fence can blend with the environment. Photo courtesy of Star Source International.

Photo courtesy of SONY Corporation.

of intrusion detection devices can be used for this purpose. If security personnel are available for surveillance purposes, **closed-circuit television (CCTV)** cameras can be used to monitor perimeter fencing (Fischer & Green, 1998).

LOCKS

Locking devices are used to deter the undetermined and delay the determined. Locks tend to increase the amount of time required for an intruder to gain access to a facility. Thus, locks increase the probability of detection and apprehension if used in conjunction with alarm systems and if human resources are available to respond to the affected area.

Key-operated locks are the most common. A notched key is inserted into a keyway containing obstacles or tumblers that can be bypassed by using the correct key. When the appropriate key is turned, a bolt, arm, or shank in the locking device is moved. In the case of a doorknob, rotating the key inside the keyway inserts or withdraws a bolt to or from a strike plate hole embedded in the door frame, thus opening or closing the lock. The lock's bolt can be spring-loaded or a deadbolt. Spring-loaded bolts (latches) automatically enter the strike when the door is closed. Deadbolts require insertion and rotation of a key or operation of a thumb latch to secure the bolt in the strike. Spring-loaded bolts, unless otherwise protected by a latch guard or metal plate, are easily compromised by slipping a knife or screwdriver between the door and the jamb, moving the bolt, thus releasing the spring. Deadbolt locks are not spring-loaded and require manual operation with a key. Deadbolt locks with an antiwrenching exterior collar and a minimum 1-inch throw into the strike plate hole provide the best security where key-operated locks are used.

Obviously, key control is a very important consideration with any key-based lock system. An inventory of the keys as well as a key assignment record is vital to system integrity. One major disadvantage to key-based systems surfaces when locks must be rekeyed frequently. Organizations with numerous locations or high personnel attrition may find it necessary to rekey often. The cost can be considerable. However, the expense associated with rekeying can be reduced by utilizing multiuse, instant rekeying lock systems. These systems allow up to 12 easy-to-complete key sequence changes during the life of the lock cylinder, thus reducing labor expenses associated with locksmith-assisted hardware changes. A special lock-change key is inserted into the keyway, rotated, and the cylinder is reprogrammed for a new key set (Southerland, 2000).

Combination locks (dial or push-button) are often used on safes, vaults, padlocks, and vehicle doors. Combination locks cannot be picked, but can be compromised if the combination to the lock is readily available to unauthorized users. **Keypad locks** generally rely on microcomputer technology and can be applied in a wide range of settings. Telephones, radios, automatic teller machines, calculators, and microwave ovens all utilize keypads to enter data and operate the device. **Electronic locks** are used where control of the locking device is maintained at a location some distance from the lock. These locks are used to control gates and visitor access to businesses and apartment buildings.

A **card-operated lock** is often used to control access to restricted areas. Cards are inserted into a card reader and a minicomputer activates the locking device. A typical card-operated lock system requires the user to place a card on, insert a card into, or swipe a card through a reader that determines the validity of the card and releases the lock if the card is valid. Some card-key access systems also record the card number and the date and time entry is granted. These systems make the controlled access decision based on preauthorization. They record and store access information and can summon assistance if necessary (Hess & Wrobleski, 1996; Tyska & Fennelly, 2000).

VISUAL ASSESSMENT AND SURVEILLANCE SYSTEMS

Where security personnel are limited, surveillance systems provide extra eyes and ears to the human observer. Convex mirrors are used to observe locations and blind corners that are normally unobservable. Article surveillance and antitheft systems incorporate the use of miniaturized electronic monitors and detection devices to reduce losses due to shoplifting, theft, and pilferage. Still picture, motion picture, and video cameras are used to record events. CCTV can be used for continuous monitoring of several locations simultaneously and can be connected to a video tape recorder for future playback. **Digitization** greatly enhances CCTV, and a vast amount of information can be stored on a compact computer disk. Through digitization, an image can be converted to a computer's digital language and stored electronically.

Closed-circuit television camera. Photo courtesy of
Panasonic Security & Digital Imaging Company.

CCTV capability enhances safety and security effectiveness and efficiency in three ways. First, advances in CCTV technology offer more opportunities for integration of CCTV systems in public as well as private institutions. CCTV can be used in a wide variety of security settings. Second, CCTV operates as an extension of the human operator's eyes and ears. Although expensive to install and maintain, CCTV can generate considerable personnel cost savings because one person can monitor numerous locations simultaneously. Often coupled with time lapse recording, pinhole lenses, opaque domes, and zoom, pan, and tilt controls, CCTV increases personnel productivity and efficiency. Third, CCTV systems can provide a permanent record of an incident or event through the use of video recording (Wimmer, 2000).

Dome camera with pan/tilt and zoom lens. Photo courtesy of
Panasonic Security & Digital Imaging Company.

Covert camera enclosures. Photo courtesy of Ultrak Corporation.

Closed-circuit television monitor. Photo courtesy of Ultrak Corporation.

Programmable keyboard CCTV controller with touch-screen liquid crystal display. Photo courtesy of Ultrak Corporation.

Digital recorder for CCTV. Photo courtesy of Panasonic Security and Digital Imaging Company.

Technological advances with CCTV have greatly enhanced surveillance capabilities. Digitization increases storage capacity, enhances high-speed communication, can compress images from four cameras into a single frame of video recording tape, and allows one person to monitor four cameras from a single four-way split screen. Some CCTV systems integrate interactive video and audio (IAVA) technology. IAVA enhances system capability because a covered area can be monitored for sight and sound. An **infrared (IR) camera** can be used for nighttime surveillance and is not inhibited by inclement weather conditions.

ALARM SYSTEMS

An **alarm** is a communicator designed to notify a receiver of impending danger. An alarm system includes an array of interconnected parts designed to function as a unit. Alarms are not new. Geese were used by the ancient Romans in the fourth century B.C. to alert humans when an enemy approached a campsite. August Pope patented one of the first electric intrusion alarms in 1853. The device consisted of electromagnetic contacts, similar to a telegraph, that could be mounted on doors and windows and connected by wire to a battery and a bell. Today, alarm systems range from simple to complex and are used to detect fire, intrusion, medical emergencies, and other threats. They can be used to secure

Door/window sensor. Photo courtesy of Interlogix, Inc.

perimeters and buildings as well as sensitive areas within a facility. They may also be used to control energy consumption.

Every alarm system consists of three basic components: a triggering device or sensor (detector) that detects a condition, an alarm system circuit that transmits information, and an **annunciator** (signal) that notifies the recipient of the detected condition. **Sensors** include simple electromechanical devices that annunciate when an electric circuit is broken, pressure devices that respond to added weight or tension, photoelectric cells that activate when a light beam is interrupted, and devices activated by motion, sound, temperature, or vibration.

Passive infrared sensors are designed to detect changes in heat or thermal energy. If a person with a body temperature of 98.6 degrees Fahrenheit passes through a protected room with a temperature of 70 degrees Farenheit, the IR sensor will detect the person's presence and activate an alarm. An **ultrasonic motion sensor** transmits extremely high (beyond a human being's audible range) sound energy that fills the volume of a protected area (e.g., room). When an object or person moves through the protected area, the motion creates a shift in the frequency of the transmitted sound energy, known as a Doppler shift. The shifted frequency is detected (sensed) by one or more receivers, and an alarm is activated. **Microwave motion sensors** are similar in operation to ultrasonic motion sensors except that microwave systems utilize high-end radio frequencies rather than sound. Microwave sensor units transmit microwave energy and detect the energy as it is reflected from objects and returned to the transmitter/receiver unit. Except where dual or multiple sensor technologies are used simultaneously, ultrasound and microwave motion detectors have limited application due to the possibility of false alarms. However, when used in conjunction with a different type of sensor, and both sensors are required to coincidentally detect an alarm condition to signal an alarm, ultrasonic and microwave sensors can be very practical (Trimmer, 1999).

Motion sensor. Photo courtesy of Interlogix, Inc.

Alarm control system touchpad. Photo courtesy of Interlogix, Inc.

The **alarm system circuit** is the communication link between the sensor and the annunciator. In some cases, the circuit also connects with an audio-video recorder or communications device. A circuit communicates via wire, radio wave, electric circuit, telephone line, fiber-optic cable, microwave, satellite, or a combination of these. Advances in fiber-optic technology greatly improved materials available for alarm circuitry. Optical fiber transfers a pulsating light through a fine glass, or fiber. Optical fiber transmission has many advantages over other types of circuits. Fiber optics are low cost, safe to operate, and immune to interference from other power sources (Hess & Wrobleski, 1996). At the end of a circuit, the annunciator notifies, or signals, a recipient that an event (intrusion, fire, medical emergency) is taking place. Annunciators include audible or silent signals, such as a light, bell, buzzer, horn, or siren, or visual text display on a computer screen.

Alarm systems fall into four basic categories. A **local alarm system**, such as a car alarm, notifies anyone who is within hearing distance. A **proprietary alarm system** is owned and operated on site by the user and requires continuous control-panel monitoring. A **public alarm system** is connected directly to a public 911 emergency dispatch center or to a local police department. A **central station alarm system**, although similar to the proprietary system, may be monitored at a remote location. Utilizing modern communications technology, a central station system can include a sensor in New York City with an annunciator in San Diego, California.

Central station systems also allow for monitoring of numerous locations simultaneously. Typically, a telephone dialer in a **central processing unit (CPU)** located at the facility where the event is occurring sends a signal through the circuit to the central station. The CPU is the brain for the system. It receives, processes, stores, and transmits information detected by the sensors. Most CPUs also have fail-safe mechanisms that notify the central station when electric power to the alarmed facility has been interrupted.

ALARM SYSTEM MANAGEMENT

An improvement in protection usually results when alarm systems are properly installed and monitored continuously. Otherwise, continuous protection can only be achieved by assigning personnel to observe the protected area. However, over time, using personnel in lieu of alarm systems is costly. Alarm systems, although expensive to purchase and install, are usually economical in the long run and provide a substantial return on the initial investment. Security professionals must recognize that alarm systems are becoming very sophisticated. The increased use of automated, personal computer (PC)-based technologies to perform critical security monitoring functions presents new challenges for the security manager. The manager must be able to effectively integrate electronic technologies into a total security management system in a way that does not conflict with an organization's operational environment. As such, the security manager's ability to control risk with minimal operational interference is determined by certain critical alarm systems design and integration decision-making functions: the relevance and completeness of the risk assessment, the degree of the security alarm system's applicability to the facility, the quality of the equipment selected and its installation, and how the system facilitates organizational operations (Gallagher & Grassie, 2000). Careful planning and management of alarm systems will help avoid the costs associated with inapplicability events such as false alarms (Wilberg Fitzsimons, 2000) while reducing costs through integrated systems design ("Sun Microsystems integrates access control worldwide," 2000).

The first step to effective **alarm system management** involves **alarm point definition**. In other words, the points where an alarm is to be connected to the security management system must be defined (identified). The security manager must

- determine how and when the facility operates and who uses the facility.
- identify assets, threats, vulnerabilities, and security countermeasure requirements.
- develop a concept of security operations.
- integrate the concept of security operations with organizational (facility) operations.
- define and program alarm point active and inactive times.

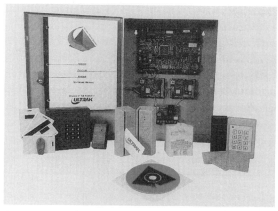

Access control system with CPU and components.
Photo courtesy of Ultrak Corporation.

After alarm points are identified and integrated with facility operations, the security manager can develop effective alarm response procedures. These procedures should be concise, unambiguous, consistent, and tailored to each specific alarm point, with consideration given to the time necessary for the response. Finally, alarm monitoring and response personnel must receive training consistent with the operational demands of the system. Without appropriate alarm systems management, even the best-intentioned capital investment in systems can become a nightmare for the security manager (Gallagher & Grassie, 2000).

Security systems integration is advancing rapidly as the availability of new technologies provide unprecedented levels of performance and effectiveness for security systems. Experts outline at least six trends in security systems integration. The first trend is toward standardization of operating systems, something often insisted upon by information technology departments to simplify support requirements. Second, computer networks, such as local area networks (LAN), are replacing dedicated security hardwire as the standard infrastructure for connecting security system components. The third trend involves card-key access and card-reader technologies. Magstripe cards continue in use where cost is a consideration. However, the overwhelming choice for new card-key access systems involves the use of proximity card technology since, patents for proximity cards and card readers are about to expire and the cost should decrease considerably. The fourth trend involves greater integration of systems so that useful information can be shared, enabling more intelligent operational decisions and often reducing costs of operation. The fifth trend involves shifting video recording and transmission standards from analog to digital technology. Higher processor power as well as increased speed and memory capacity are cited as the major reasons for the shift toward digital technology. The sixth trend is toward the development of an asset tracking system. The demand for asset tracking capability has been heightened by an increase in thefts of small high-value items

Control center with video monitors. Photo courtesy of SONY Corporation.

such as computer laptops. The challenge for the security manager involves the task of designing, managing, and maintaining sophisticated, large-scale security systems. Facing the challenge requires the development of new skills by security personnel (Coleman, 2000).

Additional information regarding alarm systems may be obtained by contacting the Central Station Alarm Association at communications@ csaaul.org or the National Burglar and Fire Alarm Association at www.alarm.org.

FIRE PREVENTION AND PROTECTION

Fire safety is probably more regulated than any other component of a safety and security program. Numerous federal, state, and local laws prescribe fire safety practices. Since fire prevention and protection principles are well established, one could assume that the application of fire safety fundamentals are very similar between and among facilities. Although similarities may exist in small facilities with common fire hazards, fire prevention and protection strategy depends primarily on the types of fire hazards present and fire exposure considerations. Through a comprehensive planning approach to fire safety, the security manager can design a fire prevention and protection program that meets the need of the facility (Schumacher, 2000).

Fire Prevention

Fire prevention is defined as all fire service activities that decrease incidents of uncontrolled fire. Fire prevention activities include fire department inspections, records and reports, investigations, facility plan review, hazard abatement, education, enforcement, company inspection programs, and fire information reporting systems (National Fire Protection Association, 2000).

The main objective of a **fire prevention inspection** is to determine if reasonable life-safety conditions exist within a given facility. Inspections are intended to identify hazards that could cause a fire or allow a fire to develop or spread. Accurate inspection documentation is an essential factor in fire prevention because inspection reports are used to enforce fire safety regulations, including those relating to violation notices, plan reviews, and issuance of permits.

Fire investigation involves fire cause determination and the investigation of criminal actions that may have contributed to a fire. Fire cause determination is important because the analysis of causes and gathered data will, over time, indicate trends in certain fire-prone areas. Moreover, the information will provide data for the development of a fire prevention program.

Facility plan review includes involvement of the public fire department during building construction. Generally, this review focuses on four areas: site plans, preliminary building plans, final building plans and specifications, and certificates for occupancy. Most sites are reviewed in conjunction with the local building, zoning, and public works departments or with authoritative state agencies. Fire officials also participate in preconstruction conferences to answer questions relating to building fire protection features, building codes, fire prevention code requirements, and other plan review processes.

If an existing facility requires an upgrade or a remodel, retrofitting the fire safety apparatus also requires special consideration and planning. The fire safety retrofit design plan should include specific elements. The plan should address applicable fire codes and standards, an identification of new fire systems arrangements, existing building characteristics and fire protection systems, a timetable for phasing in new fire safety equipment, and provision for future needs (Greene & Tappen, 2000).

How customized fire safety design principles can be incorporated with combined new construction and retrofitting is exemplified by a major project undertaken by a center for the developmentally disabled in New York State. The project added 27,000 square feet to an existing 47,000 square feet of space. In conjunction with the new construction project, the center enhanced its fire safety by expanding, upgrading, and customizing its fire alarm system. In addition to the main fire annunciator panel, three additional annunciators were located strategically throughout the facility. Anyone near one of the annunciators can view the alarm condition and take action. In lieu of traditional strobe light and blaring buzzer-type fire notification devices, strobe-only and strobe/voice notification devices were installed to minimize panic among the children in the event of a fire alarm ("Center for developmental disabilities . . .," 2000).

Fire hazard abatement involves the use of abatement codes established at the municipal level. Abatement codes focus on building, zoning, planning, electrical, plumbing, heating, air conditioning, landscaping, air pollution, and environmental protection. The codes are usually updated at 5-year intervals and are designed to correlate with the fire prevention standards of the American Insurance Association.

Fire safety education is an important ingredient to fire prevention. The two main purposes of education are fire prevention and fire reaction training. Life safety and asset protection in the event of a fire depend on good planning and proper training of employees. When a fire occurs or when a fire alarm is sounded, all occupants should react instinctively. All fire alarms should be treated as real. Plans for notification of occupants as well as fire-fighting and other emergency personnel are essential. Evacuation plans and routes must be developed and practiced.

Educating occupants about fire prevention and protection systems as well as evacuation procedures is critical to safety and injury prevention. Indoctrination of all new employees and periodic refresher training should be part of every employee's continuing education program. Fire prevention, reporting, and evacuation procedures, use of extinguishers, basic first aid, and fire drills should be part of every fire safety training session.

Some situations require the development and training of a private company fire unit or fire brigade. Facilities located in remote areas, away from public fire departments, may require an in-house firefighting team. Manufacturing facilities located in some foreign countries may not be located near adequate firefighting services. It may be necessary to create a company fire brigade made up of selected, well-trained employees who are competent to handle firefighting assignments. The size of a fire brigade will depend upon the location and size of a facility as well as on the nature of the fire risk.

Fire prevention enforcement encompasses the adoption and administration of fire prevention codes, enforcement procedures, and notices. Enforcement procedures involve compliance with fire permits, certificates, and licenses. Enforcement notices involve fire prevention personnel who inspect occupancies that have been issued warnings or notices of violation, red tag or condemnation notices, citations or summons, or warrants in violation of fire codes. It is the public fire inspector's duty to ensure that corrective action is taken so occupants are in compliance with all fire safety codes.

Company **fire inspection programs** include building surveys and the correction of common problems concerning life-safety conditions. It also involves locating and correcting fire hazards, and testing fire protection systems. These inspections may be conducted by company personnel. If situations are detected that need to be corrected, it is the inspector's duty to conduct all follow-up or reinspections (National Fire Protection Association, 2000).

Fire Protection Systems

Fire protection focuses on fire detection, containment, and suppression. Fire protection is a primary consideration during construction of new facilities as well as when upgrading existing facilities. Model building codes (statutes) and regulations for new construction have existed for many years. The codes and regulations provide for alternative methods, materials, and equipment that may be used to provide equivalent levels of safety. Performance-based fire safety design principles are used to analyze, document, and evaluate fire safety alternatives. Consultation with qualified experts and fire safety engineers is often necessary to ensure compliance with regulatory fire safety goals (Gemeny, 2000).

A fire progresses through four stages. In the incipient stage, invisible products of combustion (gases) are released and no smoke or heat is visible. In the smoldering stage, the products of combustion become visible as smoke. In the flame stage, an actual fire develops. Finally, in the heat stage, the temperature increases dramatically, the air expands, and the fire may become uncontrollable.

Fire Sensors and Alarm Systems   Four types of fire sensors (detectors) are commonly used. They respond to the different stages of fire development. The **thermal sensor** provides the least amount of advanced warning time. It senses the heat in a protected area. Some thermal sensors are preset and respond at a specific temperature. Others, known as rate-of-rise sensors, respond to rapid increases in temperature. **Infrared sensors** respond to infrared emissions in flame. **Photoelectric sensors**, commonly found in residences and many businesses, detect smoke in the environment. **Ionization sensor**, the most sensitive, respond to invisible products of combustion, such as toxic gases.

Fire alarm annunciators fall into two basic categories. Local annunciators sound at the location of the fire. Their purpose is to notify occupants of a residence or facility and summon help from those who are near enough to hear the alarm. Remote annunciator systems transmit the fire alarm signal to another location, such as a central station security counsel, 911 emergency communications center, or fire department. Remote annunciators may be monitored at some distance from the sensor location.

Fire Extinguishers and Sprinkler Systems   There are five types of portable fire extinguishers. Water, fog, and foam extinguishers are effective for Class A (ordinary combustibles) and Class B (flammable liquid) fires. Carbon dioxide CO_2) extinguishers are generally used on Class B and Class C (electrical) fires. Dry chemical extinguishers are designed to deal effectively with Class A, B, and C fires. Dry powder extinguishers are effective against Class D (combustible metals) fires.

Fire sensor. Photo courtesy of Interlogix, Inc.

Inergen fire suppression systems provide a gaseous alternative to other types of fire-extinguishing agents. Inergen systems are ideal for environments that should not be exposed to water, fog, foam, dry chemical, or powder. Inergen can be applied in vaults, computer or telecommunications facilities, or any area containing sensitive electronic equipment. Inergen is a mixture of nitrogen, argon, and carbon dioxide that suppresses a fire by lowering the oxygen level in the fire affected area to a level at which combustibles will no longer burn. It is a clean, clear, non-toxic agent that allows people to breathe normally, yet it does not support combustion. In addition, Inergen is environmentally friendly. It does not deplete the ozone, and it has no global-warming potential or atmospheric lifetime (Fireline Corporation, 2003).

Sprinkler systems provide one of the best-known protections against personal injury and property loss due to fire. Sprinklers provide excellent protection in high-rise buildings. Sprinkler systems use underground or overhead water pipes with sprinkler heads plugged with a metal strip that melts at a specified temperature. Properly installed and maintained sprinkler systems rarely fail to operate if there is an adequate water supply to support the system (National Fire Protection Association, 2000).

HUMAN PROTECTION SYSTEMS

People constitute the most significant protection resource. Although technology can be used to reduce security personnel requirements (Fischer & Green, 1998; Walsh & Healy, 1987), hardware and high-tech devices cannot totally displace the human security agent. Monitoring, critical analysis of situations, and effective intelligent response can be accomplished only through the appropriate use of personnel. Even when alarm and surveillance systems are monitored at some remote site, such as a central station, someone (a human agent) must be in place to receive an alarm signal and respond or notify appropriate response personnel.

Security personnel take many forms. Receptionists, secretaries, janitorial and maintenance workers, supervisors, executives, retail clerks, cashiers, and operations personnel can fulfill a security function. Every person can function as a deterrent to crime and all are in a position to control access and observe and report unsafe conditions and suspicious behavior. Proper security training for all personnel expands the number of people available for loss prevention (Canton, 2003).

In all but the smallest organizations, the primary responsibility for the protective function usually rests with the facility or security manager and asset protection personnel. The security force may consist of any combination of uniformed or plain clothes protection officers, investigators, CCTV and alarm console monitoring personnel, health and safety compliance inspectors, firefighters, or emergency response specialists. The security force may be proprietary, contract, or a combination of the two. Even in organizations where no one is assigned full time to asset protection duties, someone is nominally responsible for the security function.

Workforce Planning

Determining personnel requirements necessitates careful assessment and planning. If designated security personnel are required, management must determine how many are needed, what knowledge they must possess, what tasks they are to perform, and how they are to be trained. Workforce planning is not an easy task. Budgetary constraints often limit payroll dollars. Security managers must be creative and use human resources wisely, thus avoiding unnecessary expenditures.

The first step in workforce planning is to determine how many people are required. The foundation for human resource recommendations is based on the needs assessment and security survey. The assessment will reveal where and when a human agent is necessary. After personnel assignments (posts) are determined, the number of coverage hours are calculated. For example, if a human agent is to be assigned to a workstation or post, 24 hours per day, 7 days a week, the result is the equivalent of 168 clock hours. An estimated 4.5 **full-time equivalent (FTE) persons** will be needed to cover this assignment. This accounts for vacations and sick leave without unnecessary overtime. The position could be filled with any combination of full-time or part-time employees.

There are 2,080 (52 weeks × 40 hours per week) working hours available per year for each FTE. However, this calculation is based on the assumption that the position is filled by a full-time person and no vacation, holidays, or sick leave time is taken. Therefore, adjustments must be made to reduce the number of hours a full-time person is available for work if vacation, holiday, and sick leave benefits are provided. To account for 2,080 working hours, two part-time workers could fill the assignment at 1,040 hours each. If a contract service provides security personnel, the client organization need only provide the number of workforce hours exclusive of any calculation for time off.

When the number of persons or employees required is determined, it is necessary to conduct an analysis of the tasks the person in this position is expected to perform. The **job task (occupational) analysis** can be accomplished through direct observation or by comparing this position with similar positions in or outside the organization. The tasks may also be identified by interviewing current employees or other employers. The purpose of the job task analysis is to identify the job functions (duties) a worker must perform. After job functions are identified, desired job behaviors are analyzed to determine future training needs. In addition, each behavior must be analyzed in terms of the actual performance of the behavior and how the behaviors will be measured.

Next, a **job description** is created. Often referred to as a position description, it identifies the principle elements, scope of authority, and responsibilities involved in the job. The job description should be reviewed annually and revised as necessary. Closely aligned with the task analysis and job description are **job specifications**. Whereas the job description describes the major duties of a position, the job specifications outline specific skills, competencies, and personal qualifications that are necessary to perform the job adequately. The job description and job specifications may appear in the same document (Ortmeier, 1999).

After the number and qualifications of people required have been determined, the workforce information as well as the job descriptions and specifications can be referred to the human resources department or other appropriate personnel to initiate the recruitment and selection process (see Chapter 6, "Personnel Security"). In some cases, the manager to whom the new employee(s) will report may prefer to initiate the process. If plans call for contract labor, the workforce planning information is made available to security personnel vendors who wish to submit bids for the services.

A careful risk assessment and security survey should reveal the times and locations where human resources are required. The results of this analysis are used to schedule working time. Where a post must be staffed 24 hours per day, 7 days per week (continuous staffing), most organizations maintain at least three 8-hour shifts to ensure 24-hour service. Some organizations add a fourth shift for peak activity periods, as in the following example:

A Shift	2300 hours–0700 hours	(11:00 P.M.–7:00 A.M.)
B Shift	0700 hours–1500 hours	(7:00 A.M.–3:00 P.M.)
C Shift	1500 hours–2300 hours	(3:00 P.M.–11:00 P.M.)
D Shift (optional)	1900 hours–0300 hours	(7:00 P.M.–3:00 A.M.)

Organizations may also utilize what is commonly referred to as the 10 Plan: three 10-hour shifts that overlap during peak periods. Fewer people are scheduled for each shift, but a greater number are available during peak periods. Ten plans also tend to improve the morale of employees. They work four 10-hour shifts and have three days off, as in the following example:

A Shift	2400 hours–1000 hours	(midnight–10:00 A.M.)
B Shift	0800 hours–1800 hours	(8:00 A.M.–6:00 P.M.)
C Shift	1600 hours–0200 hours	(4:00 P.M.–2:00 A.M.)
D Shift (optional)	1700 hours–0300 hours	(5:00 P.M.–3:00 A.M.)

To reduce overtime costs and sick leave abuse as well as improve morale, a few organizations are scheduling 12.5-hour shifts. Under the plan, employees work three or four days a week, alternating every 7-day period. The plan requires only two shift changes every 24 hours, instead of three, reducing the number of shift changes and resulting in more time for the actual work assignment (Payton & Amaral, 1996). If employees work a shift in excess of 8 hours, state statutes should be researched to determine if state law requires overtime be paid for hours worked in excess of 8 hours per day.

Workforce schedule planning involves a comprehensive labor needs assessment, the calculation of the total number of work hours required, and a determination of the workforce's impact on the budget. The goal of workforce scheduling is to maximize coverage with minimum resources without sacrificing quality. Visually, a schedule might be presented as follows:

Position	Days	Hours	Total Hours/Week
Security Director	Vary	Vary	40
Supervisor #1	M–F	2300–0700	40
Supervisor #2	Tu–Sat	0700–1500	40
Supervisor #3	Wed–Sun	1500–2300	40
Supervisor #4	Vary	Vary	40
Assignment #1	24/7	2400–2400	168
Assignment #2	M–F	0800–1600	40
Assignment #3	M–F	1600–2400	40
Assignment #4	M–F	1200–2000	40
TOTAL			488

Since salaries and wage rates vary among positions and individuals, the total hours indicated on the schedule above cannot simply be multiplied by a flat hourly rate. Rather, the dollar amount budgeted for each position must be calculated separately. For example, if the wage rate for Assignment #2 is $10/hour, the total direct labor cost for that position is $400 per week, or $20,800 per year. Statutorily mandated and related payroll costs, training, and discretionary benefit packages could account for an additional 40 percent in indirect labor costs for each position. Thus, a $20,800 position may actually cost $29,120 per year.

Training and Education

Training and education often represent different approaches to learning. Training often refers to the development of specific skills or competencies related to tasks performed by an individual in a workplace environment. Education on the other hand encompasses general knowledge development. As a means for human resource development, emphasis should be placed on both education and training. Any personal or professional learning activity, whether education-related or training-related, designed to prepare or improve an individual or enhance performance is beneficial. Competence in leadership, human relations, written and oral communications, critical thinking, and problem solving are just as important as driving skills and dexterity in handling equipment. The success of an organization depends on its personnel. What employees know, how they perform, the values they possess, and the judgment they exercise determine outcomes for any enterprise. To ensure high productivity, quality performance, and adherence to ethical standards, education as well as training must be top priorities (Ortmeier, 1995, 1996a).

As stated in Chapter 1, formal security management-related education programs are presented by numerous colleges and universities. As security education struggles to become a discipline, some experts argue that security management curricula must focus more on the business-related aspects of the occupation. It is no secret that the role of the security manager has changed. Security managers are expected to possess business, legal, and diplomacy skills. While some educational programs claim to prepare individuals for the multidisciplinary, business-related tasks required to function effectively as a security manager, existing curricula often focus on the reactive approach necessary in many public law enforcement functions (Davidson, 2003; Longmore-Etheridge, 2000; Nalla, 2001; Ortmeier, 1994, 1995, 1996b).

The author conducted a survey that involved approximately 200 security service providers in Southern California. The purpose of the survey was to identify, from a career perspective, the training and education needs of contemporary security personnel. The survey acted as the basis for the development of a focused, comprehensive strategy to promote security management as a distinct academic discipline and to legitimize the profession at all levels of education. The results were used to incorporate security management courses into a state university's business college curricula as well as develop a security officer academy and security management associate degree at a community college.

The survey revealed that all respondents favored seminars to address specific training needs, and 98 percent favored a career education pathway (see

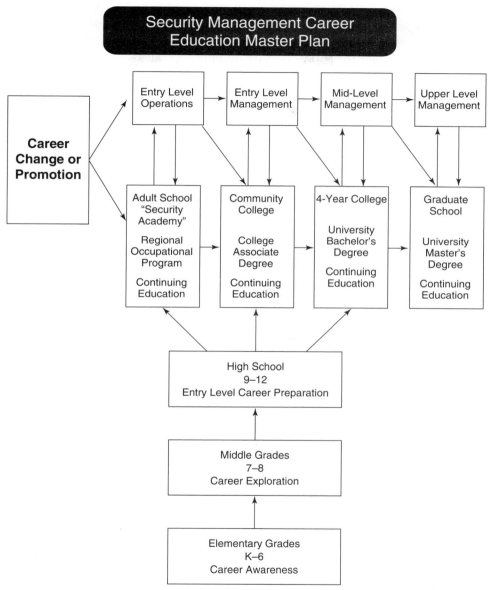

Figure 5-1 A professional education plan for a career in security management

Figure 5-1). In addition, the respondents favored security-related training and education at all educational levels. Eighty-seven percent thought high schools should include security occupations as part of their career awareness programs, and 85 percent said a security officer academy for basic training was needed. An associate degree at the community college level was favored by 95 percent of respondents, and 92 percent thought a bachelor's degree program at the university level was appropriate.

While the study produced no consensus as to what level of education security professionals should attain, survey participants largely agreed on what subjects should be studied at each level. Using a Likert scale, respondents were asked to rate the most appropriate educational level for delivering 177 subject areas identified by the Academic Program Committee of the San Diego Chapter of the American Society for Industrial Security (ASIS).

The survey addressed four educational levels, including high school, security/protection officer academy, associate degree/lower division, and bachelor's degree/upper division. Lower division refers to the first 2 years and upper division refers to the second 2 years of a 4-year bachelor's degree program. The associate degree could, with an appropriate combination of courses, function as the first 2 years of a bachelor's program.

- High school. The respondents indicated that foundation coursework in government, history, applied math, written and verbal communications, computers, hygiene, and physical education were appropriate at this level.
- Security officer academy. At this level, the respondents identified a need for technique-oriented coursework associated with self-defense; CPR and first aid; chemical weapons, baton, and firearms training (where appropriate); patrol procedures; and traffic regulation. Respondents recommended that instruction emphasize the legal aspects of security, public relations, and report writing.
- Associate degree/lower division. At the associate degree level, the competencies identified by the respondents were consistent with those of entry-level management. Here, emphasis was placed on accounting, general business practices, public and human relations, law, written communications, investigations, computer literacy, specialized security applications, public speaking, and social science.
- Bachelor's degree/upper division. At this level, the respondents indicated a need for the development of competencies appropriate to midlevel management. These competencies include business law and ethics, budgeting and finance, contracts, personnel management and labor relations, planning, organizational theory, communications, public relations, policy formulation, statistics, systems engineering, technical writing, and threat assessment and analysis.

Additional information regarding high school preparation for security careers may be obtained by contacting States' Career Clusters at www.careerclusters.org.

The respondents also indicated that working security professionals who wish to enhance policy formulation and systems integration skills may wish to pursue a masters degree in security management or business administration.

Overwhelmingly, the security professionals who responded to the study indicated a need for specialized training and education in security services. In addition, the study revealed a trend toward incorporating business-related rather than law enforcement competencies into a security management career education plan (Ortmeier, 1995, 1996b).

Teaching and Learning Strategies The methods used to teach children and teenagers are not appropriate for adults. Differences in experience, education, and levels of motivation require different approaches to adult learning methodologies. According to Knowles (1970), adult learning strategy embodies five key principles.

1. An adult accepts the material presented based on evidence, not blind faith. The learner must be aware of the credibility of the information and how it relates to the real world in which they operate.
2. The adult is active rather than passive during the learning process. Adults contribute thoughts and ideas and relate relevant personal experiences to the subject being taught.
3. Each adult's individual needs must be addressed. Although experience and education levels vary, the instructor who facilitates discussions well can provide a valuable learning experience for the most knowledgeable individual.
4. Adult learners evaluate themselves. As learning progresses, individuals conduct an internal self-assessment of their understanding of the material and how it relates to their personal situation.
5. Instructional methods that promote effective adult learning must be used. Discussion, role-playing, and the demonstration method of instruction provide an opportunity for interaction and promote an effective learning environment.

For adults, learning is a process through which the student as well as the instructor assumes responsibility for what, when, where, and how learning takes place and to whom the learning process is directed (Pike, 1992).

Program Development **Professional development** through appropriate training and education results in professional action. The ultimate goal of any professional development curriculum is to prepare individuals to perform well. To be effective, career education and training programs must be performance-based. Participants should demonstrate real-world, integrated job skills. According to the U.S. Department of Labor Secretary's Commission on Achieving Necessary Skills (SCANS), superior performance requires a three-part foundation: basic skills (reading, writing, computation, listening, and speaking); creative thinking and problem-solving skills; and personal qualities associated with responsibility, self-management, and integrity. Participants should also demonstrate the ability to identify, organize, plan, and allocate resources; work well with others; acquire and use information; understand complex relationships; and work with a variety of technologies.

Utilizing these competencies as a core, career education and training programs can be relevant to the workplace and promote critical thinking, problem solving, flexibility, teamwork, leadership, and communication. The development of a performance-based education or training program begins with an job-task (occupational) analysis. The job-task information collected and analyzed becomes the foundation for workforce training curriculum development. The analysis helps to identify general knowledge requirements, such as those articulated in the SCANS report cited previously, and specific job-related skills and desired employee qualities. The analysis will disclose what the trainees should know and be able to do, and how should they think and act.

Professional career program development can address psychomotor, cognitive and **affective skill** development. Psychomotor skills are required to perform functions such as manipulation of tools and weapons. Cognitive skill development focuses on knowledge acquisition. Knowing the law, for example, is vital to success in security occupations. Affective skill development addresses desired values and attitudes consistent with those demanded of security personnel.

After job-related competencies (skills) and human behaviors are identified, the education and training program can be developed and implemented. The first step in this process involves the creation of **instructional goals** and **instructional objectives**. An instructional goal is the learning outcome expected at the conclusion of an instructional program. Instructional goals should

- translate job outcomes into instructional outcomes by reorienting the statement to the thinking skill required and the context in which the performance occurs.
- develop outcomes around the essential functions or problems of the discipline or job area.
- reflect the breadth of application that learners may face in specific job positions.
- include the personal interactions, communications, and basic skill requirements related to performance.
- be presented in a way that emphasizes, in relevant, authentic terms, the importance of each goal.

An instructional objective describes the skills and behaviors the learner is expected to exhibit to demonstrate competence. Instructional (enabling) objectives are measurable (performance-based) and enable the learner to achieve the instructional goal. Written tests, verbal presentations, projects, collaborative activities, and practical demonstrations are often used to measure performance and progress toward meeting instructional goals. Instructional objectives

- offer a balanced core of learning in each course.

- promote a belief that in-depth study of a limited number of important topics will have a more lasting effect than a course that tries to cover many disconnected topics.

- are designed to focus on results, with multiple indicators (assessments) of performance.

- utilize authentic assessments that encourage originality, insightfulness, and problem solving, along with mastery of important information.

- ensure active learner involvement.

- avoid tracking plans that assign students to a particular level and deny some students the opportunity to acquire knowledge and skills to succeed.

- get students *doing* early in the course rather than studying all the principles and *basics* prior to performing (Nicholson, 1997).

Perhaps the most widely accepted approach to developing and classifying instructional objectives is found in the classic *Taxonomy of Educational Objectives* (Bloom, Englehart, Furst, Hill, & Krathwohl, 1956). The taxonomy serves as a guide for specifying performance outcomes. It provides a hierarchy (levels) of thinking processes that enable learners to develop an understanding of complex material.

- Knowledge. This is the simplest level and represents a mere recall of facts or other memorized information. Verbs most commonly used in knowledge-level objectives include *define, state, repeat, locate, name,* and *recognize.*

  Example: Upon the completion of this course, the learner should be able to state a definition for security management.

- Comprehension. Slightly broader than the knowledge level, comprehension-level performance standards require the learner to organize facts and select among available alternatives. Some verbs used in comprehension level objectives include *describe, identify, discuss, estimate,* and *summarize.*

  Example: Upon completion of this course, the learner should be able to identify a situation in which asset protection is required.

- Application. At this level, a learner should be able to apply skills or information learned to new and different situations. Some verbs used in application-level objectives include *solve, illustrate, demonstrate, translate,* and *interpret.*

  Example: Upon the completion of this course, the learner should be able to demonstrate asset protection techniques.

- Analysis. At this level, the learner should be able to classify and sort information. Some verbs used in the analysis level include *differentiate, criticize, catagorize, compare,* and *contrast.*

  Example: Upon completion of this course, the learner should be able to differentiate low from high loss probability.

- Synthesis. At the synthesis level, the learner must combine ideas from previous learning to create new concepts and information. Some verbs that characterize the synthesis level include *create, design, develop, organize, compose,* and *construct.*

  Example: Upon completion of this course, the learner should be able to create a loss prevention program.

- Evaluation. This is the highest level of the taxonomy, and it requires the learner to make decisions and exercise judgment based on previously known facts or opinions. Some verbs that characterize this level include *evaluate, appraise, assess, prioritize, justify,* and *recommend.*

  Example: Upon completion of this course, the learner should be able to justify the budget for a loss prevention program.

Evaluation of a trainee's progress and assessment of outcomes should be matched to the instructional objectives. Methods used to assess learner performance should replicate, as closely as possible, the actual performance standards in the workplace. Written tests should not be the only assessment tool. Projects, team activities, demonstrations, and simulations also help predict success in the actual work environment. The ultimate success of the program is measured against the individual's ability to perform and apply what was learned in accordance with the measurable standards identified in the occupational (job-task) analysis (Ortmeier, 1999).

SUMMARY

The basics of defense involve the use of systems and countermeasures to control access. Outer and inner perimeter controls, natural barriers, building exteriors and interiors, lighting, fencing, locks, and visual assessment, surveillance, alarm, and fire protection systems form the nonhuman elements of physical security and access control. Human protection systems include the use of security and other personnel to monitor nonhuman systems, manage the safety and security program, and take appropriate action when necessary. Security workforce planning involves a determination of personnel requirements, job-task analyses, the creation of job descriptions and specifications, scheduling, training, and professional career education.

KEY TERMS

affective skills	annunciator
alarm	basics of defense
alarm point definition	card-operated lock
alarm system circuit	central processing unit (CPU)
alarm system management	central station alarm system

closed-circuit television (CCTV)

combination lock

digitization

electronic lock

facility plan review

fire hazard abatement

fire inspection program

fire investigation

fire prevention

fire prevention enforcement

fire prevention inspection

fire protection

fire safety education

full time equivalent (FTE) person

infrared (IR) camera

infrared sensors

instructional goal

instructional objective

ionization sensor

job description

job specifications

job-task (occupational) analysis

key-operated lock

keypad lock

local alarm system

microwave motion sensor

passive infrared (IR) sensor

perimeter controls

perimeter lighting

photoelectric sensor

professional development

proprietary alarm system

public alarm system

sensor

thermal sensor

ultrasonic motion sensor

DISCUSSION QUESTIONS AND EXERCISES

1. Outline and describe the basics of physical security. Include outer and inner perimeter controls and the roles of protective lighting and locking devices in the description.

2. Compare and contrast visual assessment, surveillance, and alarm systems. What role does each fulfill?

3. Physical security and access control systems are not complete without a human resource component. Explain. Are dedicated security personnel necessary in all organizations?

4. Appropriate preservice and in-service career education and training are essential for security personnel. How are training and education needs determined? Does training help to reduce civil and criminal liability? How?

C H A P T E R 6

Personnel Security

LEARNING OBJECTIVES

After completing this chapter, the reader should be able to

- describe personnel security policies and techniques.
- outline a procedure for recruitment and selection of personnel.
- discuss the impact of legislation on human resource management.
- contrast management with leadership.
- identify leadership qualities and competencies.
- distinguish between law, policy, and ethics.
- articulate a professional code of conduct.

INTRODUCTION

Personnel security involves protection of human beings and protection from individuals who pose threats to others as well as the organization's physical and information assets. Personnel security and **personnel integrity** are fundamental to the protection of an organization's most valuable assets: its employees and clients. Personnel security and integrity are essential to organizational success, form the foundation for effective and ethical business practices, ensure the availability of human resources, and assist in the maintenance of high morale, economic stability, and fair and equitable treatment (American Society for Industrial Security, 1998).

Protection of people involves the application of the principles and practices of physical security, the subject of Chapter 5, as well as the protection from violence in the workplace discussed in Chapter 10. In this chapter, attention is focused on protection from people, especially employees of the organization. As such, this chapter addresses personnel selection, supervision, and integrity. Clearly, the process of security management must assure that honest, dedicated, industrious people are employed by the organization. After the initial decision to employ an individual is made, the person's emotional, mental, and physical health must be maintained and the employee's trustworthiness and reliability evaluated continuously. Hiring the right people and maintaining their integrity is a management responsibility (Pitorri, 1998).

PERSONNEL RECRUITMENT AND SELECTION

Recruitment is the process of locating and attracting suitable applicants as candidates to fill job vacancies. **Selection** involves the process of evaluating and choosing the most appropriate and qualified person from a pool of applicants.

Recruitment

Recruiting candidates to fill a position vacancy is accomplished in a variety of ways. Internally, it may be accomplished through promotion or transfer. Externally, the recruitment process may involve newspaper and trade journal advertising, college and university career fairs, the Internet, former employees, friends and relatives of employees, applications on file, labor organizations, employment agencies, and community job fairs.

Recruiting acceptable candidates is critical and can be difficult. A low birth rate in the United States, coupled with good economic times, limits the number of people available in the pool of qualified workers. In addition, lax attitudes and apathy toward drug use, theft, and loyalty often threaten the integrity of prospective employees. Numerous laws also regulate the employment procedure, making the recruitment and selection process elaborate and time consuming (Cheeseman, 2004; Lewis, Goodman, & Fandt, 2001).

The recruitment process normally begins with a request for, or submission of, a **resume** and an **application.** The resume or application can be solicited by the employer or submitted on the prospective employee's initiative. A resume is a subjective account of a person's background, while an application is more objective. A comparison of the resume with the application may help to reveal any contradictions and inconsistencies.

Employment application instruments should be objective, uniform, consistent, and job-task related. Care should be exercised in the development of application forms to ensure that information is not requested in violation of any state or federal statute. Age, birthplace, race, citizenship, religious affiliation, and arrest information is often protected by antidiscrimination and privacy laws. In addition, some public organizations, such as law enforcement agencies, may request information that cannot be requested by a private organization. For example, as a general rule, private organizations have access to and may request conviction data but not arrest records. Conviction records are public information, whereas arrest records are not (Bland & Stalcup, 1999).

An application form should not contain questions other than those pertaining to the applicant's ability to perform the job for which application is made. An appropriately constructed application form, once completed by the applicant, provides a window into the candidate's past and assists in the candidate's background verification process. Signed and dated below a statement affirming to state the truth, the application becomes a legal document. It can be used by the employer as a defense in a subsequent legal proceeding if the employee is terminated due to false or misleading information presented in the application (Lewis, Goodman, & Fandt, 2001; Pitorri, 1998).

Selection

The selection process begins with a preliminary **pre-employment screening** of the applicants. It involves a review of each resume and application package to ensure that the candidate meets the qualifications and specifications for the position. The pre-employment screening process may involve pre-employment aptitude, ability, psychological, and integrity (honesty) tests; appropriate physical agility tests; a medical examination; criminal history, driving record, and credit checks; a legally permissible polygraph examination; and an interview.

The applicant can be asked to authorize the disclosure of relevant background information by third parties. To release the prospective employer and the third parties from liability associated with disclosure of the information requested, the candidate should be required to sign an *authorization to release information document* as a condition for employment. Prospective employers should consult in-house or contracted legal counsel regarding the appropriate language to be included in the authorization to release information document.

Aptitude, knowledge, and skills tests determine suitability for the position and provide objective verification of the knowledge and skills claimed in the resume and application. The tests can help conserve resources and assist in determining the level and amount of training necessary to prepare the candidate for the position. A wide range of valid pencil and paper **psychological tests** are available that can be used to determine a candidate's emotional stability and mental health. The test procedures often include the use of staff psychologists to interpret the results. **Integrity tests** can be used to detect a propensity toward dishonesty, substance abuse, violence, or a high level of tolerance for such behavior in others (Jones & Arnold, 2003). Similar in format and application to psychological tests, several integrity testing instruments are commercially available. Test producers should provide validity data for psychological and integrity tests.

Using tests to identify attitudes toward substance abuse and theft, and to predict behavior based on these attitudes, is not always foolproof. Employers should not rely solely on the results of such tests when making hiring decisions. The tests should be viewed as complementary tools in a comprehensive pre-employment screening arsenal. Additionally, organizations risk violation of federal and many state laws if tests discriminate against anyone on the basis of race, gender, or political views (Anderson, 1999). Employers should not overlook the job application form itself as a tool for collecting information to predict behavior. If questions on an application form are presented properly, candidates often admit past misconduct (Millwee, 2000).

A growing number of employers are requiring performance-simulation tests of job applicants. Especially useful in determining an applicant's potential, performance-simulation tests address actual job behaviors. Through work sampling and assessment centers, candidates demonstrate their skills or they are evaluated as they progress through exercises or scenarios intended to simulate problems they will confront on the job (Robbins & Coulter, 2003).

A physical agility test may be required if it relates to the tasks the candidate is required to perform in the position for which application is made. Subject to limited exceptions as outlined in the Americans with Disabilities Act (ADA) as well as to limited exceptions for applicants for some government positions, medical examinations can be required only after an offer of employment has been made. Normally, the results of the medical examination are used to determine if a preexisting medical condition restricts the candidate's ability to perform the tasks in the position or if the candidate suffers from a disease that can be communicated to others (Anderson, 1999; Bland & Stalcup, 1999).

Criminal history checks are imperative, yet current laws severely restrict a private employer's ability to access arrest data. As a general rule, conviction data is a matter of public record, accessible to anyone. Many county sheriff's departments, especially those in counties that contain major urban areas, have websites through which employers can obtain local conviction data as well as the identity of those who are in jail or have outstanding arrest warrants.

Although a criminal history is not an absolute disqualifier, the prospective employer should be aware of the nature and number of convictions. Recent theft, substance abuse, or violent crime convictions should disqualify a candidate. However, if the candidate is 45 years of age and the only conviction is for shoplifting at age 19, one could assume that the candidate has been rehabilitated. Driving record checks are also important if the employee is required to operate a motor vehicle as a condition of employment.

Technological advances combined with legal authority make background checks more accurate and efficient for some industries. Financial institutions currently use electronic systems to conduct criminal history checks and reduce employee pre-screening and training costs. Federal laws require banks, brokerage houses, and insurers to conduct criminal history checks on all prospective employees who are required to handle cash or other financial assets. In the past, affected institutions fingerprinted individuals using traditional methods and submitted the fingerprint cards to the FBI, where the prints were classified manually and a felony records check was conducted. However, traditional processing methods took up to 3 months, and if the prints were not readable, a new set of prints was required. In many cases where the applicant was rejected, the prospective employee was already on the payroll and considerable time had been invested in training the new person. Utilizing the automated fingerprint identification system (AFIS), many institutions now scan fingerprints directly into a computer database that automatically classifies the prints and completes a criminal records check within minutes (Millwee, 2000).

A credit history check on the applicant should be conducted also. Late payments, nonpayments, bankruptcies, liens, and judgments against a candidate can be uncovered through a comprehensive credit reporting process. Most employees are placed in positions of trust and are charged with the responsibility for protecting assets. Although a poor credit history does not mean the new employee would steal to pay off debt, it may indicate inadequate self-management skills, poor judgment, and lack of responsibility, especially with respect to the management of financial assets. Most financial institutions will not employ individuals with poor credit histories. If they cannot manage their own money properly, they cannot be expected to manage another person's assets. Although some bad credit may be unavoidable, such as when a catastrophic illness leads to financial disaster, poor financial management is often linked to irresponsible behavior. A wise employer does not hire irresponsible people.

A thorough background investigation on a prospective employee is not complete until personal references are checked and academic credentials and employment history provided by the applicant are verified. A high percentage of resumes, job applications, and employment interviews produce something less than the whole truth. Naturally, applicants prefer that derogatory information not be uncovered. Candidate-provided references rarely release any negative information about the applicant. Therefore, prospective employers must be diligent in the search for the truth. Since applicants provide references who will speak favorably of them, the prospective employer may do well to visit and interview coworkers and neighbors of the applicant, if time and resources permit (Anderson, 1999; Lewis, Goodman, & Fandt, 2001). Additional information regarding background investigations is presented in Chapter 8.

Subject to limited exceptions discussed in Chapter 8, federal law prohibits private employers from using a polygraph or similar instrument as a pre-employment screening tool. The law does permit the use of the polygraph for screening candidates for numerous government positions, including most public law enforcement occupations. Where appropriately used, the polygraph examination is a valuable tool for verification of information supplied by an applicant.

The interview is a face-to-face encounter between the candidate and the employer's representative or screening committee. The interview provides an opportunity to observe the candidate's appearance, demeanor, and response to questions designed to probe the candidate's abilities, honesty, dependability, judgment, and initiative. During an interview, questions that may be in violation of local, state, and federal statutes relative to marital status, lifestyle, and equal employment opportunity must be avoided (Lewis, Goodman, & Fandt, 2001). Ethical dilemmas as well as various types of situations may be presented to the candidate to evaluate the candidate's problem-solving skills under pressure and predict decision-making behavior.

Some interesting scenarios develop when private organizations employ off-duty public law enforcement officers to work in a private security setting. Although the reasons (more training and the ability to exercise police powers) for employment of off-duty public law enforcement officers are legitimate and understandable, private employers should be aware of the potential legal implications that may arise when private security personnel hold public police powers. Several court cases illustrate the legal tightrope walked by private organizations that employ public police officers as private security personnel.

On October 15, 1994, Robert Abraham and Dennis Redding were observed by store security personnel shoplifting in the men's department of the Macy's store at the Cherry Hill Mall in Cherry Hill, New Jersey. The store's security personnel followed the shoplifting suspects into the mall parking lot while radioing mall security personnel for assistance. Kimberly Raso, a Cherry Hill, New Jersey, police officer working off-duty as a mall security officer, responded to the radio call. Suspect Abraham entered and started a vehicle and backed up abruptly toward Officer Raso. The officer avoided being hit by Abraham's vehicle. However, Abraham hit a parked vehicle and pulled forward toward Raso, despite Raso's repeated commands to stop. Raso again jumped out of Abraham's path, drew her weapon, and fired one shot through the driver side window. Abraham died after driving away and hitting another parked car, a parking island, and a tree. Subsequently, Robert Abraham's widow filed a multicount lawsuit against Officer Raso, the mall, the Township of Cherry Hill, and Macy's department store for assault, battery, **negligent hiring,** and violation of Abraham's constitutional right against unreasonable search and seizure by using excessive force.

Regarding the violation of Abraham's constitutional right, his widow alleged that Raso violated Section 1983 of the U.S. Code, which prohibits persons acting under the authority granted to them by the state from violating another person's constitutional rights. Generally, private organizations cannot be sued under Section 1983 because their employers do not act under the authority of state law. However, when a private entity hires off-duty police officers, it can expose itself to liability under Section 1983. In this case, the private employer was fortunate. The court determined that Raso was not liable because she identified herself as a police officer, retained police authority while off-duty per state law, and was acting in self-defense. In a different but similar case, an off-duty Seattle, Washington, police officer, employed by Safeway as a private security officer, arrested a suspected shoplifter, although the suspect did not steal merchandise. A jury found the police officer and the store liable under Section 1983 of the U.S. Code.

Similar situations appear in case law throughout the United States. Although the respondents to a lawsuit may prevail, the cost of litigation increases the cost of doing business. Adequate training is one key to limiting liability. Off-duty police officers should be trained in the law as it relates to private security operations. Secondly, and probably most important, private employers who employ off-duty police officers in a security capacity should be aware that unique legal issues arise in a public police officer-private employer relationship (Peck, 1999).

Negligent Hiring and Retention

The hiring of an employee must be more than an intuitive guess. Although state and federal privacy statutes make preemployment screening challenging, failure to complete a diligent inquiry into the suitability of persons employed may constitute **negligent hiring** and can have devastating consequences. Poor hiring decisions result in losses due to theft, high attrition rates, increased insurance claims and premiums, vicarious liability, and negligent hiring lawsuits. A thorough background investigation on a prospective employee is not a luxury, it is a necessity. As numerous court judgments indicate, employers are held liable for the actions of employees when the employer failed to investigate properly and the investigation would have uncovered the risk.

The elements of negligent hiring liability include the following:

- The person in question was an employee of the organization.
- The employee was unfit for employment in the position.
- The employer knew or should have known the employee was unfit.
- The plaintiff was injured by the employee during a contact connected with employment.
- The employer owed a duty of care to the plaintiff.
- The hiring of the employee was the proximate (legal) cause of the injury to the plaintiff (Hess & Wrobleski, 1996).

An employer may also be held liable for negligent supervision or retention of an employee. **Negligent retention** involves a situation in which the employer does not take disciplinary or remedial action after becoming aware of a risk factor. To avoid negligent retention lawsuits, the employer must thoroughly investigate claims of misconduct, such as sexual harassment and violent behavior on the part of any employee (Bland, 2000). **Sexual harassment** refers to a pattern of behavior that involves unwelcomed lewd remarks, offensive touching, intimidation, and other conduct or communication of a sexual nature that is offensive to a reasonable person (Cheeseman, 2004). Violent behavior may involve threats as well as acts resulting in physical contact (Kovacich & Halibozek, 2003).

In 2000, the Hawaii State Occupational Safety and Health Division cited Xerox Corporation for failure to have or enforce workplace violence policies that might have prevented Xerox employee Byran Uyesugi from shooting seven coworkers to death in 1999. Publicized as the worst mass killing in Hawaii history, the state alleged that Xerox allowed Uyesugi to return to work after a 1993 on-the-job violent outburst. The state's citation also stated that Xerox did not have an effective workplace violence prevention program and did not properly train managers to recognize and deal with potential employee violence ("Hawaii cites Xerox in worker shooting," 2000).

If an investigation uncovers a foreseeable threat, the employer is legally obligated to take appropriate action to remove the threat through reassignment or termination of the employee. The elements of negligent retention include the following:

- The employee was hired by the employer.
- After hiring, the employer became aware that the employee is a potential threat.
- The employer retains the employee in the position, knowing the risk.
- The plaintiff's injurious contact with the employee was connected with employment.
- The plaintiff was injured during the contact (Hess & Wrobleski, 1996).

Employer liability for the actions of an employee may extend beyond the employment relationship. If a former employee applies for a new position elsewhere, and the prospective employer contacts the former employer for a reference, the former employer should provide dates of employment only. A former employer may be held liable if a generally positive reference is provided for a former employee, despite knowledge that the person is a potential threat (American Society for Industrial Society, 1998; Hess & Wrobleski, 1996).

PERSONNEL MANAGEMENT

Appropriate recruitment and selection procedures represent only the initial steps in the personnel management cycle. The management of human resources also involves training and scheduling, supervision and leadership, performance appraisal, promotion, the development of policies and procedures, discipline, possible demotion or termination, adherence to employment law, and employee retention strategies.

Training and Scheduling

Employee training falls into three broad categories: **preservice training**, **in-service training**, and **career enhancement**. Some occupations require prescribed preservice training prior to employment. In most states, police, fire, corrections, and security personnel have specific preservice training requirements. In-service training involves apprenticeships, coursework, seminars, internships, or on-the-job training. Career enhancement includes educational experiences that focus on specific job-related training as well as those experiences that promote personal development of the individual. Substantial returns on the training investment may be realized if an organization focuses on individual career enhancement of employees. Benefits in terms of increased productivity, improved morale, and loyalty to the organization are positive by-products of an individualized career training program (Johnson, 2003; Lenahan, 2000).

Employees are scheduled according to a plan that identifies need and productivity requirements. Employee work schedules are generally based on the assumption that individuals are willing to work at 100 percent capacity. However, all employees cannot be expected to work continuously at top speed. Therefore, adequate personnel must to be assigned to a set of tasks to ensure that productivity needs are met (Ortmeier, 1999; Slater, 2000; Smith, R.V., 2000). A comprehensive discussion of training and scheduling is presented in Chapter 5.

Supervision and Leadership

The management of human resources involves both **supervision** and **leadership**. Not all supervisors make good leaders. Not all leaders make good supervisors. Ideally, good supervisors are also good leaders. The concept of leadership is often misunderstood because definitions of leadership vary and the process for leadership development is vague. However, substantial evidence exists that leads progressive thinkers to believe that leadership skills are essential for all workers in contemporary society (Drucker, 1994).

Leadership is every person's responsibility, and each employee can assume a leadership role. The chief executive officer (CEO) of an organization is probably the most important strategic initiator. The CEO plays a significant role in defining the organization's philosophy, values, mission, and priorities. The CEO is instrumental in creating the climate conducive to successful change and positive outcomes. The CEO is also in the best position to assist with the creation of a vision for the future.

Upper and middle managers should lead as well as manage. Rather than insulate themselves from line supervisors and operations personnel, upper and middle managers should interact with subordinates, assisting the latter through mentoring, coaching, and team building. Upper and middle managers are in an excellent position to act as conduits, monitoring for and adjusting the pace of change. Some people are attracted to supervisory positions for the wrong reasons. They are attracted by the power and control that comes with a position of authority. However, true leadership is not so much the exercise of power as it is the empowerment of others. Leadership is service to others that requires tremendous commitment, energy, patience, humility, and selflessness.

Line supervisors are in a pivotal leadership position to facilitate the achievement of goals. These supervisors help line personnel achieve accountability and performance objectives. It has been stated that the quantity and quality of performance can be linked directly to the quality of supervision. Line supervisors are in the best position to assume a leadership role in reviewing individual productivity, making recommendations for improvement and taking corrective action when appropriate (Baker, 2000).

Finally, regardless of the size of an organization or the number of levels of authority or supervision, it is the line person who has the most direct role in serving the mission of the organization. The line person is in the best position to directly impact the lives of the people who are served. Thus, considerable training and education resources should be expended to develop ethical leadership competencies in line as well as senior personnel. Further, ethical leadership development should be viewed as a lifelong process, not an event (Johnson, 2001; Ortmeier, 1997, 2003; Meese & Ortmeier, 2004).

The universal phenomenon called leadership has been the subject of a great deal of research from both the theoretical and the practical points of view. Leadership has been described variously as a trait, the focus of group process, the art of inducing compliance, an exercise of influence, a kind of behavior or act, a form of persuasion, a power relationship, an instrument in goal attainment, an effective interaction, a differentiated role, and an initiation of structure (Bass, 1990). Leadership has also been defined as acts or behaviors (Carter, 1953), an act which results in others acting or responding in a shared direction (Shartle, 1956), the process of arranging a situation to achieve common goals (Bellows, 1959), and the initiation and maintenance of structure through interaction (Stogdill, 1959). It has been defined as directing and coordinating work relationships while showing consideration (Fiedler, 1967), an activity which mobilizes people to do something (Heifetz, 1994), and a social meaning-making process that takes place as a result of activity or work in a group (Drath & Palus, 1994).

Leadership should not be confused with supervision or management. Leadership, a concept that is broader than supervision, occurs anytime one attempts to motivate, influence, or mobilize an individual or group. Supervision and management, on the other hand, involve directing people toward organizational goals (Hersey & Blanchard, 1982). Although supervision and leadership may be exercised or exhibited by the same individual, both represent distinct concepts. Leadership produces change by establishing direction, aligning people, motivating, and inspiring. Supervision and management bring a measure of order and consistency to organizations by planning and budgeting, organizing and staffing, and controlling (Kotter, 1990). In other words, supervision and management follow leadership (Covey, 1998).

Bennis (1993b, p. 214) distinguished leadership from management by stating that

- the manager administers; the leader innovates.
- the manager is a copy; the leader is an original.
- the manager maintains; the leader develops.
- the manager focuses on systems and structure; the leader focuses on people.
- the manager relies on control; the leader inspires trust.
- the manager has a short-range view; the leader has a long-range perspective.
- the manager asks how and when; the leader asks what and why.
- the manager has an eye on the bottom line; the leader has an eye on the horizon.
- the manager accepts the status quo; the leader challenges it.
- the manager is the classic good soldier; the leader is not dependent on others.
- the manager does things right; the leader does the right thing.

As one author stated, the leader is the one who climbs the tallest tree, surveys the situation, and cries out, "Wrong jungle!" The manager responds with "Shut up! We are making progress" (Covey, 1998).

Throughout the twentieth century, numerous theorists attempted to define leadership. An important breakthrough in understanding the concept of leadership occurred with the publication of *Leadership* by James MacGregor Burns in 1978. Burns characterized leadership as either **transactional leadership** (when one person takes the initiative, making contact with others for the purpose of the exchange of valued things) or **transformational leadership** (when one or more persons engage with others in a way that the leader and nonleader raise one another to higher levels of motivation and morality). Examples of transactional leadership through a contingent reward approach can be found in *The One Minute Manager* (Blanchard & Johnson, 1992). The function of transactional leadership is to maintain the organization's operation rather than to change it (Burns & Becker, 1988). Transformational leadership, on the other hand, focuses on the three behavior patterns of charisma, intellectual stimulation, and individualized consideration (Bass, 1985). Tichy and Ulrich (1984) presented the transformational leader as the model for future leadership excellence. They cited three identifiable activities associated with transformational leadership: creation of vision—view of a future state, mobilization of commitment—acceptance of a new mission, and institutionalization of change—new patterns of behavior must be adopted.

Although leadership originally focused on traits or inbred qualities that a person possessed since birth, today it is believed that leadership skills can be acquired or modified extensively through learning. These skills include competence to keep communication channels open and functioning effectively, interact socially, solve problems, plan, initiate action, and accept responsibility. Such skills are not inherited; they are learned (McGregor, 1960). Also critical to the success of the leader are skills in facilitation of team interaction, effective team problem solving, and training (Miskin & Gmelch, 1985).

An effective leader is likely to demonstrate excellent communications and interpersonal skills. A leader is likely to be both relations-oriented and task-oriented, manage conflict successfully, and mobilize and direct individuals toward higher objectives (Bass, 1981). Orton (1984) cited the importance of quality decision making, commitment, and the ability to employ situational strategies. Motivational, or person-oriented behaviors, tend to promote follower satisfaction, although they may not contribute to group productivity (Bass, 1981). McGregor (1966) suggested that people already possess motivation and desire full responsibility.

Leadership competence has also been expressed in terms of the ability to plan, organize, and set goals. Leaders must create clear-cut and measurable goals based on advice from all elements of a community. Likert (1967) discovered that high-producing leaders make clear what the objectives are and give people freedom to complete the task. Argyris (1964) suggested that it is in an individual's nature to be self-directed and to seek fulfillment through the exercise of initiative and responsibility. Hersey and Blanchard (1982) suggested that leadership involves goal setting, organizing, setting time lines, and directing. Contemporary experts often focus on leadership competencies. Bennis (1984, 1993a) identified four competencies of leadership:

- Management of attention—the ability to attract followers
- Management of meaning—the ability to communicate one's viewpoint or vision
- Management of trust—reliability
- Management of self—the ability to know one's skills and use them effectively

Daniel (1992) identified 13 leadership competencies. They include a goal orientation, a bottom-line focus, the ability to communicate and enforce standards, initiative, strategic influence, communication of confidence, and interpersonal sensitivity. Good leaders also develop and coach others, give performance feedback, collaborate and build teams, problem solve, project a good image and reputation, and possess self-confidence. Kotter (1993) pointed out that good leaders articulate a vision, involve people in decision making, and recognize and reward success. Drath and Palus (1994) stated that leaders must be trained to participate in, rather than exercise, leadership by learning community-oriented, meaning-making capacities, such as the capacity to understand oneself as both an individual and as a socially embedded being; the capacity to understand systems in general as mutually related, interacting, and continually changing; the capacity to take the perspective of another; and the capacity to engage in dialogue. Leaders must be flexible (W. Bridges, 1994) and demonstrate initiative, integrity, and the ability to empower others (Davids, 1995).

Essential leadership competencies can be grouped into five major categories. The communications and related interpersonal competencies category addresses one's ability to communicate with diverse populations. Through motivational competencies, a person demonstrates the ability to encourage others and build proactive relationships. Problem solving competencies focus on problem identification, critical and analytical thinking, and situation analysis. Planning and organizing competencies are used to create a vision, prioritize, delegate, and define goals and objectives. Actuation-implementation competencies address the ability to implement a vision and evaluate results (Ortmeier, 2002; Meese & Ortmeier, 2004).

In the final analysis, the real test of leadership lies in the performance of the groups being led (Bass, 1981). The competencies applied in a particular circumstance depend on the situation, the people involved, the action to be taken, and the desired results (Byrnbauer & Tyson, 1984). Leadership skills are especially important in an asset protection environment. As the primary protection officers for most organizations, security personnel must respond to threats against people and property and assume control in dangerous situations. The ability to communicate well, exercise effective judgment, reduce hostility, promote safety, and restore normal operations requires leadership competence (Ortmeier, 1997, 2002; Meese & Ortmeier, 2004).

Motivation and Management

Ultimately, what motivates others depends on the culture and situation at hand (Adler, 2002; Hellriegel, Slocum & Woodman, 2001). However, several theories that illustrate how individual differences affect motivation are useful to a manager's understanding of the reactions of people with whom they come in contact.

Abraham Maslow arranged individual motivational factors according to a hierarchy of needs. Maslow identified five types of human needs: physiological (the most basic), security, affiliation, esteem, and self-actualization (at the top of the needs hierarchy). Physiological needs include those that are basic to human survival: food, water, shelter, and clothing. Security needs address the desire for stability, safety, good health, and the absence of threats or pain. In an employment situation, security needs may be satisfied if employment is stable and expands employee competence and confidence of long-term employability. Affiliation needs include the desire for friendship, belonging, and love. When a person's affiliation needs are not met, dissatisfaction may lead to low productivity, absenteeism, stress-related behaviors, and psychological problems. Esteem needs include the desire for self-respect, personal achievement, and recognition

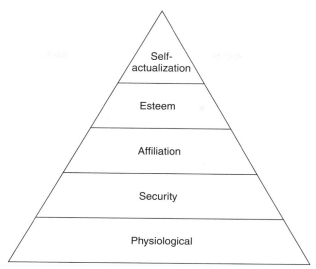

Figure 6–1   Maslow's Hierarchy of Needs

from others. To satisfy esteem needs, people desire prestige, status, and opportunities to demonstrate their competence and worth. Self-actualization needs, the highest level on Maslow's need hierarchy continuum, are achieved when one's desires for personal growth, self-fulfillment, and reaching one's full potential are realized. Maslow suggested that as one need is satisfied, motivation shifts to satisfying the next higher level of need (Maslow, 1970).

Clay Alderfer (1972) also viewed motivation from an individual needs perspective. In contrast to Maslow's five-level hierarchy of needs, however, Alderfer suggested three categories of need: existence, relatedness, and growth (Alderfer, 1972). Alderfer named his formulation Existence, Relatedness, and Growth (ERG) Theory. Alderfer's ERG theory recognized Maslow's satisfaction-progression hypothesis, but the ERG theory also contains an additional dimension called the frustration-regression hypothesis. The frustration-regression hypothesis suggests that frustration (obstacles) encountered when seeking to meet higher-level needs leads to a reemergence of lower-level needs.

In his learned needs theory, David McClelland (1971) suggested that people develop needs through interaction with the surrounding environment. Thus, social contexts influence the learning of motivational needs. This theory contrasts with Maslow's theory that a needs hierarchy is inherent to human beings. According to McClelland, understanding the differences among individual motivators depends on the presence of three key motives: affiliation, achievement, and power (McClelland, 1971).

According to expectancy theory, an individual, given choices, selects options that are perceived to provide the greatest rewards. Thus, the expectancy theory or model suggests that motivation to perform is based on an understanding of the relationship between performance and effort and the perception of the desirability of outcomes associated with different performance levels (Vroom, 1964).

Behavioral Assumptions and Leadership Style

Numerous factors and conditions operate to create behavioral assumptions that influence a person's perception of another individual or of specific circumstances (Adler & Towne, 2002). Behavioral assumptions about people and how to motivate them influence leader behavior. If a leader harbors false assumptions about people, the beliefs can cause a leader to use inappropriate motivational techniques with followers. Correct behavioral assumptions can result in positive outcomes (Fournies, 2000). Although many of the assumptions and the accompanying models for direction and control of human beings were developed for managerial personnel, the concepts apply to leaders as well.

One of the most widely quoted models for recognizing and distinguishing assumptions about motivation was developed by Douglas McGregor in the 1950s. In his classic work, *The Human Side of Enterprise,* McGregor (1960) explored theoretical assumptions about human nature and human behavior as it relates to ethics, management, leadership, and motivation. McGregor proposed that two sets of leadership or managerial assumptions regarding human behavior appear to exist. He referred to the traditional view of leadership and managerial direction and control as Theory X and the view that leadership and management should be based on the integration of individual and organizational goals as Theory Y. Theory X includes the following leadership and managerial assumptions:

- The average human being has an inherent dislike of work and will avoid work if possible.
- Because of the dislike for work, most people must be coerced, controlled, directed, or threatened with punishment to get them to put forth adequate effort toward the achievement of objectives.
- The average human being is self-centered, prefers to be directed, wishes to avoid responsibility, has relatively little ambition, and wants security above all.

McGregor suggested that Theory X leaders and managers did not account for critical factors associated with motivation. These factors include a few simple generalizations about human beings. First, human beings are "wanting" animals. As soon as one need is satisfied, it is replaced with another. Second, human needs are organized in a hierarchy of importance. Third, a satisfied need is not a motivator of behavior. According to McGregor, Theory X leaders and managers ignore these generalizations. They direct and control through the exercise of authority (McGregor, 1960).

Theory Y leaders and managers, on the other hand, operate with a different set of assumptions regarding human behavior. Theory Y assumptions include the following:

- The expenditure of physical and mental effort in work is as natural as play or rest.
- External control and the threat of punishment are not the only means for bringing about effort toward objectives. People will exercise self-direction and self-control in the service of objectives to which they are committed.
- Commitment to objectives is a function of the rewards associated with their achievement.
- The average human being learns, under proper conditions, to accept as well as seek responsibility.
- The capacity to exercise a relatively high degree of imagination, ingenuity, and creativity in the solution to problems is widely, not narrowly, distributed in the population.
- Under the conditions of modern industrial life, the intellectual potentialities of the average human being are only partially realized (McGregor, 1960).

Theory Y assumptions are dynamic rather than static and they represent significantly different implications for leadership and management than do Theory X assumptions. Theory Y assumptions focus on human growth. Theory X leaders and managers blame followers and workers for failure to achieve goals. Theory Y implies that poor productivity is more often the result of poor leadership and management. Theory Y focuses on the integration of goals: the creation of conditions through which members of a group or organization may achieve their own goals as well as the goals of the enterprise. Thus, motivation, the potential for growth, the ability to assume responsibility, and the readiness to work toward individual as well as group goals are present in all people. The leader's responsibility is to recognize, harness, and channel these characteristics toward common goals by creating a climate and methodology conducive to success (Baker, 2000; Hellriegel, Jackson, & Slocum, 2002; McGregor, 1960).

An adaptation of Theory Y, called Theory Z, was created by William Ouchi in the early 1980s. Theory Z is a leadership and management style that advocates trusting followers and employees and creating an environment in which followers and employees feel as though they are an integral part of the group or organization. According to Theory Z, a relationship of trust promotes increased productivity and goal achievement (Lewis, Goodman, & Fandt, 2001; Ouchi, 1981).

The managerial grid developed by Robert Blake and Jane Mouton (1985) identifies five leadership styles that integrate varying degrees of concern for people with concern for production and goal achievement. Blake and Mouton's five leadership styles are arranged on a grid. The impoverished leadership style (1,1) demonstrates low concern for people, production, and goal achievement. Leaders utilizing this style exert minimal effort and wish to maintain the status quo. Through the country club style (1,9) leaders demonstrate high concern for people but low concern for production and goal achievement. Leaders create a secure and comfortable environment in the hope that followers will produce. Low concern for people and high concern for production and goal achievement characterize the produce or perish leadership style (9,1). Leaders use coercive powers to achieve results and show little concern for the personal needs of followers. Through the middle-of-the-road style (5,5), leaders strive to balance follower personal needs with a concern for productivity and goal achievement. Through the team style (9,9), leaders demonstrate high concern for people as well as productivity and goal achievement. Blake and Mouton believed that 9,9 was the optimal style. The 9,9 approach is consistent with McGregor's Theory Y. Leaders at 9,9 strive for teamwork and commitment to goal achievement among team members (Blake & Mouton, 1985).

Paul Hersey and Ken Blanchard created a situational leadership model that suggests that supportive (people-centered) and directive (production- and goal-centered) leadership behaviors should be contingent on the readiness level of followers and workers (Hersey & Blanchard, 1982; Hersey, Blanchard, & Johnson, 2001). Supportive leadership behavior is consistent with open communication links between a leader and followers. Leaders listen, encourage, and involve followers in decision making. Directive leadership behaviors are consistent with situations requiring structure, control, direct supervision, and a reliance on one-way (leader-to-follower) communication. Follower readiness (maturity, experience, expertise) determines the followers ability to set high and attainable task-related goals and willingness to assume responsibility for achieving the

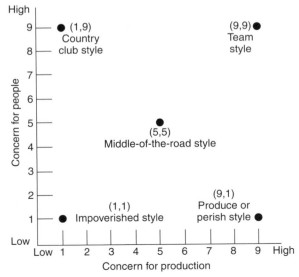

Figure 6–2   Managerial Grid

goals. The level of supportive or directive leadership behaviors is dependent on different levels of follower readiness. According to the situational leadership model, leaders use a delegating, supportive, selling, or telling style, depending on follower readiness.

Leaders use a delegating style when they view followers as mature, competent, and motivated. The supportive style is used to encourage, assist, and maintain open communication links between leader and follower. Through the telling style, the leader provides direction, encourages two-way communication, helps build confidence, and motivates the follower. The telling leadership style is used when clear and specific instructions are necessary (Hersey & Blanchard, 1982; Hersey, Blanchard, & Johnson, 2001).

Although many leadership theories include motivation of others as an objective, the stated purpose of path-goal leadership is to enhance performance and satisfaction by focusing on motivation as a primary ingredient of leadership. The underlying assumption of path-goal leadership theory is that followers will be motivated if they believe that they are capable of performing tasks assigned, that their efforts will result in a certain result, and that the rewards for completing the tasks are worthwhile. Through the application of path-goal theory, the leader's challenge is to select and implement a leadership style that best meets a follower's motivational needs.

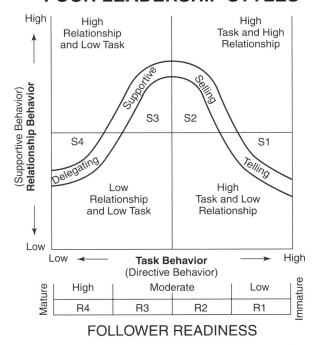

Figure 6–3   Hersey and Blanchard's Situational Leadership Model

Although complex, the application of the path-goal theory of leadership achieves follower motivation through careful consideration of leadership behaviors, follower characteristics, and task characteristics. The theory suggests that each type of leader behavior (directive, supportive, participative, or achievement oriented) has a different impact on the follower. Which leadership behavior is motivating is contingent on follower and task characteristics (Meese & Ortmeier, 2004; Northouse, 2001).

Performance Appraisal

A **performance appraisal** is a systematic assessment of how well an employee is performing. It is used to establish standards, appraise employee performance, make objective human resource decisions, and provide documentation to support those decisions (Robbins & Coulter, 2003). An objective, well-documented performance appraisal, one conducted according to legally permissible human resource policies and procedures, may be the best defense against litigation arising from claims of inappropriate discipline or wrongful termination.

The appraisal focuses on performance, not on the person, and on strengths as well as weaknesses. The appraisal process should be designed to enhance performance. The ideal appraisal process includes the supervisor's evaluation of the employee and a self-evaluation made by the employee. In addition, some formal appraisal processes include peer evaluations and evaluations of the employee by clients or consumers of the employee's services (Meese & Ortmeier 2004; Robbins & Coulter, 2003).

The appraisal meeting is one of the most important parts of the appraisal process. It is constructive, emphasizing strengths and pointing out areas for improvement, and is used as the means for achieving future goals. An appraisal meeting should be held in a trusting, private environment with adequate, uninterrupted time allotted for open, honest, and frank discussion. The content of the appraisal meeting is kept strictly confidential and shared with others on a need-to-know basis only, since the discussion may often include expressions of opinion and criticism.

Ultimately, good organizational reputation and successful achievement of an organization's goals are the result of excellent performance resulting from human effort. Regardless of the knowledge a supervisor possesses, operational success is measured through the line operator's performance. Thus, excellent performance by others is a primary goal of the supervisor (Sennewald, 2003). If an organization has a human performance problem, it probably has a supervision problem.

Promotion

Promotion serves as a means to fill job vacancies, as a reward and morale booster, and as an incentive for employees to perform better. Employees with the best records in production, quality of work, and cooperation should be the ones promoted. Due to financial constraints or the inability to measure perfor- mance objectively, salary increases or promotions may be difficult. Virtually all employees expect to be rewarded for a job well done. If promotion is difficult, even though a promotion is warranted, the progressive manager may choose to assist the employee with a transfer or new job search. If promotion from within is possible, it is accomplished through merit and ability to perform specific tasks. For those who are good candidates and seek promotion, the competition for promotion may be intense. Therefore, the promotion process should be fair, objective, and based on the candidate's ability to perform in the new position. A competitive process involves the use of standardized objective assessments of the candidate's qualifications and current performance as well as an evaluation of the candidate's strengths and weaknesses as predictions of future perfor- mance (Lewis, Goodman, & Fandt, 2001; Mosley, Megginson, & Pietri, 1993).

Failure to promote or reward employees appropriately can be extremely expensive. Arbitrary and discriminatory promotion practices can cost millions of dollars. On November 16, 2000, the Coca-Cola Company agreed to pay $156 mil- lion to settle a federal lawsuit brought by approximately 2,000 of its African- American employees. The largest dollar settlement ever in a racial discrimination lawsuit, the settlement also requires sweeping changes in, and outside monitor- ing of, Coca-Cola's promotion and compensation procedures. The changes are estimated to cost the company an additional $36 million. A $140 million cash settlement was agreed upon in a similar case involving Texaco and some of its employees in 1996 (Winter, 2000).

Discipline

The primary purpose of disciplinary action is to improve performance and be- havior rather than punish or seek revenge. The disciplinary process serves to ed- ucate the employee. Except in rare instances when immediate termination may be warranted by policy or law, a system of uniformly applied **progressive dis- cipline** should be used. Utilizing this system, corrective action progresses through the following steps: verbal warning, verbal warning noted in em- ployee's record, written reprimand, suspension, demotion or termination. The agency or business should also create a written policy that addresses uniform standards of behavior. The standards must focus on habitual tardiness and absen- teeism, actual or attempted theft of company/agency property, fighting or bod- ily injury to others, malicious mischief and harassment, intoxication on duty, possession of illegal drugs or alcohol on duty, refusal or failure to comply with supervisory instructions, inattention to duties (sleeping, idleness), violation of published safety or health rules, unauthorized possession of weapons or explo- sives, and sexual harassment.

Failure to discipline appropriately can have far-reaching negative conse- quences, especially when illegal activities are involved. Obviously, theft of an or- ganization's assets, liability associated with negligence, and settlements resulting from lawsuits exact a heavy toll from businesses and government operations. In some cases, losses result from extremely subtle activities. Even pilferage of employee's personal property, including lunch items from communal refrigerators in the workplace, impact negatively on employee morale. Low morale tends to reduce productivity, resulting in incalculable losses to an organization (Slater, 2000).

Discipline must be based on an objective standard. Several questions should be answered prior to any disciplinary action:

- Was the employee forewarned concerning consequences?
- Was the rule reasonable?
- Did the firm/agency verify the violation prior to disciplinary actions?
- Was the investigation thorough and fair?
- Is there substantial evidence of guilt?
- Were rules and penalties enforced uniformly?
- Was the disciplinary action appropriate to the situation?

If disciplinary action is warranted, employer reaction should be immediate, consistent, and fair. Disciplinary action is more likely to be viewed as fair if reasonable notice of rules of conduct is provided and employees are warned of the consequences for misbehavior. The employer representative should present the behavioral problem in specific terms by providing the date, time, and place of the incident as well as the organizational rule or policy violated. Due process requires that the employee be allowed to provide an explanation. Discussions should remain impersonal and agreement on the direction of behavioral change should be obtained (Robbins & Coulter, 2003).

Human Resource Policies and Procedures

Unique human resource situations arise that can be addressed with special policies and procedures. These situations involve problems associated with substance abuse, grievances, and claims of sexual harassment. All organizations should have written policies regarding substance abuse in the workplace. The policies must be communicated to each employee. Disciplinary procedures for policy violation must be consistent with applicable laws. Substance abuse issues are particularly sensitive, and related policies must be carefully crafted. Case law on the constitutionality of substance testing in the workplace generally is still inconclusive.

Clearly defined policies must also address employee grievances. Complaint procedures usually progress from informal to formal stages. In a nonunion organization, the procedure begins with the immediate supervisor and progresses through middle management to the chief executive officer and, possibly, an outside arbitrator. In a unionized organization, a similar process is followed in liaison with union representatives. The complaint or grievance is filed by the employee with the union steward and progresses through a union committee and the union president toward outside arbitration if warranted and necessary.

By definition, sexual harassment involves any unwelcome sexual advances, requests, conduct, or actions motivated by hostility directed toward the victim's gender. A growing number of court cases address the subject of sexual harassment. The cases and decisions generally hold that an employer is liable if sexual harassment is unreasonably condoned, improperly investigated, or left uncorrected. All organizations should have a clear, written policy on sexual harassment and should train employees adequately on the policy. For assistance with creating policies of this nature, an organization can consult the policy guidelines established and published by the U.S. Equal Employment Opportunity Commission (EEOC) in June 1999.

The policy against sexual harassment should state that the tenets apply at the worksite as well as elsewhere during any other business-related activity, such as a business trip or office party. The policy should expressly provide that there will be no reprisals against any complainant, outline complaint procedures, and require all employees to sign and date a form acknowledging receipt of the policy statement. The policy should be conspicuously posted in at least two locations at the worksite. As an added precaution and protection against claims of sexual harassment, supervisors should obtain permission from a superior or the human resources (personnel) department before any adverse employment action is taken against a subordinate (Bland, 2000).

Employer–Employee Relations Laws

A great deal of legislation governs the relationship between employers and employees. Most of the laws address prospective, current, and former employee civil rights. The following summarizes the principle legislation in this area.

- Social Security Act of 1935: This act established the social security system.
- Fair Labor Standards Act of 1938: This act established minimum wages to be paid to employees, the 40-hour workweek, and regulations regarding child labor.
- The Equal Pay Act of 1963: This law provides for equal pay for equal work for individuals of different gender working in the same job classification.
- Title VII of the Civil Rights Act of 1964 (amended in 1972): This law prohibits employers of 15 or more persons from discriminating against any individual on the basis of race, color, gender, religious preference, or national origin. None of these factors may be used in any decisions with respect to hiring, promotion, discharge, compensation, training, or any other term, condition, or privilege associated with employment. Responsibility for enforcement of the law rests with the EEOC. Many state and local governments have similar legislation that parallels the federal law.
- Executive Order 11246 of the Civil Rights Act: This presidential order amended and added the requirement of affirmative action to Title VII of the Civil Rights Act of 1964.

- Age Discrimination in Employment Act of 1967 (amended in 1986): This law prohibits employment discrimination against a person because the person is 40 or older.
- Occupational Safety and Health Act of 1970: This law provides that employers must do everything possible to protect human resources by furnishing employees with a work environment that is free of recognizable hazards likely to cause serious injury or death. The act is administered by the Occupational Safety and Health Administration (OSHA). The act applies to virtually all private employers. It does not apply to local, state, or federal employees or workers covered by some other health and safety law, such as the Federal Coal Mine Safety and Health Act or the Atomic Energy Act of 1954.
- Pregnancy Discrimination Act of 1978: This law prohibits employers from discriminating against pregnant women.
- Worker Adjustment and Retraining Notification (WARN) Act of 1988: This law requires employers to notify workers of impending layoffs.
- Drug-Free Workplace Act: Covered employers under this law must implement certain policies to restrict employee drug use.
- Americans with Disabilities Act of 1990 (amended in 1991): The ADA prohibits discrimination against a disabled person with respect to employment, public accommodations and services, and services provided by private organizations. An employer may not discriminate against a disabled person because of the disability. The ADA also prohibits testing for or inquiring about a medical or physical disability until a job is offered. Preemployment inquiries regarding substance abuse must be limited to recent and current use. The act prohibits any preemployment, promotion, or discharge test that is designed to disqualify persons with disabilities.
- The Employee Polygraph Protection Act of 1988: Subject to limited exceptions, this law prohibits or severely restricts the use of the polygraph or similar instruments by private employers. Under the act, private employers cannot use a polygraph for preemployment screening. The act further prohibits employers from requiring or requesting an employee to submit to a polygraph. A private employer cannot take any action against an employee for refusing to take a polygraph or for the results of such a test.
- Family and Medical Leave Act of 1993: This act provides that employers must allow unpaid leave for childbirth, adoption, or illness (Cheeseman, 2004; Lee, 2003; Lewis, Goodman, & Fandt, 2001; Mann & Roberts, 1997).

Employee Retention

Much has been written about employee recruitment, selection, training, supervision, and evaluation. Yet little attention is directed toward **employee retention**, an issue in times of cost containment and a critical necessity when the unemployment rate is low. During periods of cost containment, retrenchment, or downsizing due to the need to contain or reduce expenses, decisions must be made regarding which employees to retain. Thus, organizations should have written reduction in force (RIF) policies in place. Even more critical is the need to recruit and retain capable employees when the economy is doing well and labor is scarce.

A new employee's adjustment to an organization and its culture is often difficult and stressful for both the organization and the individual. Existing employees also encounter stressful situations and demands. As a benefit to the organization and employees, a strategy for retention as well as recruitment of qualified personnel is necessary. Every effort should be made to retain the most productive people since the costs associated with recruitment and training of new employees can be considerable.

Employee retention begins with policies and open lines of communication designed to ensure realistic expectations on the part of new and existing employees. Preemployment interviews might be structured so the employer representative speaks first, describing the negative as well as the positive aspects of employment with the organization. This procedure provides time for the candidate to relax during the initial phase of the interview and presents a preview of what the applicant can expect if offered a position. The job description and specifications, compensation and benefits plan, and minimum activity requirements should be discussed. Negative aspects may include extensive travel requirements, long work days, lack of support staff, and numerous time-sensitive projects. Honesty on the part of a candidate is expected. Employers should also be honest with job applicants. Lack of honesty and assurance of expectations at the beginning of an employee-employer relationship is a recipe for a costly disaster.

The next step in the employee retention process involves a proper orientation to the new employee's work environment. Prior to the new employee's start date, existing employees should be notified of the new person's impending arrival. Publication of a biographical statement and a photograph of the new employee is helpful. A staff member should be assigned as a peer guide, and the new employee should be introduced to other employees. Policies, procedures, work site arrangements, and physical layout of the facility should be explained thoroughly.

Next, training of the new employee is absolutely essential, especially where skills are deficient. Initial training involves an orientation to the organization, its products or services, culture, and expectations. Ongoing in-service training is necessary to reinforce perishable technical skills, develop new skills, and review policies. Advanced training involves job specialization and management training, as well as personal and professional career development.

Although the retention of good employees cannot be guaranteed, proper orientation and training can assist with retention. Employees who demonstrate the knowledge, ability, and skills necessary to do a job well are difficult and expensive to replace. Encouraging good employees to remain with an organization should be one of management's highest priorities (Robbins & Coulter, 2003; Smith, R.V., 2000).

PERSONNEL INTEGRITY

Maintenance of personnel integrity involves more than effective preemployment screening procedures, periodic performance appraisals, and internal security controls. Personnel integrity also involves promotion of and adherence to a **code of ethics** and appropriate standards of professional conduct.

Ethics involves moral principles and focuses on the concept of right and wrong and standards of behavior. Unlike law or organizational policy, which are formally prescribed and enforced by a controlling authority, ethics is based on moral standards, whether illegal or not. These moral standards, or ethical **values,** are formed through the influence of others. These standards are concerned with the relationships between people and how they exist in peace and harmony.

Values are fundamental beliefs upon which personal decisions and conduct are based. Societal values are based on the norms of the community. Organizational values represent the beliefs of an organization. Professional values are reflected by an occupation or discipline. Personal values are based on individual beliefs. Values may be ethical or unethical. Gang members have values, but their behavior may be unethical. Behavior may be unethical, yet not illegal. Therefore, ethics assumes a special meaning and involves the systematic reflection on, and analysis of, morality. It takes on a specific form when someone assumes the roll of a professional.

Ethical standards dictate behavior when law or precedent, which may prescribe behavior, do not exist. Whenever one possesses the power of discretional decision making, the decision should conform to what one ought to do even though law, policy, or precedent prescribing must-do behaviors is not available. The ends do not always justify the means. Conducting oneself according to an acceptable ethical standard, whether the profession has a code of ethics or not, means doing the right thing at the right time. Ethical conduct relates to qualities and actions that are morally correct, such as honesty and appropriate behavior. Unethical conduct refers to immoral behavior such as corrupt practices, dishonesty, and violation of acceptable standards.

In some cases, the law may permit or condone behavior that one might consider to be unethical. OSHA regulations, for example, establish minimum workplace health and safety standards. Yet, an employee's health and safety might be enhanced significantly if the employer sets standards that are higher than the OSHA-established minimums. Thus, the employer can adhere to the legal standard but it may be unethical to do so (Cheeseman, 2004).

Ethical behavior is based on virtues, values, morality, and appropriate choices. The premise of ethics is simple—people with high moral character make good moral choices (Johnson, 2001). A genuine moral dilemma occurs in a situation from which the decision maker cannot emerge innocent, no matter what the decision. To what extent does a morally good end justify the use of an unethical, even illegal, means to achieve this end? Can falsifying a report to achieve a good end (convicting a known internal thief) be justification for using unethical, and possibly illegal, means to achieve this end? Could inaction lead to a lawsuit by the victim of the dangerous person who was not apprehended because ethical means were not available? Hopefully, when confronted with these types of decisions, people will make the morally correct choices (Klockars, 1991).

The importance of choice in ethics is often confused with the notion that values are subjective and people merely choose their own set of values. This assumption is misleading because most ethical decisions involve a choice between already established possibilities. Personal values are rarely one's own values alone. By their very nature, values are shared and exist outside those who embrace the values. A person does not choose the alternative. Rather, the person chooses among alternatives (Solomon, 1996).

Most people live in a pluralist society, an environment with no single code of ethics but several sets of values emanating from a variety of cultures and subcultures (Solomon, 1996). Members of a criminal gang may subscribe to a particular set of values or code of ethics. They may not believe it unethical to kill a rival gang member. A security person may be reluctant to intervene to stop another's inappropriate behavior. Although it may be incorrect, this is the security person's choice. The individual challenge is to choose and follow an appropriate set of values.

Certain cognitive processes and socialization with others reinforces unethical conduct and influences the onset and proliferation of undesirable behavior. Thus, psychological and social forces help produce misconduct. However, one should not lose sight of the role of choice when engaged in unethical and unprofessional conduct. Given a security person's position of trust, unethical, even illegal, behavior results when the person makes a conscious decision to act in a way that is not appropriate to the situation. While circumstantial reasons, peer pressure, loyalties, social factors, or psychological problems may exist, the fundamental ingredient for unethical conduct is a conscious decision to abuse authority or engage in misconduct. Although the other factors may help perpetuate, justify, or excuse unethical conduct, it is an individual's conscious decision-making process that is ultimately determinative (Byers, 2000; Meese & Ortmeier, 2004).

Potential ethical problem areas in security management include corruption, discrimination, violation of rights to privacy, violation of rights under the Constitution, negligence, use of excessive force, uncivil conduct, violation of organizational policies or procedures, and violations of the professional code of ethics. Each of these areas should be addressed in recruitment and in-service training programs.

Although real or imagined unethical behavior may involve a very small number of individuals, the negative impact of this behavior can be devastating.

People engage in unethical conduct when they accept gratuities, practice racism and discrimination, misuse privileged communications and confidential information, misappropriate property, obstruct justice, engage in inappropriate behavior, and invoke a code of silence with respect to another person's unethical behavior (Foss, 2003; Meese & Ortmeier, 2004; Ortmeier, 2002).

Morally correct values are at the core of ethical behavior. Doing the right thing at the right time, delivering what is promised, taking responsibility for one's own actions, and treating others with courtesy and respect lie at the heart of ethical standards. Most institutions, agencies, and professions have a code of ethics that prescribes ethical conduct. As exemplified by the ASIS International Code of Ethics, standards of ethical behavior must emanate from the organization as well as the individual.

ASIS INTERNATIONAL CODE OF ETHICS

Preamble

Aware that the quality of professional security ultimately depends upon the willingness of practitioners to observe special standards of conduct and to manifest good faith in professional relationships, the American Society for Industrial Security adopted the following code of ethics and mandates its conscientious observance as a binding condition of membership in or affiliation with the Society:

Article I

A member shall perform professional duties in accordance with the law and the highest moral principles.

Ethical Considerations

I-1 A member shall abide by the law of the land in which the services are rendered and perform all duties in an honorable manner.

I-2 A member shall not knowingly become associated in responsibility for work with colleagues who do not conform to the law and these ethical standards.

I-3 A member shall be just and respect the rights of others in performing professional responsibilities.

Article II

A member shall observe the precepts of truthfulness, honesty, and integrity.

Ethical Considerations

II-1 A member shall disclose all relevant information to those having a right to know.

II–2 A right to know is a legally enforceable claim or demand by a person for disclosure of information by a member. Such a right does not depend upon prior knowledge by the person of the existence of the information to be disclosed.

II–3 A member shall not knowingly release misleading information nor encourage or otherwise participate in the release of such information.

Article III

A member shall be faithful and diligent in discharging professional responsibilities.

Ethical Considerations

III–1 A member is faithful when fair and steadfast in adherence to promises and commitments.

III–2 A member is diligent when employing best efforts in an assignment.

III–3 A member shall not act in matters involving conflicts of interest without appropriate disclosure and approval.

III–4 A member shall represent services or products fairly and truthfully.

Article IV

A member shall be competent in discharging professional responsibilities.

Ethical Considerations

IV–1 A member is competent who possesses and applies the skills and knowledge required for the task.

IV–2 A member shall not accept a task beyond the member's competence nor shall competence be claimed when not possessed.

Article V

A member shall safeguard confidential information and exercise due care to prevent its improper disclosure.

Ethical Considerations

V–1 Confidential information is non-public information, the disclosure of which is restricted.

V–2 Due care requires that the professional must not knowingly reveal confidential information or use a confidence to the disadvantage of the principal or to the advantage of the member or a third person unless the principal consents after full disclosure of all the facts. This confidentiality continues after the business relationship between the member and the principal has terminated.

V–3 A member who receives information and has not agreed to be bound by confidentiality is not bound from disclosing it. A member is not bound by confidential disclosures made of acts or omissions which constitute a violation of law.

V-4 Confidential disclosures made by a principal to a member are not recognized by law as privileged in a legal proceeding. The member may be required to testify in a legal proceeding to information received in confidence from the principal over the objection of the principal's counsel.

V-5 A member shall not disclose confidential information for personal gain without appropriate authorization.

Article VI

A member shall not maliciously injure the professional reputation or practice of colleagues, clients, or employers.

Ethical Considerations

VI-1 A member shall not comment falsely and with malice concerning a colleague's competence, performance, or professional capabilities.

VI-2 A member who knows, or has reasonable grounds to believe, that another member has failed to conform to the Society's Code of Ethics shall present such information to the Ethical Standards Committee in accordance with Article XIV of the Society's Bylaws (American Society for Industrial Security, 2000).

Additional information regarding codes of ethics can be obtained by contacting the University of British Columbia's W. Maurice Young Centre for Applied Ethics at www.ethics.ubc.ca/resources/business/codes.html.

SUMMARY

Personnel security involves the protection of, as well as protection from, individuals. Internally, personnel security begins with an effective recruitment, selection, and pre-employment screening strategy. Externally, it involves the use of physical security and other measures to prevent human threats against personnel and property from materializing. Employers may be held liable for negligent hiring and retention of employees. This means that employers must complete a diligent inquiry into the suitability of persons to be employed and take appropriate action in cases of employee misconduct.

Personnel management involves training, scheduling, and effective supervision of employees as well as the development of leadership competency among all employees. Performance appraisal, promotion, and discipline of employees should follow established procedures and be consistent with applicable laws and rules promulgated by regulator agencies. Human resource management policies and procedures should be clearly defined and describe how employees should behave and what conduct is prohibited. Employers must also be thoroughly knowledgeable regarding laws that affect the employer-employee relationship. The maintenance of personnel integrity is vital to short-term and strategic individual and organizational success. All employees should adhere to a code of ethics and standards of professional conduct, and appropriate values should be promoted. Ethical behavior must emanate from the organization as well as the individual employee.

KEY TERMS

application

career enhancement

code of ethics

employee retention

ethical standards

ethics

in-service training

integrity tests

leadership

negligent hiring

negligent retention

performance appraisal

personnel integrity

personnel security

preemployment screening

preservice training

progressive discipline

promotion

psychological tests

recruitment

resume

selection

sexual harassment

supervision

transactional leadership

transformational leadership

values

DISCUSSION QUESTIONS AND EXERCISES

1. Describe the role of personnel security in the protective function.
2. Outline and describe the process for recruitment and selection of personnel.
3. Numerous federal and state statutes regulate the employer–employee relationship. Most statutes are designed to establish and protect employee rights, promote safety and health, and prevent discrimination. What impact do these laws have on the ability to manage human resources? Are statutory protections a hindrance or do they assist with achievement of organizational goals?
4. Human resource management requires effective supervision as well as leadership development for all personnel. Explain. Include a description of the difference between supervision and leadership in the explanation.
5. Distinguish ethics from law and policy. What role does maintenance of personal integrity play in the personnel security arena?

Information Security

LEARNING OBJECTIVES

After completing this chapter, the reader should be able to

- define critical and proprietary information as well as intellectual property.
- identify threats to critical information.
- explain the purpose of information security management.
- assess vulnerabilities to critical information.
- evaluate information protection strategies.
- develop policies, procedures, and systems for information protection.
- distinguish between government and business information.
- define and explain the four subfields of communications security.
- discuss the need for computer security policies, procedures, and systems.

INTRODUCTION

Information is a valuable asset and the lifeblood of almost every enterprise. As a basis for political power and societal defense, information and its protection are vital to national security. Information also represents one of the most important vehicle for survival within a competitive global economy. As a business resource, information is used for internal operations and strategic planning. Additionally, information provides the knowledge base necessary to identify risks and protect people and property. Information is extremely perishable and often costly to produce and protect.

Information critical to individuals and organizations surfaces in many forms. As defined by the **U.S. Economic Security Act of 1996**, the federal law relating to the protection of U.S. economic interests, **critical information** includes

> all forms and types of financial, business, scientific, technical, economic, or engineering information, including data, plans, tools, mechanisms, compounds, formulas, designs, prototypes, processes, procedures, programs, codes, or commercial strategies, whether tangible or intangible, and however stored, compiled, or memorialized, if the owner has taken reasonable measures to keep such information confidential; and the information derives independent economic value, actual or potential, from not being generally known to, and not being readily ascertainable, acquired, or developed by legal means by the public (U.S. Economic Security Act of 1996).

Information may be defined and classified further in terms of its intended purpose and use. **Proprietary information** includes virtually any information belonging to an individual or organization. Proprietary information is identified through ownership or a possessory right. **Intellectual property** refers to information created through research and development, such as chemical formulas, software designs, and unique processes and procedures.

Threats to critical information are numerous and varied. They include threats from environmental and natural disasters, fire, accidents, and intentional as well as unintentional human actions. Information can be physically or electronically damaged, destroyed, or stolen. Authorized as well as unauthorized persons can manipulate data, deny access to authorized users, conduct economic and political espionage, and improperly destroy critical information. Bribery and extortion as well as physical and electronic eavesdropping undermine efforts to safeguard proprietary information and intellectual property. Employees, guests, vendors, foreign nationals, and computer **hackers** can sabotage databases. New vulnerabilities are created and discovered each day (American Society for Industrial Security, 1998; Boyce & Jennings, 2002; Hess & Wrobleski, 1996; Jones, 2000). No longer confined to hard copy recording and storage or oral exchanges, information can now be digitized through the use of computers and gathered, analyzed, stored, retrieved, intercepted, and manipulated electronically, without physical intrusion into the database. **Digitized information** is not distance-dependent or time-dependent. It can be transmitted around the globe in seconds. It can be transmitted or received without human presence; altered, destroyed or removed without leaving a physical evidence trace; and transported on pocket-sized computer disks.

Truly, the compromise of critical political and business information represents the greatest threat to governments and businesses today (Raum, 1999; "Seven major U.S. agencies get 'F' in computer security," 2000). Yet, complacency and carelessness on the part of many individuals and organizations often leads to the unauthorized disclosure of information. Those concerned about unauthorized intrusion often overlook risks that emanate from activities such as cellular phone use and commerce on the **Internet** (Jesdanun, 2000).

In medieval times, forces attacking a castle had to overcome numerous obstacles before penetrating defenses and reaching the inner sanctum in the heart of the castle. As technology developed, the means for penetration became more sophisticated, but the primary targets were still people and tangible assets. In the information age, however, the manipulation, theft, or compromise of personal, business, and government data represents the primary threat to individuals and organizations. Thus, in today's environment, the database, likened to the coveted heart of the medieval castle, is the inner sanctum that requires protection (Lodin, 1999).

INFOSEC RISK ASSESSMENT AND ANALYSIS

The purpose of **information security (INFOSEC)** is to protect information assets and systems against any internal or external threat that might endanger them. To accomplish information security goals, management utilizes **INFOSEC risk assessment and analysis** to determine the criticality of the information, its vulnerability, and the probability that a threat will materialize. Management must assess threats in terms of their seriousness, frequency, and immediacy. The cost of information replacement, waste, abuse, and liability associated with its unauthorized release must be evaluated. The cost effectiveness of the information safeguards recommended and implemented must also be determined.

Evaluating information assets and assessing the threats against them is not always an easy task. Such assets are often difficult to identify. In the early days of common law, information had no intrinsic value because it was not tangible. Today, the intangible asset identified as information does have value, but its worth can only be determined by calculating the political and financial impact of its loss. In addition, INFOSEC risk assessment and analysis is conducted within an environment full of uncertainty. Forecasts are often based on subjective evaluations as predictions of future events. There is no way to predict with any certainty how often an adverse event will occur or how severe the impact of the event will be.

In spite of the problems and challenges associated with INFOSEC risk assessment and analysis, the identification and safeguarding of critical information is imperative. Yet, the security manager is faced simultaneously with new threats, new technology, and new legislation. New information systems applications, software, and hardware are installed and implemented continuously. Changes in organizational structures and cultures also dictate the need for ongoing INFOSEC risk assessment and analysis. As the demand for enormous volumes of timely and accurate information increases, so do the responsibilities for threat identification and safeguards implementation (Boyce & Jennings, 2002; Carroll, 1996; Gersh, 2000).

INFORMATION PROTECTION STRATEGIES

Virtually every individual or group is aware of the need to identify and protect vital information. Although most make an effort to safeguard data and systems, some enterprises are more diligent in their efforts than others. National governments have traditionally engaged in the protection of state secrets. Private businesses, on the other hand, have been slow to develop comprehensive policies, procedures, and strategies for the protection of proprietary information and intellectual property. Because of false assumptions about the nature and possibility of potential threats, businesses lose billions of dollars annually to poor and inadequate data protection.

Discretionary and mandatory access control strategies govern approaches to information protection. Through **discretionary access control**, no one has an intrinsic right to view critical or sensitive information. Rather, access is allowed on a need-to-know basis. One is allowed to view only that which is vital to completion of assigned tasks. The problem with discretionary information access control is that the authorized user may inadvertently grant access to an unauthorized user. Discretionary access control is often used in private business enterprises.

Mandatory access control strategies can, on the other hand, trace their origins to restrictive legislation. The National Security Act of 1947, the Atomic Energy Act of 1954, and the National Security Decision Directive 145 of 1985 provide the foundation for mandatory access control policy. Two types of control structures, hierarchical and nonhierarchical, are established by the policy. The hierarchical structure includes four categories for classified information:

- Top Secret. Unauthorized disclosure of information in this category would cause *grave damage* to the United States.
- Secret. Unauthorized disclosure of information in this category could cause *damage* to the United States.
- Confidential. Unauthorized disclosure of information in this category would be *prejudicial to the interests* of the United States.
- For Official Use Only. Unclassified but sensitive. Unauthorized disclosure of this information would compromise trade secrets, give a contractor a competitive bidding advantage, or circumvent the Privacy Act of 1974.

Nonhierarchical INFOSEC falls within one of two categories: caveats and compartments. In government security operations, caveats refer to the nationality of the author or viewer of the classified information or object. Examples of caveats include NOFORN (no foreign access) and US/UK EYES ONLY (only United States and United Kingdom viewers allowed). Compartments refer to the subject matter of the information or object. Through background investigations, individuals are cleared to view material at different hierarchical levels based on a determination of the cleared person's reliability and loyalty to the government. The clearances correspond to the security categories assigned to the information or objects (Boyce & Jennings, 2002; Carroll, 1996).

A preoccupation with competition, maximizing net profit, increasing shareholder equity, or the process of juggling multiple tasks often relegate information protection to last place on most organizations' priority list. The prevailing attitude among many is that theft or inadvertent destruction of information cannot or will not happen to them. However, as has been demonstrated, substantial evidence suggests that lax INFOSEC can and does result in critical information loss. Consequently, many businesses, large and small, file for bankruptcy each year because they fail to anticipate the possibility of information loss and to implement adequate precautionary measures to protect this vital asset.

The business community might save itself considerable time, effort, and money by adopting information protection strategies that replicate those employed in government operations. Paralleling government efforts, **operations security (OPSEC)** involves information risk assessment and business intelligence activities in a process through which business operations are analyzed to identify potential intelligence indicators that competitors might scrutinize to gain a competitive advantage. OPSEC views operations from an adversary's perspective in an effort to seek out an organization's vulnerabilities and protect its critical information (OPSEC Professionals Society, 2000). This means that business people must think like criminals, anticipating the threat. Private businesses seeking government contracts for classified projects are often required to submit OPSEC plans along with their bids. Ingredients to the development and implementation of an OPSEC plan include

- an identification and valuation of the critical information.
- identification and analysis of a potential threat, including the threat's motivation and capabilities.
- an evaluation of the organization's information vulnerabilities.
- an assessment of the impact of a materialized threat as well as a cost-benefit analysis of any protective measure implemented.
- implementation of the most cost-effective protective measure options (countermeasures) (Jelen, 1994).

In 1988, President Ronald Reagan signed National Security Decision Directive 298, which established the National Operations Security Program. The program is used to identify, control, and protect unclassified information associated with U.S. national security programs and activities. If not protected, the information could be used by adversaries or competitors against the interests of the

United States. The directive names the Director of the National Security Agency (NSA) as the person in charge of interagency OPSEC training. The directive also includes a provision for the establishment and maintenance of the **Interagency OPSEC Support Staff (IOSS)**. The IOSS includes representatives from the NSA, FBI, CIA, U.S. Department of Energy, U.S. General Services Administration, U.S. Department of Defense, and other government organizations. The IOSS provides training to members of the security, intelligence, law enforcement, acquisitions, and research and development communities (Interagency OPSEC Support Staff, 2000).

Information security countermeasure expenditures are easily justified when the cost–benefit ratio is calculated. Utilizing the guidelines associated with determining vulnerability to loss, coupled with the criticality and probability of loss as outlined in Chapter 4, the potential negative economic impact of the loss can be affirmed. The return on investment (ROI) or value-added contribution (VAC) is determined by comparing the cost of the countermeasure against the financial damage that could result if an information loss occurred.

As previously mentioned, business information may be classified utilizing a system that replicates government security classification systems. According to Carroll (1996), it takes little thought to develop a protocol for classifying valuable business information that parallels a government system.

- *Company confidential, special control* is assigned to the business equivalent of top secret information. This classification is awarded to material with a loss value of 10 percent of the company's annual net profit.
- *Company confidential* information parallels government's secret classification. Compromise of company confidential information could result in a loss value of 1 percent of annual net profit.
- *Private confidential* information parallels government's confidential classification and refers to information that, if compromised, could embarrass an individual or damage the public reputation of the company.
- *Internal use only* (restricted) information refers to material that does not fit easily into one of the first three categories.

A distinction must be made between government and private business information. At the government level, unclassified information falls within the public domain and must be released, upon request, under the conditions set forth in the U.S. Freedom of Information Act. Private businesses, on the other hand, subject to certain exceptions, retain ownership of or a possessory right to information. Thus, private organizations are not required to release proprietary information to the public (Carroll, 1996).

Information protection goes beyond procedural controls involved in security classification systems. Complementary physical access controls, policies, personnel security, and computer logic protection are also necessary. Physical security, for example, is a basic first line defense requirement for any information protection program. Security personnel, employee and guest identification systems, surveillance and alarm systems, automatic door controls, fences, lighting, signage, and Crime Prevention through Environmental Design (CPTED) all contribute to the protection of information.

Policies lie at the foundation of any information protection program. They serve to guide and inform employees and outsiders on how the program works and to whom it applies. Policies address minimum information protection standards and set forth procedures to be followed as information technology advances. Authorization policies establish permission levels for access to information. Special audit assignments describe provisions for information protection oversight responsibilities. Legal protection policies remind staff of special agreements in place to maintain confidentiality and rights to privacy (American Society for Industrial Security, 1998). Policies should also address procedures for destroying or disposing of information that is no longer needed. Too often, critical information is discarded carelessly. In most jurisdictions, discarded materials placed in a trash can or dumpster are considered abandoned property, thus belonging to no one. An adversary may remove the discarded materials and use the information against its former owner. Shredding or pulping documents and appropriate deletion of information stored in an electronic medium helps to prevent adversarial access to information.

Unauthorized persons often view or have access to intellectual property, trade secrets, and sensitive information. Therefore, personnel security is also an integral part of the information protection program. Effective preemployment screening is a essential. Personnel integrity must be maintained, and minimum standards of professional conduct must be adhered to. Security managers, in conjunction with other personnel, can establish guidelines for classifying critical information. The guidelines should address the specific protection level associated with each classification and ensure that classification levels are conspicuously posted on critical material. Passwords, coding, and physically secured areas should be utilized along with a record of who possesses critical information and why. Such information is shared on a strict need-to-know basis.

Subject to certain exceptions discussed in Chapter 6, "Personnel Security," employees can be required to sign **information-protection-related agreements**. Nondisclosure agreements, usually directed toward individuals with authorized access to critical information, prohibit disclosure of the information to individuals or organizations not specified in the agreement. Secrecy agreements are used to prevent release of information by those who inadvertently come into contact with the information. Noncompete agreements are used to prevent an employee from leaving the company and obtaining employment with a competitor. Noncompete agreements have some legal limitations. The agreement cannot deny an individual the right to earn a living, even with a competitor. However, such agreements may be enforceable if the competitor is nearby or the former employee transfers company information to the new employer. Those who wish to create information-protection-related agreements are advised to consult with legal counsel regarding language appropriate for each agreement.

Other personnel-security-related information protection tools include the use of seals, audio visual equipment restrictions, and financial records controls. Tamper-evident seals and other indicative systems can be used as a deterrent and indicate when controlled access to information has been breached. The use of cameras and audio-video recording equipment on site can be restricted. Access to accounting, shipping, receiving, payroll, bank records, income, and similar financial information should be restricted to those who have an absolute need to view and use the information (Carroll, 1996).

Many types of proprietary information and intellectual property can be protected through the use of copyrights, patents, and trademarks. A **copyright** seeks to prevent unauthorized use of virtually any creative writing or expression that can be physically observed. Materials that may be copyrighted include items such as books, periodicals, lectures, videos, maps, musical compositions, drawings, and works of art. A copyright infringement occurs whenever one copies a substantial and important part of a copyrighted work without permission. However, under the fair use doctrine, the law does permit limited unauthorized use of copyrighted materials. Fair use applies to brief quotations of copyrighted material used in a news report, for review in a scholarly work, in a parody, or by a teacher or student to illustrate a lesson. For individuals, a copyright expires 70 years after the death of the creator. For business copyright registrants, a copyright expires 120 years from the date of creation or 95 years from the date of the first publication, whichever is shorter.

A **patent** protects a novel, useful, and nonobvious invention from unauthorized replication or use. The subject matter for patents includes processes, machines, compositions of matter, improvements to existing processes, machines, and compositions of matter, designs of articles for manufacture, living material invented by a person, and asexually reproduced plants. Patent infringement occurs when the replication or use of a patent is unauthorized. Under the public use doctrine, a patent may not be granted if an invention is used by the public more than one year prior to the patent's application filing (Cheeseman, 2004). Twenty-year terms are granted to patents on processes and manufactured articles. Design patents have a 14-year life term.

A **trademark** protects against unauthorized use of a distinctive mark, name, word, symbol, or device that identifies the product of a particular commercial enterprise. In addition, trade names (service marks) and quality certification marks can be protected by trademarks. The term for the original registration of a trademark is 10 years. Trademark registrations can be renewed for an unlimited number of 10-year terms. However, once a trademark becomes a common term (generic name) for a product or service, it loses its federal trademark law protection (Cheeseman, 2004).

Although an appropriate integration of physical and information security is necessary to protect sensitive and critical information, most organizations still separate physical and information security operations. However, as organizations pass through the twenty-first century, many realize that the principal asset in need of security is the organization's information. Thus, the role of organizational security may change to reflect the need to integrate all aspects of security into a comprehensive asset protection program. Physical, information, and computer (logical) access will be controlled by a single entity. One large company is leading the trend toward this type of integration. Microsoft Corporation of Redmond, Washington, combined its physical, information, and corporate security groups under the chief information security director (Gersh, 2000).

COMMUNICATIONS SECURITY

Communications security (COMSEC) includes all efforts to protect information transmitted by voice, electronic impulse, wire, microwave links, fiber optic lines, and satellite systems from unauthorized interception (Hess & Wrobleski, 1996). An interception can be accomplished by wiretapping, through interception of electrical impulses radiated (emanated) from computer equipment, and by concealing audio or visual transmitters on the victim's premises (bugging).

Communications security subfields include line, transmission, cryptographic, emanations, and technical security. Communications line security involves protection of telephone cables, junction boxes, switches, modulator-demodulator sets (modems), local area networks (LANs), and telephone space radio. **Line security** is effective only on lines within an individual's or organization's control. **Encryption** of communications through **cryptography** is the best method for defeating an assault by unauthorized communications line interception (wiretapping). Additionally, communications lines and equipment should be inaccessible or secured within locked or guarded perimeters. Tamper-resistant telephones and communications apparatus are also recommended.

Wiretaps are difficult to detect. Most make no noise, and they consume very little detectable energy. Especially vulnerable are **space radio communications**. These include cellular phones, marine and mobile radio telephones, microwave radio relays, satellite radio, and high-frequency radio used in remote locations of the world. Although interception of microwave and satellite signals typically requires special equipment, cellular phone and radio telephone communications can be monitored with devices purchased at a local retail electronics store. Therefore, line transmissions and telephones should not be used for communicating extremely sensitive information. Meeting in person may be the best alternative.

Transmission security involves policies and procedures that place an adversarial interceptor at a disadvantage. Authentication of the parties to the transmission, communications logs, speech privacy equipment (scramblers), and access control are primary communications transmission protection mechanisms. No telephone number that provides direct access to a computer should ever by published. Computer hackers can capture telephone numbers from computers with dial-up service.

Cryptography is the science of secret writing, and **cryptographic security** involves a transformation (secret writing) of the data being transmitted to render it unintelligible to an unauthorized interceptor. Cryptography involves the use of nonexclusive codes and **ciphers**. A code can represent a complete message, such as the Associated Public-Safety Communications Officers (APCO) 10-code system used by most police and security dispatchers (Adams, 2001). A cipher is the one-to-one correspondence between the characters in the actual message (plain text) with the characters or symbols in the secret writing equivalent (crypto text). Converting plain text to crypto text is referred to as an **encryption**, while conversion of crypto text to plain text is referred to as a **decryption**. If the same character or symbol key is used for encryption and decryption, the cipher is symmetric. If different keys are used, the cipher is asymmetric. The only unbreakable cipher is a randomly produced cipher that is used only once. With time and perseverance, virtually any multiple-use cipher can be compromised (broken) by a knowledgeable and determined person.

A detailed explanation of cryptography and cryptographic security is beyond the scope of this book. The foregoing simply provides a brief explanation of the science and uses of secret writing. No security system, policy, or procedure is absolute. Cryptopgraphic security is no exception. It must not be viewed as a substitute for other information protection procedures or good physical or personnel security. When part of the overall security package, cryptography can be an asset protection tool, but only when it is used infrequently and reserved for the most sensitive information. When purchasing crypto devices and software, the manager must realize that someone, at least the manufacturer, has a key to the cipher.

Cryptography is one of the most secure methods of preventing unauthorized interception of data communications. Therefore, the hostile attacker must resort to acquiring the data before it is encrypted. Since traditional methods, such as wiretapping, require some physical intrusion, the attacker can resort to interception of emanations (emissions) from electronic equipment. Acoustical (sound) and electromagnetic (electrical and mechanical parts interplay) emanations from equipment can be captured by the directional pickup devices available today. Utilizing **emanations security** to prevent compromise of information through the capture of acoustical emanations, rooms that contain computer and other radiating electronic communications equipment can be constructed with sound deadening materials such as acoustical tiles. Emanations security can also be enhanced if one uses nonradiating electronic equipment or equipment designed to shield radiating electronic equipment from outside emanations interception.

Technical security in communications involves prevention of adverse technical surveillance through the use of intrusion devices. Technical surveillance devices include microphones and wires as well as mechanical instruments used to listen through a heating duct or conduit. Carrier current devices, which capture voice communications by utilizing a facility's internal electric wiring system, visual-optical (CCTV) devices, and telephone bugging instruments are also used. Communications security defenses against technical surveillance include physical inspection (search) for devices, electrical wiring and equipment inspections, metal and harmonic detectors for electronic bugs, and instruments that detect electronic emanations from bugging devices (Carroll, 1996).

COMPUTER SECURITY

Since the early 1970s, computer technology has dramatically changed the way information is acquired, transmitted, analyzed, stored, and retrieved. It has changed the work world and is part of almost everyone's daily life. Computerized cash registers exist at most retail checkout counters. Onboard computers are used to detect problems in late-model vehicles. Sophisticated systems manipulate national defense information and manage global financial transactions.

Along with the increased use of computers has come a commensurate increase in computer-related crime. No longer limited to interference by a few high-tech hackers (unauthorized computer database intruders), numerous forms of computer-related crime are now common. **Computer crime** is limited only by the ingenuity of the criminal and the offender's knowledge of computer technology. With computers, funds can be stolen from financial institutions without physical intrusion. Business trade secrets and classified government information can be obtained without physically penetrating a business or country. Personal information stored in electronic databases can be manipulated, destroyed, or used for unethical or illegal purposes.

Computer crime is defined generally as any crime committed with computer technology. It may involve the actual destruction of computer hardware and software, or it may be used as a tool in a criminal enterprise. More commonly, it involves unauthorized access (or exceeding authorization) to the computer's database. Computers have been used to steal patient records ("Hacker steals patient records," 2000), credit card and bank account numbers, and to commit fraud, theft, burglary, embezzlement, espionage, sabotage, and even murder. Computers are also used in support of criminal enterprises associated with child pornography, prostitution, gambling, illegal drugs, money laundering, and organized crime. Misuse of computers in the workplace, such as computer game-playing and personal communications, divert and consume employee production time.

Internet access increases risk and threats to sensitive and proprietary information (Boni & Kovacich, 2000). As the Internet becomes the primary electronic vehicle for transmitting information throughout the world, thousands more new users log onto the World Wide Web each day. With the vast amount of information in transit and little thought given to its security, the opportunities for data theft and destruction increase. Studies indicate that over 40 percent of computer software and equipment are prone to a computer virus (disruptive software infections). Twenty-two percent contain passwords that can be breached by a computer hacker in less than seven minutes (Adams, 2000b). To gain access to computer databases, the hacker or cybercriminal searches for the path of least resistance, exploiting security-related weaknesses that provide unimpeded access to targeted networks (Lam, Beekey, & Cayo, 2003).

Currently, the total indirect and direct costs associated with computer crime may approach hundreds of billions of dollars annually. Losses can be devastating and the threat often originates with unknown sources. On March 2, 1998, the night before Microsoft Chairman Bill Gates was scheduled to testify at a Congressional committee hearing, a computer hacker launched a massive attack against computers using Microsoft network software. The hacker targeted computers in government and universities running Windows NT software (Bigelow, 1998). On May 19, 1998, a group of seven hackers testified before a U.S. Senate Government Affairs Committee that they could destroy the foundation of the Internet within 30 minutes by interfering with the links between long distance carriers. According to the hackers, poor computer security can be blamed on the multitude of Internet networks, inadequate security measures in software programs, and lack of government regulation (Bigelow, 1998). According to the Congressional General Accounting Office, U.S. State Department computers, the Federal Reserve System, individual credit and medical records, utilities, and stock exchanges are also at risk.

The personal computer, now found in most businesses and many homes, linked through cyberspace by the Internet, eliminates the need for an actual physical intrusion into a business, government agency, or personal residence. Advances in technology have created a virtual world with no physical boundaries or barriers. Virtual organizations, that exist mostly in cyberspace, have been created. These organizations exist but are not represented in a physical form. This phenomenon presents new challenges for the security manager.

Although the average individual personal computer user has little to worry about, hackers pose one of the greatest threats to computer systems. Kevin Mitnick, named to the FBI's most-wanted list, was captured in 1995 in Raleigh, North Carolina, after a nationwide hunt aided by Tsutomu Shimomura, a researcher at the University of California–San Diego (UCSD), Supercomputer Center. The Mitnick case highlighted the damage a single hacker can cause. Mitnick stole computer passwords, damaged UCSD and University of Southern California computers, allegedly pilfered software and product plans valued in the millions of dollars from high-tech companies, and installed programs that caused severe damage (Krasnowski, 1997). Other than UCSD, some of Mitnick's victims included Motorola, Novell, Nokia, and Sun Microsystems. Although it was never proven, Mitnick was alleged to have penetrated the computer system at the North American Air Defense Command. At sentencing, Mitnick was ordered to pay $4,125 to the companies that suffered millions of dollars in damages and ordered to serve 3 years 10 months in prison. With credit for time served awaiting trial, Mitnick was released from prison on January 21, 2000, under the condition that he not use computers, software, cell phones, televisions, modems, or other computer system or Internet-accessible equipment for a period of 3 years.

The Mitnick case is not an isolated incident. On March 29, 1996, federal authorities identified Julio Cesar Ardita, a 21-year-old Buenos Aires, Argentina, student, as the person who tapped into sensitive research on satellites and penetrated computer systems in at least six countries. Ardita gained access to U.S. government computers, including the U.S. Navy's system, and to numerous university computer laboratories. On August 13, 1996, a computer hacker vandalized the U.S. Justice Department's Internet home page. The hacker posted obscenities and antigovernment graffiti on the Department's Web site. In August 1998, a security risk was discovered in Qualcomm's popular Eudora electronic mail software. By exploiting a flaw in the software, a hacker disguised a program to look like a harmless address on the Internet. Computer users who clicked on the address would inadvertently allow hackers access to the innocent user's own computer.

On August 30, 1999, a hacker gained access to millions of email messages by exploiting a flaw in the software program used by Microsoft to run its free Hotmail Web service for 40 million people worldwide. The hacker revealed how access was gained and forced Microsoft to shut the service down to make necessary repairs. In October 1999, computer security experts discovered an electronic reconnaissance program designed to infect Windows-based personal computers without the user's knowledge and to transmit the captured data to a Russian Web site.

In February 2000, electronic vandals crippled some of the world's most popular Internet sites by using dozens of powerful computers to flood the sites with false data. The hackers created the virtual traffic jams by penetrating less secure computer workstations and servers with high-speed Internet connections and installing stealth programs on the hijacked computers. Next, the hackers activated the programs, flooding target sites with bogus requests, thus jamming the target sites. Buy.com, Yahoo!, eBay, ETrade.com, Amazon.com, and the Cable News Network (CNN) fell under the attack before computer security technicians were able to shield the computers from assault. Before service was restored, the companies lost sales to millions of customers. The attacks on the Web sites also caused stock prices to drop on some of the high-technology companies.

In March 2000, Max Butler, a computer expert working as an informant for the FBI, faced charges himself for allegedly hacking into U.S. Department of Defense, U.S. Air Force, NASA, and other sensitive computer databases. In May 2000, Canadian police arrested a 15-year-old Montreal-area hacker for disabling CNN's Web site on February 8, 2000 (Koerner, 2000). The boy subsequently pleaded guilty to 56 computer crime-related charges. From his bedroom overlooking a golf course, the boy penetrated numerous Web sites, including those of Yahoo.com, Amazon.com, and eBay.com, causing an estimated $1.7 billion in damages (Brooke, 2001).

In May 2000, **software viruses** swamped computer networks around the world. The viruses were spread through Microsoft Outlook email applications. The virus arrived disguised as a "joke" or "I LOVE YOU" email with an attached file. When the unsuspecting user opened the attachment, the virus emailed itself to everyone on the computer's address book and attacked music, graphics, and other files on the computer's hard drive. The virus hit over 82 million computers and infected 2.6 million email sites, causing an estimated $6.7 billion in damage (Markoff, 2000).

On September 21, 2000, a 20-year-old Mission Viejo, California, man was arrested by U.S. authorities for allegedly hacking into computers operated by the National Aeronautics and Space Administration's Jet Propulsion Laboratory in Pasadena, California, as well as computer systems in such prestigious universities as Harvard, Stanford, and Cornell. The man also allegedly penetrated hundreds of other computers throughout the United States and, in some cases, used stolen credit card numbers to purchase thousands of dollars worth of merchandise (Lota, 2000).

On October 25, 2000, Microsoft security personnel discovered a computer system penetration that allowed access to source codes (software blueprints) under development. No software was compromised in this case. With source codes in their possession, however, competitors could write programs to challenge Microsoft products. The codes can also be used to identify software flaws, making database break-ins and virus infection easier (Johnson, 2000). In 2001, antiglobalization computer hackers penetrated the computer systems of the World Economic Forum in Davos, Switzerland. More than 3,000 of the world's top executives, bankers, politicians, scholars, and journalists were in attendance. The hackers obtained the names, email addresses, and phone numbers of 27,000 people along with 1,400 credit card numbers and 3,200 passwords (Giussani, 2001). At the height of the energy crisis in the spring of 2001, a key computer system used to monitor electricity transmission throughout the state of California was targeted by hackers. Although the hackers experienced limited success, the incident exposed security weaknesses within the system ("Hackers target state's electricity," 2001).

Utilizing an email wiretap, individuals and organizations can surreptitiously obtain business intelligence and proprietary information from another group. For example, if company A wants to acquire company B, company A can email a purchase proposal to company B. Included in the email is an invisible computer code designed to forward internal company B email to company A. As the target company's employees communicate with each other regarding the proposal, a copy of each email is sent to company A. According to one expert, such email wiretaps may become more common than computer viruses (Hopper, 2001).

According to FBI statistics, the number of reported Internet fraud cases tripled during 2002. Nearly 50,000 Internet fraud complaints were referred to prosecutors. The most common complaint involved online auction fraud, followed by nondelivery of merchandise, credit card fraud, fictitious investment schemes, and Internet identify theft. The FBI's Internet Fraud Complaint Center, operated in cooperation with the National White Collar Crime Center, also received nearly 40,000 nonfraud complaints involving unsolicited email, child pornography, and computer intrusions (Anderson, 2003).

Such disruptions illustrate how vulnerable computer systems are and how reliance on technology can be devastating. As individuals and organizations are enticed to place their personal, financial, political, planning, and medical information online and into computer databases, consideration must be given to the security of the systems and the data they contain. Unauthorized computer system intruders can easily falsify their digital fingerprints, thus making offenders difficult to trace and locate. In addition, the high-tech workplace itself is often an antisecurity environment. In an effort to promote ingenuity, industriousness, wealth, and a casual no-holds-barred workplace culture, many organizations are lax on computer security procedures development and enforcement. Even when computer security is a priority, experts trained to protect systems and software are unavailable (McCollum, 2000).

The security of computer databases is probably one of the greatest challenges facing business and government in the twenty-first century. During testimony before the U.S. Congress in 1997, FBI Director Louis Freeh intimated that the greatest threat facing U.S. national security was economic crime, most of which could occur through the illegal use of computer technology. In a government computer security audit conducted in 2000, one-fourth of the U.S. government's 24 major agency computer systems failed the review. The U.S. Departments of Justice, Interior, Labor, and Health and Human Services were among the agencies cited for poor computer security. In one agency, all 1,100 computer users had access to sensitive information, while in another agency, 20,000 users without written authorization had access to one system ("Seven major U.S. agencies get 'F' in computer security," 2000).

Threats against government agencies and personnel do not always originate from likely sources. On December 4, 2000, threatening email was sent to President Clinton via the Internet from a small town of about 4,000 in Nebraska. The email originated in the community's only parochial high school. A student was using one of the school's computers—against school policy—to check messages on his private email account. The student left the computer unattended for a few moments. In his absence, two other boys used the student's email account to send the threatening message to the White House. The Secret Service traced the email to the school's computer and the innocent student's email account. No charges were filed. However, the case demonstrates the seriousness and far-reaching implications of seemingly minor pranks. The expense associated with the U.S. Secret Service investigation and the harm caused by lax security measures on the innocent student's part illustrate the impact of poor computer security ("Threatening email traced to computer at CC," 2000).

Security for computer systems must include strategies to protect the equipment, software, and information stored in the database. Physical security is used to prevent fire or access to computer terminals. Administrative controls can be implemented to maintain accountability for those who have legitimate access to the system and database. Logical controls may be used to restrict access to information stored in the database. Passwords and data encryption are examples of logical controls. **Firewalls**, the electronic security tools that screen traffic before allowing access to computer networks, can be used to restrict access to databases (Boyce & Jennings, 2002; Hutchinson & Warren, 2001; Lodin, 1999). Intrusion by **computer viruses** and **malware** (malicious software) can be prevented through the use of antivirus and malware-unfriendly software (Harley, 2000). Backup duplicate files should be maintained to prevent total loss of data due to criminal activity, accident, or natural disaster. Internet privacy can be protected through appropriate technological advances, self-regulation by e-commerce organizations, and government regulation. Carroll (1996) suggests 10 principles for safeguarding sensitive computer information:

1. The simple security principle. No person shall view information that has a classification that exceeds the person's security clearance.
2. The nonaccessibility principle. No sensitive information will be released to any person or object except according to established procedures.
3. The lattice principle. The classification of an information item or clearance of a person or process shall consist of its (their) hierarchical classification or clearance plus the sum of all compartment classifications or clearances.
4. The star (*) principle. No person shall write or submit classified information to another person or object whose classification is lower than the subject classified information.
5. The first integrity principle. No computer program will accept information from a less privileged (lower level) computer program.
6. The second integrity principle. No computer program shall write into a higher privileged program.
7. The labeling principle. All classified information items are clearly labeled with their classification in human-readable and machine-readable formats.
8. The tranquility principle. The security classification of information can be changed only according to established procedures.
9. The audit ability principle. All relevant security-related actions performed on sensitive information items will be recorded in an indelible record.
10. The trusted software principle. Trusted software will be permitted to violate principles if necessary.

Identification of vulnerabilities and investigation of computer crime are often difficult because traditional criminal identification and investigative methods are inappropriate. Most law enforcement agency expertise focuses on street crime, not computer crime. Cyperspace and computer security and investigations require different skills. The computer nerds of today will be the sophisticated information technology hackers of tomorrow. However, resources are available to security professionals and computer systems administrators.

Some of these resources include the Computer Emergency Response Team (CERT), Systems Administration, Networking, and Security (SCANS) and its Global Incident Analysis Center, and the FBI's National Infrastructure Protection Center (NIPC) (Sniffen, 2001). Organizations and businesses may report Internet-related crime to their local law enforcement authority or the federal investigative authority responsible for enforcement of Internet-crime-related statutes. The types of cyber crimes that can trigger involvement of federal agencies include the following:

- Computer intrusion (i.e., hacking) and password trafficking—FBI, NIPC, or Secret Service
- Theft of trade secrets or Internet harassment—FBI
- Counterfeiting—U.S. Secret Service
- Child pornography, trademark or copyright infringement—FBI or U.S. Customs Service, if imported
- Internet fraud—FBI, Federal Trade Commission, or Securities and Exchange Commission, if securities fraud
- Internet bomb threats or illegal trafficking of explosives or firearms—FBI or Bureau of Alcohol, Tobacco, and Firearms (ATF) ("How to report Internet crimes," 2000)

The FBI has established regional computer crime laboratories to retrieve computer data that can be used as evidence (Hughes, 2000). In 2002, President Bush signed the Cyber Security Research and Development Act into law. The legislation dedicated more than $900 million over 5 years to research and education programs designed to help secure the nation's technology infrastructure against terrorists and computer hackers ("Bush signs Cyber Security Act," 2002). In addition, information is available on several computer-security news Web sites, including Security Watch, Packet-Storm, and Security-Focus. Purdue University maintains the computer-security-research–oriented CERIAS Web site. Princeton University's Secure Internet Programming Laboratory and the University of California, Davis' Computer Security Laboratory are also valuable resources (Neeley, 2000).

Computer security information sources:

The Federal Computer Incident Response Center (Fed CIRC) at www.fedcirc.gov
The National Infrastructure Protection Center at www.nipc.gov
The National White Collar Crime Center at www.cybercrime.org

The training and education of cybersecurity professionals is also an essential element in protecting computer and information systems. To this end, the National Science Foundation (NSF), in collaboration with the American Association of Community Colleges (AACC), developed a plan to establish cybersecurity-workforce foundation-skill standards, certification assessments, and cybersecurity training programs. The plan proposes to establish and maintain comprehensive cybersecurity education programs as well as continue professional training for cybersecurity personnel (American Association of Community Colleges, 2002).

SUMMARY

Critical information includes all forms and types of tangible and intangible information. The protection of critical information is vital to organizations, nations, and individuals. Threats to critical information include environmental and natural disasters, fire, accidents, and intentional and unintentional human actions. The purpose of INFOSEC is to protect information assets and systems. Through assessment and analysis techniques developed through OPSEC and COMSEC, threats to information can be evaluated and strategies implemented to protect critical information. Effective information security policies and procedures lay the foundation for information protection.

The introduction of computers dramatically altered the manner through which information is collected, transmitted, analyzed, stored, and retrieved. Crimes committed with computers is increasing for many reasons, not the least of which is that physical contact with a victim or actual intrusion into a protected area are not necessary. Protection of computer systems and databases includes the use of physical security as well as administrative and logical controls. Computer security breaches require nontraditional investigative skills.

KEY TERMS

cipher

communications security (COMSEC)

computer crime

computer virus

copyright

critical information

cryptographic security

cryptography

decryption

digitized information

discretionary access control

emanations security

encryption

firewall

hacker

information

information-protection-related agreements

information security (INFOSEC)

INFOSEC risk assessment and analysis

intellectual property

Interagency OPSEC Support Staff (IOSS)

Internet

line security

malware

mandatory access control

operations security (OPSEC)

patent

proprietary information

software virus

space radio communications

technical security

trademark

transmission security

U.S. Economic Security Act of 1996

DISCUSSION QUESTIONS AND EXERCISES

1. What is the purpose of information security (INFOSEC)?

2. Define and contrast critical information, proprietary information, and intellectual property.

3. Identify three threats to critical information and describe strategies to protect the information. What role does risk assessment play in the information protection function?

4. How should information protection strategies be evaluated?

5. What is communications security (COMSEC)? Describe the four COMSEC subfields. How does COMSEC differ from other protection strategies?

6. What should be included in an operations security (OPSEC) plan?

7. Outline and describe the strategies for protecting computer systems and databases.

8. Discuss methods for protecting *personal* information, including data that may be stored in one's personal computer.

9. Traditional criminal identification and investigation methods are inappropriate for computer-related crime. Explain.

CHAPTER 8

Investigations, Intelligence Operations, and Reporting

LEARNING OBJECTIVES

After completing this chapter, the reader should be able to

- list and describe the common elements of the investigative process.
- discuss the types of human resource investigations.
- describe elements of personal injury and property damage investigations.
- outline the procedure for collection and preservation of evidence.
- analyze evidence gathered in a civil or criminal investigation.
- describe situations in which surveillance and undercover assignments are warranted.
- identify business crime activity.
- describe business crime prevention techniques.
- locate and develop sources of information.
- discuss procedures for information gathering and analysis.
- evaluate information gathered from public and private sources.
- identify impermissible investigative conduct.
- describe industrial espionage techniques.
- compare and contrast business intelligence with counterespionage.
- outline procedures for documentation.

INTRODUCTION

Central to the tasks and functions of loss prevention, asset protection, and the security management process is the need to gather information and accurately document and report findings of fact. Thus, investigations, intelligence operations, and reporting are critical. An investigation should be conducted any time a loss occurs or a threat materializes. Intelligence is gathered to maintain a competitive edge and identify potential criminal activity. The results of an investigation or intelligence operation must be reported in a fashion that enhances organizational decision-making capabilities.

INVESTIGATIONS

The Basics

An **investigation** is a systematic process through which information is gathered, analyzed, and reported. An investigation facilitates decision making (American Society for Industrial Security, 1998). An investigation involves an investigator who conducts an inquiry for a particular purpose (Walsh & Healy, 1987). It is a systematic inquiry into the facts surrounding an event, condition, or situation (Ortmeier, 2002).

An investigation is warranted when an accident occurs, when unexplainable property losses are discovered, or when personal misconduct or criminal activity is observed or reported. In addition, an investigation is a necessary ingredient in the process of gathering information on prospective employees and business partners. Background investigations are integral to business and criminal intelligence operations. Through a systematic inquiry, the investigator collects information, identifies and analyzes problems, determines facts, preserves evidence, and reports findings in an objective manner. Subsequent to an incident, the investigator must determine who was involved and what, when, where, how, and why the incident occurred. As a preventive tool, the investigator can use the systematic inquiry to identify potential problem individuals, predict behavior, and forecast events.

The investigative process is an art as well as a science. Through training, education, experience, and intuitive judgment, a good investigator re-creates events and facilitates decision making. Utilizing the personal qualities of honesty and open-mindedness in collaboration with excellent human relations, communications, and critical thinking skills, a good investigator adds value to organizational outcomes (O'Hara & O'Hara, 2003).

Types of Investigations

Several types of investigations are conducted in a security and protective services environment. These investigations focus on noncriminal and criminal events as well as predictions of future behavior and activity. They may be conducted to ensure compliance with safety laws and regulations, support litigation activities, assess protective system vulnerabilities, follow up on consumer complaints, prevent accidents, trace and locate a criminal suspect, or identify the source of any unexplained loss. In a business environment, an investigation can focus on customer service, finance, purchasing, sales and marketing operations, human resources, or information systems protection, or it may be conducted in support of litigation activities (American Society of Industrial Security, 1998).

Human Resource Investigations In the personnel arena, typical **human resource investigations** include those related to employee backgrounds, workplace violence, employment discrimination, worker compensation claims, substance abuse, and wrongful termination. Background investigations on prospective employees should be part of the pre-employment screening process. As a due diligence requirement, an organization should verify information contained in a candidate's employment application. Failure to exercise due diligence could result in the development of a liability connection between the new employee and the organization. Criminal, credit, previous employment, academic, and other background history information must be authenticated. Untruthful statements and deception practices by the applicant provide clues to the job candidate's integrity, ethics, and propensity toward improper, even criminal, behavior. In some instances, it is also appropriate to update background information on those seeking promotion within the organization. Additional information regarding background investigations for employees is presented in Chapter 6.

Employers are required by law to investigate claims of sexual harassment and unlawful employment discrimination. Failure to conduct a thorough investigation and take prompt corrective action in a case of sexual harassment can have severe consequences. Inaction and inappropriate action on the part of employers have led to multimillion dollar civil judgments for plaintiffs in sexual harassment lawsuits. Likewise, employers must investigate, and have been held civilly liable for, claims of unlawful employment discrimination. Such claims are based on alleged discriminatory practices in selection, promotion, retention, and working conditions of employees. Discrimination against a person because of age, gender, race, ethnicity, lifestyle, or disability is prohibited by law.

Employers must investigate threats of harm against employees as well as claims of unsafe working conditions. Employers have been held liable for injuries or deaths resulting from workplace violence and failure to correct safety hazards. Liability may attach if the employer is aware, or should know, that employees are in danger because of the possibility of violent acts perpetrated by other employees, outsiders, or as a result of hazardous working conditions.

In the area of worker's compensation, the need for an investigation arises from two types of situations. The first involves injuries to employees that have arisen out of employment (AOE). Typical AOE injuries are those that develop over an extended period of time, such as stress or lung disease. The other type of injury that may give rise to a worker's compensation claim and investigation is an injury that occurs during the course of employment (COE). A COE injury is attributed to a single act or event, such as an accident or fall.

Individuals under the influence of alcohol, drugs, or other substances are less productive, experience poor attendance, create hazardous situations, and do poor quality work. Those who abuse substances in the workplace are high risk and may have a propensity toward theft, injuries, and property damage. A key to dealing effectively with substance abuse in the workplace is the ability to recognize the symptoms of abuse and take corrective action through counseling and appropriate discipline. However, the symptoms of chemical abuse are often subtle, and direct confrontation of the abuses can subject the employer to legal challenges. Often, the best evidence is produced through an undercover investigation or **surveillance** activity.

Investigations relating to claims of wrongful termination result from allegations of discriminatory action on the part of an employer or from a discharge arising out of a false accusation of dishonesty or substance abuse in the workplace. In the event of a lawsuit, the plaintiff will often claim that the employer's investigation of the allegation was inadequate or improperly conducted. As a defense, the employer must present proof of a proper investigation into the allegations, with sufficient cause for the termination, meticulous documentation of the history of the employee's wrongdoing, coupled with the warnings given and reasonable actions taken by the employer.

A timely human resource investigation, coupled with the action warranted, can reduce organizational liability for the inappropriate actions of an employee. In this regard, the education of, and support from, senior management is critical to success. Security managers must strive to educate senior management regarding the human resource policies, procedures, investigations, and corrective actions necessary to mitigate liability. In addition, new employees as well as existing employees should be informed and reminded of behaviors that may trigger a human resource investigation.

Finally, information or evidence discovered during the course of a human resource investigation should be disclosed according to applicable laws and organizational policy. Unless legally required to disclose the information to an external agency, sound management practice may indicate that internal distribution, on a need-to-know basis, is preferable to any form of public disclosure.

Personal Injury and Property Damage Investigations   Personal injury and property damage can result from an unintentional accident, a collision, or through the intentional act (or omission to act) of another human being. Personal injury involves physical harm to an individual. Property damage involves harm to or destruction of property. An investigation must be conducted if personal injury is involved. Injury or damage scenes should be approached with caution if hazardous materials are present, electric power lines are exposed, or natural gas lines are broken. After all injured parties at the scene have received necessary emergency medical treatment, the investigation of the incident may proceed. Witnesses should be interviewed separately to avoid cross-contamination of statements. The person conducting the interviews should avoid leading questions that imply an answer. Rather, witnesses should be asked what they observed and responses should be recorded verbatim if possible.

When interviews are complete, the investigator will examine the scene, record measurements, photograph the area, if appropriate, and prepare follow-up written reports on the incident. In some cases, it may be necessary to reconstruct the event to determine the exact cause of the injury or damage. Ultimately, the goal of any personal **injury investigation** or **property damage investigation** is to prevent similar occurrences in the future. Information collected during the course of the investigation can be used to improve procedures and protective systems (Ortmeier, 1999).

Criminal Investigations The purposes of a **criminal investigation** are to determine if a crime was committed, identify and locate the suspect, and recognize, collect, and preserve evidence that may establish guilt or innocence of the accused. A criminal investigation is successful when all available physical evidence is collected and preserved properly, witnesses are intelligently interviewed, and the suspect, if willing, is effectively interrogated. All leads must be properly developed and the investigation must be documented.

Criminal statutes describe criminal behavior and prescribe punishments for conviction. Each element of an offense must be established in the incident under investigation to determine if a crime occurred. If a crime has been committed, the investigator must distinguish misdemeanors from felonies. The powers to arrest differ between felonies and misdemeanors. Failure to arrest properly could result in civil and possible criminal liability for false arrest or false imprisonment.

A suspected perpetrator can be identified in a number of ways. The suspect may be apprehended at the scene, or an individual may provide the investigator with an admission or confession subsequent to the incident. Eye witnesses to the crime may be available. Circumstantial evidence in the form of a motive, opportunity to commit the crime, or trace evidence that can place the suspect at the crime scene may also be available. If the suspect is not present at the crime scene, it will be necessary to trace and locate the perpetrator.

Crime suspects are rarely in hiding. Their identity or location is simply unknown. Before notifying law enforcement authorities or launching a search for a fugitive, the investigator must ensure that the legal requirements for a possible arrest have been satisfied and all pertinent background information and identification data on the suspect have been gathered. The investigator should collect as much information as possible regarding the suspect's history. Criminal records, if available, provide information regarding aliases used, convictions, and the nature of previous offenses. Other forms of trace information include telephone, city, and crisscross directories, credit bureaus, motor vehicle records, identification data from the U.S. Immigration Service, passport or military records, informants, county assessors and recorders offices, and friends and acquaintances (O'Hara & O'Hara, 2003).

Evidence collected must meet certain legal tests to maintain its evidentiary value. The courts will examine the chain of custody of the evidence and will want to know where, when, and by whom the evidence was located and how it was preserved for in-court presentation. Therefore, evidence must be carefully collected, marked for future identification, and preserved. Investigators should wear latex gloves when collecting evidence to avoid possible contamination. Without destroying the integrity of the evidence, small as well as large items should be permanently marked for identification wherever possible.

All physical evidentiary items should be placed in appropriate containers and the containers marked with identifying information. Small delicate items should be wrapped in cotton and placed in an envelope, bottle, or box. The investigator who discovered the evidence should place an identifying mark or initials on the evidence as it is collected. All containers should be sealed and identified with the appropriate evidence or property tag. Each item should be logged into the investigative report. To maintain the chain of custody of evidence, items must be secured and transported properly.

Surveillance and undercover operations are usually necessary when conventional investigative methods fail to produce enough evidence. Surveillance involves the observation of a person, place, or object. Surveillance is time consuming, expensive, and requires tremendous patience, alertness, and resourcefulness. Surveillance is most successful when the surveillant's appearance and activities do not attract attention from the subject or the public (F. Green, 2000). However, the type of surveillance conducted depends on the nature of the investigation and the circumstances. Stationary, or fixed, surveillance, the stakeout, is used when the subject is at a specific location. Observations may be made from a vehicle, natural hiding places, or areas within a building. Surveillance technology in the form of video cameras and recording devices can substitute for a human surveillant, provided legal requirements are met. A moving surveillance (tail) is used to maintain observation of a moving subject. A close (tight) tail is used when it is extremely important not to lose sight of the subject. Rough (loose) tails are used when keeping the subject under constant observation is not necessary (O'Hara & O'Hara, 2003).

Audio and video monitoring are common surveillance methods. This usually involves electronic monitoring of conversations through wiretap or use of video cameras. However, since wiretaps and similar activities are considered searches, court authorization and a search warrant is required if conducted by law enforcement (government) personnel. The courts are reluctant to issue warrants for electronic surveillance unless there is a demonstrated need and all other investigative procedures are exhausted. For private sector personnel, electronic surveillance is not subject to restrictions under any government exclusionary rule. However, such nongovernmental surveillance activity may be subject to privacy laws, the criminal law, and lawsuits. In the private sector, electronic undercover surveillance is not legally appropriate if the subject has a reasonable expectation of privacy.

An **undercover investigation** is a surveillance through which the surveillant, using an assumed identity or cover, makes personal contact with a subject. Undercover surveillance is justified when criminal activity is suspected but no hard evidence of a crime exists. The surveillant gains the confidence of the subject in the hope of obtaining incriminating evidence. Undercover assignments are expensive and can be dangerous. Surveillants must exercise care to avoid detection. Criminals are paranoid and suspicious of people around them. Subjects of a surveillance may be aware of possible undercover activity (Bennett & Hess, 1991).

Surveillance may be conduced by internal security staff or through the use of personnel from external security and investigations firms (Lewis, Goodman, & Fandt, 2001). There are dozens of large contract firms and hundreds of small companies throughout the United States that provide undercover and surveillance services. Retail outlets, financial institutions, lodging establishments, restaurants, automobile dealerships, and manufacturers are among the types of organizations that often use contracted undercover operatives to identify internal criminal activity, monitor the quality of customer service, and verify product knowledge on the part of employees (F. Green, 2000).

Business Crime Investigations   Crimes are committed by and against for-profit, nonprofit, and not-for-profit organizations. Most organizations are for-profit business enterprises that produce and sell goods and services. None are immune from crime in the form of business asset theft or damage. A criminal investigation, whether conducted internally or by an external agency, is warranted whenever criminal activity is suspected or identified.

Criminal investigations in businesses and similar organizations can be viewed from at least three perspectives. First, crimes in the form of **fraud, embezzlement**, and theft are committed against business organizations by employees. Second, crimes such as arson, vandalism, robbery, burglary, and theft are committed against business by outsiders. Third, crimes involving regulatory noncompliance, price-fixing, tax evasion, and commercial bribery are committed by employees and others on behalf of business organizations.

Many of the losses due to crime in a business environment are the result of a fraudulent scheme or activity. Business-related frauds are often perpetrated through the dishonesty of a party to a business transaction. The parties to the transaction may be employers or employees, buyers or sellers, financiers or borrowers, stockholders or corporations, principals or agents. Frauds are perpetrated through embezzlement, misrepresentations on financial statements, false claims and bankruptcy, bid rigging, inflating expense accounts, feigned accidents and injuries, and numerous computer and Internet-related activities. Fraudulent schemes include charity, investment, personal improvement, business opportunity, and telemarketing scams. They also include identity theft and countless forms of misrepresentation.

Basically, fraud involves practically any scheme or device used by one person to deceive another. Perpetrators of fraud utilize false suggestions, forgery, false pretenses, misappropriation, suppression of the truth, surprise, tricks, and lying. Fraudulent behavior can be civil or criminal, or both. It can be prosecuted in criminal court, rectified in civil court, or it may be unactionable, where a buyer has no legal recourse (caveat emptor—let the buyer beware). Most criminal statutes on fraud specify certain types of fraudulent behavior, such as embezzlement, larceny by trick, false pretenses, defrauding an innkeeper, bad checks, forgery, and uttering (passing) a forged instrument. The uncommon characteristic of each of these offenses is the method used or the time frame wherein the perpetrator forms the intent to permanently deprive someone else of property. A common characteristic is the possessory right to whatever the subject of the fraud is. In an embezzlement case, for example, the perpetrator already has legal possession of the property because of a relationship of trust. Subsequent to the lawful possession, however, the embezzler breaches the trust and misappropriates the property. Bank officers, cashiers, and bookkeepers embezzle. On the other hand, if a person obtains property from another through a misrepresentation of the facts, lawful possession does not pass and the perpetrator commits the crime of false pretenses. A broker who knowingly sells worthless or nearly worthless stock at an inflated price commits the fraud-related offense of theft by false pretenses.

In an effort to consolidate fraud-related crimes and simplify prosecution, many states merge these offenses and larceny into the statutory offense of theft. Under such statutes, criminal liability is incurred when a court can establish that the perpetrator unlawfully took property from another and did not intend to return it. The fact that the intent to permanently deprive the possessor of the property was formed before, during, or at the time of the taking is immaterial under these statutes. This eliminates the need to prosecute under separate statutes dealing with the crimes of larceny, embezzlement, false pretenses, larceny by trick, and the like.

A common and likely fraudulent scheme involves some form of internal theft by an employee. An internal theft may be disguised to mask the criminal activity, giving it the appearance of legitimacy. Secreting merchandise or product in a purse or briefcase are examples of a disguise. Other common forms of internal theft involve **accounts payable diversions** as well as **cash conversion, inventory conversion**, and **receivables conversion**. Accounts payable diversions are disbursement frauds committed by an employee who processes payroll information, refunds, discounts, rebates, or purchases. Flaws in accounts payable processing systems and poor controls provide the opportunity for personnel to convert practically anything into cash or negotiable instruments. A cash conversion involves theft of liquid assets such as currency and negotiable instruments such as checks. Cash conversions occur most often because there are too few controls on persons handling liquid assets or there is little separation of responsibility for the accounting function. Cash conversions are common when the same person is responsible for receiving and recording incoming receipts, recording sales, making bank deposits, reconciling bank and financial statements, and issuing credit memos.

Inventory and product conversions are usually accomplished by the internal thief who does not have ready access to liquid assets or the accounting function. Inventory or products are stolen. Thus, thieves convert the items to their own use (conversion). Receivables conversion occurs when an employee steals a customer's cash payment and covers the amount stolen with a payment received from another customer. Typically, the scheme involves keeping cash from customer A and waiting until the next day to credit the company with receipts from customer B. Referred to as *lapping receivables,* the scheme requires an element of ingenuity and attention to detail. Computerized point of sale and inventory systems have done little to prevent receivables conversion, although patterns of illegal behavior on the part of the internal thief are easier to detect (Bologna & Shaw, 1997).

Embezzlement is another common form of internal theft. As compared to larceny, where the intent to permanently deprive someone of property is formed before or at the time of the taking, embezzlement is the appropriation of property by a person to whom it has been legally entrusted. Embezzlers, therefore, hold positions of trust and have a fiduciary responsibility for property in their possession. Embezzlements often go undetected, and when detected, they are rarely prosecuted. When prosecuted, the penalty after conviction is often significantly less than for other fraud or theft-related offenses. Like most other crimes, embezzlement occurs when motive and opportunity to commit the crime are present, and a capable guardian for the property, such as adequate security measures, is absent. Embezzlers often rationalize their behavior as necessary because of their circumstances, as compensation for being underpaid, or as a loan to be replaced at some future date. Embezzlers tend to have low self-esteem, compulsive personalities, or excessive lifestyles.

Prevention of employee fraud and embezzlement goes beyond security systems and procedural controls. Appropriate organizational culture and values, codes of conduct, and management's creation of an environment of trust and cooperation also promote a climate that helps to prevent employee theft. Yet, even in the best environments, internal theft can and does occur. Usually, detection involves identification of an intentional financial irregularity or discrepancy. Sometimes, detection occurs because transactions and dollar amounts in transactions are at variance with norms, or expectations in the normal course of business. Most often, the internal theft of cash or negotiables is discovered through an audit.

Audits generally take two forms: **financial audits** and **fraud examinations**. Financial audits involve an evaluation of the accounting system. Transactions are examined to evaluate the timeliness, accuracy, and completeness of the transaction recording. Financial auditors do not examine each transaction. They sample transactions and confirm that the records are free of material (significant) errors. Fraud examinations, on the other hand, require the investigator to think in terms of how the financial controls could be compromised by an ingenious criminal mind (Bologna & Shaw, 1997).

The fraud examiner searches for any discrepancy, whether significant or not. Although minor errors may be the result of an honest mistake, the discovery of a relatively insignificant misstatement may lead to a disguised criminal scheme. A cashier who is over or short by a small amount at the end of a shift may be prone to simple mistakes. Numerous overages and shortages over a period of weeks may be the result of inattention to detail. At the very least, the cashier has a cash-handling problem. At the most, the cashier is under ringing (or not ringing) merchandise, mentally recording the amount of excess cash in the register, and removing the overage at the end of the shift.

Information Gathering and Analysis

Sources of information in an investigation include physical evidence, specialized databases, victims, witnesses, suspects, records, informants, and the Internet. Records include statutes and local, state, and federal law enforcement and other government data. Public databases generally accessible to everyone include records associated with motor vehicles, driving, criminal convictions, worker compensation claims, diplomas, degrees, and credentials, credit history, military service, licenses issued, bankruptcy, and civil litigation. Private individual and business records as well as various publications may also be valuable sources of information. Access to records may be gained through permission, the legal process, the information's status as a public record, and through computerized databases.

Informants are an important source of information and are indispensable in many criminal investigations. When informants are utilized, care should be exercised to evaluate their motives, as well as the information provided, to ensure reliability. In a criminal prosecution, the reliability (veracity) of informant information is critical. Failure to test the reliability of informant-supplied information could result in the suppression of evidence derived from the informant's information (O'Hara & O'Hara, 2003). A basis for the informant's knowledge must also exist. In other words, the informant must be in a position to know the facts asserted (Acker & Brody, 1999).

The Internet is an excellent vehicle for gathering information. Search engines (tables of content for the World Wide Web) provide useful windows to view Web sites throughout the world. All search engines operate in a similar fashion. They run computer software programs that search the content of Web sites. They create an index in a large database consisting of key words from Web site pages they examine. When a user enters key words, the search engines compare the key words entered with the Web site pages in the database and deliver the results to the user in the form of links. The key words or phrase entered should be specific to narrow the search parameters and to allow the search engine to identify Web sites relevant to the purpose of the search. Popular search engines include the following:

- www.yahoo.com
- www.excite.com
- www.lycos.com
- www.hotbot.com
- www.wisdomdog.com
- www.altavista.com
- www.content.overture.com
- www.askjeeves.com
- www.webcrawler.com
- www.dogpile.com
- www.google.com
- www.infoseek.com
- www.multicrawl.com

Government agencies maintain Web sites that contain considerable resources and Internet links of interest to the security professional. In addition, government regulations and laws pertaining to security management can often be accessed through government agency Web sites. Noteworthy government Web sites include the following.

- *www.fedworld.gov.* This Web site is a clearinghouse for government information.
- *www.fbi.gov.* This is the FBI's Web site and it contains information about FBI programs, including the National Infrastructure Protection Center (NIPC), the Awareness of National Security Issues and Response (ANSIR) program, and the Uniform Crime Report (UCR).
- *www.treas.gov/usss.* This is the U.S. Secret Service Web site that provides information about financial crimes such as counterfeiting and electronic fraud.
- *www.nacic.gov.* This is the Web site for the National Counterintelligence Center (NACIC) that provides information about trends in foreign and domestic espionage against American businesses.
- *www.dss.mil.* This is the home page for the Defense Security Service (DSS). This Web site can assist companies in search of government contracts.
- *www.xsp.org.* The Extranet for Security Professionals Web site offers an opportunity to exchange sensitive, unclassified information over a strongly encrypted network.

- *www.nsi.org*. This is the Web site for the National Security Institute. The Institute posts travel advisories.
- *www.travel.state.gov*. This is the U.S. State Department's Bureau of Consular Affairs Web site. It also contains travel advisories.
- *www.loc.gov*. This is the Library of Congress Web site that contains valuable and timely information about pending legislation and statutes.

Each state government also has a Web site. A search engine may be used to locate a state's Web site.

Security professionals can obtain updated information on new computer viruses by accessing the Web sites of the major antivirus software producers. These include

- www.symantec.com
- www.networkassociates.com
- www.sophos.com
- www.datafellows.com
- www.norman.com (Norman Data Defense Systems)

Current events information and news are available through news services such as Excite's NewsTracker at nt.excite.com and Yahoo!'s News Clipper at my.yahoo.com. In addition, ASIS International offers a security news and legal update service through ASISNET, located at www.asisonline.org. Free information regarding security-related topics can be found at www.security management.com. In addition to ASIS, several other professional security organizations have Web sites. They include

- *www.classmgmt.com*. The National Classification Management Society.
- *www.scip.org*. The Society of Competitive Intelligence Professionals.
- *www.ifpo.org*. The International Foundation for Protection Officers.
- *www.cfenet.com*. The Association of Certified Fraud Examiners (Uttenweiler, 1999).

Role of Forensic Science

Traditionally, the term *instrumentation* has been applied to laboratory analysis of physical evidence found at the crime scene. Instrumentation evolved into the fields of forensic science and criminalistics. Instrumentation, forensic science, and criminalistics are terms that are often used interchangeably. However, forensic science involves the application of the physical as well as some social and business sciences to the investigation of crime. Sophisticated laboratory procedures and analyses are currently available, and more are being developed. Psychological profiling, anthropology, forensic accounting, spectrographic analysis, biology, chemistry, DNA analysis, and new ballistics testing technology are used in contemporary criminal investigations. The use of digital imaging as an investigative tool has also increased (Blitzer & Jacobia, 2002). Thus, forensic science may be defined as the application of science to the enforcement of law, and it has become extremely important to investigations in the twenty-first century.

One of the most significant advances in forensic science in the latter half of the twentieth century was the development of DNA (deoxyribonucleic acid) profiling technology (Senna & Siegel, 2001). Contained within a gene, DNA is a molecule that is present in all forms of life. It is unique to the life form, determines the organism's traits, and assists with the development of a genetic fingerprint specific to the organism from which the molecules are taken. Blood, semen, and body tissues are good sources of human molecular cells containing DNA. Human biological samples collected at crime scenes can be used to develop a DNA profile. Comparison samples taken from victims and suspects can be profiled and analyzed to determine if both samples have a common origin. For example, the DNA profile developed from a semen sample taken from a rape victim can be compared to the DNA profile of blood taken from the rape suspect (Adams, Caddell, & Krutsinger, 2004; Lee, Palmbach, & Miller, 2001; Ortmeier, 2002; Saferstein, 2001).

Impermissible Investigative Conduct

Several issues arise when conducting investigations in private businesses and non-law enforcement settings. These issues focus on **impermissible investigative conduct** surrounding searches, **surreptitious investigative methods**, use of the polygraph, and arrest and detention of suspected law violators. Searches of desks, lockers, and other areas under the direct control of employees, for example, raise serious questions regarding the right to privacy. If work areas are subject to search, employees should be given clear, written notice that such searches may occur. The search policy should be contained in an employee handbook and posted prominently in work areas. It is inadvisable to search a locked desk drawer or locker of an employee without the employee's consent. To prevent claims of invasion of privacy, an employee may be asked to sign a release form documenting the employee's consent to a search. The physical search of a person is not permissible in private businesses.

Many statutory provisions severely restrict an employer's ability to use surreptitious (secret) investigative methods such as electronic monitoring (wiretapping), eavesdropping, and undercover investigations. Other than cases involving interception of telephone conversations, there are few definitive court rulings that describe the limits (if any) of any employer's monitoring of employees by electronic means. However, several invasion of privacy actions have been filed against employers who monitored electronic mail or similar messages transmitted between employees. The courts have consistently held that organizational email systems are the property of the organization.

Electronic mail (email) has emerged as an extremely popular and useful communications tool, especially in the workplace. Yet, email systems and their ancillary Internet links are also subject to abuse by employees. As a result, many organizations restrict and monitor employee email communications and Internet usage, limiting communications to that which is related to the job. Some argue that the monitoring constitutes a violation of one's constitutional right to privacy. However, the U.S. Constitution does not grant private, nongovernmental employees a right to privacy. The Fourth Amendment to the Constitution restricts governmental intrusions. Nevertheless, private employers may, through their words or actions, create an employee expectation to privacy which can form the foundation for an invasion of privacy lawsuit. To reduce the probability of a privacy lawsuit, employers are advised to create, communicate, and enforce a written policy regarding use of organizational email systems. To decrease the expectation of email privacy, employers should use the policy to inform employees that computer systems, accompanying software, and email communications are organizational property, not the personal property of the employee. Employees should be informed that all email messages will be treated as business messages and that the employer reserves the right to review these e-mail messages. Employers should also inform employees that personal passwords do not establish a right to privacy. The policy should thoroughly define what types of communication are considered impermissible. Discriminatory, obscene, derogatory, sexually explicit, and defamatory communications of any kind should be prohibited. The policy should also specify the consequences for email system misuse, and the policy should be uniformly enforced. Finally, the employee should be required, in writing, to acknowledge receipt of, and consent to, the organizational email communications policy (Aronsohn, 2003).

Federal legislation that impacts electronic monitoring in the workplace includes the Omnibus Crime Control and Safe Streets Act of 1968. Federal courts have held that an employer can violate the act by secretly recording telephone calls made by employees on the employer's telephone system. A provision of the act contains an exemption for "system providers," such as employers who provide and maintain electronic communication systems.

Some states prohibit eavesdropping on any confidential employee communication. **A confidential communication** includes any communication carried on under circumstances reasonably indicating that any party to the communication desires it to be confined to the parties involved in the communication. The term does not include communications made in a public gathering, such as an office party. Furthermore, it does not apply to any public utility engaged in the business of providing communication services. Generally, these statutes provide that the use of devices for purposes of eavesdropping constitute an invasion of privacy. The statutes define eavesdropping as intentionally tapping or making any unauthorized connection, whether physically, electronically, or otherwise; or willfully and without the consent of one party to the communication, or in any unauthorized manner, read, or attempt to read or to learn the contents or meaning of any message or report. In a few states, such as California and Maryland, all parties to the communication must consent to the eavesdropping or recording of the conversation. Furthermore, evidence obtained in violation of the law is inadmissible in any judicial, administrative, legislative, or other proceeding. Accordingly, even if an employer uncovers significant information about the employee, the employer will not be able to use such information if a provision of the eavesdropping statute has been violated.

Some statutes also place severe restrictions on an employer's ability to monitor employee performance. They often prohibit employers from conducting any monitoring of employee email, Internet movements, or computer file use without first informing employees of the employer-organization's policy. One suggestion is to give employees advanced written notice that monitoring can occur. Employees must give their full and voluntary consent in writing prior to monitoring.

At present, there are no definitive reported court cases limiting an employer's right to conduct a legitimate undercover investigation. Undercover investigations are most appropriate when an employer suspects theft or substance abuse is actually taking place within the organization. When undercover operatives are used, the investigation must have an effective infrastructure. The investigations team must maintain good communication linkages. The case must also be managed to ensure that it remains focused and is executed properly. Appropriate participants in the undercover investigation include the undercover operative, the case manager, the client, an employment law attorney, and applicable law enforcement personnel. Written, email, or v-mail (digitally transmitted audio-video via the Internet) reports should be submitted daily by the operative. Telephonic contact with the case manager should also be made on a daily basis to clarify and expand the written reports as necessary. All reports, materials, and evidence collected should be organized into a case file for possible courtroom presentation (Ferraro, 2000).

State and federal laws also place severe restrictions on the use of polygraphs or similar devises by private employers. The federal statute contains a general exception for ongoing investigations involving economic loss and exceptions for employers in specific industries. Significant provisions of state and federal law prohibit employers from demanding or requiring that any applicant or employee take a polygraph test, a "lie detector" test, or any other similar test or examination as a condition of employment or as a condition of continued employment.

Specifically, the federal **Employee Polygraph Protection Act** of 1988 prohibits employers from directly or indirectly requiring, requesting, suggesting, or causing any employee or prospective employee to take or submit to any lie detector test; using, accepting, referring to, or inquiring about the results of any lie detector test; or discharging, disciplining, discriminating against, or denying employment or promotion to, or threatening any such action against, any employee or prospective employee who refuses, declines, or fails to take a lie detector test. In addition, an employer may not base an employment decision upon the results of any lie detector test. Actually, lie detectors do not exist. However, the term "lie detector" is often applied to instruments such as a polygraph, voice stress analyzer, psychological stress evaluator, or any other similar device.

Exemptions under the Employee Polygraph Protection Act include the following:

- Government Exemption. The act does not apply to the United States government or any state or local government. Further, the act does not apply to the federal government in the performance of any counterintelligence function or any test given to employees of private employers who have contracts with the Department of Defense.
- Private Employer/Investigative Exemption. A private employer may request an employee to submit to a polygraph test if all of the following conditions are met: The test is administered in connection with an ongoing investigation involving economic loss to the employer's business; the employee had access to the property; the employer has reasonable suspicion that the employee was involved; and the employer gives fair notice to the employee that a request for a test may occur.
- Security Service Exemption. The federal act does not prohibit the use of a polygraph test by private employers whose primary business consists of providing armored car personnel, security system personnel, or other security personnel.
- Drug Security, Drug Theft, or Drug Division Investigations Exemption. The federal act does not prohibit the use of a polygraph test by an employer authorized to manufacture, distribute, or dispense certain controlled substances.

There are additional restrictions on the use of exemptions. The employer investigation exemption does not apply if an employee is discharged, disciplined, denied employment or promotion, or otherwise discriminated against in any manner on the basis of the analysis of a polygraph test chart or the refusal to take a polygraph test without additional supporting evidence. Under the exemption for security services, drug security, drug theft, or similar investigation, an employer may not use the results as the sole basis for an adverse employment action. Furthermore, during the actual testing phase, the examiner may not ask any questions that were not presented in writing for review to the examinee before the test. Finally, a private employer may disclose information from a test only to the examinee or any other persons specifically designated in writing by the examinee or any court (Cheeseman, 2004; Hess & Wrobleski, 1996; Simonsen, 1998).

Finally, unlawful detention issues, such as false arrest and false imprisonment, often arise when someone's freedom of movement is restricted in a significant way. Unless placed under a criminal or civil (citizen's) arrest, it is unlawful to detain persons against their will. **Unlawful detention** could result in criminal as well as civil liability. Readers should consult their respective state statutes for specific detention requirements in their jurisdictions.

The legal restrictions placed on the investigative conduct of the public police, as agents of government, are distinguished from the legal restrictions placed on similar conduct of private security personnel. The Bill of Rights (the first 10 amendments to the U.S. Constitution) place restrictions on the conduct of representatives of government, not the behavior of private persons. Thus, the laws of arrest and rules of evidence, as well as the legal aspects of interrogation, search, and seizure, often vary between the public and private sectors. Additional information regarding these legal aspects is contained in Chapter 3.

INTELLIGENCE OPERATIONS

Business Intelligence

In a competitive environment, loss prevention goes beyond identification of and protection from obvious threats. The successful business cannot operate in a vacuum. The business must also protect against loss due to competition. In this vein, **business intelligence (BI)** involves the process of collecting, analyzing, and disseminating competitive information and other data that can be used to meet business organization objectives. Remaining in business and staying ahead of the competition are legitimate business objectives. Legally appropriate business intelligence activities help meet the objectives.

Sole proprietorships, partnerships, and corporations benefit from successful anticipation of the competition's tactics and strategies. Through tactical intelligence operations, one seeks to identify and analyze short-range activities of similar businesses. **Tactical business intelligence** focuses on actual rather than perceived or advertised schemes of competitors. Pricing policies and terms of sale, for example, must be in line with the competition and consistent with the marketplace.

Strategic business intelligence seeks to forecast the long-range implications of business activities. Long-range predictions of the competition's activities involve the identification of new target markets as well as the number of competitors available in the future. It involves an analysis of the competitors' capabilities, assets, methodologies, and skills. It provides information to assess the value of alliances and assists a business with the creation of a corporate vision.

Business intelligence also involves the use of counterintelligence to protect the organization from internal and external intelligence-gathering threats. Business intelligence, sometimes referred to as **competitive intelligence**, is not **industrial espionage (IE)**. Business intelligence is a legitimate activity. Industrial espionage, on the other hand, involves the use of illegal, unethical, and fraudulent means to obtain proprietary information and intellectual property.

The business intelligence process involves the gathering and analysis of raw data about the competition. Illegal industrial espionage includes activities such as theft of a competitor's information through traditional methods or computer access, extortion, commercial bribery, or employment of the competition's personnel to extract information. Legitimate business intelligence activities can be conducted without resorting to any illegal methods. Intelligence is gathered by observing the competition and by accessing other individuals and organizations external to the competition.

Sources of information include a competitor's finance, accounting, and human resources personnel as well as marketing and sales executives, operations managers, and staff. They can be observed in an effort to discover information about sales promotions, employee recruitment campaigns, training programs, labor contracts, distribution channels, pricing practices, physical plant, warehouse, and distribution center utilization, advertising, customer service, employee morale, and corporate security operations.

Sources of information external to target competitor organizations include credit agencies, chambers of commerce, better business bureaus, distributors, industry experts and information brokers, market research organizations, trade associations, and competitor customers. If a competitor is a corporation with stock that is publicly traded, financial statements may be available. The U.S. Freedom of Information Act of 1966 requires public as well as many private corporations to disclose information about finances and operations. Information on patents or the development of items to be patented can be obtained from the U.S. Patent Office (Pitorri, 1998).

Organizations that conduct business in the global marketplace, especially those with a physical presence in a foreign country, must consider local conditions to protect personnel and organizational assets. Several contract services provide up-to-date information on political conditions, criminal activity, and corruption as well as investing, licensing, and commercial trade in the international arena. Organizations can subscribe to database services that provide comprehensive guides to foreign laws and regulations, operating conditions, rules on foreign investment, labor availability, and price control policies. These services, some of which are available online or through U.S. government agencies, cover the latest business developments in major and emerging world markets.

> Information regarding political and commercial conditions in foreign countries may be obtained by contacting the Northwestern University Library's Economist Intelligence Unit at www.library.northwestern.edu/reference/instructional_services/e

Criminal Intelligence

Criminal intelligence involves gathering information about actual as well as possible criminal activity and threats to an organization and its assets. Whereas business intelligence typically refers to information about competitors gathered legally, criminal intelligence focuses on the activities of individual criminals and organized criminal groups. Security personnel gather criminal intelligence information as part of risk assessment and analysis designed to prevent the criminal threat from materializing. Paramount among the criminal threats to information assets is the threat of industrial espionage.

COUNTERESPIONAGE

Industrial espionage is a term often used to describe illegal activities that are designed to obtain trade secrets, proprietary information, and intellectual property. **Counterespionage** refers to those activities designed to prevent espionage from occurring. Generally, counterespionage involves the application of appropriate physical, personnel, and information security measures as well as a thorough investigation of all actual or attempted security breaches. Industrial espionage awareness and prevention training programs should reach all staff. Security policies must also be enforced at all staff levels. Comprehensive risk assessments and periodic reviews of the assessment process greatly enhance the organization's ability to identify weaknesses in the security system. Persons responsible for the security function must be thoroughly knowledgeable regarding illegal espionage methodologies (American Society for Industrial Security, 1998).

Industrial espionage threats stem from several sources. A business's own employees are possible, albeit improbable, sources. Employees who are disgruntled or experiencing financial difficulties may steal information and give or sell it to a competitor. In a highly competitive environment, other companies and their personnel may resort to crime to obtain vital information. Some nations, even allies of the United States, are possible perpetrators of industrial espionage. Heads of state in nations with crumbling economies (or no economic base at all) often promote state-sanctioned industrial espionage. Unhappy citizens may overthrow a government. If a country does not possess the technology to compete in the global marketplace, it could easily resort to industrial espionage to obtain the requisite technology to improve its economic position and keep its citizens from revolting.

Agents who participate in business espionage activities come from diverse backgrounds and numerous countries. Current and former employees, customers, competitors, contract vendors, business partners, and former government intelligence officers are involved with industrial espionage. Since the end of the Cold War in the early 1990s, many former Soviet Block intelligence agents shifted their focus from gathering political and military information to collecting United States and Western ally proprietary information and intellectual property. Secret economic data that has taken years of research to develop and millions of dollars to produce are typical targets of these former intelligence agents.

The current goals of the Russian intelligence service (KGB) as well as many other foreign nationals is to gather technical, scientific, and other forms of economic data from U.S. businesses. The U.S. Central Intelligence Agency (CIA) has identified several friendly and not-so-friendly nations as perpetrators of economic espionage activities. In addition to former Soviet Union countries, China,

Iran, North Korea, and Cuba as well as Canada, France, Israel, Germany, India, South Korea, Japan, and Taiwan have been customers of stolen U.S. technology or have agents responsible for losses suffered by American businesses. One former French official indicated that the United States and France are allies in political and military matters only, not in economic or technical environments.

Whether the perpetrators of industrial espionage are employees or outsiders, domestic or foreign, they operate because businesses and organizations are vulnerable. Espionage agents take advantage of the vulnerabilities by identifying weaknesses in security systems and exploiting them. These agents utilize overt as well as covert (clandestine) avenues of attack. Almost 90 percent of an espionage agent's activity involves collection of information from and through overt sources. Trade publications and product shows, employment interviews and online information services are excellent sources for overt information collection.

Common **covert operations** used to gather information include penetration of telephone and facsimile lines, examining trash, employee subversion, use of secret listening devices, secret insertion of an agent into the targeted organization, computer hacking through the Internet, and reverse engineering of a product. Conversations, computer modem transmissions, and facsimiles over telephone lines can be intercepted. Unshredded documents can be retrieved from trash. Employees can exchange information for money, sex, and other reasons. Undercover agents, although costly, can surreptitiously penetrate an organization by posing as contractors, salespersons, or new employees. Agents have penetrated organizations by obtaining employment with the janitorial services vendor who holds the cleaning contract with the targeted enterprise. Once inside, the undercover agent, posing as a janitor, is free to roam the business, especially at night, collecting, examining, and analyzing documents, operations, and data visible on desks and available through open computer terminals. Undercover agents also frequent local gyms, restaurants, and bars where target company employees exercise, dine, and party. The agents eavesdrop on conversations and, in some cases, pose as employees of the target organization.

Virtually any organization or agency can be the target of industrial espionage. From a business perspective, the most frequent targets include companies engaged in global commerce, biotechnology, high technology, manufacturing of computers and electronics, and firms whose success is based on unique products, patents, or formulas (Pitorri, 1998). The Internet and other computer network information systems increase the risk of cyber-based threats (Boni & Kovacich, 2000).

REPORTING

Most people dread the thought of note-taking and report writing. They either do not understand the importance of **documentation** or they do not appreciate the slow, deliberate process demanded by good writing (Thaiss & Hess, 1999). A security person's ability to document facts surrounding an incident, interview, accident, investigation, or criminal activity reflects on the writer's professionalism and the organization's ability to solve a problem. Probably no other single activity in loss prevention is more important than effective documentation and quality report writing.

Security personnel are required to perform writing tasks on a continuous basis. They must be able to take notes, incorporate notes into reports, summarize statements of witnesses, record formal confessions, and enter information on report forms. Personnel must write in-depth narrative accounts containing complete sentences and paragraphs (investigative reports, supplemental/follow-up reports), and enter information into activity logs. They are often required to write press releases, memoranda, correspondence, and draft material for policy and training manuals.

Documentation Methods

Documentation can be accomplished through traditional note-taking and report writing methods. If physical, technical, and legal requirements permit, documentation may also occur through the use of audiotape, videotape, stenography, computer-assisted recording devices, or an combination of methods. If computers are used, care must be exercised to ensure that confidentiality is maintained and access is restricted on a need-to-know basis. Computer disks that have been erased still retain information that can be retrieved through technical means. Additionally, other electronic mediums, such as email and the Internet, are not secure from message interception.

Notes

Notes are created in the normal course of business or in the field while investigating an incident. Notes are the primary source documents for a subsequent report. Notes should be made contemporaneous to an incident, during the course of the activity, or immediately after an incident occurs. These notes are often referred to as field notes because they are recorded on the job in the field (Parr, 1999). Since memories fade and are imperfect, notes must be written and maintained in the course of virtually every occupation. Notes are personal to the author and may be used to refresh one's memory, as the foundation for a report, and as supporting evidence in a judicial proceeding (O'Hara & O'Hara, 2003).

Reports

Reports can become part of an official record and often form the foundation for the history of an incident. Reports may be viewed by other employees, supervisors, the media, attorneys, the courts, insurance companies, and other organizations. They may be scrutinized in the judicial process, provide evidence for litigation against the report writer, support a petition, or lay the foundation for a defense against a lawsuit or criminal charge. Reports can help to determine future courses of action and are used as the basis for promotion, discipline, and evaluation. Report writing should be taken seriously. Reports with misspelled words, poor grammar, punctuation errors, inaccuracies, or omissions are potentially costly. Defective reports also cast doubt on the professionalism of the author. Although they vary in form and content, reports have one common purpose: to communicate information in a clear, concise, and accurate manner. They should always be written with the audience or potential readers in mind. Effective reporting is a matter of reducing to writing the pertinent facts concerning a problem or event.

Contact reports are used to document information acquired during an encounter with another person or persons. **Incident reports** and crime reports are used to document the occurrence of an event or reported criminal activity. **Narrative reports** and supplemental reports are used to narrate what happened, record witness statements, and document additional information acquired subsequent to an original report. Accident and traffic collision reports are used to document the circumstances surrounding an accident or vehicle collision. **Organization-specific reports** are written and completed in the normal course of business. The latter includes inspection reports, audit reports, and security surveys. Memoranda and letters are used for interdepartmental and other general correspondence.

The types of reports used by an organization depend on the nature of the organization's activity and its documentation requirements. Most existing organizations have reporting forms or formats in place. New organizations seeking to develop report forms and procedures should consult with existing organizations for information. Report form books and form tools in computer software packages are also commercially available.

General Writing Principles

Writing must be reasonably fluent, well developed, and organized, showing sufficient command of the language used to communicate the information. All essential information must be included in a report (who, what, where, when, how, why). The report must be free of errors in typing, grammar, punctuation, spelling, and word choice that diminish its value or usefulness. A writer should choose the correct language, use proper sentence structure, be completely accurate, include all facts, and distinguish facts from hearsay, conclusions, judgments, and personal opinions. A report writer should strive for clarity; be concise, fair, and complete; and record the sequence of events in chronological order. The writer should record the names, addresses, and if possible, social security numbers of all involved in an incident. Narratives should include an introduction, body, and conclusion.

At a minimum, investigative reports should contain information describing how the author became involved in the situation, the facts necessary to accurately describe what happened, identification of parties involved, statements of the parties involved, specifics relative to the scene of the incident, descriptions of physical evidence as well as property damaged or stolen, and actions taken by the personnel at the scene (California Commission on Peace Officer Standards and Training, 1999). To ensure that the report is complete, the report writer should strive to include the date of the report, file or case number (if applicable), subjects involved, type of report, and complainant (if any). Other necessary information includes the name and identification of the person writing the report; office or department of origin; report status (open, pending, supplemental, closing); individuals to whom the report is sent; a narrative, including all facts acquired and all developed leads; and conclusions and recommendations. If applicable, the report might also include undeveloped leads and photographs, sketches, copies of documents, evidence receipts, and computer disks (O'Hara & O'Hara, 2003).

In an attempt to sound official, personnel often adopt a writing style and use language that is elaborate, redundant, obscure, and full of jargon and legalese (Adams, 2001). Clear, concise, simple, commonly used vocabulary is best. In report writing, the author of the report should present accurate information with brevity and clarity as guides to readability. Writers should avoid using words of more than two syllables, and sentences should not exceed ten words. Examples of jargon and wordy phrases (and their concise English counterparts) include the following:

- executed a stop (stopped)
- in the vicinity of (near)
- verbal confrontation (argument)
- inquired (asked)
- proceeded to the location (went to _____)
- terminate (end)
- approximately (about)
- initiated (began)
- related (said)
- party (person)
- in view of the fact that (because)
- for the purpose of (to)
- conducted an investigation (investigated)
- upon an individual basis (individually)
- pursuit of alleged perpetrator (ran after suspect)
- maintained visual contact (watched)
- exited the vehicle (got out of the car)

Correct spelling, word usage, punctuation, and capitalization are also essential ingredients to good report writing. Mistakes in these areas lead readers to believe that the writer is undereducated, poorly trained, careless, and unprofessional. The writer should not rely on computer spell-check programs, either. Inappropriate words that are not identified by a spell-check software program (Hess, 1997) include those *italicized* in the following sentences.

- He went to the *sight* of the accident.
- The *breaks* on the car did not work.
- It was a *miner* incident.
- He injured his left *feet.*
- She did not *no* where the suspect went.
- The item was found in the car's *truck.*
- He was unable to *here.*

Reports should be written to express a thought accurately and clearly, not to impress the reader. The language used in normal conversation is the language of a report. The vocabulary and style used should approximate what and how the writer would communicate if telling a story. First-person rather than third-person voice is recommended in report writing. For example, the author should write "I asked to see the report" rather than "The supervisor asked for the report" (Ortmeier, 1999).

SUMMARY

An investigation is a systematic process used to determine the causes of accidents and losses as well as the facts surrounding personal misconduct and criminal activity. Investigations are also used to research the background of potential employees and business partners. Common types of investigations in a security setting include those associated with human resources, personal injury, property damage, and crime. Effective information gathering and analysis procedures are critical to any investigation. Impermissible investigative conduct emanates from invasions to privacy, improper use of the polygraph and similar instruments, and unlawful arrest and detention of suspected law violators.

Intelligence operations include the gathering of business and competitive intelligence as well as criminal intelligence. Counterespionage refers to those activities designed to prevent espionage from occurring. Utilizing numerous methods, current and former employees, business associates, and external agents are involved in business espionage activities.

Effective and efficient documentation is critical to the success of any security operation. Utilizing a variety of methods, security personnel document the circumstances surrounding incidents, interviews, interrogations, and continuous activities. As the primary source documents for the creation of a report, notes should be made contemporaneous to an event. Reports are part of an official record of an event or activity and form the foundation for the history of an incident. Report writers (authors) should practice generally accepted report writing principles to avoid suspicion and inquiries into the writer's professional capabilities.

KEY TERMS

accounts payable diversion

business intelligence

cash conversion

competitive intelligence

confidential communication

contact report

counterespionage

covert operations

criminal intelligence

criminal investigation

documentation

embezzlement

Employee Polygraph Protection Act

financial audit

fraud

fraud examination

human resource investigation

impermissible investigative conduct

incident report

industrial espionage

inventory conversion

investigation

narrative report

organization-specific report

personal injury investigation

property damage investigation

receivables conversion

strategic business intelligence

surreptitious investigative methods

surveillance

tactical business intelligence

undercover investigation

unlawful detention

DISCUSSION QUESTIONS AND EXERCISES

1. What elements are common to the investigative process?
2. Under what circumstances is a civil or criminal investigation warranted?
3. Describe the proper procedure for the collection and preservation of evidence in criminal investigations.
4. When are surveillance and undercover operations necessary?
5. Business crime often differs from traditional street crime. Describe the types of crime that businesses are most likely to encounter.
6. Discuss the procedure for developing, locating, evaluating, and analyzing information.
7. What constitutes impermissible investigative conduct?
8. What is business intelligence? How does it differ from industrial espionage?
9. Documentation is vital to the success of every security operation. How can appropriate documentation be assured?

CHAPTER 9

Specific Security Applications: Part I

LEARNING OBJECTIVES

After completing this chapter, the reader should be able to

- identify security threats unique to specific industries and government operations.
- describe asset protection priorities as well as loss prevention policies, procedures, and systems associated with the following:
  - airline and airport security
  - banking and financial institution security
  - computer security
  - contract services
  - courthouse and courtroom security
  - disaster recovery
  - educational institution security
  - entertainment security
  - executive protection
  - government security
  - healthcare security
  - hospitality security
- evaluate specific security environments, applications, and services.

INTRODUCTION

Although many threats and general security management principles apply across a broad spectrum of public and private environments, some threats as well as security services and practices are unique, with specific applications. Further analysis of unique and specific security requirements often yields even greater variance in loss prevention philosophy and practice among similar organizations and institutions. This chapter explores several unique security environments, applications, and services.

AIRLINE AND AIRPORT SECURITY

The terrorist attacks of September 11, 2001, resulted in an increased emphasis on airline and airport security. However, long before 9/11, several other incidents illustrated the need for and the uniqueness of airline and airport security. A 6-foot 2-inch, 250-pound incoherent man shed his clothes and mumbled threats while he broke into an in-flight Alaska Airlines cockpit on March 16, 2000. The man attacked the crew and grabbed for the aircraft's controls before he was subdued by the copilot and some terrified passengers. On December 29, 2000, a deranged man tried to seize the cockpit controls of a British Airways 747 jumbo jet en route from London to Kenya. The man bit the captain's ear and finger, sending the aircraft into a dive of several thousand feet before he was subdued by passengers and crew (Fisher, 2000).

Deregulation of commercial airlines during President Reagan's administration led to increased competition, lower airfares, and increased air travel by the public. Competitive pressures forced many airlines to reduce meal portions and flight attendant crews, resulting in poor service and disgruntled passengers. Other cost-cutting measures led to poor aircraft maintenance, which resulted in reduced safety.

Many airports are 24-hour cities. The approximately 425 commercial airports in the United States are all considered high security risks, with the highest risk airports located in large urban areas. Airports accommodate millions of people annually, and aircraft typically cross numerous jurisdictional boundaries (Garbera, 1998).

Airline and airport security developed primarily as a result of the skyjackings that occurred during the 1960s. The United States government's initial response was to place sky marshals (deputy U.S. Marshals) on commercial airline flights. Carry-on luggage and passengers were screened by metal detectors and security personnel contracted by the airlines. In addition, bomb threats, actual bombings, the taking of hostages, terrorist activities, even disruptive behavior from passengers created a need for increased security in the air travel and transport industry. Air cargo theft, airline ticket fraud, theft of passenger luggage and items from vehicles in parking lots, traffic control problems, and the potential for fire and major disasters are commonplace in some airports. Not all criminal activity in airports originates with external sources. Theft, sabotage, and personal injury also result from employee actions. Disgruntled and terminated employees are responsible for much of the property damage and, in at least one documented case, the death of innocent people.

Although air travel is still one of the safest modes of human transportation, incidents such as the bombing of Pan Am Flight 103 over Lockerbee, Scotland, in 1989, the Atlantic Ocean crash of TWA Flight 800 in 1996, and the terrorist attacks of 2001, generated tremendous publicity and concern for airline passenger safety. Numerous other air disasters spotlighted the need for air security and safety:

- On August 6, 1997, 228 people aboard a Korean Air Boeing 747 were killed when the jetliner crashed in Guam.
- On February 2, 1998, 104 people were killed when DC-9 Cebu Pacific Air Flight 387 crashed into a mountain as it prepared to land in the southern Philippines.
- On February 16, 1998, 196 people aboard the aircraft and 6 people on the ground were killed when a China Airlines Airbus A-300–600R crashed while approaching the airport in Taipei, Taiwan.
- On September 2, 1998, 229 people were killed when Swissair Flight 111 crashed off the coast of Nova Scotia. The MD-1 was en route from New York to Geneva.
- On December 11, 1998, 101 people were killed when a Thai Airways Airbus A310–200 crashed during landing at an airport approximately 300 miles south of Bangkok, Thailand. Forty-five people aboard the aircraft survived.
- On February 24, 1999, 61 people were killed when a China Southwest Airlines plane crashed 250 miles south of China's Zhejiang province. The aircraft was a Russian-built TU-154.
- On October 31, 1999, 217 people were killed when EgyptAir Flight 990 crashed into the Atlantic Ocean 60 miles south of Nantucket, Massachusetts. The flight was en route from New York to Cairo.
- On January 30, 2000, 169 people were killed when Kenya Airways Flight 431 crashed into the ocean after takeoff from Abidjan, Ivory Coast. Ten people survived the crash of the Airbus 310.
- On January 31, 2000, Alaska Airlines Flight 261, a McDonnel Douglas MD 83, bound from Puerto Vallarta, Mexico, to San Francisco, crashed into the Pacific Ocean about 40 miles northwest of Los Angeles International Airport. Eighty-eight passengers and crew members were killed.

In 1972, the **Federal Aviation Administration (FAA),** the federal agency responsible for regulating air transportation in the United States, began to require specific minimum security measures at major airports. These measures included

- screening of all persons and baggage entering aircraft departure areas.
- the availability of law enforcement support with the ability to respond to screening points within 5 minutes.
- the development of security plans by airlines and airport management.
- the development of airport disaster plans.

In 1987, the FAA assumed the responsibility for enforcing comprehensive safety and security standards and programs for airports and the airline industry. In 1988, with the enactment of Federal Aviation Regulation (FAR) 107.14, the U.S. government required heightened access controls at commercial airports and restricted access to commercial aircraft. Subsequent to the TWA Flight 800 crash in 1996, the White House Commission on Aviation Safety and Security (the Gore Commission) was formed. It recommended uniform standards for the selection, training, certification, and recertification of airport boarding area passenger and luggage screening personnel and screening companies. Congress reacted with the passage of Public Law 104–264 in October, 1996. The law mandated additional security features and screening. The screening was designed to ensure that dangerous articles and explosive devices were not introduced into controlled areas. However, the wage rate and training provided to screening personnel was often minimal because many airlines responsible for screening did not wish to pay more than necessary. The airlines maintained they were in the transportation business, not the security business (Vincent, 2000).

On February 7, 1997, the White House Commission on Aviation Safety and Security issued its report. The report included 57 recommendations, 31 of which dealt with improvements in security for the traveling public (Thomason, 2000). The commission recommended that the federal government consider aviation security a national security concern. Subsequently, the President of the United States included $100 million in the fiscal year 1999 budget request for upgrades in civil aviation security. The FAA used the money to continue installation of explosive detection systems and devices as well as hardened cargo containers to control explosions that could occur in the baggage compartments of commercial aircraft.

In February, 1998, the U.S. Department of Transportation issued a status report on the commission's recommendations. The report indicated that the following actions had been taken:

- The U.S. Department of Defense established a task force to assess the possible use of surface-to-air missiles against commercial aircraft.
- The U.S. Department of Transportation strengthened its relationship with other departments and agencies to assess the possible use of chemical and biological weapons against commercial airlines.
- The FAA gave cleared security personnel access to classified information regarding terrorist threats.

- The FAA collaborated with the U.S. State Department to provide airport security training to personnel in foreign countries served by U.S. airlines.
- The FAA proposed a program to improve compliance with international security standards at airports.
- The FBI increased the number of agents assigned to counterterrorism activities (Doherty, 1998).

In the late 1990s, a trend to improve security at airports included the development of **passenger profiling techniques.** The techniques were used to identify smugglers and possible terrorists. Profiling came under attack by some as a violation of civil liberty and for being discriminatory in its application. This led the U.S. Justice Department to develop guidelines to prevent any future discrimination.

Airline security personnel and U.S. Customs agents with dogs trained to seek out passengers, luggage, and cargo that possess or contain drugs and explosives became common at major airports. Additionally, some airlines initiated extensive security training programs for their employees. Positive identification of passengers, baggage/passenger matching, and random baggage searches became part of the preboarding passenger screening procedure.

In spite of increased security, airport screening methods still appeared inadequate due primarily to low pay, high-turnover, and minimal benefits and training for airline-contracted screening personnel. A U.S. General Accounting Office (GAO) report issued in March, 2000, indicated that many other countries, including Canada, France, Belgium, the United Kingdom, and the Netherlands, had better-trained screening personnel. The responsibility for passenger and luggage screening in these countries lies with the government or the airport, not the airlines. Thus, screeners were paid more, received better training and benefits, and experienced lower attrition. As a result, they possessed a higher skill level and detected more suspicious objects than did their U.S. counterparts (Vincent, 2000). As screening technology advanced, many security personnel were replaced with screening equipment. The use of biometrics, automated scanners, and access control integration represented new airport security trends (Zunkel, 2000).

Of the many initiatives designed to combat the threat of terrorism in the skies, one FAA project involved the installation of explosive detection equipment in airports. As the FAA upgraded safety and security regulations, new explosive detection technology was developed and implemented. The new equipment, installed in several unnamed airports, included FAA-certified explosive detection systems, automated dual-energy x-ray machines, and trace explosive detection devices. Other FAA initiatives included deployment of agency security personnel in foreign countries, research into making aircraft more resistant to explosive detonations, and expanded passenger bag matching (Major, 1999).

A major problem at U.S. airports was the fragmentation of the responsibility for security. Apparently, no single entity, whether it be the airlines, the FAA, or the jurisdiction within which the airport facility is located, was able to assume overall responsibility for the security function. Although all domestic aviation activities were licensed, certified, or supervised by the FAA, the airport security duties were performed by the local police agencies and private security companies. In addition, domestic airports are not federal facilities, despite the federal authority overriding their operations. Thus, lack of standard operating procedure at many airports added to the confusion. Recommendations for improvement included placement of the overall security function within the federal government, with uniform passenger, luggage, and cargo screening standards under the auspices of the FAA (Slepian, 2000).

The dramatic and deadly events of September 11, 2001, changed the course of commercial aviation security in the United States. In response to the terrorist attacks of 9/11 and the obvious need to improve airline and airport security, the federal government began to assume responsibility for the security function in November 2001. Congressional action on November 16 led to the passage of the **Aviation and Transportation Security Act of 2001.** The law federalized aviation security and centralized responsibility under the newly created **Transportation Security Administration (TSA).** The TSA officially assumed its duties on February 17, 2002. Currently, the TSA oversees U.S. airline and airport security. It provides trained federal employees for passenger and baggage screening and it supplies sky marshals (air marshals) for unnamed commercial flights (Salant, 2002; U.S. Department of Homeland Security, Transportation Security Administration, 2003).

Federalization of commercial aviation resulted in the removal of contract private security personnel from passenger- and baggage-screening points. They were replaced with twice as many federal TSA employees, who earn almost two times the salary of their private-sector counterparts. The impact of this transition has yet to be measured. Some have argued that federalized passenger screening has not delivered a noticeable improvement in air passenger safety (Dalton, 2003).

BANKING AND FINANCIAL INSTITUTION SECURITY

The nature of banking has changed dramatically. Gone are the days when states limited bank branches and financial transactions took place at a physical location. The personal computer, electronic fund transfers, automatic teller machines, debit cards, and the paperless money trail have revolutionized the banking and finance industry. The distinction between **financial institutions** such as commercial banks, savings and loans, credit unions, brokerage houses and insurance companies has also become increasingly blurred.

Financial institutions provide attractive targets for the skilled (and unskilled) criminal. Robbery, burglary, embezzlement, loan fraud, manipulation of funds, computer hacking, and credit card and check fraud are major threats. Losses to financial institutions are direct, since the object of the theft is money, not goods or services. Losses from fraud alone are estimated to exceed $30 billion annually.

In an effort to reduce the vulnerability of financial institutions, the U.S. Congress passed the **Bank Protection Act** in 1968. The act focused on minimum security measures at all federally insured financial institutions. The act required

- a person to be designated as the bank security officer.
- the development of comprehensive security programs and implementation of protective programs that would meet or exceed federal standards.
- maintenance of bait money (currency with serial numbers recorded).
- periodic removal of excess cash from teller areas and bank premises.
- security-conscious opening and closing procedures.
- stringent security inspections.
- cooperation and liaison with the FBI and other law enforcement agencies (Hess & Wrobleski, 1996).

The use of technology to commit crime against financial institutions represents a major threat to financial assets. Banks and other institutions have increased their risk exposure because they are connected internally and externally through online banking services and electronic fund transfers. Unauthorized use of an electronic database by an employee may result in invasions to privacy. Data manipulation through computers is particularly dangerous. Account and loan balances as well as credit lines can be altered or completely deleted. Financial institution Internet Web sites can be penetrated (hacked) and the content altered to display false or slanderous information. Through denial of service attacks, a hacker can electronically flood the institution's computer with email

Photo courtesy of Wackenhut Corporation.

messages, shutting down the system. Insertion of computer viruses is always a concern, and confidential customer information can be obtained and redirected to different accounts or sold to illegitimate users. Some hackers offer to sell stolen information back to the financial institution or delete a virus for a fee, thus extorting money from the institution. Comprehensive personnel, and physical and information protection strategies can help prevent these types of incidents and crimes from occurring in banks and other financial institutions (Spivey, 2001).

COMPUTER SECURITY

An in-depth examination of computer security is presented in Chapter 7.

CONTRACT SERVICES

Contract security services are addressed in Chapter 1.

COURTHOUSE AND COURTROOM SECURITY

The continuing growth of local, state, and federal judicial systems has forced existing court facilities to accommodate an increase in human activity. Expanding space requirements has pressured jurisdictions to construct new courtroom buildings, expanding the courts and increasing the number of judicial personnel, litigants, jurors, and a variety of ancillary activities associated with legal proceedings. In addition to litigation activities, courthouses contain other government agencies, receive deliveries, have adjacent or underground parking areas, are transfer points for defendants and convicted criminals, and function as venues for public ceremonial events.

In recent years, incidents of assault, bombings, and homicide have increased in American courthouses. Spectators become unruly, demonstrators may protest a judicial decision, defendants try to escape, witnesses are threatened, juries are tampered with, and judges, prosecutors, and courthouse staff receive death threats. The most vulnerable areas include courtrooms, judges' chambers, probation and parole offices, clerk of court offices, and areas where pro-defense and pro-prosecution witnesses may encounter one another. Courthouse building exteriors and perimeters must be protected against a possible bombing attack. After the bombing of the Alfred P. Murrah federal building in Oklahoma City in 1995, virtually all government buildings were identified as potential targets for terrorists (Thomas, 2001).

Bailiffs or court security officers keep order in most of the nation's courtrooms. In some states, county marshals or deputy sheriffs provide security for the courts. Security of federal courthouses and courtrooms is the responsibility of the U.S. Marshals Service. In an effort to increase the level of security, access

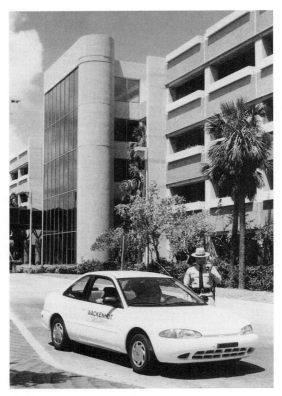

Photo courtesy of Wackenhut Corporation.

control devices and metal detectors have been installed at entry points in many courthouses. Surveillance systems, duress alarms, security glass, contracted security officers, and armed courtroom security personnel provide additional protection.

DISASTER RECOVERY

Several types of natural and environmental disasters are potential threats to people and property. No place in the world is immune from the possibility of a catastrophic event that could result in injuries, loss of life, and destruction of property. For the security manager, prevention of loss due to a disaster is a critical responsibility. In addition, organizations must have policies, procedures, and protection systems in place that assist with the restoration of normal operations as soon as possible after a disaster.

Mitigating damages subsequent to a catastrophic event led to the development of **disaster recovery** as a new specialty within the field of security management. In some large organizations, such as international telecommunications companies, individuals may be tasked with the sole responsibility for developing and implementing disaster management plans. Poor customer service and loss of market share are potential consequences of a failure to return to normal operations in a timely fashion.

Disasters can impact every aspect of organizational life, and each aspect must be addressed in the recovery effort. Public emergency responders must be assisted with traffic control and crowd management. The site must be secured and communications reestablished. Injured people may be trapped in the facility. Hazmat teams must isolate hazardous materials, and on-site crisis counseling may be necessary.

Unlike disaster response, disaster recovery requires balancing the need to return the affected area to normalcy with the strategic goal of reducing vulnerability. Because disaster recovery has long-lasting effects and is usually expensive, numerous stakeholders from government, business, and the community should be involved in the recovery process (Haddow & Bullock, 2003).

EDUCATIONAL INSTITUTION SECURITY

Statistically, educational institutions are safer than homes. Yet, private and public schools, colleges and universities are not immune from the hazards and risks that threaten other types of institutions. Behaviors demonstrated in schools are typically reflective of the society and the community a specific school serves (Dunn, 1999). As a result, campus security departments have been formed to protect property, students, faculty, and staff. Local police agencies provide additional protection, and in some cases, an educational institution may create its own standalone police department.

Educational institution security is a relatively recent development. Most colleges and universities did not have formalized security or police departments prior to World War II. However, as student populations became more politicized in the late 1950s and throughout the 1960s, the threat of civil disorder became more evident. Anti-Vietnam War sentiment and the radical behavior of some during the civil rights movement led to violent demonstrations and riots on several college campuses.

During the 1970s and 1980s enrollment in institutions at all educational levels increased dramatically. Violent crime, sexual assaults, unlawful homicide, and theft increased along with the increase in student populations. Gang and drug activity in elementary and secondary schools and escalating crime rates on college and university campuses created new challenges in learning institutions (Simonsen, 1998). In kindergarten through twelfth grade institutions (K–12, elementary, and secondary schools), vandalism, burglaries, and arson are major problems. Many teachers report hearing violent words and observing aggressive behavior in children as early as kindergarten. Classroom teachers are spending more time helping students learn the social skills that young people previously learned from their parents (Hess & Wrobleski, 1996). Schools have also been successfully sued for failure to provide a safe and secure environment. In some cases, the suits arise because of the discovery of a sexually intimate relationship between a teacher and an underage student.

Although reported violence in the schools decreased in the 1990s (Mc-Queen, 2000), crimes in schools increased overall in the past quarter century. The U.S. Bureau of Justice Statistics and the National Center for Education Statistics report an increase in gang activity and violent crime in the schools. According to these reports, gang activity increased between 1989 and 1995. Students victimized by violent crime increased 25 percent (Arnette & Walsleben, 1998). Consider these alarming statistics for the 1999–2000 school year in the United States. On average, 13 students per day were suspended, expelled, or arrested for taking firearms to school. More than 5,000 bomb threats and over 1 million acts of violence occurred (Kenworthy & O'Driscoll, 2000).

Violence in the schools can become deadly. On March 24, 1998, Andrew Golden, age 11, and Mitchell Johnson, 13, killed four elementary school students and a teacher in Jonesburro, Arkansas. On April 21, 1998, 15-year-old Kipland P. Kinkel, wearing a trenchcoat and carrying three guns, ran through a crowded Springfield, Oregon, high school cafeteria firing a rifle from his hip. Twenty-three students were injured, 19 of whom were hit by gunfire. Two students died from their wounds. The bodies of Kipland's parents were later found in his home. He had shot them both. On the same day, a 15-year-old boy in Onalaska, Washington, ordered his girlfriend off a bus and took her to his home, where he shot himself in the head and died. In another incident on April 21, 1998, a 15-year-old Jersey Village, Texas, student was shot in the leg in a high school classroom. The gunshot originated in another student's backpack containing a firearm that discharged accidentally.

In one of the worst and most publicized incidents of school violence to date, two students, Eric Harris, 18, and Dylan Klebold, 17, went on a lethal rampage at Columbine High School in Littleton, Colorado, on April 20, 1999. Harris and Klebold killed 12 fellow students and a teacher before taking their own lives. Other killings at schools by young people age 18 and under occurred in the 1990s in the following locations:

05–02–99	Conyers, Georgia
05–19–98	Fayetteville, Tennessee
04–24–98	Edinboro, Pennsylvania
12–15–97	Stamps, Arkansas
12–01–97	West Paducah, Kentucky
10–01–97	Pearl, Mississippi
02–19–97	Bethel, Alaska
02–02–97	Moses Lake, Washington
11–15–95	Lynnville, Tennessee
10–23–95	Redlands, California
10–12–95	Blockville, South Carolina

02-01-93   Amityville, New York

01-18-93   Grayson, Kentucky

On March 5, 2001, Charles "Andy" Williams, a 15-year-old freshman at Santana High School in Santee, California, a suburb of San Diego, opened fire on fellow students, faculty, and staff on his high school's campus at 9:20 A.M. Reloading his .22 caliber revolver at least four times, young Williams fired about 30 shots, killing 2 boys and wounding 11 other students, a campus security supervisor, and a student teacher. Charles Williams was allegedly seeking revenge for being teased and bullied by students at Santana High School (McDonald, 2001a). On March 22, 2001, 18-year-old student Jason Hoffman opened fire with a shotgun at Granite Hills High School in El Cajon, California, injuring five people. Granite Hills is in the same school district as Santana High School and is located approximately six miles south of the Santana campus. Hoffman was angry with school officials. Richard Agundez Jr., an El Cajon police officer assigned to the Granite Hills High School, responded quickly to the incident and wounded and subdued Hoffman during a brief gun battle (McDonald, 2001b).

The shootings at Santana and Granite Hills high schools marked the first times since January 29, 1979, that such an incident occurred in a San Diego area school. Twenty-two years earlier, Brenda Spencer, a 16-year-old, used a scoped rifle her father gave to her for Christmas to shoot at employees and students outside San Diego's Cleveland Elementary School. From her home across the street from the school, she killed 2 and wounded 9 because she said she did not like Mondays (Wolf Branscomb, 2001). In one of the worst school killings of its type anywhere, an expelled student entered his former school in Erfurt, Germany, on April 27, 2002, armed with a shotgun and a handgun. The student methodically killed 17 people before killing himself.

According to a study conducted of 15 school shooting incidents occurring since the early 1990s, the profile of the violent offender in schools includes the following characteristics:

- White male between 11 and 18 years of age.
- Product of a broken home.
- No symptoms of severe mental problems.
- No history of serious behavioral problems.
- Small in stature.
- Teased and bullied by student peers.
- Had access to firearms and often dressed in military-style clothing.
- Threatened violence before shooting (Washburn & Hasemyer, 2001).

As a result of a federal law passed in 1994, all 50 states enacted legislation that requires a one-year suspension for students who take guns to school.

Successful strategies to reduce the incidence of crime and regulate non-criminal conduct in K–12 schools focus on behavior codes, graffiti removal, crisis management, conflict prevention, and more active parental and community involvement. Some school districts, especially in tough inner-city neighborhoods, have their own police or security departments. Many also use metal detectors and a few use high-tech options such as biometrics and finger scanning to identify authorized students and personnel (Michel, 2000). Crime Prevention through Environmental Design (CPTED) has lso been applied successfully in the schools. Thousands of angry and disturbed young people enter school buildings every day and do not express their anger in a tragic way. Ultimately, the key to crime prevention in the schools may rest with a process of identifying the symptoms and treating the causes of potentially violent behavior in young people. Apparently, violence occurs more often in schools where minor infractions of school policies are ignored. Order maintenance in the schools sets the stage for a secure learning environment (Dunn, 1999).

Legislation and several types of collaborative programs have been developed by national, state, and local governments to create a safe environment in the schools.

- Most states have, through legislation, **created safe-school zones**. These zones include school transportation systems and off-campus school activities. The safe-school zones give rise to zero-tolerance policies focusing on weapons and drugs.
- Federal regulations enacted in 1994 require drug- and alcohol-use testing for all school bus drivers.

Chain link fences are used to enclose some school campuses. Photo courtesy of Star Source International.

- School districts are collaborating with the courts, probation agencies, and youth-service professionals to share information and monitor students who have criminal records.
- School districts are developing crisis prevention and intervention policies and procedures.
- Many schools now have security personnel, security devices, and criminal background checks on perspective employees, and have enlisted parents and volunteers to monitor facilities and school activities.

Since 1999, the U.S. Secret Service and the U.S. Department of Education have collaborated to identify potential threats and prevent violence in schools. These federal agencies embarked on the Safe School Initiative. Their efforts resulted in the development of a guide to managing threatening situations and creating safe school environments. The guide, *Threat Assessments in Schools,* is available through the U.S. Secret Service at www.secretservice.gov/ntac or the U.S. Department of Education at www.ed.gov/offices/OESE/SDFS (U.S. Department of Justice, Secret Service, & Department of Education, 2002).

Numerous other resources are available to assist with the development of school safety and security programs. Some organizations and their accompanying Web sites relating to school safety include the following:

- Center for the Study and Prevention of School Violence, www.colorado.edu/UCB/Research/cspv
- Creating Safe and Drug-Free Schools: An Action Guide, www.ed.gov/offices/OSDF/actguid/
- Early Warning, Timely Response: A Guide to Safe Schools, www.ed.gov/offices/OSERS/OSEP/products/earlywrn.html
- National Crime Prevention Council, www.ncpc.org
- National Resource Center for Youth Services (College of Continuing Education, University of Oklahoma), www.nrcys.ou.edu/default.htm
- National School Safety Center, www.nssc1.org
- Office of Juvenile Justice and Delinquency Prevention, www.ojjdp.ncjrs.org/
- Partnerships Against Violence Network, www.pavnet.org
- Report on School Safety (US DOE), www.ed.gov/pubs/AnnSchoolRept98/
- Safe and Drug-Free Schools Program Office, www.ed.gov/offices/OSDFS/index.html
- The American Academy of Experts in Traumatic Stress, Comprehensive School Crisis Response Plan, www.schoolcrisismanagement.info/
- The Safe Schools Coalition, www.thesafeschools.org
- U.S. Department of Education emergency planning Web site, www.ed.gov/emergencyplan

- Youth Risk Benefit Survey, Centers for Disease Control and Prevention, www.cdc.gov/nccdphp/dash

Unlike K–12 schools, colleges and universities (**postsecondary institutions**) have longer instructional days and unique problems. Some are residential campuses with dormitories, apartments, and single-family residences. In addition to the types of crime problems that commonly occur on K–12 campuses, postsecondary institutions may experience muggings, sexual assaults, illegal drug use, domestic and child abuse, and homicides. On August 15, 1996, Frederick Martin Davis, a 36-year-old engineering graduate student at San Diego State University, killed three professors. Apparently upset over the progress of his masters thesis, he hid a 9 mm handgun in a classroom first aid kit before he methodically killed the professors who were members of his thesis review panel. On October 28, 2002, a man who was failing courses in the nursing school of the University of Arizona at Tucson shot 3 of his professors to death, then killed himself. On May 9, 2003, a gunman killed 1 and injured several others when he opened fire at the business school of Case Western Reserve University in Cleveland, Ohio.

Noncriminal problems and incidents occur at postsecondary institutions also. Nonpayment of dormitory and apartment rent, traffic and parking congestion, alcohol abuse and suicide create challenges for campus-based protective services.

On college campuses, the professionalization and expansion of protective services coupled with increased student involvement in the preventive function have made a positive impact on crime and noncriminal problems. In addition, the **Crime Awareness and Campus Security Act** of 1990 requires postsecondary institutions to collect and disseminate campus crime statistics to students, parents, faculty, and staff. On August 16, 1990, the U.S. Department of Education printed final regulations that implemented amendments to the Drug-Free Schools and Communities Act enacted by Congress on December 12, 1989. The amendments required each institution of higher learning, as a condition to participation in a federal financial aid to students program, to certify that it had adopted and implemented a program to prevent the unlawful possession, use, or distribution of illicit drugs and alcohol by students and employees (Hess & Wrobleski, 1996).

Published guides to colleges and universities provide details on safety and security measures to prospective students and parents (*Peterson's Guide to . . .*, 2000; *Profiles of American . . .*, 2000). In 1998, Congress passed the Jeanne Clery Act, a federal law aimed at improving the reporting of crimes committed on college campuses. By October 17, 2000, colleges and universities throughout the United States were required to post their crime statistics on the U.S. Department of Education's Internet Web site, www.ope.ed.gov/security. The primary purpose of the Clery Act was to ensure accurate reporting of crime on college campuses. According to federal officials, postsecondary institutions traditionally underreported crime in spite of the 1990 federal law requiring submission of crime data. The Clery Act closed a number of loopholes through which colleges could exclude some reported crimes. The act expands the definition of a campus to include city streets and other properties that meander through college campuses. Colleges and universities are also required to survey local police, dormitory leaders, and rape crisis centers for criminal allegations that may not have been reported to college officials. All criminal complaints, proven or not, must be documented and reported under the 1998 law ("An education in crime stats," 2000).

ENTERTAINMENT SECURITY

As more individuals reach retirement age and the United States becomes more technologically advanced, the amount of leisure time available increases. As a result, people seek out mediums for entertainment. Sporting events, recreational facilities, theme parks, racetracks, movie studios and theaters, ocean liners, and casinos provide diversion venues for the leisure seeker. These venues also pose unique threats and provide opportunities for criminal activity. Organizations sponsor conventions, rock concerts, parades, festivals, and political rallies that draw large crowds and create problems related to order maintenance as well as crowd and traffic control. Theft, medical emergencies, and gate-crashing also create a need for security personnel, equipment, and procedures.

Accidents, theft, assault, robbery, vandalism (during and after hours), bomb threats, and terrorism pose threats to persons and property at sporting events. Personnel, alarm systems, and closed-circuit television surveillance equipment are the major sources of security at these events. Sporting events tend to draw fans who may become unruly and consume alcohol or drugs. Emotional highs may lead to aggressive behavior.

Some events draw huge crowds. The Olympic Games in Atlanta in 1996 drew an estimated 14,000 athletes and officials and over 2 million visitors. In 1998, Super Bowl XXXII in San Diego attracted upwards of 100,000 ticket holders, concession workers, celebrities, party crashers, and media people along with intoxicated persons, thieves, car burglars, and ticket scalpers. A force of 1,000 police and security officers was assembled to deter criminal activity and arrest violators. Super Bowl XXXIV at the Georgia Dome in Atlanta on January 30, 2000, placed over 70,000 fans in the stadium. Security planning for the event began almost 1 year earlier. By the time of the game, systems were in place to prevent and protect against everything from accidents to biological and chemical attacks, terrorist bombings, sniper fire, and other types of violence (Adams, 2000a). Since 9/11, security at large public events has been expanded. The 2002 Winter Olympics in Salt Lake City, Utah, was staffed with 12,000 security personnel equipped with 1,300 metal detectors. The cost of security at the 2002 Olympic games approached $350 million, twice the cost of the entire 1980 Winter Olympics in Lake Placid, New York (Zeigler, 2002).

Security problems in recreational areas and theme parks have increased in the past several years. Park rangers in national parks spend an increasingly disproportionate amount of time performing law enforcement duties. State, county, and city parks have also experienced an increase in security-related problems. Theft, illegal drug activity, vandalism, and assault have become more common. Theme parks such as Disneyland and Disney World, Busch Gardens, Sea World, and Universal Studios draw millions of people each year. The environment is designed so visitors feel a sense of security. Programs are also designed to anticipate trouble. Physical barriers and surveillance systems blend with the environment and go unnoticed by the average visitor. Security personnel focus on public relations, emergency response, shoplift prevention, and traffic control.

Racetracks, particularly horse or dog racing tracks, face unique security problems. In addition to theft, robbery, auto theft, and assaults, animals must be protected and visitors must be protected from con artists, drunks, and pickpockets. Some racetracks employ proprietary security personnel while others use a contract service. Still other racetracks employ a hybrid security force with a permanent proprietary staff supplemented by contract security personnel during the racing season. Security personnel are used to protect cash in betting areas; control vehicular and pedestrian traffic; control crowds; prevent thefts from patrons; protect horse and dog owners, riders, and handlers; respond to medical emergencies; and prevent illegal gambling. Peculiar security and safety situations, although not necessarily criminal, may arise at racetracks (Hess & Wrobleski, 1996). In 1998, the California House Racing Board investigated incidents in which an extraordinary number of horses sustained fatal injuries. The investigation focused on the physical condition of the horses as well as the condition of racetracks.

Photo courtesy of Star Source International.

The nature of entertainment has also changed dramatically. Television brought audio-visual entertainment into almost every living room in the country. The movie industry and the development of the Internet also provide mediums for entertainment. However, as a result of this expansion of technology, problems associated with the protection of celebrities and intellectual property have also increased. Celebrities have been stalked, even killed, by fanatical fans, and movies have been pirated.

Counterfeit movies and compact disks (CDS) are a serious problem. The **Motion Picture Association of America (MPAA),** an entertainment industry professional organization, estimates that millions of dollars are lost each year due to video pirating (Balint, 2000). Although inferior in quality, pirated videos are offered for sale at significantly lower prices at flea markets and through street vendors and fraudulent distributors. With new digital technology, the fake videos are easily copied. First-run movies are also copied by individuals who sit in movie theaters with video cameras when new films are released. The MPAA has offices in over 70 countries, staffed with people who work to prevent piracy and open legitimate distribution networks. Actual total losses due to pirating are difficult to estimate. Diminished consumer satisfaction due to low-quality pirated movies cannot be determined. Local, state, and federal sales and income taxes are also diverted (Simonsen, 1998).

Cruise ships and riverboats also experience unique security problems. Ships and boats are usually in motion when operating, and steep, narrow passageways and stairwells create special hazards. Probably the greatest threats to cruise lines and riverboat operations is the potential for accidents, medical emergencies, slip-and-fall claims, and the resulting liability and lawsuits. And, although thieves cannot escape unless a ship or boat is in port, theft remains a major threat in marine entertainment mediums.

Gaming has also become a favorite pastime for many Americans. Lotteries, casinos, and other wagering mediums in some form are permitted and regulated in more than 60 percent of the states. Billions of dollars exchange hands each year in gaming environments. Theft, pilferage, cheating, and organized crime are constant threats in wagering establishments.

In a casino, patrons may not pay close attention to their coins, tokens, handbags, or other personal items. Continuous surveillance, videotaping of suspicious people, and security personnel are used to monitor patrons and employees to identify thieves. **Casino security** consists of a three-pronged attack involving surveillance of patrons and employees, physical security, and investigations of potential employees as well as reports of theft, narcotics, gaming violations, and white collar crime. Armed and unarmed security officers, surveillance personnel, and gaming commission investigators are involved in the security and safety effort (Major, 1998).

The vast majority of gaming casinos are open 24 hours per day, 365 days each year. Customers can arrive at one of these casinos at any time, searching for a pleasurable experience. Legitimate patrons usually carry large sums of cash and have credit cards, travelers checks, jewelry, and luggage in their possession.

They are extremely vulnerable and may become victims of theft. A determined thief does not limit targets to legitimate customers. Con artists working individually and in groups are a threat to all casino games. Some thieves insert slugs (a piece of metal the size of a coin or token) into gaming slot machines. Other thieves attempt to compromise slot machines by "stringing." This procedure involves the attachment of a very thin monofilament, such as fishing line, to a coin. The coin is inserted into the coin acceptor of a slot machine. The operator manipulates the line to activate the machine repeatedly with the same coin. Additionally, table card games, and other games are subject to various types of theft (Nichter, 2000).

Casinos use a five-part strategy to prevent or detect theft through the casino's games. Through the command component, casinos organize security and surveillance. Through the control component, the casino utilizes security and surveillance to influence circumstances for a favorable outcome. Good communication is the component used to link elements and personnel. Compliance is the most vital component of the antifraud strategies. Compliance with house rules and agency regulations is a necessity. A significant amount of the losses to casinos result from irregular or minimal compliance with rules and regulatory agency policy (Nichter, 2000).

EXECUTIVE PROTECTION

Executive protection encompasses all activities designed to maintain the safety, security, and health of a human asset. Executive kidnapping is a potential threat in any part of the world, even in the United States. It has become a criminal industry in some countries. The risk of kidnaping, injury, or death is not only possible, but may be probable in some areas of the world. On August 10, 1996, Sanyo executive Mamoru Konno was kidnaped in Tijuana, Mexico, and held for nine days. Konno, in charge of a Sanyo factory in Mexico, was kidnapped from his car shortly after leaving a company-sponsored baseball game on the eastern edge of Tijuana. Fortunately, Konno was released unharmed after a $2 million ransom was paid. In August 1998, Daniel Arizmendi Lopez, when asked by a Mexican judge to state his occupation, allegedly identified himself as a kidnapper. Some authorities credit Lopez with the abduction of approximately 200 wealthy business people and their family members over a 5-year period. On September 11, 1999, Chung Yin Ng, a 72-year-old Chinese-born businessman was kidnapped in Tijuana and held for a $1 million ransom until he was rescued by Baja California state judicial police. Six men, including an associate of the victim, were arrested in connection with the kidnaping.

Organizations that assign human assets to work in foreign lands must ensure the health, safety, and security of personnel. Protection teams often accompany executives. In progressive security-conscious organizations, the human asset is briefed on potential dangers and trained to avoid high-risk areas and a conspicuous appearance. In addition to the threat of kidnaping and murder, healthcare services in many foreign venues are substandard. A failure to receive adequate medical care immediately after the onset of a sudden illness can be fatal. Some companies maintain, or establish contractual arrangements with, highly trained teams that specialize in medical evacuation of personnel from foreign countries.

Since trends suggest that the United States and its citizens are preferred targets for terrorists, human assets will continue to be potential victims of terrorism. The possibility of terrorist activity demands precautionary measures. Cooperation between and among nations is also essential to counterterrorism operations. To this end, the globe's intelligence communities and criminal justice systems must assume additional responsibility for counterterrorism and personal protection (Martin, 2003).

GOVERNMENT SECURITY

Security at and for government facilities and agencies is a large, yet less visible, asset protection function. Traditionally, security at local, county, and state government facilities has been provided by the police, sheriffs' departments, state police and highway patrol agencies, and local or county marshals. The U.S. Secret Service protects the President and numerous other officials. U.S. State Department security personnel provide protection to the U.S. Secretary of State, State Department personnel, and many foreign diplomats. In U.S. government facilities and courts, security is provided by Federal Protective Officers, Park Police, Capitol Police, and U.S. Marshals. Recently, a trend toward privatization of public services has led several agencies to outsource for many of their security personnel.

Security of personnel, property, and sensitive information is critical to a functioning government and, at the federal level, necessary to national security. Virtually all federal law enforcement agencies are involved, some to a greater extent than others, with the provision of security services. Protection of the President and presidential candidates as well as foreign ambassadors and dignitaries is always a requirement. Classified information must be protected against espionage. Government facilities must be protected from sabotage and terrorism. National parks also require attention because they encounter a multitude of safety and security problems due to their increased use.

Serious damage and injury, even death, can occur in and around government facilities in spite of sophisticated security and police protection. The U.S. Capitol building in Washington, D.C., has been the scene of random violence since the early 1800s. Crime in the Capitol building occurs even though security devices and armed Capitol Police are present. On July 24, 1998, two 18-year veterans of the Capitol Police force were killed and a visitor seriously wounded when a gunman opened fire after bypassing a metal detector at a Capitol building entrance. This was the first time the Capitol Police lost officers on duty since the inception of the agency in 1828.

Risks to government facilities are not confined to the boundaries of the United States or its territories. U.S. military bases, embassies, and missions throughout the world are potential targets. In fact, the U.S. Department of State receives over 30,000 reported threats to its facilities each year (Raum, 1999). On June 25, 1996, a truck bomb exploded outside a housing complex near Dhahran, Saudi Arabia, killing 19 Americans and injuring more than 500 Americans and Saudis. On August 7, 1998, bombing attacks on two U.S. embassies in East Africa occurred within 10 minutes of each other. A bomb blast was detonated at 10:35 A.M. in a parking lot adjacent to the U.S. Embassy in Nairobi, Kenya, killing over 240 people, 12 of whom were American, and injuring over 5,000. At 10:40 A.M., a second bomb exploded in Dar es Salaam, Tanzania, 450 miles from Nairobi. The second blast claimed the lives of 10 people and injured over 70. The bombings were believed to be the responsibility of a small, sophisticated, fundamentalist, Middle Eastern terrorist group, financed and led by Osama bin Laden, that has targeted U.S. installations (Shenon, 1999).

On August 20, 1998, the United States used approximately 75 Navy warship-based cruise missiles to retaliate against bin Laden by attacking a pharmaceutical factory in Sudan and a suspected terrorist training camp in Afghanistan. Both sites were believed to be facilities operated by the bin Laden terrorist group. Subsequently, the United States heightened security at U.S. airports and government facilities and warned U.S. citizens of the possibility of future terrorist attacks. Later, on October 12, 2000, bin Laden's group was cited as responsible for the bombing of the Navy ship USS *Cole* in Yemen that left 17 sailors dead (Sniffen, 2000). Finally, followers of bin Laden hijacked four commercial airlines on September 11, 2001, flying two of the commandeered aircraft

Photo courtesy of Wackenhut Corporation.

into New York City's World Trade Center, one into the ground in Pennsylvania, and one into the Pentagon in Arlington, Virginia ("America under attack," 2001).

The bombing incidents in East Africa on August 7, 1998, did not represent the first time U.S. embassies were targeted by terrorists. Other incidents in recent history include the following:

02-16-96   Athens, Greece: rocket-grenade attack; terrorist group suspected.

09-13-95   Moscow: rocket-propelled grenade fired; minor damage.

07-27-93   Lima, Peru: bomb exploded in bus outside embassy; one person killed.

01-31-91   Lima, Peru: bomb attack from rocket launcher.

03-23-88   Bogota, Columbia: rocket-propelled grenade launched by guerrilla group; causes minor damage.

06-09-87   Rome: rocket fired on embassy by Japan-based Red Army terrorists; minor injuries.

03-27-86   La Paz, Bolivia: dynamite exploded on roof of embassy.

02-18-86   Lisbon, Portugal: car bomb exploded outside embassy.

09-20-84   Beirut, Lebanon: suicide car bomb killed 16.

12-12-83   Kuwait City: suicide truck bomb killed 6, injured 12; 17 pro-Iranian terrorists convicted.

04-18-83   Beirut, Lebanon: suicide car bomb killed 63.

International terrorists may accomplish their goals with only one or two bombings every few years. Subsequent to each bombing, the United States tightens security and supports a new offensive against terrorists. The result is less freedom of movement for people and heightened security that costs millions, if not billions, of dollars. The expenditures cause an economic drain on the nation's economy and lessens the quality of life for many Americans.

Although the Cold War ended in the early 1990s, U.S. government officials learned that complacency can result in negative consequences. Lax security at the Los Alamos National Laboratory in New Mexico threatened to compromise U.S. nuclear secrets. Even the Central Intelligence Agency is not immune from breaches in security. Revelations early in the year 2000 raised concerns that John Deutch, who directed the CIA from May 1995 to December 1996, used an unclassified computer in his home to work on highly secret classified material. A CIA inspector general's investigation also revealed that the home computer containing the classified material was used to gain access to unsecured Internet pornographic sites ("Security fears cited over prior CIA chief," 2000). In another security breach in early 2000, undercover GAO investigators, using fictitious law enforcement identification credentials, were able to penetrate 19 secured federal facilities, including the Washington, D.C., FBI building, the Pentagon, and the CIA headquarters in Langley, Virginia ("'Cops' test security, get in CIA, other buildings," 2000).

In response to the threat of terrorism, the U.S. Department of Homeland Security (DHS) was created in 2002. Representing the largest transformation of the U.S. government since the 1947 creation of the U.S. Department of Defense, the DHS consolidated 22 scattered domestic agencies with nearly 180,000 employees into one department on March 1, 2003. The DHS is organized into four major directorates.

The *Border and Transportation Security Directorate* consolidates major security and transportation operations. It includes the following federal agencies:

- U.S. Customs Service (formerly in Treasury Department)
- Immigration and Naturalization Service (part) (formerly in Justice Department)
- Federal Protective Service (formerly in General Services Administration)
- Transportation Security Administration (formerly in Transportation Department)
- Federal Law Enforcement Training Center (formerly in Treasury Department)
- Animal and Plant Health Inspection Service (part) (formerly in Agriculture Department)
- Office for Domestic Preparedness (formerly in Justice Department)

The *Emergency Preparedness and Response Directorate* oversees domestic disaster preparedness training and coordinates government disaster response. Its agencies include the following:

- Federal Emergency Management Agency
- Strategic National Stockpile and National Disaster Medical Systems
- Nuclear Incident Response Team
- Domestic Emergency Support Teams
- National Domestic Preparedness Office

The *Science and Technology Directorate* seeks to utilize all scientific and technological advantages to secure the U.S. homeland. The following agencies are part of this effort:

- CBRN Countermeasures Programs (formerly in Energy Department)
- Environment Measurements Laboratory (formerly in Energy Department)
- National BW Defense Analysis Center (formerly in Defense Department)
- Plum Island Animal Disease Center (formerly in Agriculture Department)

The *Information Analysis and Infrastructure Protection Directorate* analyzes intelligence and information from other agencies (including the CIA, FBI,

NSA) involving threats to homeland security and evaluates vulnerabilities in the nation's infrastructure. It includes the following:

- Critical Infrastructure Assurance Office (formerly in Commerce Department)
- Federal Computer Incident Response Center (formerly in General Services Administration)
- National Communications System (formerly in Defense Department)
- National Infrastructure Protection Center (formerly in FBI, Justice Department)
- Energy Security and Assurance Program (formerly in Energy Department)

The Secret Service and the Coast Guard, both previously in the Treasury Department, are now located in the DHS, remaining intact and reporting directly to the Secretary. In addition, the Immigration and Naturalization Service (INS) adjudications and benefits programs report directly to the Deputy Secretary as the Bureau of Citizenship and Immigration Services (U.S. Department of Homeland Security, 2003). Currently, the U.S. liaison to the International Police Organization (INTERPOL) is located in the U.S. National Central Bureau of INTERPOL in the U.S. Department of Justice (U.S. Department of Justice, 2003).

HEALTHCARE SECURITY

As a profession, healthcare security developed gradually over the past 100 years. During the first half of the twentieth century, healthcare security was limited to the minor role hospital maintenance staff played in providing security. In the 1950s, off-duty police officers were used to provide security in emergency rooms and other sensitive areas. As police agency budgets stabilized (and, in some cases, shrunk) during the 1960s and off-duty police time became more constrained, hospitals assumed a more direct role in the provision of safety and security services. In 1968, the **International Association of Healthcare Security and Safety (IAHSS)** was established to provide a professional forum for healthcare security managers. Today, virtually every major urban hospital, as well as many other auxiliary **healthcare facilities**, have proprietary safety and security personnel (Simonsen, 1998).

Healthcare is the fifth largest industry in the United States. Over 30,000 healthcare facilities administer care to millions of people. The healthcare facilities include about 6,000 hospitals in the U.S., ranging from 25 to 2,500 beds, as well as public and private hospitals, clinics, medical offices, **nursing homes,** and extended care and outpatient facilities that must provide a safe and secure environment for patients, staff and visitors. The facilities must also prevent loss of assets. In fact, the **Joint Commission for Accreditation of Healthcare Organizations (JCAHO)** requires minimum security standards for hospitals. As

Photo courtesy of Star Source International.

security-related problems in hospitals increase, the JCAHO stiffens and increases minimum standards for hospital security.

Major urban medical centers function much like small cities. They never close. Each has retail outlets, pharmacies, restaurants, and offices, and many have multiple buildings. In addition, many patients are unable to care for themselves, much less protect themselves from dangerous situations. Theft, fire, natural disasters, accidents, personal attacks, and sexual assaults are constant threats. Shoplifting may occur in the gift shops, patients or visitors may become violent, and power failures may threaten life-support systems. Drugs are stolen from pharmacies, cars from parking lots, and babies from maternity wards ("University Health Care provides health, safety and security for patients," 2000). Rival gang members may pursue an injured gang member into an emergency room for revenge. Family planning clinics may be subjected to civil disturbances, forcible assaults, bombings, and homicides.

Access control is difficult in many healthcare facilities. Numerous entrances and exits coupled with busy medical staffs and a constant flow of newcomers help create an environment where control and surveillance of pedestrian traffic is difficult. Hospitals and other healthcare facilities are also held liable when accidents and crime occur as the result of inadequate security (Hess & Wrobleski, 1996). A safe environment reduces exposure to risks and limits liability.

Healthcare facilities, including hospitals and medical centers, tend to be a reflection of the environments within which they are located. If they are located in high crime rate areas, the threat of crime is great and the offense rate on or near facility property is also high. With the rapid growth of home healthcare, new, more diverse problems have developed. Healthcare professionals, working

Photo courtesy of Star Source International.

alone, must enter dangerous neighborhoods. Another trend is the use of computers and the sharing of patient and personnel data between departments and among healthcare organizations. Data transmission interceptions and access to electronic mail and Internet connections threaten the privacy of countless individuals (Dolan, 1999).

Increasing and, in some cases, out-of-control costs associated with healthcare led to public outcry and subsequent regulatory controls in the late 1900s. The result was a trend toward cost containment and managed care. Traditional methods of financing healthcare were replaced with collaborative mechanisms to share resources and monitor healthcare expenses, income, and profit. Health maintenance organizations (HMOs) emerged to operate healthcare institutions as businesses rather than social service agencies. This movement focused on cost reduction. As security requirements increased, the loss prevention manager was faced with the challenge of doing more with fewer resources. JCAHO and the Occupational Safety and Health Administration (OSHA) increasingly require security assessments and plans upon which a healthcare facility is evaluated. Yet, with fewer resources, the security manager may be faced with serious plan implementation constraints. Even more exacerbating is the situation in which the person normally responsible for the protection function is not a security professional but someone whose training and education has been in facilities management or human resources rather than protection services.

Policies, procedures, equipment, and strategies for preventing losses in healthcare facilities are as numerous as the facilities are diverse. Photo identification badges for staff assist with access control. Electronic surveillance systems monitor patients, staff, and visitors. Security personnel patrol the buildings and parking lots and are part of emergency reaction teams. Many healthcare facilities provide Professional Assault Response Training (PART) to security and other emergency response employees. PART involves a comprehensive and systematic approach designed to minimize risks associated with assaultive behavior of patients, visitors, and others in a healthcare environment. PART emphasizes the roles of supervision, policy enforcement, and deescalation of conflict. The training focuses on identification of the symptoms and motives of violent behavior, the development of alternative courses of action, a determination of levels of dangerousness, response techniques, and use of force. PART helps healthcare employees develop the skills necessary to manage risk associated with assaultive behavior, mitigate liability, maintain a safe environment, and conform to legislatively mandated training requirements (Professional Growth Facilitators, 2000).

Special security practices protect electronic databases and computer-based information storage and transmission systems. Biometrics is being used to positively identify patients and staff. Loss prevention and self-protection training is being provided to more staff, especially those who work alone in a community health environment. Healthcare security personnel conduct internal investigations, inspections, audits, and surveys. They provide other interdepartmental support, such as escort and mail services. They also develop safety and security plans, test emergency protection systems, and control access.

Security in a healthcare environment is an absolute necessity. First, hospitals and other healthcare facilities have a moral responsibility to serve the public. This obligation requires the provision of a safe and secure environment. Second, healthcare enterprises have a legal responsibility to protect persons and property. The legal duty to protect is even greater when patients are unable to care for themselves. Negligence on the part of hospitals has led to compensatory damage awards by juries as well as high punitive damage awards not typically covered by liability insurance carriers. Third, accreditation and regulatory requirements of JCAHO and OSHA, coupled with numerous other federal, state and local statutes, require security in healthcare facilities. Fourth, healthcare organizations have a fiduciary responsibility to maintain a sound financial position. Thus, cost containment through the prevention of loss due to crime, waste, and natural phenomena is necessary. Fifth, good public and employee relations are maintained, in part, through the provision of a safe and secure environment (Colling, 1999).

Extended or assisted care facilities, the largest segment of which is often referred to as nursing homes, face the same general threats that confront hospitals. Although usually smaller in size and scope than hospitals, nursing homes serve a segment of the population that is often physically or mentally incapacitated. Natural and environmental disasters, fire, theft of resident property, and patient abuse are common threats to safety and security in nursing homes. The Medicare and Medicaid programs produced unique security concerns. Some facilities are alleged to have solicited kickbacks as a precondition for certain business arrangements. Some documented cases uncovered the involvement of organized crime with the Medicare and Medicaid programs.

Since most nursing homes and assisted care facilities are small, the protective function is usually assigned to a nonsecurity professional, often the business manager for a facility. In addition, budgetary realities dictate the need for personnel multitasking in small healthcare facilities. Thus, the safety and security function is often given a low priority. However, through the use of alarms, CCTV, controlled access systems, policies, and procedures, increased protection of people, property, and information can be realized. Liaison with local, state, and federal public safety agencies as well as a thorough investigation of all injuries, losses, and security violations can help minimize protection problems (Colling, 1999).

HOSPITALITY SECURITY

The **hospitality industry** consists of bars and lounges, restaurants, lodging establishments, and similar facilities. Although bars and restaurants are subject to many types of crimes, especially robbery, burglary, and disruptive behavior, it is in the lodging industry where the crime rate has climbed most dramatically. Theft, both internal and external, prostitution, assaults, rape, drug activity, and in some instances, homicide have increased. Lawsuits against hotels and motels due to inadequate security have also increased.

In an effort to make lodging establishments more attractive and improve customer convenience and satisfaction, many hotel and motel operators sacrificed safety and security. Lack of internal controls have led to an increase in theft of hotel and motel property such as cash, linens, supplies, dishes, and silverware. Guests and guest rooms are targets of the internal thief as well. Externally, professional thieves and burglars, prostitutes, drug dealers, rapists, and auto thieves find that lodging establishments are very attractive targets. Guests themselves steal ashtrays, towels, and linens for souvenirs and vandalize hotel and motel property. Credit card and check fraud, shoplifting, and nonpayment of room charges are also commonplace (Simonsen, 1998).

Losses are not always due to criminal activity. Accidents, fire, natural disasters, and poor inventory control also contribute to the depletion of lodging industry assets. Litigation costs and adverse judgments from lawsuits also affect the profitability of lodging facilities. Courts have held motels and hotels liable for theft of guest property and injuries and assaults on guests by employees as well as outsiders.

Security measures in lodging establishments should focus on strict key control, comprehensive pre-employment screening, CCTV and alarm systems, and safety programs to prevent injury to employees and guests. Guest room door locks should be rekeyed when keys are lost or not returned by a registered guest. Consideration may be given to the installation of a card-key access system to replace traditional keyed locks. Background checks on all prospective employees may uncover poor employment and criminal conviction histories, credit problems, and propensity toward chemical abuse. A well-planned and executed fire prevention strategy coupled with appropriate fire alarm and extinguishing equipment will reduce heavy losses, injuries, or deaths due to fire.

In many cases, a common response to an increase in criminal activity from outsiders against lodging establishments is to employ or add security personnel. In the long term, however, enhanced security may be achieved more inexpensively through incorporation of technology into a hotel or motel's security system. CCTV is an excellent complement to the security function. Surveillance and alarm systems reduce the need for human patrol and may be monitored continuously at or near the registration desk.

Some establishments incorporate contract-service interactive CCTV to monitor lobby activity and deter or detect robberies and other violent activity. Contract-service personnel located at a central station can view the lobby and front desk at regular intervals, usually about every 15 minutes. Lodging personnel can also notify the contract service by pressing an alert button located inside the front desk. This action immediately presents the establishment's front desk on the central station's CCTV monitor and notifies proper authorities. The event

Courtesy of Wackenhut Corp.

is also videotaped and stored as an aid to a subsequent investigation and possible prosecution (Stover, 2000).

SUMMARY

Common threats as well as safety and security principles and practices apply across the broad spectrum of public and private enterprises. However, some threats and security measures are unique to specific environments. Airlines transport and airports process millions of people and tons of cargo annually. Aircraft are vulnerable and may cross numerous state and international boundaries. Thus, aviation security is a national security concern. The nature of banking and financial transactions has changed dramatically, increasing targets of opportunity for the would-be criminal. Courthouses and courtrooms are no longer safe havens where adversaries can settle disputes without fear of disruption, injury, or death. Disaster recovery specialists develop and implement plans to assist organizations with resumption of normal activity after a major catastrophe.

Although educational institutions as a whole are safe environments, an increase in violent crime led to the development of safety and security programs in elementary and secondary schools as well as colleges and universities. The entertainment industry blossoms as more people seek leisure time activities. Sporting events, recreational facilities, theme parks, gaming casinos, and other entertainment venues serve millions of people. Computer technology and the Internet have created a need to prevent fraudulent appropriation of intellectual property.

The development of the global marketplace and an increase in international travel led to a need to protect people in transit and those who visit unsafe areas of the world. Security of personnel and critical information is an essential element of all governmental operations. Healthcare, the fifth largest industry in the United States, encompasses over 30,000 facilities. The sick, injured, and dying typically cannot care for themselves. Thus, the healthcare security business is expanding. Hospitality environments, especially lodging establishments, are targets for various types of crime committed by employees, guests, and unwanted visitors.

KEY TERMS

Aviation and Transportation Security Act of 2001

bailiff

Bank Protection Act

casino security

Crime Awareness and Campus Security Act

disaster recovery

executive protection

Federal Aviation Administration (FAA)

financial institution

healthcare facility

hospitality industry

International Association of Health-care Security and Safety (IAHSS)

Joint Commission for Accreditation of Healthcare Organizations (JCAHO)

Motion Picture Association of America (MPAA)

nursing home

passenger profiling techniques

postsecondary institutions

safe-school zone

Transportation Security Administration (TSA)

DISCUSSION QUESTIONS AND EXERCISES

1. Although commonalities exist, numerous unique hazards threaten specific types of industries and organizations. Explain.

2. Choose one specific security application from this chapter. List the types of crime and other hazards that threaten the operation, and design measures to prevent the threats from materializing.

Specific Security Applications: Part II

LEARNING OBJECTIVES

After completing this chapter, the reader should be able to

- identify security threats unique to specific industries and government operations.
- describe asset protection priorities as well as loss prevention policies, procedures, and systems associated with the following:
  - industrial security
  - library and museum security
  - office building security
  - privatization of public services
  - residential security
  - retail loss prevention
  - transportation security
  - utility security
  - workplace violence prevention
  - zoo and aquarium security
- evaluate specific security environments, applications, and services.

INTRODUCTION

Although a comprehensive exploration of every unique security environment and service is beyond the scope of a single book, Chapters 9 and 10 are designed to introduce the reader to numerous security applications. This chapter continues with a discussion of specific security environments, applications, and services.

INDUSTRIAL SECURITY

Industrial security focuses primarily on the protection of the manufacturing process. Accidents, natural disasters, internal theft, sabotage, and espionage constitute the major threats to industrial complexes. Accidents may result in process downtime, property damage, personal injury, even death. Natural disasters can destroy an entire industrial facility.

Internal theft is a major contributing factor to losses in and around industrial manufacturing facilities. Theft of tools, raw materials, component parts, finished products, equipment, time, and technology are the primary means through which dishonest employees contribute to loss. Vulnerable areas include loading docks, shipping and receiving areas, warehouses, tool storage areas, trash containers, distribution points, and data systems (Fennelly, 1992).

Although the Cold War is over, espionage and sabotage remain very real threats to manufacturing organizations. Industrial espionage occurs when trade secrets, proprietary information, or intellectual property are stolen. Sabotage occurs when the manufacturing process is intentionally disrupted or when machinery or products are intentionally destroyed. Likely suspects to espionage or sabotage are disgruntled employees, competitors, and in some cases, foreign governments.

Under contract to the U.S. Government, many private organizations and numerous colleges and universities conduct classified research and produce classified material for government consumption. To ensure compliance with federally mandated security parameters, these private industries and academic institutions participate in the National Industrial Security Program (NISP). NISP security-compliance regulations apply to contractors performing for numerous government agencies, including the U.S. Department of Defense (Kovacich & Halibozek, 2003).

LIBRARY AND MUSEUM SECURITY

Due to the rare and sometimes irreplaceable nature of **library** and **museum** inventories, special attention must be given to criminal as well as noncriminal hazards. Theft, vandalism, fire, floods, leaking roofs, and the environment are common threats to library collections and museum pieces. Libraries contain a

Photo courtesy of Wackenhut Corporation.

wide variety of out-of-print works, compact computer disks (CDS), audiovisual materials, and manuscripts. Museums contain rare, often irreplaceable, items. Irreplaceable and rare items and materials should be maintained in closed areas where access is easily restricted. Mutilation of books and periodicals may be reduced by providing copier machines to patrons. Unauthorized removal of library works may be prevented through the use of electronic markings in books and alarm sensors at exit points. Museum pieces can be monitored via CCTV and through the use of security personnel in areas accessible to the public.

Theft of priceless rare items and works of art has been identified as second only to international drug trafficking in terms of dollar value per criminal transaction. In many cases, major thefts are the product of a contractual arrangement between the thief and the illegitimate consumer (Hough, 1999). The most frequently stolen works in museums and art galleries tend to be small items that can be concealed easily. As with libraries, most museum thefts occur while the facility is open to the public. Museums and art galleries must also be vigilant regarding purchases of additional pieces for the collection. Acquisitions should be authenticated to deter and detect criminals who specialize in the creation of fraudulent pieces or the disposition of stolen works.

Comprehensive physical security programs, continuous inventory control procedures, and authentication and appraisal of new works can greatly reduce losses to museums and galleries. Maintaining appropriate air quality and temperature standards will also preserve rare items (Hess & Wrobleski, 1996).

OFFICE BUILDING SECURITY

Originally, the United States was an agrarian (agricultural) society. However, mass migration, immigration, and the industrial revolution of the last half of the nineteenth century and the early 1900s led to the development of cities and urban areas. In the latter half of the twentieth century, a technological revolution occurred. The United States, and most of the industrialized world, was transformed. Technologically advanced, service-related, information-based economies replaced industrial, labor-intensive, blue-collar economies. Today, white collar workers comprise a substantial portion of the workforce. These workers are typically housed in offices and office buildings that may be scattered throughout metropolitan areas.

Most office buildings are open to the public and provide convenient entry and exit points. Unless one agency or company occupies an entire building, several tenants will occupy a single facility. As a result, during normal business hours, few office buildings restrict access to lobbies, different floors, individual business offices, or restrooms.

Major **office building security threats** include fire (Craighead, 2003), poor or inadequate evacuation routes, terrorist activity, bombs or bomb threats, theft, burglary, robbery, sexual assault, and executive kidnaping. Office equipment, supplies, payroll checks, cash, and proprietary information are often the targets for thieves and burglars. Women may be assaulted in the restrooms or parking areas. Corporate executives may be targeted for kidnaping.

The risk of loss or injury in office buildings can be minimized in several ways.

- Security personnel, contract or proprietary, should be employed.
- Liquid assets, such as cash and valuables, and sensitive proprietary information can be stored in vaults.
- Restrooms should be locked with passkeys restricted to tenants and their guests.
- Maintenance and custodial personnel should be properly screened prior to employment.
- Common areas and parking facilities should be patrolled regularly.
- Access control and surveillance systems may be utilized.
- Fire drills and inspection of fire prevention and protection equipment should occur on a regular basis.

Photo courtesy of Wackenhut Corporation.

Subsequent to the World Trade Center terrorist bombing in New York City in 1993, several high-rise office building management teams increased security. Measures implemented or improved included access control, security patrols, staff awareness training, new policies and procedures, contingency planning, window glazing, and forms of perimeter fortification. During the 7 years subsequent to the 1993 incident, $60 million was spent at the World Trade Center to improve security and counter the threat of terrorism. However, it appears that only the high-profile facilities made measurable security improvements. In spite of the bombings at the World Trade Center in 1993 and the Murrah federal building in Oklahoma City in 1995, many office building security managers still believed their facilities were relatively immune from terrorism (Gips, 2000). The security measures in high-rise office buildings remained relatively loose during normal business hours. This false sense of security was shattered on September 11, 2001. Since the loss of New York's World Trade Center on 9/11, many high-rise facilities throughout the United States have improved security and safety measures dramatically (Craighead, 2003).

Ultimately, the type, amount, and cost of security measures employed in and around an office building will depend on the size, location, and nature of the facility. The number of tenants, the type of businesses involved, and crime rate within the area must also be considered when planning a safety and security program for an office building (Hess & Wrobleski, 1996).

PRIVATIZATION OF PUBLIC SERVICES

In principle, **privatization of public services** in some cases may be in the best interests of society in general and taxpayers in particular. However, some experts express reservations about privatization, because the privatized activities are the responsibility of the criminal justice system (public law enforcement, courts, corrections). At issue is relegation of responsibility for two precious citizen possessions to private, for-profit organizations: personal liberty and life itself (Robinson, 1999). Constitutionally, it may not be possible to delegate most crime-related law enforcement responsibilities to the private sector. However, many non-crime-related activities and services currently performed by the public police may appropriately be transferred, under contract, to private organizations through privatization of public services. In this regard, there appears to be a growing interdependence between the public and private sectors. Federal, state and local government expenditures for private sector services has increased dramatically over the past several years. In many areas of the country, the private sector is involved in activities such as traffic and parking enforcement, preventive patrol, community policing, animal control, court security, prisoner transport, and corrections.

As a result of stabilized and shrinking governmental budgets, some publicly provided services are being shifted to private providers who, through efficient business strategies and less bureaucracy, are able to cut costs and provide equivalent services on a more effective basis. It is estimated that by the year 2035, 50 percent of all law enforcement responsibilities will be assumed by private security companies (Tafoya, 1994). Caution must be exercised to insure the provision of quality public services by the private providers.

Some of the most visible efforts to privatize public services have been in the area of corrections. Private providers such as the Corrections Corporation of America, Pinkerton, and the Wackenhut Corrections Corporation are involved in the construction and operation of jails and prisons throughout the United States. By the mid-1990s, approximately 80 privately run jails and prisons were operating within the United States. In addition, hundreds of private community-based corrections programs (halfway houses, drug treatment centers, small residential institutions, work and study release programs) operate throughout the United States. In most cases, the private companies meet or exceed the quality of government-provided services while reducing costs.

Many examples of public–private cooperation and effective privatization efforts exist. During the spring of 1997, the Dallas, Texas, police department, as part of a huge anticrime offensive, solicited assistance from the city's 15,000 private security officers. The police department asked the private forces to act as additional eyes and ears for the police. Rapport and a communications system was established between the public and the private sectors. Apparently, this collaboration was effective in reducing the crime rate, especially among juveniles. In addition, private security personnel, under contract to local, county, state, and the national government, transport prisoners and provide security for courthouses in many areas of the United States. Private court security officers are also used quite extensively by the U.S. Marshals service to secure federal courthouses and courtrooms. The sharing of information between private security and public law enforcement has also increased ("Operation Cooperation," 2001).

On the international scene, private U.S. corporations, under contract to the federal government, provide security services and personnel for U.S. embassies and missions throughout the world. These companies establish security programs that supplement U.S. Marines assigned to the U.S. government facilities in foreign countries. Typically, the private security operations are managed on-site by U.S. nationals with operations-level personnel recruited and employed from the host country's local labor market (Simonsen, 1998).

RESIDENTIAL SECURITY

Individuals spend a majority of their time in a residential environment. People eat, sleep, socialize, and sometimes work in single family homes, apartments, condominiums, and multipurpose facilities. The residence may be in a single- or multi-family dwelling. It may be located in the inner city, a suburb, or rural area. It may be part of a planned community or public housing facility. Residents often provide for their own security. Others, however, may employ contract or proprietary security personnel services.

Safety and security threats in a residence include accidents, medical emergencies, fire, theft, burglary, vandalism, assault, homicide, and damage or personal injury resulting from natural disasters. The home is actually a very unsafe place and vulnerability increases when residents are asleep. Of all fire deaths each year, approximately one-half occur in the home. The residence is also an ideal target for burglars because the possibility of being caught is minimal. Nationally, only about 15 percent of all residential burglaries are solved. Most burglaries are committed when the home is unoccupied and the possibility of detection and apprehension is minimized. In addition, many homicides are committed in the home, often as a result of a long history of domestic conflict (Barlow, 2000).

Most safety and security problems in a residence are preventable. Early warning fire detectors and adequate preplanned escape routes greatly reduce fire deaths. Physical security in the form of lighting, good locks on doors and windows, access control, and secure storage of valuables can deter or minimize the impact of an unauthorized intrusion.

Residents should adhere to the following as a **residential burglary prevention strategy:**

- The residence should not look unoccupied.
- Key control should be maintained and doors and windows kept locked.

- Lights and a radio should be left on while residents are away. Timing devices may be used to control lights.
- Strangers should not be admitted to the residence.
- Residents should know their neighbors. Trusted neighbors may check on the home and retrieve mail and newspapers during an absence.
- An inventory of valuables should be kept and provided to the police if a burglary occurs.
- Notes indicating an absence should not be left where visible.
- Travel plans should not be broadcast.
- An alarm system may be considered. The most inexpensive alarm is a large dog that barks at strangers.

In an effort to create a more secure environment, many residential areas are supervised through neighborhood watch programs or are gated to restrict access. Some employ security patrols. In addition, multi-unit buildings and housing facilities may utilize alarm systems, surveillance equipment, or interior and exterior patrols. They can be constructed, utilizing Crime Prevention through Environmental Design (CPTED) principles, with consideration given to security and safety. Through local community policing efforts, resources are often available to assist residential property managers in their efforts to secure property and deter illegal activity. A training program prepared by the United States Department of Justice, Office of Justice Programs, emphasizes cooperation among property owners, managers, tenants, and law enforcement agencies to help neighborhoods fight residence-related crime (U.S. Department of Justice, Bureau of Justice Assistance, 2000).

RETAIL LOSS PREVENTION

Introduction

Losses in retail operations may occur in several ways. Administrative errors and inaccurate record-keeping account for up to 20 percent of all retail losses. Natural disasters in the form of floods, tornadoes, and hurricanes certainly take their toll. Looting during civil disturbances and riots have also left their mark on history. Products developed for human consumption can be intentionally or unintentionally contaminated (Nocella, 2000). However, losses due to theft, both internal and external, account for the greatest continuous economic drain on retail establishments.

Theft-related losses may force a retail operation into bankruptcy. To compensate for actual losses, a retail outlet is required to generate, through additional sales, many times the amount of the loss. For example, if the store operates on a 5 percent net profit margin and experiences an actual loss of $50, it must generate additional sales of $1000 to offset the loss and break even. Similarly, if the same store experiences a $500 loss, it must generate additional sales of $10,000 before profitability returns.

Inventory shrinkage is the major problem in retail environments. Shrinkage is defined as the reduction in inventories not accounted for through sales or other legitimate activity. It is the difference between the inventory that is on hand for sale and what the retail establishment indicates should be available for sale. The most significant causes of retail shrinkage are internal and external theft.

Internal Theft

The primary cause of inventory shrinkage to most retailers is internal theft (C. Bridges, 1994). Over 40 percent of all retail losses due to theft are internal in nature. Approximately 30 percent is due to external sources, while 20 percent is due to administrative error (Hollinger & Dabney, 1995). Employees have direct access to cash and merchandise, often work alone, and are familiar with retail loss prevention measures.

Employees may deplete the resources of a retail establishment in several ways. These include

- theft of cash.
- price alterations or switching.
- abuse of the refund system.
- undercharging of, or not charging for, merchandise to a friend or relative.
- theft of merchandise.
- kickbacks from vendors.
- intentionally damaging merchandise to purchase later at a discounted price.
- failing to record sales on the cash register and pocketing the cash from a customer.

Internal theft can be prevented, or at least reduced, through the establishment of sound preemployment screening procedures, strict cash handling procedures and refund policies, random audits, a code of conduct for employees, and management's attention to employee behavior. In addition, independent honesty shopping services may be employed to test employee cash-handling procedures and customer service. The honesty shopper, posing as a customer, observes employee behavior and reports to management on sales personnel efficiency, courtesy, and violations of store policies and procedures (Fischer & Green, 1998).

External Sources of Loss

Retail losses from external sources are due to vandalism, burglary, robbery, **credit card fraud** and **coupon fraud, bad checks,** and **shoplifting.** Shopping centers and malls face unique challenges because they incorporate privately owned space where the general public gathers. Public demonstrations and disturbances can deter normal customer activity. Thus, shopping center owners and security personnel must balance private property interests with the public's right to gather and exercise constitutional rights such as freedom to associate and freedom of speech (Fickes, 2000).

Vandalism and burglary may be prevented through the use of adequate exterior lighting, physical security, and subscription to a central station alarm service. When not preventable, losses due to robbery may be greatly reduced by limiting the amount of cash on hand in cash registers and other robbery targets. Stores that are open 24 hours are especially vulnerable to robbery. The Occupational Safety and Health Administration (OSHA) recommends that stores with late-night open hours take extra precautions. Improved lighting, increased staffing, video cameras, alarms, floor deposit safes, bullet-resistant glass, and employee training can prevent or at least reduce the impact of nighttime robberies.

Credit card fraud resulting from the use of a stolen or fictitious credit card may be reduced through a careful examination of the credit card and the signature of the cardholder accompanied by verification of the signature and positive identification of the purchaser. Some form of photo identification is appropriate for this verification. Coupon fraud occurs when customers (or employees) redeem coupons for cash in lieu of the purchase of the item for which the coupon was issued (Nocella, 2000).

Bad checks fall into four broad categories: forged or altered, nonsufficient funds, no account, and incorrectly completed checks. Postdated, out-of-town, second party, illegible, and counter checks are considered high risk. Since most checks are written and cashed in a retail environment, the potential for heavy dollar loss is great. Furthermore, only a small percentage of the dollar loss due to bad checks is ever recovered. Therefore, effective **check cashing procedures** are critical. Check cashing procedures include a thorough examination of the check and a positive identification of the check casher. Acceptable forms of identification for check cashing purposes include current photo driver's licenses, government or military identification, passports, and state or national identification cards (Fischer & Green, 1998).

Shoplifting, by employees as well as outsiders, is considered to be the most frequent crime committed against retailers. Shoplifting occurs whenever persons lawfully or unlawfully present on the retail premises misappropriate merchandise to their own use. It is one of the fastest growing theft-related crimes. Shoplifters fall into three broad categories: amateurs (the largest group), kleptomaniacs (compulsive thieves), and professionals. **Shoplifting methods** are limited only by the ingenuity of the thief. Common methods include hiding items under or in clothing, purses and briefcases; switching price tags; placing items in another product's packaging; use of a booster box or shopping bag; or wearing the item out of the store. Some bold thieves may simply grab the merchandise and run from the store. If a retail establishment's policy is to apprehend shoplifters, at least one employee on duty should receive adequate training to handle shoplifters. The employee must be knowledgeable regarding state and local laws associated with a retail merchant's authority to detain, search, or arrest suspected shoplifters. Shoplifter apprehensions can easily result in a physical confrontation that should be avoided (Fischer & Janoski, 2000).

An effective **shoplifting prevention strategy** includes deterrence and detection through the use of appropriate displays of merchandise, surveillance equipment and people, package and fitting room inspections, properly enforced refund procedures, locking devices, and alarms. However, the most effective deterrent is adequate, well-trained, and observant sales personnel. Shoplifting is an opportunity crime. If the potential thief suspects that detection and apprehension is a strong possibility, the shoplifter may not risk being caught.

Retail losses may also be prevented through an effective **refund policy**. Ideally, refunds should be tightly controlled and issued from a centralized service desk. To prevent refund abuse by customers as well as employees, retail merchants can develop a database of individuals who request refunds. Suspicious refunds are checked against the database to determine how often the person seeking a refund attempts to return merchandise. Additionally, when a refund is requested, a check of the inventory list may verify if the item returned was actually sold. **Transaction reports,** which include sales records, voided sales receipts, and other activity performed by the cash registers each day, may also be used where refunds are made from the cash registers and other points of sale. Loss prevention personnel should audit these reports to identify suspicious activity (Hess & Wrobleski, 1996).

Several challenges face those responsible for retail loss prevention. Rapidly evolving technology and its use, such as the Internet and retail sales online, present unique challenges to retailers. Additionally, an aging consumer population will demand different types of products and increase the need for safety and possibly emergency medical response capability in physical retail outlets. New retail formats must address store layout, the use of television as a sales medium, the ability to accept foreign currency, and the increased value of brand names and reputation. Crime will continue to be a major concern for retailers. Computer criminals are likely to take advantage of emerging technology and the new retail formats. Employee theft will continue to outpace theft due to external shoplifters. Organized groups of current and former employees are likely to steal merchandise in large volume. Merchandise warehousing and delivery systems may be particularly vulnerable. Effective retail personnel pre-employment screening and on-the-job integrity training will significantly reduce losses due to internal employee theft (Hayes, 2000).

In the future, retail merchants are more likely to rely on the use of technology as a means to prevent crime rather than apprehend shoplifters after the fact. Retailers will still apprehend shoplifters to recover merchandise. However, shoplifter apprehension is reactive, creates safety problems, and increases the probability of lawsuits associated with false arrest and false imprisonment. To avoid these problems, retailers are more likely to use technology in a proactive approach to asset protection. Increasingly, retailers will use electronic article surveillance systems, merchandise alarms, access control, cash protection and transaction exception reporting systems, CCTV, as well as identification and recognition systems for customers and retail employees (Hayes, 2000).

TRANSPORTATION SECURITY

Over a 3-year period, one major urban area's public transit system experienced losses estimated at between $160,000 and $1,000,000 due to employee theft. The losses resulted from thefts from bus fare boxes and black market sales of counterfeit and stolen public transit passes. Money was stolen from bus fare boxes when the transit system's busses were cleaned each day. In one case, a fare box repair person confessed to using a key from the transit agency's accounting office to unlock fare boxes to obtain cash. The fare box repair person worked honestly for the transit company for 6 years before becoming an internal thief. After the stealing commenced, the employee admitted to thefts totaling approximately $56,000 (Arner, 2000b).

The transportation of persons and goods by air, land, and sea represents one of the largest industries in the United States. Aircraft, railroads, trucks, buses, automobiles, ships, and barges transport millions of people as well as millions of tons of raw materials and finished products each year. The remainder of this section focuses on the threats to, and protection of, **cargo** transported for commerce.

Photo courtesy of Wackenhut Corporation.

Cargo refers to any object that is moved through the transportation system. The system includes not only the aircraft, vehicles, and vessels used to move materials but also the facilities and equipment used to load, store, and unload the materials. Internal and external theft, burglary, vandalism, and truck hijacking are common threats. Theft can occur anywhere within the distribution system. Shipping and receiving areas, containers in transit, warehouses, depots, terminals, and piers are common targets for the thief.

The U.S. Department of Transportation estimates that losses due to cargo theft may approach $2 billion annually. The Department also estimates that approximately 80 percent of the losses are due to internal theft, 15 percent to external sources, and 5 percent to hijacking. Only about 20 percent of stolen cargo is ever recovered. A vast majority of the losses occur in warehouses and distribution centers through theft by those who are authorized to be in the area. In some cases, organized gangs place part-time or temporary workers into target companies. Once inside, the gang's members provide information about shipments that leads to cargo thefts worth millions of dollars each. In addition, the increased use of computers and electronic documentation has made cargo a tempting target for thieves as well as domestic and international organized crime syndicates. Automated files contain sensitive shipping information that can be accessed electronically by hackers or through collusion with employees.

Most stolen cargo is returned illegally to the marketplace, where it is sold at a tremendous discount. Thus, product manufacturers incur a loss twice: once as a result of the theft and again when a legitimate sale is lost as the stolen goods are sold on the black market. Cargo theft reached epidemic proportions during the 1970s. This led the U.S. government to establish the Office of Transportation Security (OTS) within the U.S. Department of Transportation. Cargo theft de-

Photo courtesy of Wackenhut Corporation.

creased in the 1980s, due largely to the efforts of OTS. In 1983, the agency was dissolved and replaced with the **National Cargo Security Council (NCSC),** a voluntary organization consisting of government and private industry representatives. The NCSC functions as a clearinghouse for cargo theft information. Cargo theft increased during the 1990s. Apparently, organized criminal groups were attracted to the low-risk, high-profit nature of cargo theft because tough law enforcement and conviction sentencing strategies focused on illegal drugs rather than cargo theft (Badolato, 2000).

Cargo security measures that may prevent, or at least reduce, losses due to theft include personnel and physical security; a system of accountability and proper documentation through purchase orders, invoices, shipping documents, and receiving slips; secure packaging; policies and procedures; and prosecution of criminal offenders (Fischer & Green, 1998). Testing of all drivers for drugs and alcohol is required by federal law since January 1, 1996. Surveillance, undercover operations, access control, and a system of seals also serve preventive and detection functions.

In the late 1990s, concern developed over the quality and credentials of truck drivers. The FBI and investigators in several states uncovered a commercial driver's license bribery scheme. Apparently, hundreds of truck drivers licensed in Illinois and Florida bribed department of motor vehicle officials and workers at truck driving schools to falsify commercial driving exams. Most states allow drivers to exchange licenses without retesting. Many of the drivers with licenses obtained with a fictitious test score exchanged Illinois and Florida licenses for permits in several other states, making unsafe drivers difficult to locate.

Many of the larger cargo carriers employ proprietary as well as contract security personnel. The railroad industry employs approximately 3,500 in-house private security officers and police. In some states, railroad security personnel are commissioned as peace officers with full police powers while on duty and on railroad property. Local, county, and state law enforcement agencies as well as the FBI and U.S. Bureau of Customs also provide assistance.

To combat cargo theft, liaison between carriers and collaboration among government and industry representatives is especially helpful. All interested and affected parties must work together to develop effective reporting systems, promote knowledge of cargo theft, support task forces, encourage the development of law enforcement expertise relating to cargo theft, use cargo security technology, increase prosecutions, and stiffen penalties for cargo theft (Badolato, 2000).

In May 2003, as part of an effort to prevent terrorist incidents, the U.S. Transportation Security Administration began checking the backgrounds of 3.5 million truckers who haul hazardous materials. Trucks carry over 90 percent of the almost 1 million daily shipments of hazardous materials in the United States. Over 60,000 materials are listed as hazardous. The list includes a wide range of substances, from nail polish, gasoline, and corrosives to nuclear waste. Those who are deemed mentally incompetent, illegal immigrants, and those with recent convictions for possession of controlled substances may not transport hazardous materials (Miller, 2003).

UTILITY SECURITY

The utility industry faces extremely diverse security and access control challenges. Major urban utility administrative facilities, remote production and transfer facilities, massive infrastructure, and unprotected personnel in the field create enormous exposure. Administrative buildings must be protected because they house corporate offices, financial centers, data systems, human resources, and customer centers. Access control and protection of remote facilities, power lines, and gas and water pipes are difficult. In addition, most utility company personnel are in the field, installing, servicing, and maintaining the utility's infrastructure (J. N. Smith, 2000).

The field of utility security can be traced to World War II when the protection of utilities against sabotage and direct attack was considered vital to the war defense effort. Utility facilities were protected by armed troops. Today, even though government troops are not employed, utilities are considered vital to national security and comprehensive security programs have been implemented to protect this valuable infrastructure.

Without adequate water supplies, sewage systems, natural gas and electric power, an industrialized society cannot function. Modern economies, and the people who live and work within them, depend on (and often take for granted) the services provided by private and public utility companies. Coal, oil, gas, and hydro- and nuclear-powered electricity generating facilities, transmission lines and transformer substations, sewage treatment plants, reservoirs, pipelines, and gas wells make up an elaborate system a modern nation needs to survive.

Utility operations often cover vast areas and serve millions of people. In the lower 48 states, a national electric power grid is divided into three independently operated regions: east, west, and Texas. Each region is subdivided into smaller units and electric power is traded between units. The western power grid alone serves 65 million customers in 14 states, 2 Canadian provinces, and parts of Mexico (K. Green, 2000).

Security threats to utility providers and their facilities include natural disasters, accidents, employee theft of tools and time, vandalism to substations, trespassing, robbery at utility payment collection centers, energy theft by circumventing meters, and terrorism. On October 24, 1997, sabotage was blamed for an outage that cut electric power to San Francisco's downtown area. The blackout stopped clocks, elevators, and traffic signals. Entire neighborhoods lacked public transportation because the city's bus system is powered by electricity. Human and animal attacks on field meter readers and collection agents is also a potential problem.

Increased demand for electricity can strain power grids. More electricity is being consumed and few generating plants are under construction to keep up with the demand. During the summer of 2000, the national electric power system, already strained from increased demand to supply computers and the high-tech industry, became overloaded when a heat wave engulfed the United States. Beginning in the fall of 2000, the demand for electricity exceeded supply, forc-

Photo courtesy of Wackenhut Corporation.

ing prices to increase and resulting in blackouts in some areas, especially California (Mendel, 2001).

Operators of the 103 nuclear power facilities in the United States have been cautioned to remain especially vigilant to any suspicious activity that could signal the possibility of a terrorist attack. The FBI warned that people observed photographing or flying aircraft close to a nuclear facility could pose potential threats. The federal government, though the U.S. Nuclear Regulatory Commission, has also increased the training requirements for nuclear facility security personnel, and it has mandated additional classified security measures to protect facilities against sabotage and terrorist attacks ("FBI issues alert to nuclear plant operators," 2003).

Economic loss, injuries, and deaths may be prevented through the use of policies, procedures, and measures designed to protect utility company property, employees, and customers. Effective use of appropriate physical, personnel, and operations security techniques may also reduce the impact of a negative event. Specific **utility security measures** employed by utility providers include the following:

- Losses due to natural disasters are reduced through the establishment of emergency preparedness plans, the development of redundant systems and procedures for rapid recovery from a disaster.

- Accident prevention programs are developed and implemented. Employee training and protective equipment are necessary ingredients to an effective program.

- Company tools and equipment are subject to detailed inventory control. A major utility company was able to reduce losses due to employee theft by instituting a tool loan program for employees.

- Vandalism at substations is reduced through the installation of conspicuous CCTV cameras.

- Robbery at payment collection centers is reduced by limiting the amount of cash on hand and encouraging the use of the mail and electronic funds transfers from checking and savings accounts for bill payment.

- Energy theft is reduced or eliminated by monitoring energy usage and comparing the recorded usage at a specific site to comparable norms at similar sites.

- Meter readers are trained to avoid confrontational situations and are skilled in conflict deescalation techniques.

- Terrorism may be prevented through increased vigilance, target hardening, and improved training for security personnel.

In healthcare facilities as well as some critical industries and government operations, life can be preserved and property loss minimized when emergency backup utility sources are available. Loss of electric power and inadequate water supplies can lead to injuries, death, expensive downtime, and threats to national security, safety, and the environment.

WORKPLACE VIOLENCE PREVENTION

Workplace violence occurs between employees and may be the result of unsafe working conditions or may stem from a relationship that exists outside the workplace (Siegel, 2001). Violence is identified as the third leading cause of injury or death in the workplace. According to available data, over 2 million U.S. residents are victims of violent workplace crime each year. A higher than average number of workplace violence victims are employed in retail sales, law enforcement, teaching, healthcare, transportation, and private security. The most common type of victimization is assault. Homicide results in over 1,000 cases annually. About 40 percent of victims of workplace violence report they were acquainted with the perpetrator, with women more likely than men victimized by someone they knew (Warchol, 1998).

Workplace violence can occur in virtually any workplace and at any time. Often, incidents of workplace violence occur when they are unlikely or least expected. In San Diego, California, on June 10, 1998, a 26-year-old man dressed as a woman fatally shot his female therapist and then himself. Apparently, the man was distraught because his therapist refused to write a letter endorsing his request for a sex change operation. Numerous shootings occurred in the workplace in 1999:

01-14-99   Di-Kieu Duy, 24, armed with a firearm, killed one person and wounded another in a Salt Lake City office building.

03-18-99   Walter V. Shell, 71, killed his attorney and one of the lawyer's clients in Johnson City, Tennessee. He blamed the lawyer for a $100,000 loss in a dispute over his ex-wife's will.

04-15-99   Serfei Babarin, 71, used a firearm in the Mormon Family History Library in Salt Lake City to kill two people and wound four others before he was killed by police.

05-20-99   Six students at Heritage High School in Conyers, Georgia, were wounded by T. J. Solomon, a 15-year-old sophomore who fired 14 shots from a .22-caliber rifle and a .357 Magnum handgun.

06-03-99   Four employees of a Las Vegas grocery store were shot to death. Zane Floyd, 23, an ex-Marine and part-time nightclub bouncer, was arrested as he left the store.

06-11-99   Joseph Brooks, Jr., 27, killed his former psychiatrist and a woman at the doctor's Southfield, Michigan clinic. Four others were wounded before Brooks killed himself.

07-16-99   In San Diego, California, a morning robbery left a merchant dead in a parking lot shortly after a mall security guard observed the victim changing a tire. The merchant was on his way to a bank to deposit sales receipts.

07-29-99   Frustrated investor Mark O. Barton, 44, killed 9 people and wounded 13 at two brokerage firms in Atlanta, Georgia. Then he killed himself.

08-05-99   Alan Eugene Miller, 34, was charged with killing two coworkers at their office in Pelham, Alabama, and killing a third person at a company where he worked previously.

09-14-99   In Anaheim, California, Dung Trinh, 43, walked into a hospital and started shooting several hours after his mother passed away. The West Anaheim Medical Center shooting left three workers dead.

09-15-99   In Fort Worth, Texas, a man shouting obscenities and mocking religion, walked into a church service for teenagers and opened fire. He killed seven before he killed himself in a church pew.

On May 24, 2000, a Wendy's Restaurant in New York City became the scene of a blood bath. Two gunman wrapped plastic bags around victims' heads and fatally shot five of them in the face at point blank range. The killers, one believed to be a former Wendy's employee, fled the restaurant with $2,000 and two unopened safes. On June 21, 2000, a San Leandro, California, sausage factory owner was accused of killing three government food inspectors at his downtown facility. The factory owner was furious with the government's scrutiny of his operation.

On December 26, 2000, the day after the Christmas holiday, a 42-year-old Internet software tester, Michael McDermott, arrived at work at his usual time and spoke normally with several coworkers. At approximately 11:00 A.M., police responded to McDermott's workplace, Edgewater Technology, Incorporated, and arrested him without incident. Apparently upset over U.S. Internal Revenue Service plans to garnish his wages for back taxes, McDermott used a semiautomatic assault rifle, a 12-gauge shotgun, and a pistol to kill seven of his coworkers. McDermott had caused a disruption in the accounting department a week preceding the incident. Most of the victims in the shooting worked in the accounting department ("Seven killed in office rampage," 2000).

On February 5, 2001, 66-year-old William D. Baker, a former employee of truck diesel engine manufacturer Navistar International Corporation, walked into his former employer's plant in Melrose Park, Illinois, and began shooting with an AK-47 assault rifle. Baker had entered the facility carrying a golf bag used to conceal the assault rifle, a .38 caliber revolver, a Remington shotgun, and a .30 caliber hunting rifle equipped with a scope. When the incident was over, four people were killed, four injured, and Baker lie dead from a self-inflicted gunshot wound. Baker had worked at the plant for 39 years before being terminated amid allegations he was involved in a plot with two coworkers and three other men to steal diesel engines and parts from Navistar. In November 2000, Baker was convicted in U.S. district court of one count of conspiracy to commit theft of interstate shipments. Baker was scheduled to begin a prison term for the conviction the day after the shootings occurred (Rodriguez, Yates, & Marx, 2001).

On July 8, 2003, Doug Williams, an employee at the Lockheed Martin aircraft parts factory in Meridian, Mississippi, killed 5 and wounded 9 fellow employees before killing himself. Armed with a shotgun, Williams opened fire after attending a company meeting on workplace ethics. Prior to the shooting, Williams had several confrontations with management and other employees, and he had stated that he wanted to kill people. The shooting was the deadliest workplace violence incident in the United States in almost three years.

In 1992, the U.S. Center of Disease Control (CDC) listed workplace homicide as a serious public health problem. The CDC, in collaboration with the National Institute of Occupational Safety and Health, cited six factors that increase the likelihood of workplace homicide:

1. contact with the public
2. working alone or in small groups
3. delivery of passengers, services, or goods
4. the exchange of money

5. working in high-crime-rate areas
6. working late nights or in the early morning hours

Statistics indicate that retail sales workers have the highest risk of injury on the job (Warchol, 1998). In fact, one half of all occupational homicides occur at night in small retail outlets. In June 1996, OSHA released guidelines for workplace violence prevention in nighttime retail establishments. Re-released to the public on April 28, 1998, the guidelines include the following suggestions for reducing homicides in small retail stores:

- Maintain video surveillance.
- Provide silent and personal alarms.
- Improve visibility through adequate lighting, installation of mirrors, and low-profile store fixtures.
- Install drop safes and signs indicating little cash is on hand.
- Establish emergency procedures, communications systems, and training and education programs.
- Restrict customer access by reducing store hours or closing portions of the store.
- Lock doors not in use.
- Increase staffing during high-risk periods.
- Install bullet-resistant enclosures for clerks.
- Take precautions when employees must access remote locations such as freezers and outside garbage containers.

In cases where workplace violence is committed by nonstrangers, the perpetrator may be a coworker, supervisor, client, or domestic partner. Workplace violence perpetrators tend to be loners, white males, 25 to 50 years old, and individuals with a history of violence. They are fascinated with weapons, antagonistic toward others, depressed, paranoid or psychologically imbalanced, self-destructive, and may be substance abusers. Often, the perpetrator is faced with job termination or layoff. In other cases, the offender may react violently to the leadership style of a supervisor. In some incidents, the perpetrator retaliates against a person who rejected romantic advances or reported the offender for sexual harassment (Siegel, 2001).

Organizations should do everything reasonably possible to mitigate the opportunity for a violent episode (Dalton, 2003). Employees should be trained to recognize the symptoms of workplace violence and the profile of potential perpetrators (Harwood, 1998). Organizations should also develop comprehensive plans to prevent or reduce the impact of workplace violence (Hess & Wrobleski, 1996). Failure to do so may result in management liability for injuries or deaths to victims. A **workplace violence prevention plan** should include

- policies and procedures for prevention and response to workplace violence incidents.
- training of employees regarding the policies and procedures as well as the symptoms of potentially violent behavior.
- liaison with community resources.
- physical and personnel security.
- effective preemployment screening.
- enforcement of codes of conduct.
- provision for assistance programs for employees with behavioral problems (Batza & Taylor, 2000; Lynch, 2000; May, 2000).

There are several personal communication skills an individual can use to diffuse and reduce conflict that could lead to a workplace violence incident. Attitude is important and one should treat an angry or verbally abusive person with respect. However, a potential victim must set limits on behavior, not tolerate verbal abuse, maintain personal safety, and seek assistance as soon as possible. Victims should attempt to remain calm, focus attention on the perpetrator, utilize delaying tactics, and accept criticism in a positive manner. Victims should also identify avenues of escape in the event a verbally abusive person becomes violent; place solid, bullet resistant objects between themselves and the violent person; and comply with a violent person's commands if other options are not available (Albrecht, 2001).

Workplace violence is very costly in terms of dollars as well as the potential for injury or death. Over 10,000 serious incidents each year cost organizations approximately $250,000 per incident. Approximately 30,000 medium severity incidents each year cost about $25,000 per occurrence. Tens of thousands of less severe incidents cost organizations about $10,000 for each incident (American Society for Industrial Security, 1998).

Although productivity appears to be increasing, physical and psychological stress in the workplace is increasing as well. Pushed by longer workweeks, larger workloads, and pressure to produce more, job-related stress can lead to depression, anxiety, and illness. The trauma associated with the stress can result in harassment, verbal abuse, and physical violence events. Job-related stress should be a major concern for employers, especially since the courts are increasingly likely to hold organizations liable for hostile work environments. Even verbal abuse in the workplace can cost an employer hundreds of thousands of lawsuit judgment dollars if the behavior is tolerated (Fest, 2001).

ZOO AND AQUARIUM SECURITY

A **zoological park** or **aquarium** is defined as any permanent cultural institution that owns and maintains wildlife that represent more than a token collection and, under the direction of a professional staff, provides its collection with

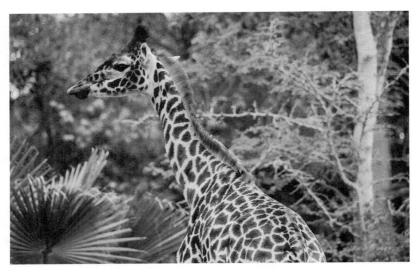

Photo courtesy of Star Source International.

appropriate care and exhibits them in an aesthetic manner to the public on a regularly scheduled, predictable basis (American Zoo and Aquarium Society, 2000). Zoos and aquariums also exhibit, conserve, and preserve the earth's fauna in an educational and scientific manner. Based on this definition, there are 172 zoos and aquariums in North America.

Facilities that house rare and exotic plants, animals, fish, and other wildlife have special security needs. Many of the plant and animal species are near extinction. Precautions must be taken to insure their safety and good health. They must be protected from environmental disasters, mistreatment by human beings, and assaults from predators. Some zoological parks are small, while others cover hundreds of acres. The Zoological Society of San Diego, in addition to its world famous zoo, maintains an 1,800-acre wildlife preserve, The Wild Animal Park, that contains more than 2,500 animals comprised of 250 different species.

Zoos open to the public are subject to vandalism, accidents, health-related emergencies, theft, and shoplifting (Bagott, 2003). Ticket and credit card fraud, auto theft, and violence against persons are potential threats in zoological parks. Bus and tram rides require safety considerations. Close encounters with dangerous wildlife, users of automatic teller machines, endangered species, and food service area health regulations necessitate special protection, security, and safety precautions.

In 1999, Atlanta, Georgia, zoo officials were faced with several challenges in their 10-year quest to house giant pandas at the facility. Pandas in the wild are found only in the central region of China and their fate is controlled by the Chinese government. However, since 1972, Chinese officials have loaned pairs of pandas to zoos to conduct research. In addition to stringent health, safety, and habitat requirements, Chinese officials wanted the Atlanta zoo to provide continuous audio-video monitoring of the pandas and allow open access to the moni-

Photo courtesy of Star Source International.

toring by Chinese researchers. Through integration of CCTV and Internet tech-nology, continuous monitoring of the pandas is provided and the Chinese can observe the pandas at any time (White, 2001).

On December 27, 2000, two female koalas, ages 7 and 15, were reported stolen from the San Francisco Zoo. Although the zoo has a 24-hour security op-eration, the koalas were discovered missing by an animal keeper. Apparently, the thieves stole the marsupials during the previous evening. The suspect(s) climbed onto the koala exhibit roof, penetrated a skylight, and entered the koala facility through a furnace door. Zoo officials were extremely concerned for the rare creatures' safety because the stress associated with improper care could be deadly. Koalas do not drink water. They require a specialized diet, consisting only of the freshest tips of eucalyptus buds, the bearlike creatures' main source of water. In addition, the koalas have no body fat. Therefore, the temperature of a koala's environment must be maintained at a constant 65 to 70 degrees (Mason, 2000). On December 28, 2000, two teenage boys were arrested and charged with burglary, possession of stolen property, and felony theft in con-nection with the koalas' disappearance. Apparently, the 2 boys took the koalas to give to their girlfriends ("Two teens arrested in theft of koalas," 2000).

As zoos and aquariums seek to place visitors closer to wildlife in a natural habitat, traditional physical barriers, such as glass enclosures and cages, are being eliminated. As a result, the risk of improper interactions with wildlife as well as the possibility of wildlife theft increases. Birds and snakes are most vul-nerable, especially as objects of theft, because they are easy to conceal and sell (Bagott, 2003).

Many zoos and aquariums are accredited by the American Zoo and Aquar-ium Association (AZA). To be accredited, all aspects of wildlife care must be highly professional. In addition, the zoo or aquarium must demonstrate significant support through donations, volunteerism, and membership. Other factors that are heavily considered in the accreditation process include fiscal viability, educational activities, operations, strategic plans, physical facilities, visitor services, management of the collection, participation in conservation and research programs, safety and emergency procedures, and security measures (American Zoo and Aquarium Society, 2000).

Critical to the success of any zoo or aquarium security program is planning and personnel training. Contingency plans that can be activated quickly provide guidance for personnel in an emergency, especially in the event of an animal's escape. A comprehensive training program, for facility staff as well as security personnel, creates security awareness and helps promote rapid and appropriate responses to crime and emergency situations (Bagott, 2003).

SUMMARY

Internal theft is a major contributor to losses in and around industrial facilities. Libraries, museums, and art galleries require special security measures due to the rare and often irreplaceable nature of their contents. Most office buildings are open to the public, providing easy access for criminal offenders. The privatization of public services is expanding as private providers assume safety and security responsibilities under contract to public jurisdictions. Most safety and security problems in a residence are preventable, and since people spend most of their time in and around their home, residential security should be a priority. Retail establishments incur losses in a variety of ways, with internal theft identified as the primary cause of losses due to theft. Most losses in the transportation industry are due to theft, damage, or destruction of cargo transported in commerce. Private and public utility systems are deployed over very large areas. Thus, the utility industry faces diverse security and access control challenges. Many workplace violence incidents can be prevented if workplace safety plans are developed and implemented, symptoms of violence are identified, preventive action taken, and disruptive behavior dealt with appropriately. Zoological parks and aquariums contain rare and exotic wildlife species requiring unique safety and security measures.

KEY TERMS

aquarium	coupon fraud
bad check	credit card fraud
cargo	industrial security
cargo security measures	inventory shrinkage
check cashing procedure	library

DISCUSSION QUESTIONS AND EXERCISES

1. Security organizations within retail operations often differ in their approaches to loss prevention. Some focus most protection resources toward externally motivated crime prevention while others emphasize internal theft prevention. Is one approach better than the other? How should protection resources be allocated in any organization?

2. Choose one specific security application from this chapter. List the types of crime and other hazards that threaten the operation, and design measures to prevent the threats from materializing.

GLOSSARY

Accident An unfortunate event caused unintentionally by a human agent.

Accounts payable diversion Disbursement fraud committed by person who processes payroll information, refunds, discounts, rebates, or purchases.

Administration Process through which two or more people collaborate to accomplish a predetermined goal.

Administrative law The branch of public law created by administrative agencies and presented in the form of rules and regulations that dictate duties and responsibilities of individuals and organizations.

Affective skills Desirable values and attitudes.

Alarm Communicator designed to notify a receiver of impending danger.

Alarm point definition Identified points through which an alarm system is connected to a security management system.

Alarm system circuit Communication link between alarm sensor and annunciator.

Alarm system management Alarm point definition (identification) and integration with facility operations, the development of effective alarm response procedures, and training of alarm monitoring and response personnel.

Annunciator Signaling device that notifies recipient of detected alarm condition.

Appellate court Reviews cases and decisions appealed to it from a trial court or lower appellate court.

Arraignment Generally, the pretrial judicial hearing at which a defendant enters a plea to a criminal charge.

Aviation and Transportation Security Act of 2001 Federal law that created the Transportation Security Administration (TSA).

Bad check Forged, altered, or incorrectly completed check or a check drawn on a nonexistent account or an account with insufficient funds.

Basics of defense Involves use of policies, procedures, people, equipment, architectural design, and strategies to prevent loss and deter, detect, deny, delay, or detain the person or agent that may cause harm to the enterprise.

Budget A plan expressed in financial terms; list of possible expenditures.

Business intelligence Competitive intelligence; process of collecting, analyzing, and disseminating competitive information and other data to meet business objectives.

Capital expenditures Refers to depreciable assets, such as equipment and buildings.

Card-operated lock Utilizes cards with magnetic strips inserted into a card reader connected to a microcomputer that activates the locking device.

Career enhancement Educational experiences that focus on specific job-related training as well as those experiences that promote individual personal development.

Cargo Any object moved through the transportation system.

Cash conversion Theft of liquid assets, such as currency, and negotiable instruments, such as checks.

Central processing unit (CPU) Receives, processes, stores, and transmits information detected by alarm sensors.

Central station alarm system Similar to a proprietary alarm system control center; however, the alarm system is monitored from a facility at a remote location. The central station may monitor several alarm systems simultaneously.

Challenge for cause A challenge to a potential trial juror's qualifications that must be accompanied by a reason; there is no limit to the number of challenges for cause.

Cipher One-to-one correspondence between characters in an actual message (plain text) with the characters in a secret writing equivalent (crypto text).

Civil disorder Occurs when an individual or group disrupts the normal peace and tranquility of a community or the operations of a business or organization.

Civil liability May occur when a person is harmed or injured through the action or inaction of another. The harm may or may not be the result of criminal activity.

Classification of fire Class A, ordinary combustible; Class B, flammable liquid; Class C, electrical; Class D, combustible metal.

Closed-circuit television (CCTV) Video surveillance system closed to external transmission.

Code of ethics Standards of professional conduct.

Code of Hammurabi First written law (circa 2100 B.C.) designed to prescribe responsibilities of the individual to a group. The code also specified punishment for offenses.

Combination lock Dial or push-button lock commonly used with safes, vaults, padlocks and vehicle doors.

Common law Unwritten law based on custom or tradition.

Communications security (COMSEC) All efforts to protect information transmission from unauthorized interception.

Compensatory damages Designed to compensate a petitioner in a lawsuit for actual losses incurred.

Competitive intelligence Business intelligence.

CompStat Computer-driven statistics used in planning and management.

Computer crime   Generally, any crime committed utilizing computer technology.

Computer virus   A destructive software program designed to invade a computer system and alter stored information or modify the computer system's operations.

Confidential communication   Any communication carried on under circumstances reasonably indicating that any party to the communication desires it to be confined to the parties involved in the communication.

Conspiracy   Criminal plan involving at least two people. In some states, requires an act toward the completion of the intended (planned) crime.

Contingency plan   Plan implemented only if a certain event, such as a natural disaster, occurs.

Contract   Legally binding voluntary agreement between or among parties through which promises are made for a valuable consideration.

Contract security service   Security organization that provides security services to individuals or other organizations for a fee.

Copyright   Protects against unauthorized use of virtually any creative writing or expression that can be physically observed.

Cost-benefit analysis   A systematic process through which one attempts to determine the value of the benefits derived from an expenditure and compare the value with the cost.

Counterespionage   Activities designed to prevent espionage from occurring.

Coupon fraud   Occurs when customers or employees redeem coupons for cash in lieu of the purchase of the item for which the coupon was issued.

Court of last resort   A state's highest court; U.S. Supreme Court.

Courts of general jurisdiction   Courts that can try any state case brought before them.

Courts of limited jurisdiction   Courts that are limited in the types of cases they are authorized to try.

Covert operations   Undercover, secret, or surreptitious operations.

Credit card fraud   Economic crime utilizing a credit card or credit card accounts.

Crime   Offense against a society; an intentional act, or omission to act, in violation of the criminal law, committed without defense or justification and punished by society as a felony, misdemeanor, or infraction.

Crime Awareness and Campus Security Act   1990 federal law requiring postsecondary educational institutions to collect and disseminate campus crime statistics.

Crime Prevention through Environmental Design (CPTED)   Theory and practice associated with protecting people and the environment through the proper design of facilities and communities.

Crimes against persons Offenses committed by physical contact with the victim, in the presence of the victim with the victim's knowledge, or by placing the victim in fear of immediate harm; violent crime.

Crimes against property Offenses committed when victim is not present or is unaware that the crime is being committed; nonviolent crime.

Criminal intelligence Gathering information about actual as well as possible criminal activity and threats to a society or to an organization and its assets.

Criminal investigation An investigation that focuses on actual or suspected criminal activity.

Criminal negligence A form of criminal intent; the actor can foresee the result and fails to exercise the degree of care that a reasonable and prudent person would exercise in similar circumstances.

Critical information All forms and types of information as defined in the U.S. Economic Security Act of 1996.

Cryptography Science of secret writing; transformation of data to render it unintelligible to an unauthorized interceptor.

Cyber Security Research and Development Act of 2002 Federal law that established computer security research centers; intended to create programs to defend against terrorists that may target vital communications networks.

Decryption Conversion of crypto text to plain text.

Degrees of proof Standards by which guilt or liability must be established in criminal and civil cases.

Delphi Technique Process through which several individuals or experts provide input on an issue and arrive at consensus on a prediction or list of needs or priorities.

Digitization The conversion and electronic storage of an image or information to a computer's digital language.

Disaster recovery Addresses ability to recover from a disaster in a manner that does not adversely impact continuity of operations.

Discretionary access control Access to information is allowed on a need-to-know basis.

Documentation Any medium used to create a record of an event or communication.

Dynamic risk Exists when threat conditions fluctuate.

Economic crime A violation of the criminal law designed to reward the offender financially.

Electronic lock Remotely controlled electronic locking device typically used to control gates and access.

Elements of planning Needs assessment, development of alternative courses of action, and selection of an action plan.

Emanations security Prevents compromise of information through capture of acoustical emanations.

Embezzlement   Fraudulent appropriation of property by a person to whom the property has been entrusted.

Employee Polygraph Protection Act   1988 federal law that severely restricts the use of the polygraph or similar instruments by private sector organizations.

Employment law   Refers to common law and statutory provisions that regulate the employment relationship.

Encryption   Conversion of plain text to crypto text.

Environmental crime   Human activity that violates an environmental crime statute.

Environmental disaster   Term associated with exposure to hazardous materials, conventional and nuclear power failures, and gas line or water main breaks.

Ethical standards   Standards that dictate behavior when law or precedent, which may prescribe behavior, do not exist.

Ethics   Involves moral principles and focuses on the concepts of right and wrong and standards of behavior.

Evaluation   Process used to measure performance, compare performance with stated objectives, report results, and take corrective action.

Evidence   Information used to make a decision. In a judicial proceeding, includes testimony, writings, material objects, and other items presented to prove or disprove the existence or nonexistence of a disputed fact.

Executive protection   Activities designed to maintain the safety, security, and health of a human asset.

Expressed contract   Written or verbal contract in which all terms are explicitly stated.

Facility plan review   Fire department review of plans during facility construction.

Felony   A crime for which the potential penalty may be a fine and/or imprisonment of more than one year, or death.

Financial audit   Evaluation of an accounting system; transactions are sampled to confirm records are free of significant errors.

Financial institution   Bank, credit union, brokerage house, insurance company, or any other institution in which financial transactions are the primary focus.

Fire hazard abatement   Involves use of fire abatement codes typically established at the municipal government level.

Fire inspection program   Fire safety surveys, testing of fire systems.

Fire prevention   Policies and practices designed to prevent a fire from occurring.

Fire prevention enforcement   Adoption and administration of fire prevention codes, enforcement procedures, and notices.

Fire protection Procedures and fire suppression systems and activities designed to minimize harm to persons and property after a fire has started.

Fire triangle Heat, fuel, and oxygen necessary for a fire to occur.

Firewall In computer security, the electronic tool used to restrict access to computer databases.

First (initial) appearance Nonadversarial proceeding before a magistrate (judge) to set bail.

Foreign Corrupt Practices Act (FCPA) Federal law that prohibits payments of bribes by U.S. companies to foreign government officials.

Fraud examination Search of accounting records for any error or discrepancy, significant or not, to determine if financial controls could be compromised.

Full-time equivalent (FTE) person Equivalent to a person, or combination of persons, assigned to work full time (40 hours per week).

Hacker An expert at programming and solving problems with a computer; can refer to a person who illegally accesses restricted databases.

Healthcare facility Hospital, medical center, health clinic, nursing home, or similar facility.

Highway Patrol A state agency with primary responsibility for traffic law enforcement and safety.

Homeland Security Act of 2002 Federal law that created the U.S. Department of Homeland Security and consolidated 22 separate federal agencies from several departments into one, effective March 1, 2003. The purpose of the consolidation is to better coordinate the defense of the United States and improve liaison with state and local governments and the private sector.

Hospitality industry Hotels, motels, restaurants, and similar institutions.

Human error Unintentional, human mistake.

Human resource investigation All types of investigations related to the management of human resources.

Hybrid security organization A security operation that employs proprietary security staff as well as contract security personnel to supplement proprietary staff.

Identity theft A crime committed when an imposter fraudulently uses another's personal identification information to obtain credit, merchandise, or services in the name of the victim.

Impeachment In a judicial proceeding, refers to an attack on the credibility of a witness; possible result of cross-examination of a witness.

Impermissible investigative conduct Illegal or unethical investigative conduct.

Implied contract Contract resulting from the actions of the parties.

Indemnity/hold harmless clause Clause in a contract through which the indemnified person or organization is held harmless for the action/inaction of another.

Index crimes Contained in Part I of the Uniform Crime Report (UCR): murder, forcible rape, robbery, aggravated assault, burglary, larceny (theft), auto theft, arson.

Indictment Formal criminal charge issued by a grand jury.

Industrial espionage Use of illegal, unethical, and fraudulent means to obtain proprietary information and intellectual property.

Industrial security Focuses primarily on the protection of the manufacturing process.

Information In a criminal proceeding, the formal criminal charge issued by a prosecutor in a state felony case.

Information-protection-related agreements Nondisclosure, secrecy, and noncompete agreements designed to prevent unauthorized disclosure of information.

Information security (INFOSEC) Security of information creation, processing, storage, retrieval, transmission, dissemination, and disposition. The protection of information assets and systems against any threat.

Infraction Minor civil or criminal offense not amounting to a misdemeanor or felony.

Infrared (IR) camera Detects changes in infrared light radiation from area covered by camera.

Inherent risk Unavoidable risk due to nature of activity.

In-service training Continuous professional training for employees.

Instructional goal Learning outcome expected at the conclusion of an instructional program.

Instructional objective Enabling objective; describes skill or behavior the learner is expected to exhibit to demonstrate competence.

Intangible standards Characteristics that are difficult to measure. Examples include attitude, morale, and reputation.

Integrity test Used to detect a person's propensity toward dishonesty, substance abuse, violence, or high level of tolerance for such behavior in others.

Intellectual property Information created through research and development, such as chemical formulas and software designs.

Intentional torts Willful tort activity. Examples include assault, false imprisonment, and defamation of character.

Interagency OPSEC Support Staff (IOSS) Interagency group that provides OPSEC-related training to security, intelligence, law enforcement, acquisitions, and research and development personnel.

Intermediate appellate courts Appellate courts between trial courts and courts of last resort.

Internet   An interconnected system of computer networks.

Inventory conversion   Unauthorized conversion of inventory to one's own use.

Inventory shrinkage   Reduction in retail inventory not accounted for through sales or other legitimate activity.

Investigation   A systematic process through which information is gathered, analyzed, and reported.

Ionization sensor   Senses virtually all products of combustion, including heat, flame, smoke, and invisible toxic gases.

Job description   Position description; identifies the principle elements, scope of authority, and responsibilities involved in a job.

Job specifications   Outline specific skills, competencies, and personal qualities necessary to perform a job adequately.

Job task (occupational) analysis   Identifies the job functions (duties) a worker is expected to perform.

Key-operated lock   Most common lock; utilizes notched key inserted into the lock's keyway.

Keypad lock   Generally, a lock that utilizes microcomputer technology. Keypad similar to touch pad on Touch-Tone phone.

Law Enforcement Assistance Administration (LEAA)   Now defunct federal program, established through the Omnibus Crime Control and Safe Streets Act of 1968, that provided federal monies to fight crime and improve the criminal justice system.

Law Enforcement Education Program (LEEP)   Now defunct federal program that provided grants and interest-free loans to preservice and in-service law enforcement personnel to attend college.

Leadership   Occurs anytime one motivates, influences, or mobilizes an individual or group.

Line item budget   Detailed budget that includes a description and the cost of each item.

Line security   Involves protection of telephone cables, modems, local area networks (LANS), and similar communications systems.

Local alarm system   When activated, produces an alarm signal in the immediate vicinity of the protected premises.

Malware   Malicious software used to inflict damage to, or insert a virus into, a computer database.

Mandatory access control   Origins traced to restrictive legislation. Hierarchical and nonhierarchical classifications for information. Information requires clearance to view.

Metropolitan Police Act   1829 British law, promoted by Sir Robert Peel, that established first public, full-time police department in the world.

Microwave motion sensor Similar in operation to ultrasonic motion sensor except microwave systems utilize high-end radio frequencies rather than sound.

Miscellaneous expenses In a budget, those expenses not assigned to any other established expense category.

Misdemeanor Crime for which the potential penalty may be a fine and/or confinement for up to one year.

National Crime Victimization Survey (NCVS) Random-sample survey conducted to determine unreported crime and other information.

National Incident-Based Reporting System (NIBRS) Enhanced UCR; requires and provides more detailed information than UCR.

National law enforcement agencies Federal agencies; have broad territorial and narrow subject matter jurisdiction.

Natural disaster Sudden, extraordinary misfortune caused by a force of nature.

Negligence Generally, a lack of due care or diligence that an ordinary, reasonable, and prudent person would have exercised in similar circumstances.

Negligent hiring Possible liability associated with failure to complete a diligent inquiry into the suitability of a person for employment.

Negligent retention Possible liability associated with employer's failure to take disciplinary or remedial action after becoming aware that an employee is a risk factor.

Numerical standards Quantifiable standards such as numbers, statistics, percentages.

Objective measures Used in risk assessment, planning, and evaluation. Include audits, inspections, surveys, marketing, and reports.

Occupational Safety and Health Act Federal law created to protect worker health and safety.

Operating expense Expense incurred as a result of organizational operations. Examples include rent, utilities, contract services, training, insurance, and licensing fees paid.

Operations security (OPSEC) Risk assessment activities designed to identify potential vulnerabilities that an adversary may exploit to obtain critical information.

Organized crime Refers to relatively permanent group of individuals that systematically engage in illegal activities and provide illegal services.

Passive infrared (IR) sensor Detects changes in infrared light radiation in protected area.

Patent A novel, useful, and non-obvious invention protected by the Federal Patent Statute from unauthorized replication or use.

Peel, Sir Robert The British Home Secretary credited with creating the first full-time police department in the world in London in 1829.

Peremptory challenge A challenge to a potential trial juror's qualifications for which no reason need be given; limited in number.

Performance appraisal   Systematic assessment of employee performance.

Performance-based budget   Includes measurable units tied to objectives; allows for cost-benefit analysis.

Perimeter controls   Refers to barriers, illumination systems, and personnel used to monitor or control a facility's perimeter.

Personal injury investigation   Investigation focusing on event that causes harm to an individual.

Personal property   Refers to property other than real property (real estate).

Personnel expenses   All expenses associated with wages, salaries, payroll taxes and employee benefits.

Personnel integrity   Refers to honesty and appropriate behavior.

Personnel security   Protection of persons associated with an organization as well as protection from individuals who seek to harm the organization.

Photoelectric sensor   Detects objects, including smoke, in an environment.

Physical security   Tangible objects, lighting, surveillance and alarm systems, and security personnel devoted to access control.

Pinkerton, Allan   Established the first national private security and investigations company in the United States in 1851.

Planning   The process of formulating a detailed program for action.

Policy   General statement that describes goals or states an organization's position on issues or topics.

Postsecondary institutions   Colleges, universities, and other post-high-school education and training institutions.

Preemployment screening   Preemployment selection processes.

Preliminary hearing   In the pretrial stages of a criminal proceeding, hearing at which the judge determines if probable cause exists that a crime was committed and that the person charged committed the offense.

Preservice training   Training provided prior to an employee's assumption of duties.

Private administration   Refers to the administration of private organizations.

Private citizen powers to arrest   Private person's powers of arrest, as compared with those of a public peace officer.

Private justice system   Rules, regulations, standards of conduct, and punishments established by private enterprises.

Private person's search authority   Refers to limitations placed on a private person's authority to conduct a search (as compared to a public peace officer).

Private police   Private security; protective services typically financed through private funding sources.

Privatization of public services   Public services provided by private organizations (contractors).

Procedure   Outlines steps to be followed consistently in a definite order.

Products of combustion   Flame, heat, smoke, and toxic gases.

Professional development   Training, education, and experiences designed to assist a person to perform well.

Progressive discipline   Corrective action progressing through several steps, i.e., verbal warning, written reprimand, suspension, demotion or termination.

Property damage investigation   Focuses on damage to property, rather than harm to a person.

Proprietary alarm system   Owned and operated on-site by the protected user.

Proprietary information   Virtually any information belonging to an individual or organization.

Proprietary security   Security program controlled and financed directly by the protected organization.

Proximate cause   Legal cause; the actor can foresee (anticipate) the consequences of an act or omission to act.

Psychological tests   Used to determine an individual's emotional stability and mental health.

Public administration   Refers to administration of public and quasi-public organizations.

Public alarm system   Typically, an alarm system connected directly to a public 911 emergency dispatch center or police department.

Public law enforcement   Generally refers to peace officers working with a city, county, state, federal, or other public police or law enforcement agency.

Punitive damages   Designed to punish a respondent in a lawsuit.

Pure risk   Potential for harm or loss with no possible benefit.

Quality assurance   Continuous quality improvement; initiative designed to promote and assure quality.

Real property   Land and anything permanently (or semipermanently) attached to land.

Receivables conversion   Occurs when employee misappropriates a customer's cash payment and covers the theft with a payment received from another customer.

Repeat-use (standing) plan   Implemented each time a given situation or incident occurs. Unless modified, repeat use plans change little over time.

Return on investment (ROI)   Net cost savings that result from security measures employed.

Risk   Possibility of suffering harm or loss; exposure to probability of loss or damage; an element of uncertainty.

Risk assessment   Critical, objective analysis of an organization's entire protective system.

Risk management techniques   Strategies and tactics designed to eliminate risk, reduce the probability loss will occur, or mitigate damage, if threat materializes.

Roles of public law enforcement Keep the peace, maintain order, police public property, and respond to and investigate crime.

Roles of the security manager Managerial, administrative, preventive, investigative.

Security Freedom from risk or harm; safety.

Security management Multifaceted and interdisciplinary management tactics and strategies designed to secure persons, property, and information and prevent losses from any source.

Security survey Risk assessment tool used to evaluate an organization to identify risks and security hazards/deficiencies.

Sensor Device that senses a specific condition, such as motion, sound, temperature, or vibration.

Sheriff Historically, the chief law enforcement officer of a county.

Shoplifting Misappropriation (theft) of retail merchandise.

Single-use plan A plan that is used once and no longer needed when the objectives of the plan are accomplished.

Solicitation A crime that involves requesting another to commit a crime.

Space radio communications Includes communications systems and equipment such as cellular phones, marine and mobile radio telephones, microwave radio relays, satellite radio, and high-frequency radio.

Speculative risk Potential for benefit or loss, depending on consequences of activity or inactivity.

Static risk Constant and unchanging risk, as in the possibility of an earthquake or severe storm.

Statute Written law that is the product of legislative activity.

Strategic business intelligence Seeks to forecast the long-range implications of business activities.

Strategic plan Long-range plan.

Street crime Generally, refers to crimes such as murder, rape, robbery, assault, burglary, larceny (theft), auto theft, and arson.

Strict liability Liability attached even though the person liable was not at fault or did not intend any harm.

Subjective measures Used in risk assessment, planning, and evaluation. Include expert opinion, forecasting, and the Delphi Technique.

Substance abuse Refers to the inappropriate ingestion of toxic and controlled substances into the human body.

Supervision Management; involves directing people toward organizational goals.

Supplies and materials expenses Refers to objects with a life expectancy of less than one year; includes office supplies, computer software, fuel, etc.

Surreptitious investigative methods Secret (undercover) investigative methods.

Surveillance   Covert or overt observation of persons or property.

Symptoms of substance abuse   Significant changes in personal appearance, sudden and irrational changes in behavior, or similar changes in human behavior.

Tactical business intelligence   Focuses on actual rather than perceived or advertised schemes of competitors.

Tactical plan   Short-range plan.

Tangible standards   Standards that are quite clear, specific, identifiable, and generally measurable; typically expressed in terms of dollars, numbers, physical properties, and time.

Task Force Report of Private Security   Published by the National Commission on Criminal Justice Standards and Goals in 1976, this report recommended minimum training and licensing requirements for private security.

Technical security   Term used to describe the development and implementation of countermeasures identified in risk assessments; prevention of adverse technical surveillance caused by the use of intrusion devices.

Terrorism   Use of violence or threats to intimidate or coerce.

Thermal sensor   Senses heat in a protected area.

Thief takers   Forerunners of bounty hunters; provided for in British Highwayman Act of 1692.

Tort   A civil, rather than criminal, wrong for which the law provides a remedy.

Trademark   Protects against unauthorized use of a distinctive mark, name, word, symbol, or device that identifies the goods of a particular commercial enterprise.

Traditional budget   A budget that includes a simple percentage increase over the previous budget.

Transactional leadership   When one takes the initiative, making contact with another, for the purpose of the exchange of valued things.

Transaction report   Sales records, voided sales receipts, and other activities performed by cash registers each day.

Transborder   Crosses borders. Generally refers to event in one country that impacts the environment in another country.

Transcript   A written record; typically refers to a written record of a judicial proceeding.

Transformational leadership   When one engages another in a way that the leader and nonleader raise one another to higher levels of motivation and morality.

Transmission security   Policies and procedures that place an adversarial interceptor at a disadvantage.

Transportation Security Administration (TSA)   Federal agency with primary responsibility for commercial aviation and transportation security.

Trial court   Court where criminal or civil trial takes place.

Ultrasonic motion sensor Transmits and detects extremely high (beyond a human's audible range) sound energy.

Uniform Crime Report (UCR) Document published by the FBI that includes crime statistics reported voluntarily to the FBI by law enforcement agencies throughout the United States.

Unintentional tort Emanates from a situation in which person liable did not intend harm but the person failed to exercise the care of an ordinary, reasonable, and prudent person.

Unlawful detention Detention of one person by another without lawful authority.

USA Patriot Act of 2001 Officially titled the Uniting and Strengthening America by Providing Appropriate Tools Required to Intercept and Obstruct Terrorism, this federal law broadens law enforcement criminal investigative authority.

U.S. district court Trial court in the federal (national) court system.

U.S. Economic Security Act of 1996 Federal law relating to the protection of U.S. economic interests, including the protection of critical information.

U.S. Supreme Court Court of last resort in the United States. The only court created by the U.S. Constitution.

Value Moral standard; formed through the influence of others.

Value-added contribution (VAC) Value security contributes to the organization.

Vicarious liability Liability incurred as a result of situations in which organizations or third parties may be held liable for the intentional or unintentional actions of others with whom they have a relationship.

Virtual security organization The security function is integrated with the entire operation or merged with another department.

Voir dire examination "Speak the truth" examination of a prospective trial juror to determine juror's suitability for jury service. The prospective juror's qualifications may be challenged for cause or a party may exercise a peremptory challenge.

White collar crime Offense committed by a person or group in the course of an otherwise respected and legitimate occupation or financial activity. Generally refers to crimes such as corruption, bribery, tax evasion, embezzlement, industrial espionage, and other economic crimes.

Workplace violence Violence upon a person that occurs in the workplace.

Zero-based budget (ZBB) Budget process through which each program within a budget period must justify its existence and expenditures.

Zoological park Permanent cultural institution that owns and maintains wildlife that represent more than a token collection and exhibits the collection to the public.

APPENDIX A

Correlation of ASIS International Syllabus for Introduction to Security for Business Students with *Security Management: An Introduction, 2nd edition*

ASIS International Syllabus Module		Relevant Text Chapters
I	The Context for Security	1, 4, 9, 10
II	Risk Assessment	4
III	Legal Aspects of Security Management in America	3
IV	Investigations	2, 8
V	Personnel Integrity and Protection	6
VI	Technical Management	4, 5
VII	Information Protection	7
VIII	Business Intelligence	8

APPENDIX B

Safety and Security Survey Instrument

A safety and security survey involves a critical and objective audit, assessment, and analysis of an entire organization to identify hazards and deficiencies. A survey instrument, such as this checklist, is typically used to identify the organization's vulnerabilities. Utilize the following nomenclature to evaluate each area.

S = Satisfactory
U = Unsatisfactory
N/A = Not applicable

GENERAL

Nature of business/agency: _____

Facility name: _____

Address: _____

Survey date: _____

Hours of operations: _____

Facility contact person: _____

Phone number: _____

Fax number: _____

Email address: _____

Environment: (check one)

Urban industrial ＿＿ Urban residential ＿＿ Suburban industrial ＿＿
Suburban residential ＿＿ Rural ＿＿

Survey conducted by: ＿＿＿＿＿＿＿＿＿＿＿＿＿＿＿＿＿＿＿＿＿＿

Surveyor's address: ＿＿＿＿＿＿＿＿＿＿＿＿＿＿＿＿＿＿＿＿＿＿

Surveyor's phone: ＿＿＿＿＿＿＿＿＿＿＿＿＿＿＿＿＿＿＿＿＿＿

Surveyor's email: ＿＿＿＿＿＿＿＿＿＿＿＿＿＿＿＿＿＿＿＿＿＿

COUNTRY (where facility is located)	**S**	**U**	**N/A**
Political conditions	—	—	—
Crime rates	—	—	—
Personnel safety	—	—	—
Availability of labor	—	—	—
Economic conditions	—	—	—
Medical treatment availability	—	—	—
Public firefighting availability	—	—	—
Public utilities	—	—	—
Public transportation	—	—	—
Public roadways	—	—	—
Flood susceptibility	—	—	—
Earthquake susceptibility	—	—	—
Fire susceptibility	—	—	—
Hurricane susceptibility	—	—	—
Tornado susceptibility	—	—	—
Severe weather susceptibility	—	—	—

Comments

＿＿＿＿＿＿＿＿＿＿＿＿＿＿＿＿＿＿＿＿＿＿＿＿＿＿＿＿＿＿
＿＿＿＿＿＿＿＿＿＿＿＿＿＿＿＿＿＿＿＿＿＿＿＿＿＿＿＿＿＿
＿＿＿＿＿＿＿＿＿＿＿＿＿＿＿＿＿＿＿＿＿＿＿＿＿＿＿＿＿＿
＿＿＿＿＿＿＿＿＿＿＿＿＿＿＿＿＿＿＿＿＿＿＿＿＿＿＿＿＿＿

COMMUNITY (neighborhood)	**S**	**U**	**N/A**
Crime rates	—	—	—
Aesthetic qualities	—	—	—
Public police protection	—	—	—
Fire protection	—	—	—
Emergency medical services	—	—	—
History of civil unrest	—	—	—
Graffiti/vandalism	—	—	—

Comments

_____

_____

_____

_____

PHYSICAL SECURITY

Facility Perimeter	S	U	N/A
Fencing	___	___	___
Landscaping	___	___	___
Parking	___	___	___
Employee parking area illumination	___	___	___
Visitor/guest parking area illumination	___	___	___
Employee parking area monitoring	___	___	___
Visitor/guest parking area monitoring	___	___	___
Lighting (all areas properly illuminated?)	___	___	___
Vehicular traffic pattern	___	___	___
Pedestrian traffic pattern	___	___	___
Trash removal	___	___	___
Protection from adjacent occupancies	___	___	___
Proper Signage	___	___	___

Comments

_____

_____

_____

_____

Building

Describe type of construction, building design, number of entrances/exits, windows, roof construction, number of stories, adjacent occupancies. Photographs or video of building are helpful.

_____

_____

_____

_____

_____

_____

	S	U	N/A
Common walls with adjacent occupancies	——	——	——
Exterior door construction	——	——	——
Exterior door locks	——	——	——
Door lock operation	——	——	——
Exterior window construction	——	——	——
Window height above ground	——	——	——
Window security	——	——	——
Roof access restrictions	——	——	——
Building exterior lighting	——	——	——
Emergency lighting system	——	——	——
Shipping/receiving area monitoring	——	——	——
Emergency exits	——	——	——
Emergency exits unobstructed	——	——	——
Interior door construction	——	——	——
Interior wall construction	——	——	——
Antitheft systems/mechanisms	——	——	——

Comments

_____

_____

_____

_____

_____

_____

Access Control	S	U	N/A
Intrusion detection	——	——	——
Building entrances minimized	——	——	——
Employee entrance monitoring	——	——	——
Visitor/guest entrance monitoring	——	——	——
Interior door locks	——	——	——
Key control system	——	——	——
Key sign-out/assignment system	——	——	——
Keys accounted for	——	——	——
Key safeguards	——	——	——
Employee distinguishableness	——	——	——
Visitor/guest supervision	——	——	——

Restricted access to sensitive/vulnerable areas   ___   ___   ___
Computer/data storage area restrictions   ___   ___   ___
Key storage area restrictions   ___   ___   ___
Mechanical/utility room restrictions   ___   ___   ___
Telecommunications room restrictions   ___   ___   ___
Mailroom restrictions   ___   ___   ___
Executive office suite restrictions   ___   ___   ___
Vendor access   ___   ___   ___
Vault/safe security   ___   ___   ___
Controlled substance security   ___   ___   ___
Hazardous material security   ___   ___   ___
Cash/liquid asset protection   ___   ___   ___
Proper signage to direct visitors   ___   ___   ___

Comments

_____

_____

_____

_____

Alarm and Surveillance Systems

Does facility have an alarm system?   Yes _____   No _____
If yes, type: Local _____ Central Station _____ Police connected _____

	S	U	N/A
Alarm coverage	___	___	___
Emergency power source	___	___	___
Frequency of alarm tests	___	___	___
Frequency of false alarms	___	___	___
Penalties assessed by government for false alarms	___	___	___
Alarm response	___	___	___

Alarm response provided by _____

Does facility have closed circuit television (CCTV)? Yes _____ No _____

	S	U	N/A
Lighting compatibility with CCTV	___	___	___
CCTV monitoring	___	___	___
CCTV video recording	___	___	___

Comments

_____

_____

_____

_____

_____

Fire Protection

Fire alarm system: manual _____ automatic _____ none _____

	S	U	N/A
Sprinkler system	——	——	——
18' ' clearance below sprinkler head	——	——	——
Fire extinguishers	——	——	——
Fire suppression in computer facilities	——	——	——
Fire alarm system testing	——	——	——
Fire suppression system testing	——	——	——
Gas line protection	——	——	——
Electric power cord protection	——	——	——
Fire doors functional	——	——	——
Flammable material storage	——	——	——
Fire notification plan	——	——	——
Fire evacuation plan	——	——	——
Fire exits unobstructed	——	——	——
Fire exits secured from outside	——	——	——
In-house fire brigade	——	——	——
Fire safety policy/procedures	——	——	——
Street number/address prominently displayed	——	——	——

PERSONNEL SECURITY	S	U	N/A
Employee background investigations	——	——	——
Previous employer verification	——	——	——
Personnel records security	——	——	——
Exit interviews at employee termination	——	——	——
Organization property retrieval at termination	——	——	——
Employee/visitor safeguards against:			
Accidents	——	——	——
Theft	——	——	——
Assault	——	——	——
Workplace violence	——	——	——

Comments

_____

_____

_____

_____

INFORMATION SECURITY	S	U	N/A
Critical information identification	___	___	___
Critical information security	___	___	___
Information hardcopy destruction	___	___	___
Employee nondisclosure agreement in place	___	___	___
Intellectual property identification	___	___	___
Intellectual property security	___	___	___
Client/customer list protection	___	___	___
Access to computers restricted	___	___	___
Access to computer transmissions restricted	___	___	___
Portable personal computers/laptop security	___	___	___
Email access restrictions	___	___	___
Internet connection security	___	___	___
Electronic document destruction procedures	___	___	___
Software licensing	___	___	___
Prohibition against installing outside software without authorization	___	___	___
Terminated employees immediately denied access	___	___	___
Disaster recovery plan	___	___	___
Duplicate data files maintained at remote location	___	___	___
Password security	___	___	___
Information security indoctrination/training	___	___	___
Cellular phones used to access confidential proprietary information?	___	___	___
Cellular phone communication protection	___	___	___

Comments

_____

_____

_____

_____

INVESTIGATIONS, INTELLIGENCE, AND SECURITY

Background Investigations	S	U	N/A
Employees (new)	——	——	——
Employees (existing)	——	——	——
Vendors/contractors	——	——	——
Partnerships with other organizations	——	——	——
Security clearances	——	——	——

Comments

_____

_____

_____

_____

Incident Investigations	S	U	N/A
Investigation of any loss	——	——	——
Accidents	——	——	——
Safety hazards	——	——	——
Crime	——	——	——
Natural disasters	——	——	——

Comments

_____

_____

_____

_____

Intelligence	S	U	N/A
Competition counterintelligence	——	——	——
Criminal intelligence	——	——	——
Foreign travel intelligence	——	——	——

Comments

_____

_____

_____

_____

Reporting Procedures	**S**	**U**	**N/A**
Background investigations documentation	——	——	——
Background investigation confidentiality	——	——	——
Security Activity Log maintenance	——	——	——
Recording of incidents	——	——	——
Incident reported to proper manager/authority	——	——	——
Adherence to reporting procedures	——	——	——

Comments

_____

_____

_____

_____

OPERATIONS	**S**	**U**	**N/A**
Audit procedures	——	——	——
Employee locker/workspace inspections	——	——	——
Accounting function separation	——	——	——
Package control system	——	——	——
Opening time ambush controls	——	——	——
Closing time ambush controls	——	——	——
Receiving area security	——	——	——
Shipping area security	——	——	——
Delivery driver controls	——	——	——
Shipping/receiving area separation	——	——	——
Equipment inventory	——	——	——
Contractor/vendor audits	——	——	——
Customer/guest/visitor service	——	——	——

Comments

_____

_____

_____

_____

POLICIES AND PROCEDURES	**S**	**U**	**N/A**
Mission statement	——	——	——
Vision statement	——	——	——
Organizational goals	——	——	——
Organizational values	——	——	——

	S	U	N/A
Quality improvement initiatives	—	—	—
Employee code of conduct (ethics)	—	—	—
Employee misconduct policies	—	—	—
Disciplinary procedures	—	—	—
Termination procedures	—	—	—
Search/inspection policies	—	—	—
Removal of organization property	—	—	—
Bomb threat procedures	—	—	—
Evacuation procedures	—	—	—
Severe weather procedures	—	—	—
Natural disaster procedures	—	—	—
Contraband detection	—	—	—
Chemical abuse policy	—	—	—
Drug testing policy	—	—	—

Comments

_____

_____

_____

_____

SECURITY INDOCTRINATION/TRAINING	**S**	**U**	**N/A**
Indoctrination (new employees)	—	—	—
Training (existing employees)	—	—	—
Executive protection	—	—	—
Foreign travel training	—	—	—

Comments

_____

_____

_____

_____

LIAISON ACTIVITIES	**S**	**U**	**N/A**
Contact with local police maintained	—	—	—
Contact with sheriff maintained	—	—	—
Contact with state police/highway patrol maintained	—	—	—
Contact with fire department maintained	—	—	—

Contact with appropriate federal agency
maintained   ——   ——   ——

Articulation/collaboration with other security
organizations   ——   ——   ——

Comments

_____

_____

_____

_____

REFERENCES

Access Control & Security Systems Integration. (1999). *1999 salary survey*. Atlanta, GA: Security Lock Distributors.

ACKER, J. R., & BRODY, D. C. (1999). *Criminal procedure: A contemporary perspective*. Gaithersburg, MD: Aspen Publishers.

ADAMS, C. (2000a, March). Super security: Preparing for the big game takes months of effort. *Access Control & Security Systems Integration, 43* (3), 14, 16, 18.

ADAMS, C. (2000b, November). The Internet and security: Survey reveals possible lapses in judgment. *iSecurity*, p. 22.

ADAMS, T. F. (2001). *Police field operations* (5th ed.). Upper Saddle River, NJ: Prentice Hall.

ADAMS, T. F., CADDELL, A. G., & KRUTSINGER, J. L. (2004). *Crime Scene Investigation* (2nd ed.). Upper Saddle River, NJ: Prentice Hall.

ADLER, F., MUELLER, G. O. W., & LAUFER, W. S. (2003). *Criminal Justice: An Introduction* (3rd ed.). New York: McGraw-Hill.

ADLER, N. J. (2002). *International Dimensions of Organizational Behavior* (4th ed.). Cincinnati: Thomson Learning.

ADLER, R. B., & TOWNE, N. (2002). *Looking out/looking in* (10th ed.). Fort Worth, TX: Harcourt College Publishing.

AGRON, J. (1999). Lessons learned. In J. Agron & L. Anderson (Eds.), *Under siege: Schools as the new battleground* (pp. 10-12). Atlanta, GA: Access Control & Security Systems Integration.

AINSWORTH, B. (2000, December 19). Drug measure a challenge to carry out. *San Diego Union Tribune*, p. A3.

ALBANESE, J. S. (1996). *Organized crime in America*. Cincinnati: Anderson.

ALBANESE, J. S. (2000). *Criminal justice 2000 update*. Needham Heights, MA: Allyn & Bacon.

ALBRECHT, S. (2001, January 3). Guns at work in the wake of Wakefield. *San Diego Union Tribune*, p. B7.

ALDERFER, C. P. (1972). *Existence, relatedness and growth: Human needs in organizational settings*. New York: The Free Press.

America under attack. (2001, September 11). *Newsweek Extra Edition, 88* (12-A), 1-64.

American Association of Community Colleges. (2002). *Protecting information: The role of community colleges in cybersecurity education*. Washington, DC: Community College Press.

American Institute of Architects. (2003). *Building security through design*. [Online]. Available: www.aia.org/security.

American Society for Industrial Security. (1998). *ASIS International presents introduction to security for business students*. Alexandria, VA: American Society for Industrial Security.

American Society for Industrial Security. (2000). *Code of ethics*. Alexandria, VA: American Society for Industrial Security.

American Zoo and Aquarium Society. (2000). *Accreditation fact sheet 2000*. [Online]. Available: http://www.aza.org/dept/accred/accredfacts.htm.

An education in crime stats. (2000, November 15). *Law Enforcement News, 26* (543), 1, 10.

ANDERSON, C. (2003, April 10). FBI reports internet fraud tripled last year. *San Diego Union Tribune*, p. A15.

ANDERSON, T. (1999, June). Treading lightly through the hiring thicket. *Security Management, 43* (6), 35-36, 38-41.

ANDERSON, T. (2000, May). Taking stock of the states. *Security Management, 44* (5), 74-79.

ANDERSON, T. (2002, December). On the money. *Security Management, 46* (12), 49-50, 68-69.

ARGYRIS, C. (1964). *Integrating the individual and the organization.* New York: Wiley.

ARMOUR, S. (2003, February 10). Wal-Mart takes hit on worker treatment; Lawsuits, unions slam megaretailer. *USA Today*, p. B01.

ARNER, M. (2000a, October 16). Crime rate falling in this county and in U.S.—for now. *San Diego Union Tribune*, p. A1.

ARNER, M. (2000b, December 31). Worker thefts hit transit agencies. *San Diego Union Tribune*, pp. B1, B4.

ARNETTE, J. L., & WALSLEBEN, M. C. (1998, April). Combating fear and restoring safety in schools. *Juvenile Justice Bulletin*. Washington, DC: U.S. Department of Justice, Office of Juvenile Justice and Delinquency Prevention, pp. 11-12.

ARONSOHN, A. J. (2003, April). E-Snooping. *Loss Prevention & Security Journal, 3* (4), 36-37.

ASIS (American Society for Industrial Security) International Guidelines Commission. (2003). *General security risk assessment guidelines.* Alexandria, VA: ASIS International.

BADOLATO, E. V. (2000, July). Smart moves against cargo theft. *Security Management, 44* (7), 110-112, 114-115.

BAGOTT, J. (2003, May). It's all happening at the zoo. *Security Management, 47* (5), 46-50, 52, 54, 56.

BAILIN, P. (2000, November). Gazing into security's future. *Security Management, 44* (11), 60-63, 65, 67.

BAKER, T. E. (2000). *Effective police leadership: Moving beyond management.* Flushing, NY: Looseleaf Publications, Inc.

BALINT, K. (2000, September 8). Copyrights take a licking on Net frontier. *San Diego Union Tribune*, pp. A1, A23.

BARLOW, H. D. (2000). *Criminal justice in America.* Upper Saddle River, NJ: Prentice Hall.

BARNES, S. (2000, December 29). Freezing weather's icy grip continues in Midwest, South. *San Diego Union Tribune*, p. A12.

BASS, B. M. (1981). *Stogdill's handbook of leadership: A survey of theory and research.* New York: The Free Press.

BASS, B. M. (1985). *Leadership and performance beyond expectations.* New York: The Free Press.

BASS, B. M. (1990). *Handbook of leadership.* New York: The Free Press.

BATZA, D., & TAYLOR, M. (2000, December). James got his gun. *Security Management, 44* (12), 74-79.

BELLOWS, R. M. (1959). *Creative leadership.* Englewood Cliffs, NJ: Prentice Hall.

BENNETT, W. W., & HESS, K. M. (1991). *Criminal investigation* (3rd ed.). St. Paul, MN: West Publishing.

BENNIS, W. G. (1984, September). The four competencies of leadership. *Training and Development Journal, 38* (9), 14-19.

BENNIS, W. G. (1993a). *An invented life: Reflections on leadership and change.* Reading, MA: Addison-Wesley.

BENNIS, W. G. (1993b). Managing the dream: Leadership in the 21st century. In W. E. Rosenbach & R. L. Taylor (Eds.), *Contemporary issues in leadership* (3rd ed.) (pp. 213-218). Boulder, CO: Westview Press.

BENTLEY, S. W. (1997, October). An alliance is born. *Security Management, 41* (10), 77, 78, 80.

BIGELOW, B. V. (1998, March 4). Hacker attack hits computers across nation. *San Diego Union Tribune*, p. A1.

BLAKE, R. R., & MOUTON, J. S. (1985). *The managerial grid.* Houston, TX: Gulf.

BLANCHARD, K., & JOHNSON, S. (1992). *The one minute manager.* New York: Morrow.

BLAND, T. S., (2000, January). Get a handle on harassment. *Security Management, 44* (1), 62, 64-67.

BLAND, T. S., & HARKAVY, M. S. (2000, September). It's all in their heads. *Security Management, 44* (9), 92–94, 96.

BLAND, T. S., & STALCUP, S. S. (1999, June). Accurate applications. *Security Management, 43* (6), 38–39.

BLITZER, H. L., & JACOBIA, J. (2002). *Forensic digital imaging and photography*. Boston: Academic Press.

BLOOM, B., ENGLEHART, M., FURST, E., HILL, W., & KRATHWOHL, D. (1956). *Taxonomy of educational objectives: The classification of educational goals. Handbook 1: Cognitive Domain*. New York: David McKay.

BOLOGNA, J., & SHAW, P. (1997). *Corporate crime investigation*. Woburn, MA: Butterworth-Heinemann.

BONI, W., & KOVACICH, G. (2000). *Netspionage: The global threat to information*. Woburn, MA: Butterworth-Heinemann.

BOYCE, J. G., & JENNINGS, D. W. (2002). *Information assurance: Managing organizational IT security risks*. Boston: Butterworth-Heinemann.

BRIDGES, C. (1994, July). A pound of prevention for a ton of merchandise. *Security Management, 38* (7), 22–23.

BRIDGES, W. (1994, September 19). The end of the job. *Fortune, 130*, pp. 62–64.

BRODY, D. C., ACKER, J. R., & LOGAN, W. A. (2001). *Criminal law*. Gaithersburg, MD: Aspen Publishers.

BROOKE, J. (2001, January 19). Web hacker pleads guilty to attacking huge sites. *San Diego Union Tribune*, p. A16.

BROWN, S. E., ESBENSEN, F. A., & GEIS, G. (1996). *Criminology: Exploring crime and its context* (2nd ed.). Cincinnati: Anderson.

BUNNING, R. L. (1979). The Delphi technique: A projection tool for serious inquiry. In *The 1979 annual handbook for group facilitators* (pp. 174–181). San Diego, CA: University Associates.

BURNS, J. M. (1978). *Leadership*. New York: Harper & Row.

BURNS, L. R., & BECKER, S. W. (1988). Leadership and decision making. In S. M. Shortell & A. D. Kaluzny (Eds.), *Health care management: A text in organization theory and behavior* (2nd ed.) (pp. 142–186). New York: Wiley.

BURSTEIN, H. (1996). *Security: A management perspective*. Englewood Cliffs, NJ: Prentice Hall.

Bush signs Cyber Security Act. (2002, December 5). *Government Security*. [Online]. Available: http://govtsecurity.securitysolutions.com.

BYERS, B. (2000, September/October). Ethics and criminal justice: Some observations on police misconduct. *ACJS (Academy of Criminal Justice Sciences) Today, 21* (3), 1, 4–7.

BYRNBAUER, H., & TYSON, L. A. (1984, September). Flexing the muscles of technical leadership. *Training and Development Journal, 38* (9), 48–52.

CALDWELL, G. E. (2000, June). Selling security's mission in a corporate environment. *Security Technology & Design, 10* (6), 12–14, 16.

California State. (2000). *Penal Code*. Sections 1–632.

California State. Bureau of Security and Investigative Services. (2003). *Assembly Bill (AB) 2880: Increased training and fee increase for security guards*. West Sacramento, CA: Bureau of Security and Investigative Services.

California State. Commission on Peace Officer Standards and Training. (1999). *Regular peace officer basic course*. Sacramento, CA: Commission on Peace Officer Standards and Training.

CANTON, L. G. (2003). *Guard force management* (Updated edition). Boston, MA: Butterworth-Heinemann.

CARROLL, J. M. (1996). *Computer security* (3rd ed.). Woburn, MA: Butterworth-Heinemann.

CARTER, L. F. (1953). Leadership and small group behavior. In M. Sherif & M. O. Wilson (Eds.), *Group relations at the crossroads* (pp. 312–322). New York: Harper.

Center for developmental disabilities installs access control, CCTV, fire alarms. (2000, September). *Access Control & Security Systems Integration, 43* (10), 81–83.

CHAN, A. (2003, January). Web-based loss prevention: The fast track to controlling shrink. *Loss Prevention & Security Journal, 3* (1), 12–14.

CHEESEMAN, H. R. (2004). *Business law* (5th ed.). Upper Saddle River, NJ: Prentice Hall.

Chenkin v. Bellevue Hospital Center, N.Y.C., ETC, 479 F. Supp. 207 (1979).

China's piracy plague. (2000, June 5). *Business Week*, pp. 44–46.

CHUVALA, J., III, & FISCHER, R. J. (Eds.). (1991). *Suggested preparation for careers in security/loss prevention*. Dubuque, IA: Kendall/Hunt.

CLEMMER, J. (1992, April). 5 common errors companies make starting quality initiatives. *Total Quality, 3*, 7.

CLIFFORD, M., & EDWARDS, T. D. (1998). Defining "environmental crime." In M. Clifford (Ed.), *Environmental crime: Enforcement, policy, and social responsibility* (pp. 5–30). Gaithersburg, MD: Aspen Publishers.

COLE, G. F., & SMITH, C. E. (2001). *The American system of criminal justice* (9th ed.). Belmont, CA: Wadsworth/Thomson Learning.

COLEMAN, J. (2000, August). Trends in security systems integration. *Security Technology & Design, 10* (8), 38–40, 42–44.

COLEMAN, J. W. (1994). *The criminal elite: The sociology of white collar crime*. New York: St. Martin's Press.

COLLING, R. L. (1999). *Hospital and healthcare security* (4th ed.). Woburn, MA: Butterworth-Heinemann.

COLLINS, P. A., RICKS, T. A., & VAN METER, C. W. (2000). *Principles of security and crime prevention* (4th ed.). Cincinnati: Anderson.

CONLON, M. (2000, December 21). No letup seen as freeze menaces much of U.S. *San Diego Union Tribune*, p. A14.

'Cops' test security, get in CIA, other buildings. (2000, May 26). *San Diego Union Tribune*, p. A10.

COVEY, S. R. (1998). *The seven habits of highly effective people*. New York: Simon & Schuster.

CRAIGHEAD, G. (2003). *High-rise security and fire life safety* (2nd ed.). Boston, MA: Butterworth-Heinemann.

CROWE, T. D. (2000). *Crime prevention through environmental design* (2nd ed.). Woburn, MA: Butterworth-Heinemann.

CUNNINGHAM, W. C., STRAUCHS, J. J., & VAN METER, C. W. (1990). *The Hallcrest report II: Private security trends 1970–2000*. Boston, MA: Butterworth-Heinemann.

CUNNINGHAM, W. C., & TAYLOR, T. H. (1985). *The Hallcrest report: Private security and police in America*. Portland, OR: Chancellor Press.

DALTON, D. R. (1995). *Security management: Business strategies for success*. Boston, MA: Butterworth-Heinemann.

DALTON, D. R. (2003). *Rethinking corporate security in the post-9/11 era: Issues and strategies for today's global business community*. Boston: Butterworth-Heinemann.

DANIEL, T. (1992, March). Identifying critical leadership competencies of manufacturing supervisors in a major electronics corporation. *Group and Organizational Management: An International Journal, 17* (1), 57–71.

DAVIDS, M. (1995, January/February). Where style meets substance. *Journal of Business Strategy, 16* (1), 48–55, 57–60.

DAVIDSON, M. A. (2003, June). It is what you know. *Security Management, 47* (6), 69–70, 72, 74–75.

DEUTCH, J. (1997, September 22). Terrorism. *Foreign Policy*, p. 10.

DOHERTY, K. (1998, May). Beyond the Gore commission: What next? *Access Control & Security Systems Integration, 41* (5), 1, 42–43.

DOLAN, T. G. (1999, August). Healthcare security: A very insecure profession. *Security Technology & Design, 9* (8), 10–12, 14.

DORNING, M. (2000, August 28). U.S. violent crime rate dropped again last year. *San Diego Union Tribune*, p. A2.

DRATH, W. H., & PALUS, C. J. (1994). *Making common sense: Leadership as meaning-making in a community of practice*. Greensboro, NC: Center for Creative Leadership.

DRUCKER, P. F. (1994, November). The age of social transformation. *The Atlantic Monthly*, pp. 53–80.

DUNN, M. (1999). Critical elements in school security. In J. Agron & L. Anderson (Eds.), *Under siege: Schools as the new battleground* (pp. 13–14, 16). Atlanta, GA: Access Control & Security Systems Integration.

DUNPHY, H. (2003, May 1). Terrorist attacks worldwide declined substantially in 2002. *San Diego Union Tribune*, p. A22.

End in Sight. (2003, November 2). S*an Diego Union Tribune,* pp. A1, A10.

EPSTEIN, J. (1998). State and local environmental enforcement. In M. Clifford (Ed.), *Environmental crime: Enforcement, policy, and social responsibility* (pp. 145–168). Gaithersburg, MD: Aspen Publishers.

FAGIN, J. A. (2003). *Criminal justice.* Boston: Allyn & Bacon.

FAY, J. J. (1999). *Model security policies, plans and procedures.* Woburn, MA: Butterworth-Heinemann.

FAY, J. J. (2000, August). SICM: A risk management tool. *Security Technology & Design, 10* (8), 22–24, 26.

FBI issues alert to nuclear plant operators. (2003, May 6). *Security Beat, 3* (18). [Online]. Available: www.securitysolutions.com.

FENNELLY, L. J. (1992). *Security applications in industry and institutions.* Woburn, MA: Butterworth-Heinemann.

FENNELLY, L. J. (2004). *Handbook of loss prevention and crime prevention* (4th ed.). Boston: Butterworth-Heinemann.

FERRARO, E. F. (2000, July). Ordinary people. *Security Management, 44* (7), 48–50, 99–101.

FEST, G. (2001, January 22). Desk rage. *San Diego Union Tribune*, pp. C1, C2.

FICKES, M. (2000, November). Soapbox at the mall. *Access Control & Security Systems Integration, 43* (12), 1, 26, 28.

FIEDLER, F. E. (1967). *A theory of leadership effectiveness.* New York: McGraw-Hill.

FIRDAUS, I. (2002, October 13). Bombing at Bali nightclub kills 182. *San Diego Union Tribune*, pp. A1, A18.

Fireline Corporation. (2003). *Inergen systems.* [Online]. Available: www.fireline.com. Baltimore, MD: Fireline Corporation.

FISCHER, R. J., & GREEN, G. (1998). *Introduction to security* (6th ed.). Woburn, MA: Butterworth-Heinemann.

FISCHER, R. J., & JANOSKI, R. (2000). *Loss prevention and security procedures: Practical applications for contemporary problems.* Woburn, MA: Butterworth-Heinemann.

FISHER, I. (2000, December 30). Passengers save jet from attacker, deadly free fall. *San Diego Union Tribune*, pp. A1, A10.

FLEISSNER, D., & HEINZELMANN, F. (1996, August). *Crime prevention through environmental design and community policing.* Washington, DC: National Institute of Justice.

FOSS, B. (2003, January 1). Pain of scandals may yield benefits. *San Diego Union Tribune*, pp. C1, C8.

FOURNIES, F. (2000). *Coaching for improved work performance.* New York: McGraw-Hill.

GAINES, L., KAUNE, M., & MILLER, R. L. (2001). *Criminal justice in action: The core.* Belmont, CA: Wadsworth/Thomson Learning.

GALLAGHER, F. J., & GRASSIE, R. P. (2000, September). Alarm management: The key ingredient in effective security management operations. *Security Technology & Design, 10* (9), 12–14, 16, 18.

GARBERA, D. (1998, May). Protecting airports from themselves. *Access Control & Security Systems Integration, 41* (5), 1, 48.

GARCIA, M. L. (2000, June). Truth and consequences. *Security Management, 44* (6), 44–48.

GEMENY, D. F. (2000, August). Performance-based design: An overview. *Security Technology & Design, 10* (8), 64–66, 68.

GERSH, D. (2000, November). Untouchable value. *iSecurity*, pp. 16, 18–20.

GIGLIOTTI, R., & JASON, R. (1999). Approaches to physical security. In L. J. Fennelly, *Handbook of loss prevention and crime prevention* (3rd ed.). Boston: Butterworth-Heinemann.

GIPS, M. A. (1998, February). Where has all the money gone? *Security Management, 42* (2), 32–36, 38–40.

GIPS, M. A. (2000, May). Building in terrorism's shadow. *Security Management, 44* (5), 42–44, 46–50.

GIUSSANI, B. (2001, February 5). Hackers hit blue-chip World Economic Forum. *San Diego Union Tribune*, p. A1.

Global crime cartels are tech-savvy, U.S. says. (2000, December 16). *San Diego Union Tribune*, p. A12.

GOETSCH, D. L., & DAVIS, S. (1995). *Implementing total quality*. Englewood Cliffs, NJ: Prentice Hall.

GREEN, F. (2000, November 26). Workplace gumshoes. *San Diego Union Tribune*, p. H2.

GREEN, K. (2000, August 3). Weather, consumers help avert blackouts. *San Diego Union Tribune*, pp. A1, A19.

GREENE, J. D., & TAPPEN, A. R. (2000, July). Designing retrofit fire alarm systems: Part 2. *Security Technology & Design, 10* (7), 60–63.

HABERER, J. B., & WEBB, M. L. W. (1994). *TQM: 50 ways to make it work for you*. Menlo Park, CA: Crisp Publications.

Hacker steals patient records. (2000, December 12). *San Diego Union Tribune*, p. A3.

Hackers target state's electricity. (2001, June 10). *San Diego Union Tribune*, p. A3.

HADDOW, G. D., & BULLOCK, J. A. (2003). *Introduction to emergency management*. Boston: Butterworth-Heinemann.

HAKIM, S., & BLACKSTONE, E. A. (1997). *Securing home and business: A guide to the electronic security industry*. Woburn, MA: Butterworth-Heinemann.

HALL, M. (2003, January 23). 'Rent-a-cops' rarely trained or investigated. *USA Today*, p. 1A.

HALLIGAN, M. R. (2000, September). Inevitable disclosure. *Security Management, 44* (9), 94.

HANCOCK, B. W., & SHARP, P. M. (2004). *Criminal Justice in America: Theory, practice, and policy* (3rd ed.). Upper Saddle River, NJ: Prentice Hall.

HARDEN, B. (2002, October 23). Sniper plays taunting game with police and news media. *San Diego Union Tribune*, pp. A1, A18.

HARLEY, D. (2000, August). Living with viruses. *Security Management, 44* (8), 88, 90, 92–94.

HAROWITZ, S. L. (2003, January). The new centurions. *Security Management, 47* (1), 50–52, 54, 56–58.

HARR, J. S., & HESS, K. M. (2003). *Seeking employment in criminal justice and related fields* (4th ed.). Belmont, CA: Wadsworth/Thomson Learning.

HARRELL, A. V., & TAYLOR, R. B. (1996, May). *Physical environment and crime*. Washington, DC: National Institute of Justice.

HARWOOD, E. (1998, June). Going to work on workplace violence. *Access Control & Security Systems Integration, 41* (6), 1, 31–33.

Hawaii cites Xerox in worker shooting. (2000, November 8). *San Diego Union Tribune*, p. A10.

HAWKINS, S. (2000, March 29). Texas twister kills four people, hurts 36 in Fort Worth. *San Diego Union Tribune*, p. A8.

HAYES, R. (2000, April). An inventory of what's in store. *Security Management, 44* (4), 72, 74, 76.

HEIFETZ, R. A. (1994). *Leadership without easy answers*. Cambridge: The Belknap Press of Harvard University Press.

HELLRIEGEL, D., JACKSON, S. E., & SLOCUM, J. W., JR. (2002). *Management: A competency-based approach* (9th ed.). Cincinnati, OH: South-Western/Thomson Learning.

HELLRIEGEL, D., SLOCUM, J. W., JR., & WOODMAN, R. W. (2001). *Organization behavior* (9th ed.). Cincinnati, OH: South-Western College Publishing.

HENRY, V. E. (2002). *The COMPSTAT paradigm: Management accountability in policing, business and the public sector*. Flushing, NY: Looseleaf Law Publications.

HERSEY, P., & BLANCHARD, K. H. (1982). *Management of organizational behavior: Utilizing human resources*. Englewood Cliffs: Prentice Hall.

HERSEY, P., BLANCHARD, K. H., & JOHNSON, D. E. (2001). *Management of organizational behavior: Leading human resources* (8th ed.). Upper Saddle River, NJ: Prentice Hall.

HESS, K. M. (1997, December). The ABCs of report writing. *Security Management, 41* (12), 123–124.

HESS, K. M., & WROBLESKI, H. M. (1996). *Introduction to private security* (4th ed.). Minneapolis, MN: West.

HODGE, B. J., ANTHONY, W. P., & GALES, L. M. (2003). *Organizational theory: A strategic approach* (7th ed.). Upper Saddle River, NJ: Prentice Hall.

HOLLINGER, R. C., & DABNEY, D. A. (1995). *1994 national retail security research project.* Gainesville, FL: University of Florida.

HOPPER, D. I. (2001, February 6). E-mail wiretaps drive privacy advocates buggy. *San Diego Union Tribune*, pp. C1, C3.

HOUGH, W. O. (1999). Proactive security is called for. In R. R. Robinson (Ed.), *Issues in security management: Thinking critically about security* (pp. 158–162). Woburn, MA: Butterworth-Heinemann.

HOUSE, R. J. (1996). Path-goal theory of leadership: Lessons, legacy, and a reformulated theory. *Leadership Quarterly, 7* (3), 323–352.

How to report Internet crimes. (2000, March). *Security Management, 44* (3), 34.

HUGHES, J. (2000, November 15). FBI regional computer lab has new San Diego headquarters. *San Diego Union Tribune*, p. B3.

HUTCHINSON, B., & WARREN, M. (2001). *Information warfare: Corporate attack and defence in a digital world.* Boston: Butterworth-Heinemann.

INBAU, F. E., FARBER, B. J., & ARNOLD, D. W. (1996). *Protective security law* (2nd ed.). Woburn, MA: Butterworth-Heinemann.

INCIARDI, J. A. (2000). *Elements of criminal justice* (2nd ed.). New York: Harcourt College Publishers.

Interagency OPSEC Support Staff. (2000). *About us.* [Online]. Available: http://www.ioss .gov/html/About.html.

Is LA's crime honeymoon over? Gangs blamed for surge in violent crime rate. (2000, July/August). *Law Enforcement News, 26,* (537–538), p. 8.

JACOBSON, R. V. (1997, September). Look through the risk management window to add up security costs. *Access Control & Security Systems Integration, 40* (9), 59–62.

JEFFERY, C. R. (1972). *Crime prevention through environmental design.* Beverly Hills, CA: Sage Publications.

JELEN, G. F. (1994, October). OPSEC for the private sector. *Security Management, 38* (10), 67–68.

JESDANUN, A. (2000, August 21). Personal data, privacy concerns clash online. *San Diego Union Tribune*, p. A5.

JOHNSON, C. E. (2001). *Meeting the ethical challenges of leadership: Casting light or shadow.* Thousand Oaks, CA: Sage Publications.

JOHNSON, D. L., KLEHBAUCH, J. B., & KINNEY, J. (1994, February). Break the cycle of violence. *Security Management, 38* (2), 24–28.

JOHNSON, G. (2000, October 25). FBI starts probe into Microsoft break-in. *San Diego Union Tribune*, p. C1.

JOHNSON, J. W. (2003, February). Get the most from your guard force. *Security Management, 47* (2), 73–74, 76, 79–80.

JONES, D. (2000, August 2). Businesses battle over intellectual property. *USA Today*, pp. 1B–2B.

JONES, J. W., & ARNOLD, D. W. (2003, February). Trends in personnel testing: A loss prevention perspective. *Loss Prevention & Security Journal, 3* (2), 14–16.

JOPECK, E. J. (2000, August). Five steps to risk reduction. *Security Management, 44* (8), 97–98, 100–102.

KAKALIK, J. S., & WILDHORN, S. (1971). *The Rand report on private security.* Santa Monica, CA: The Rand Corporation.

KAKALIK, J. S., & WILDHORN, S. (1972). *Private police in the United States: Findings and recommendations.* Washington, DC: U.S. Government Printing Office.

KENWORTHY, T., & O'DRISCOLL, P. (2000, April 14). A year after the tragedy, a new culture revolves around security and intervention. *USA Today*, p. 1A.

KLOCKARS, C. B. (1991). The Dirty Harry problem. In C. B. Klockars & S. D. Mastrofski (Eds.), *Thinking about police: Contemporary readings* (2nd ed.) (pp. 413–423). New York: McGraw-Hill.

KNOWLES, M. S. (1970). *The modern practice of adult education: Andragogy versus pedagogy*. New York: Association Press.

KOERNER, B. I. (2000, May 1). Finally, an arrest: But how much damage do cyberattacks cause? *U.S. News & World Report*, p. 48.

KOTTER, J. P. (1990). *A force for change*. New York: The Free Press.

KOTTER, J. P. (1993). What leaders really do. In W. E. Rosenbach & R. L. Taylor (Eds.), *Contemporary issues in leadership* (3rd ed.) (pp. 26–35). Boulder, CO: Westview Press.

KOVACICH, G. L., & HALIBOZEK, E. P. (2003). *The manager's handbook for corporate security: Establishing and managing a successful assets protection program*. Boston: Butterworth-Heinemann.

KRASNOWSKI, M. (1997, December 14). Jailed hacker asking for keys. *San Diego Union Tribune*, p. A3.

KRASNOWSKI, M. (2000, November 10). Fraud charges against Keating dropped. *San Diego Union Tribune*, p. A3.

KREISHER, O. (1999, October 3). Panel warns of turmoil, terrorism. *San Diego Union Tribune*, p. A3.

KROEKER, M. A. (2001, September). Proper design helps stem crime. *Community Links, 7* (3), 15–16.

LAM, F., BEEKEY, M., & CAYO, K. (2003, February). Can you hack it? *Security Management, 47* (2), 83–84, 86, 88.

LEE, H. C., PALMBACH, T., & MILLER, M. T. (2001). *Henry Lee's crime scene handbook*. Boston: Academic Press.

LEE, S. (2003, January). Drug testing brings rights and responsibilities. *California Chamber of Commerce Labor Law Update*. [Online]. Available: www.calchamber.com.

LENAHAN, M. (2000, September). Training in tandem. *Security Management, 44* (9), 67–71.

LEWIS, P. S., GOODMAN, S. H., & FANDT, P. M. (2001). *Management: Challenges in the 21st century* (3rd ed.). Cincinnati, OH: South-Western College Publishing.

LIKERT, R. (1961). *New patterns of management*. New York: McGraw-Hill.

LIKERT, R. (1967). *The human organization*. New York: McGraw-Hill.

LODIN, S. (1999, October). Firing up data defenses. *Security Management, 43* (10), 68–70, 72–73.

LOHR, S. (2002, May 27). In new era, corporate security looks beyond guns and badges. *New York Times*, pp. C1, C3.

LONGMORE-ETHERIDGE, A. (2000, August). Long day's journey into knowledge. *Security Management, 44* (8), 61–64.

LOTA, L. (2000, September 22). Hacker, 20, accused of invading NASA, university computers. *San Diego Union Tribune*, p. A4.

LYMAN, M. D. (2002). *The police: An introduction* (2nd ed.). Upper Saddle River, NJ: Prentice Hall.

LYNCH, M. (2000, December). Go ask Alice. *Security Management, 44* (12), 68–70, 72–73.

MAJOR, M. J. (1998, March). A casino's three-pronged approach to security. *Security Technology & Design, 8* (3), 27, 29–33.

MAJOR, M. J. (1999, June). An explosive issue: Airports install high-tech explosives detectors to combat terrorism. *Security Technology & Design, 9* (6), 10–12, 14, 16.

MANISCALCO, P. M., & CHRISTEN, H. T. (2002). *Understanding terrorism and managing the consequences*. Upper Saddle River, NJ: Prentice Hall.

MANN, R. A., & ROBERTS, B. S. (1997). *Smith and Robertson's business law* (10th ed.). New York: West.

MANN, T. (1999, October). Seven steps to successful contracting. *Security Management, 43* (10), 46–48, 50–51.

MARKOFF, J. (2000, May 5). E-mail worm-virus sent messages worldwide. *San Diego Union Tribune*, pp. A1, A23.

MARTIN, G. (2003). *Understanding terrorism: Challenges, perspectives and issues.* Thousand Oaks, CA: Sage Publications.

MASLOW, A. H. (1970). *Motivation and personality* (2nd ed.). New York: Harper & Row.

MASON, M. (2000, December 28). Koalas' lives at risk after theft. *San Diego Union Tribune*, pp. A3, A6.

MAURER, R. D. (2000a, January). The evolving role of the security director. *Security Technology & Design, 10* (1), 12–14, 16.

MAURER, R. D. (2000b, August). Outsourcing: An option or a threat? *Security Technology & Design, 10* (8), 12–14, 18, 20.

MAURER, R. D. (2000c, December). Where will security be in 2010? *Security Technology & Design, 10* (12), 12–14, 16.

MAY, J. (2000, October). A tragedy in the making. *Access Control & Security Systems Integration, 43* (11), 42–43.

MCCLELLAND, D. C. (1971). *Motivational trends in society.* Morristown, NJ: General Learning Press.

MCCOLLUM, K. (2000, March 24). Colleges struggle to train experts in protecting computer systems. *The Chronicle of Higher Education*, p. A-45.

MCFADDEN, R. D. (2000, December 31). Blizzard snarls Northeast. *San Diego Union Tribune*, pp. A1, A20.

MCDONALD, J. (2001a, March 6). Two killed, 13 wounded in rampage; suspect smiled as he fired, witnesses say. *San Diego Union Tribune*, pp. A1, A6.

MCDONALD, J. (2001b, March 24). Five injured in teen's rampage at Granite Hills. *San Diego Union Tribune*, pp. A1, A22.

MCGREGOR, D. (1960). *The human side of enterprise.* New York: McGraw-Hill.

MCGREGOR, D. (1966). *Leadership and motivation.* Cambridge: Massachusetts Institute of Technology Press.

MCQUEEN, A. (2000, October 27). School violence decreases, study finds. *San Diego Union Tribune*, p. A9.

MEESE, E., & ORTMEIER, P. J. (2004). *Leadership, ethics, and policing: Challenges for the 21st century.* Upper Saddle River: Prentice Hall.

MENDEL, E. (2001, January 27). Davis touts plan to end energy ills. *San Diego Union Tribune*, pp. A1, A20.

MEREDITH, R. (1997, January 9). VW will pay $100 million to GM, settle spying suit. *San Diego Union Tribune*, p. C1.

MICHALOWSKI, R. (1998). International environmental issues. In M. Clifford (Ed.), *Environmental crime: Enforcement, policy, and social responsibility* (pp. 315–340). Gaithersburg, MD: Aspen Publishers.

MICHEL, R. (2000, September). Learning curve: Access control ensures a safe educational facility. *Security Products, 4* (9), 30–32, 34.

MILLER, L. (2003, May 3). U.S. to check background of truckers who haul hazardous goods. *San Diego Union Tribune*, p. A7.

MILLWEE, S. (2000, February). You have not because you ask not: Cost effective screening that works. *Security Technology & Design, 10* (2), 12–14, 16.

MISHRA, R. (1998, March 18). Drug addicts need treatment, not punishment, doctors say. *San Diego Union Tribune*, pp. A1, A21.

MISKIN, V., & GMELCH, W. (1985, May). Quality leadership for quality teams. *Training and Development Journal, 39* (5), 122–129.

MOSES-SCHULZ, D. (1997, April). Private security comes on board. *Security Management, 41* (4), 59, 60, 62, 63, 65.

MOSLEY, D. C., MEGGINSON, L. C., & PIETRI, P. H. (1993). *Supervisory management: The art of empowering and developing people.* Cincinnati: South-Western Publishing.

Most drug abusers have steady jobs. (1999, September 9). *San Diego Union Tribune*, p. A6.

NALLA, M. K. (2001, Spring). Designing an introductory course in private security. *Journal of Criminal Justice Education, 12* (1), 35-52.

NASON, R. R. (2000, October). Threats for the new millennium. *Security Technology & Design, 10* (10), 12-14, 16, 18.

National Advisory Commission on Criminal Justice Standards and Goals. (1976). *Task force report: Private security.* Washington, DC: U.S. Government Printing Office.

National Fire Protection Association. (2000). *NFPA fire prevention code handbook.* Quincy, MA: National Fire Protection Association.

NEELEY, D. (2000, July). The hacker files. *Security Management, 44* (7), 124, 126, 128, 131.

NEMETH, C. P. (2001). *Law and evidence: A primer for criminal justice, criminology, law, and legal studies.* Upper Saddle River, NJ: Prentice Hall.

NEMETH, C. P. (2004). *Criminal law.* Upper Saddle River, NJ: Prentice Hall.

NEWMAN, B. (Writer), & KURTIS, B. (Producer). (1997). *Investigative reports: The new face of crime* (Videotape). New York: A&E Television Networks.

NICHOLSON, L. G. (1997). *Instructor development training: A guide for security and law enforcement.* Boston: Butterworth-Heinemann.

NICHTER, D. A. (2000, September). The house rules. *Security Management, 44* (9), 74-82, 84-86, 88.

NOCELLA, H. N. (2000, December). Clipping coupon fraud. *Security Management, 44* (12), 40-42, 44, 46, 48.

NORTHOUSE, P. G. (2001). *Leadership: Theory and practice* (2nd ed.). Thousand Oaks, CA: Sage Publications.

O'HARA, C. E., & O'HARA, G. L. (2003). *Fundamentals of criminal investigation* (7th ed.). Springfield, IL: Charles L. Thomas.

Operation Cooperation. (2001, January/February). *ASIS (American Society for Industrial Security) Dynamics,* (157), 1, 4.

OPSEC Professionals Society. (2000). *OPSEC Professionals Society overview.* [Online]. Available: http://www.opsec.org/Overview.html.

ORTMEIER, P. J. (1994, September 22). Address. Speech presented at the annual conference of the American Society for Industrial Security, Las Vegas, NV.

ORTMEIER, P. J. (1995, September–November). Security management: a career education master plan. *California Security, 1* (8), 8-9.

ORTMEIER, P. J. (1996a, May). Placement in employment. *The Cohort of San Diego State University,* pp. 1-2.

ORTMEIER, P. J. (1996b, July). Adding class to security. *Security Management, 40* (7), 99-101.

ORTMEIER, P. J. (1996c). *Community policing leadership: A Delphi study to identify essential competencies.* Ann Arbor, MI: University Microfilms International.

ORTMEIER, P. J. (1997, October). Leadership for community policing: Identifying essential officer competencies. *The Police Chief, 64* (10), 88-91, 93.

ORTMEIER, P. J. (1999). *Public safety and security administration.* Woburn, MA: Butterworth-Heinemann.

ORTMEIER, P. J. (2002). *Policing the community: A guide for patrol operations.* Upper Saddle River, NJ: Prentice Hall.

ORTMEIER, P. J. (2003, February). Ethical leadership: Every officer's responsibility. *Law Enforcement Executive Forum, 3* (1), 1-9.

ORTON, A. (1984). Leadership: New thoughts on an old problem. *Training, 21* (28), 31-33.

OUCHI, W. (1981). *Theory Z: How American business can meet the Japanese challenge.* Reading, MA: Addison-Wesley.

PAPI, V. (1994, February). Planning before disaster strikes. *Security Concepts,* pp. 6, 19.

PARR, L. A. (1999). *Police report writing essentials.* Placerville, CA: Custom Publishing.

Path of destruction. (1992, May 10). *Los Angeles Times,* p. A31.

PAYTON, G. T., & AMARAL, M. (1996). *Patrol operations and enforcement tactics* (10th ed.). San Jose, CA: Criminal Justice Services.

PEAK, K. J., & GLENSOR, R. W. (2002). *Community policing and problem solving: Strategies and practices* (3rd ed.). Upper Saddle River, NJ: Prentice Hall.

PEARSON, R. (2000, September). Security's new golden rule: automation, integration and consolidation. *Security Technology & Design, 10* (9), 20–21, 24, 26, 28.

PECK, D. H. (1999, October). When police walk the security beat. *Security Management, 43* (10), 38–40, 42, 45.

PERRY, J. L. (Ed.). (1996). *Handbook of public administration.* San Francisco: Jossey-Bass.

PETERS, T. (1987). *Thriving on chaos.* New York: Knopf.

Peterson's guide to four-year colleges. (2000). Lawrenceville, NJ: Thomson Learning.

PETTERSON, R. (2003, February 18). Blizzard causes havoc in Northeast; 28 dead. *San Diego Union Tribune,* pp. A1, A12.

Picture of drug use by young mixed. (2000, September 1). *San Diego Union Tribune,* p. A6.

PIKE, R. W. (1992). *Creative training techniques handbook.* Minneapolis: Lakewood Publications.

PITORRI, P. (1998). *Counterespionage for American business.* Woburn, MA: Butterworth-Heinemann.

President's Commission on Law Enforcement and Administration of Justice. (1967). *Task force report: Police.* Washington, DC: U.S. Government Printing Office.

PRICE, J. E., HADDOCK, M. D., & BROCK, H. R. (1996). *College accounting* (8th ed.). New York: Glencoe, McGraw-Hill.

Professional Growth Facilitators. (2000). *Preparation for a violent emergency . . . It's not a choice.* San Clemente, CA: Professional Growth Facilitators.

Profiles of American colleges (24th ed.). (2000). Hauppauge, NJ: Barron's Educational Series, Inc.

PURPURA, P. P. (2003). *The security handbook* (2nd ed.). Boston: Butterworth-Heinemann.

Rand Corporation. (1999). *The benefits and costs of drug use prevention: Clarifying a cloudy issue.* Santa Monica, CA: RAND Corporation, Drug Policy Research Center.

RAUM, T. (1999, February 5). U.S. found vulnerable to bombing attacks. *San Diego Union Tribune,* p. A11.

RAYMOND, W. D., & HALL, D. E. (1999). *California criminal law and procedure.* Albany, NY: West/Thomson Learning.

RETTIE, D. F. (1995). *Our national park system.* Chicago: University of Illinois Press.

REVKIN, A. C. (2001, January 6). November–December coldest such span in U.S. since 1895. *San Diego Union Tribune,* p. A9.

ROBBINS, S. P., & COULTER, M. (2003). *Management* (2003 update). Upper Saddle River, NJ: Prentice Hall.

ROBINSON, R. R. (1999). Privatization of services. In R. R. Robinson (Ed.), *Issues in security management: Thinking critically about security* (pp. 193–194). Woburn, MA: Butterworth-Heinemann.

RODRIGUEZ, A., YATES, J., & MARX, G. (2001, February 6). Former employee opens fire, kills 4, self in Illinois factory. *San Diego Union Tribune,* pp. A1, A7.

RUTLEDGE, D. (2000). *California criminal procedure* (4th ed.). Incline Village, NV: Copperhouse Publishing.

SAFERSTEIN, R. (2001). *Criminalistics: An introduction to forensic science* (7th ed.). Upper Saddle River, NJ: Prentice Hall.

SALANT, J. D. (2002, February 18). Federal government takes over airport security. *San Diego Union Tribune,* pp. A1, A14.

SCHAUB, J. L., & BIERY, K. B., JR., (1994). *The ultimate security survey.* Woburn, MA: Butterworth-Heinemann.

SCHMALLEGER, F. (2003). *Criminal justice today: An introductory text for the 21st century* (7th ed.). Upper Saddle River, NJ: Prentice Hall.

SCHMALLEGER, F. (2004). *Criminal justice: A brief introduction* (5th ed.). Upper Saddle River, NJ: Prentice Hall.

SCHUMACHER, J. (2000, October). How to resolve conflict with proper systems integration. *Security Technology & Design, 10* (10), 36–40, 42–43.

SCOTT, M. S. (2000). *Problem-oriented policing: Reflections on the first 20 years.* Washington, DC: U.S. Department of Justice, Office of Community Oriented Policing Services.

Security fears cited over prior CIA chief. (2000, February 4). *San Diego Union Tribune*, p. A1.

SENNA, J. J., & SIEGEL, L. J. (2001). *Essentials of criminal justice* (3rd ed.). Belmont, CA: Wadsworth/Thomson Learning.

SENNEWALD, C. A. (2003). *Effective security management* (4th ed.). Boston: Butterworth-Heinemann.

Seven killed in office rampage. (2000, December 27). *San Diego Union Tribune*, pp. A1, A19.

Seven major U.S. agencies get 'F' in computer security. (2000, September 12). *San Diego Union Tribune*, p. A8.

SHARTLE, C. L. (1956). *Executive performance and leadership*. Englewood Cliffs, NJ: Prentice Hall.

SHENON, P. (1999, January 8). Years of security lapses blamed in 2 embassy bombings. *San Diego Union Tribune*, p. A15.

SIEGEL, L. J. (2001). *Criminology: Theories, patterns, and typologies* (7th ed.). Belmont, CA: Wadsworth/Thomson Learning.

SILBERMAN, M. (Ed.). (1996). *The 1996 McGraw-Hill team and organization development source book*. New York: McGraw-Hill.

SIMONSEN, C. E. (1998). *Private security in America: An introduction*. Upper Saddle River, NJ: Prentice Hall.

SIMONSEN, C. E., & SPINDLOVE, J. R. (2000). *Terrorism today: The past, the players, the future*. Upper Saddle River, NJ: Prentice Hall.

SIMONTON, G. M. (1998, May). Embracing officer authorization. *Access Control & Security System Integration, 41* (5), 40.

SLATER, P. (2000, April 3). Thefts eat away at office morale. *San Diego Union Tribune*, p. C1.

SLEPIAN, C. G. (2000, November). Security up in the air. *Security Management, 44* (11), 54-56, 58-59.

SMITH, G. B. (2000, June 15). Mob families muscled in on Wall St., charges say. *San Diego Union Tribune*, p. A12.

SMITH, J. N. (2000, November). Powering up access control. *Security Management, 44* (11), 68-70, 72-73.

SMITH, R. V. (2000, December). Sheparding your resources: Retaining employees in the new economy. *Security Products, 4* (12), 36-39.

SNIFFEN, M. J. (2000, November 18). FBI pleased with progress in Cole probe. *San Diego Union Tribune*, p. A9.

SNIFFEN, M. J. (2001, January 6). Companies cooperate with FBI in fighting computer crime. *San Diego Union Tribune*, p. A11.

SOLOMAN, R. C. (1996). *A handbook for ethics*. Fort Worth, TX: Harcourt Brace College Publishers.

SOMMER, C. J. (2003, March). Survival of the fittest: Corporate success is dependent on strategic synergy. *Loss Prevention & Security Journal, 3* (3), 16-17.

SOUTHERLAND, R. (2000, June). Protected against the enemy within. *Access Control & Security Systems Integration, 43* (7), 29-30.

SPIVEY, J. (2001, January). Banks vault into online risk. *Security Management, 45* (1), 132-134, 136, 138.

STOGDILL, R. M. (1959). *Individual behavior and group achievement*. New York: Oxford University Press.

STOVER, J. B. (2000, May). When security doesn't add up. *Security Management, 44* (5), 80, 82-83.

SUKIENNIK, G. (2001, January 8). Juries send message with damage case awards. *San Diego Union Tribune*, p. A1.

Sun Microsystems integrates access control worldwide. (2000, October). *Access Control & Security Systems Integration, 43* (11), 1, 30, 32, 34.

SUTHERLAND, E. (1949). *White collar crime*. New York: Dryden.

SWANSON, C. R., TERRITO, L., & TAYLOR, R. W. (1998). *Police administration: Structures, processes, and behavior* (4th ed.). Upper Saddle River, NJ: Prentice Hall.

TAFOYA, W. L. (1994, May/June). The future of law enforcement: A chronology of events. *Criminal Justice International*, p. 4.

TAYLOR, M. (2000, November). Security in the strike zone. *Security Management, 44* (11), 38–40, 42, 44–45.

THAISS, C., & HESS, J. E. (1999). *Writing for law enforcement*. Boston: Allyn & Bacon.

The Economist Intelligence Unit. (2000). *Latest country analysis*. [Online]. Available: http://www.eiu.com/.

THOMAS, L. (2001, January). Security measures for the Miami federal courthouse. *Security Products, 5* (1), 54.

THOMASON, R. (2000, September). Airport security for the new millennium. *Security Technology & Design, 10* (9), 52, 54, 56, 60.

Threatening email traced to computer at CC. (2000, December 20). *West Point News*, pp. A1, A3.

TICHY, N., & ULRICH, D. (1984). The leadership challenge—a call for the transformational leader. SMR Forum. *Sloan Management Review, 26* (1), 59–68.

TRIMMER, H. W. (1999). *Understanding and servicing alarm systems* (3rd ed.). Woburn, MA: Butterworth-Heinemann.

Truth, DARE and consequences: What impact is anti-drug effort having? (1998, April 15). *Law Enforcement News, 24* (487), pp. 1, 10.

Two teens arrested in theft of koalas. (2000, December 29). *San Diego Union Tribune*, p. A3.

TYSKA, L. A., & FENNELLY, L. J. (2000). *Physical security: 150 things you should know*. Woburn, MA: Butterworth-Heinemann.

United States. Congress. (1968). *Omnibus Crime Control and Safe Streets Act*. Washington, DC: U.S. Government Printing Office.

United States. Congress. (1988). *Employee Polygraph Protection Act*. Washington, DC: U.S. Government Printing Office.

United States. Congress. (1996). *Economic Security Act*. Washington, DC: U.S. Government Printing Office.

United States. Congress. (2001). *USA Patriot Act of 2001 (Public Law 107-56)*. Washington, DC: U.S. Government Printing Office.

United States. Congress. (2002, November 25). *Homeland Security Act of 2002*. Washington, DC: U.S. Government Printing Office.

United States. Department of Homeland Security. (2003). *DHS Organization*. [Online]. Available: www.dhs.org.

United States. Department of Homeland Security. Transportation Security Administration. (2003). *Aviation and Transportation Security Act (ATSA) Public Law 107-7*. [Online]. Available: www.tsa.gov.

United States. Department of Justice. (1988). *Uniform crime reporting: National incident-based reporting system, vol. 1: Data collection guidelines*. Washington, DC: U.S. Government Printing Office.

United States. Department of Justice. (2003). *U.S. National Central Bureau Home Page*. [Online]. Available: www.usdoj.gov.

United States. Department of Justice. Bureau of Justice Assistance. (1997). *East bay public safety corridor partnership*. Washington, DC: U.S. Department of Justice, Office of Justice Programs.

United States. Department of Justice. Bureau of Justice Assistance. (2000, March). *Keeping illegal activity out of rental property: A police guide for establishing landlord training programs*. Washington, DC: United States Department of Justice, Office of Justice Programs.

United States. Department of Justice. Bureau of Justice Statistics. (1992, December). *Drugs, crime and the justice system*. Washington, DC: U.S. Government Printing Office.

United States. Department of Justice. Bureau of Justice Statistics. Office of Justice Programs. (1997, May). *Criminal Victimization in the United States 1994*. Washington, DC: National Criminal Justice Reference Service.

United States. Department of Justice. Federal Bureau of Investigation. (1997). *Uniform crime report*. Washington, DC: U.S. Government Printing Office.

United States. Department of Justice. Private Security Advisory Council to the Law Enforcement Assistance Administration. (1977). *Reports to the LEAA*. Washington, DC: U.S. Government Printing Office.

United States. Department of State. (1999). *Patterns of global terrorism*. Washington, DC: U.S. Government Printing Office.

United States. Department of Treasury. Bureau of Alcohol, Tobacco, and Firearms. (2000). *Bomb threats and physical security planning guide*. [Online]. Available: http://www.atf.treas.gov.

United States. Department of Treasury, Secret Service, & Department of Education. (2002). *Threat assessment in schools: A guide for managing threatening situations and to creating safe school climates*. Washington, DC: U.S. Department of Education.

United States. General Accounting Office. (2001). *Combating terrorism: Selected challenges and related recommendations*. Washington, DC: U.S. General Accounting Office.

University Health Care provides health, safety and security for patients. (2000, October). *Access Control & Security Systems Integration, 43* (11), 44.

UTTENWEILER, W. L. (1999, October). Working the Web. *Security Management, 43* (10), 75-78.

VINCENT, B. (2000, May). Protection at $5.75 an hour. *Access Control & Security Systems Integration, 43* (6), 1, 47-48.

VROOM, V. H. (1964). *Work and motivation*. New York: John Wiley & Sons.

Wal-Mart loses overtime pay lawsuit. (2002, December 20). *The Olympian*. [Online]. Available: www.theolympian.com/home/news/20021220/business/314505html.

WALSH, T. J., & HEALY, R. J. (1987). *Protection of assets manual*. Santa Monica, CA: The Merrit Company.

WARCHOL, G. (1998). *Workplace violence, 1992-1996*. Washington, DC: Bureau of Justice Statistics.

WASHBURN, D., & HASEMYER, D. (2001, March 9). New threats raise alarm: Violence study shows Willams 'fits the pattern.' *San Diego Union Tribune*, pp. A1, A23.

WASSERMAN, G. A., MILLER, L. S., & COTHERN, L. (2000, April). *Prevention of serious and violent juvenile offending*. Washington, DC: United States Department of Justice, Office of Justice Programs, Office of Juvenile Justice and Delinquency Prevention.

WHITE, S. (2001, January). Nature watch. *Security Products, 5* (1), 50.

WILBERG FITZSIMONS, E. (2000, September 28). False alarms trigger fines. *San Diego Union Tribune*, p. B1.

WILSON, C. E. (2002, March). Bulking up for security. *Access Control & Security Systems, 45* (3), 38-40, 43-44.

WIMMER, R. (2000, January). Assessing CCTV's roles in public venues. *Security Technology & Design, 10* (1), 32-34.

WINTER, G. (2000, November 17). Black Coke employees to receive $156 million. *San Diego Union Tribune*, p. A2.

WOLF BRANSCOMB, L. (2001, March 9). A fatal day in 1979. *San Diego Union Tribune*, p. A24.

ZEIGLER, M. (2002, February 16). Olympic security sky-high. *San Diego Union Tribune*, pp. A1, A12.

ZUCKERMAN, E. (2003, February 22). Nobody had a chance. *San Diego Union Tribune*, pp. A1, A16.

ZUNKEL, D. (2000, September). Maintaining secure airports: An evolutionary process. *Security Technology & Design, 10* (9), 62-64, 66, 68.

INDEX